A GUIDE TO

# SHARKS & RAYS

# A GUIDE TO
# SHARKS & RAYS

TIMOTHY C. TRICAS, KEVIN DEACON,
PETER LAST, JOHN E. MCCOSKER,
TERENCE I. WALKER, LEIGHTON TAYLOR

CONSULTANT EDITOR
LEIGHTON TAYLOR

FOG CITY PRESS

Published by Fog City Press
814 Montgomery Street
San Francisco, CA 94133 USA

Copyright © 1997 US Weldon Owen Inc.
Copyright © 1997 Weldon Owen Pty Limited
This edition 2002

CHIEF EXECUTIVE OFFICER John Owen
PRESIDENT Terry Newell
PUBLISHER Lynn Humphries
MANAGING EDITOR Janine Flew
ART DIRECTOR Kylie Mulquin
EDITORIAL COORDINATOR Tracey Gibson
EDITORIAL ASSISTANT Kiren Thandi
PRODUCTION MANAGER Caroline Webber
PRODUCTION COORDINATOR James Blackman
BUSINESS MANAGER Emily Jahn
VICE PRESIDENT INTERNATIONAL SALES Stuart Laurence
EUROPEAN SALES DIRECTOR Vanessa Mori

PROJECT EDITORS Helen Bateman, Bronwyn Sweeney
COPY EDITOR Lynn Cole
EDITORIAL ASSISTANTS Edan Corkill, Miriam Coupe,
Vesna Radojcic, Shona Ritchie
DESIGNERS Clive Collins, Kylie Mulquin, Mark Thacker
JACKET DESIGNER John Bull
PICTURE RESEARCHER Annette Crueger
ILLUSTRATORS Martin Camm, Gino Hasler, Ngaire Sales,
Roger Swainston, Genevieve Wallace

ISBN 1 877019 48 8

Printed by Kyodo Printing Co. (S'pore) Pte Ltd
Printed in Singapore

A Weldon Owen Production

*If there is magic on this planet, it is contained in water ...
Its substance reaches everywhere; it touches the past and
prepares the future; it moves under the poles and wanders
thinly in the heights of air. It can assume forms of
exquisite perfection in a snowflake, or strip the living to a
single shining bone cast upon the sea.*

*The Immense Journey,*
LOREN EISELEY (1907–77), American anthropologist and writer

# INTRODUCTION

S harks are perhaps the least understood creatures in the animal kingdom. Objects of fear and fascination, they have inspired a complex mythology and a daunting array of misconceptions.

In the last quarter of the 20th century, when conservation groups were campaigning to save the whales, sharks were still being slaughtered in their millions by commercial fishing enterprises, their reputation as man-eaters fueled by the media. Now is our chance to elevate and expand our vision of sharks from demon-like characters in movies and cartoons to interesting and adaptable creatures that have survived from Earth's earliest history to dominate a most vital niche in the oceans of our planet.

This book aims to set the record straight on sharks and their relatives. *A Guide to Sharks and Rays* is a detailed reference source that will enlighten and inspire. It presents the current thinking on the ecology, biology, and behavior of sharks and rays. It also takes you on a journey to some of the most beautiful locations around the world where it is possible to encounter and marvel at many species of sharks and rays.

Ignorance and fear still sometimes override commonsense and respect for these creatures, but the more people take the time to observe and learn about them, the better will be our understanding of the contribution their kind makes to us and to our ocean ecosystems.

THE EDITORS

... *A dark*

*Illimitable ocean without bound,*

*Without dimension, where length, breadth, and highth*

*And time and place are lost.*

*Paradise Lost,*
MILTON (1608–74), English poet

# CHAPTER ONE
# UNDERSTANDING SHARKS *and* RAYS

# THE FASCINATING WORLD
## *of* SHARKS *and* RAYS

*Sharks and rays touch the lives of nearly all organisms that
live in their seemingly inhospitable marine environment.*

From the perspective of a land-dwelling human, the world's oceans represent an intimidating, hostile, enigmatic environment. Our terrestrial habitats are dwarfed by the oceans, which cover more than three times as much surface area.

The seas are a diverse three-dimensional environment, ranging from the warm, sunlit shallows of tropical reefs to near-freezing waters of abyssal trenches. Laden with salty minerals that sting our eyes and make the water undrinkable, the oceans are quite unlike our clear, gaseous atmosphere. They are often clouded by silt or microscopic plankton, which can reduce visibility to only a few feet. So it is not surprising that humans find it an inhospitable habitat.

### WATERY WORLD

Suspended in this alien world are the fishes, the most successful group of vertebrates

in Earth's history. Estimates put their numbers at more than 25,000 living species, and for many, there is a rich fossil record from which we can trace their evolution.

Within the group is a wide array of relatively recently evolved bony fishes that inhabit nearly every aquatic environment on Earth. For example, herbivorous parrotfishes and surgeonfishes harvest microscopic algae on tropical coral reefs, while large tunas and billfishes cruise the open oceans where they feed on small fishes and squid.

But the lives of each of these species are touched by a unique group of boneless fishes known as the sharks and rays, which can compete directly with them for food resources, or in many cases prey directly upon them.

The elasmobranch fishes consist of about 800 species of living shark, ray, and skate. Unlike the skeletons of their bony cousins, the body frames of elasmobranchs are composed primarily of cartilage, a light and flexible support material. Most of their fossil

**LITTLE CHANGED** *A fossil ray (above) (Cyclobatis longicaudatus) from the Cretaceous, and an early Permian shark fossil (left) (Orthacanthus senckenbergianus), share features with descendants such as the whale shark (below left).*

record comes from a few calcified body parts, such as teeth, spines, or vertebrae. Occasionally, whole fossilized skeletons, formed under fortuitous geological conditions, provide a glimpse of their evolution between ancestor and modern form. Today, paleontologists believe the direct descendants of modern sharks date back more than 400 million years.

## DESIGN ELEGANCE

Their long evolutionary history and lack of bone can give the false impression that sharks and rays are primitive animals. On the contrary, the elasmobranch fishes, thought to have descended from bony ancestors, show remarkable adaptations for a successful life in nearly all marine communities. Most living species have a protrusible upper jaw and specialized dentition that make them very proficient predators. The sensory system is extremely well developed, and the brain is large.

The reproductive system and behaviors are often highly specialized, and in many ways are more similar to birds and mammals than to the other fishes. These characteristics have made the sharks and rays successful organisms in a diversity of marine habitats.

## THE RAYS

Closely related to sharks, rays (also known as batoids) fill many ecological niches. They are thought to be a sister group of the sawsharks, and are represented by more than 450 species. Some batoids, such as guitarfishes, skates, and electric rays, have well-developed dorsal and caudal fins, and strong tails. Others, such as the stingrays, eagle rays, and devilrays, have greatly reduced tails that usually have only a rudimentary caudal fin, if any. These fishes range in size from small bottom-dwelling stingarees that may be only the size of a human hand, to the massive manta rays that swim in the open ocean and are more than 20 feet (6 m) in wingspan.

They are found in nearly all marine habitats and are also common in many estuaries, freshwater rivers, and lakes. While most skates and rays eat invertebrates that live in soft sediments, some butterfly rays feed only on small fishes, and many mantas feed primarily on plankton. Much remains to be learned about the behavior and biology of these most remarkable fishes.

## SHARKS AND HUMANS

Even in today's world most people are under the impression that sharks live in a secretive environment far removed from our daily lives. In reality, humans and sharks have major interactions with sometimes dire consequences for these fishes. In the early part of this century, sharks and rays supported small regional fisheries in many parts of the world. However, the recent human population explosion and improved fishing technologies have resulted in the massive harvesting of sharks and rays around the world. In addition to their food value, there is now a major international market for fins, especially those of the shortfin mako shark pictured above, which are used to make shark fin soup. There is a smaller market for cartilaginous shark skeletons used in health-food remedies. While many shark stocks have recently suffered a serious decline in numbers, some countries are starting to regulate shark harvests in the hope of maintaining a sustainable shark fishery. Individual, national, and international cooperation are necessary to ensure the shark's survival.

# THE OCEANS—THEIR HABITAT

*The lives of the sharks and rays are shaped by the nature of the diverse habitats in which they occur.*

In many ways, the ocean realms in which sharks and rays live are stable, predictable, and forgiving. The daily fluctuation in temperature is usually low because of the water's good heat retention, and mass movement of water is constant due to slow wind-driven currents or coastal upwellings.

Atmospheric storms cause destructive physical disturbances, but these are usually limited to the upper few yards of the water column, and can be avoided by short vertical migrations. The photoperiod of shallow-water species is set by the movements of the Sun and phases of the Moon. Many deep-dwelling species live in constant darkness while others are surrounded periodically by low levels of light.

Despite the ocean's many amenable features, it also imposes some unique challenges. Unlike the Earth's gaseous atmosphere, water presents a very dense environment and calls for an efficient power engine and hydrodynamic design to produce rapid movements during swimming. The high salt content of the oceans constantly removes water from the soft body tissues, and requires efficient water barriers and physiological mechanisms to replace it.

Compared to air, the oceans have a relatively low oxygen content, so ingenious oxygen-extraction factories have evolved in the gills. Relatively low visibility in the marine environment has resulted in many specializations of the eye, and the evolution of specialized sensory organs.

## DIFFERENT HABITATS

Many habitats are recognized in the world's oceans, with distinct boundaries for the different species of shark and ray. On a horizontal scale, habitats can be distinguished as coastal and open water. In the higher latitudes, intertidal and coastal-reef habitats are composed largely of rock and rubble substrates, on which grow vast beds of macroalgae that present habitats for small fish prey and invertebrates.

Vast stands of kelp forests stretch along the shores of many temperate coastlines, where they provide a good habitat for food items and shelter. In tropical regions, living corals and coraline algae build calcium carbonate reefs that support a high density of invertebrate and fish organisms. Between these reef areas of most seas are found stretches of beaches that support a rich variety of sand-dwelling

**HOME GROUNDS** *The megamouth shark (above) inhabits the mesopelagic zone to great depths and is rarely seen. The whitetip reef shark (right), on the other hand, is easily sighted in the coral environment that suits its way of life.*

worms, mollusks, crustaceans, and small fishes.

Also adjacent to many temperate and tropical reef areas are sea-grass beds, which may cover the sandy bottom. These harbor a rich diversity of organisms. The productive waters of back bays and inland estuaries provide rich food resources for sharks and rays, and also important habitats for mating, pupping, and nursery grounds for their young.

## CONTINENTAL SHELVES

The coastal regions of major landmasses and islands are usually surrounded by a shallow submarine shelf made primarily of sediments and rocky outcroppings. These can extend many miles seaward and hundreds of feet deep. These regions are usually inhabited by large populations of numerous species of shark, ray, and skate. At its most seaward extent, the shelf usually breaks to a descending slope, which on the upper reaches attracts large elasmobranch populations that decline in numbers with increasing depth.

Pelagic waters differ from other marine habitats by being separate from the bottom and therefore have little habitat diversity. The epipelagic zone, which begins near shore and extends out to the open oceans, ranges from the surface to about 330 feet (100 m) deep.

This zone receives abundant sunlight, which in near-shore areas with nutrient upwellings supports a rich supply of phytoplankton, zooplankton, and small

**TAKING COVER** *A juvenile lemon shark (above) is a common sight in shallow mangrove swamps, especially those near tropical reefs. The Pacific electric ray (below) seeks the cover of a kelp forest for its foraging expeditions.*

planktivorous fishes. Many species of shark and ray take advantage of these highly productive waters for their food resources. In the nutrient-poor epipelagic waters far out to sea, only a few species of shark and perhaps only one ray are found.

## GOING DEEPER

Below the productive surface waters is the mesopelagic zone, where daytime light levels fade into darkness and cannot support phytoplankton populations. This extends down to about 3,300 feet (1,000 m) and is characterized by a decline in oxygen and nutrient levels, and water

temperature, which makes this a relatively inhospitable environment. As a result, many of the invertebrates and small fishes that inhabit this region make daily migrations (usually at night) up into the epipelagic zone to feed. This includes many species of small sharks and a few pelagic rays that prey on small fishes, crustaceans, and cephalopods near the surface.

## AND DEEPER

The bathypelagic zone extends from below the mesopelagic to the ocean floor. This habitat is populated by relatively few organisms adapted for a slow, dark, cold life. Although many species of shark are collected at depths below 3,300 feet (1,000 m), few could live exclusively in this area because of lack of food. More deep-water sharks and skates are found near the bottom, especially below the mesopelagic zone. Here sharks feed on bottom dwellers and mesopelagic fishes that venture close to the bottom. There is also a considerable invertebrate community, which provides food for many species of skate.

# MYTHS *and* LEGENDS

*For many years humans have viewed sharks and rays as mysterious villains;*

*only today are we able to begin to dispel such myths.*

For thousands of years, the natural behavior and nature of sharks and rays were shrouded in mystery by their inaccessible environment. Until recently, most information came from untrained observers who provided only brief glimpses and often biased interpretations. With the advent of scuba and other technologies, humans are now able to observe these animals directly for prolonged periods in their natural environment.

Today's sharks have inherited an unflattering and unjustified reputation that crosses many human cultures. Records of aggressive interactions between sharks and humans

in the Western world can be traced back to the ancient Greeks, but they are conspicuously absent in Egyptian history. Many descriptions record the shark's fearsome nature. Herodotus recorded attacks by sharks on shipwrecked Persian sailors in about 500 BC. Around AD 50, Pliny the Elder wrote about the shark hazard to Mediterranean sponge divers. Today, many scholars believe that the word "shark" is derived from the German word *schurke*, meaning villain or scoundrel.

Sharks and rays usually appear in cultures that have

strong ties to the ocean. Some beliefs are more superstition than fact, while others are integral to cultural mores or religion. In eastern Africa, boat builders anoint a new hull with oil extracted from hammerhead sharks, which is thought to bring good fortune to its seafaring crew. Many fishers in the Mediterranean believe that if a thresher shark crosses the bow of a boat, bad luck will follow. A similar belief is held by many Japanese fishers. Chinese myths tell of a god that takes the form of a shark to scare its believers. Chinese pearl divers respected and avoided the shark as the vicious guardian of the pearls.

Perhaps the best recorded shark legends come from the Pacific cultures of Polynesia.

**SEA MONSTERS** *The "wonderful fish" (above) captured off Maine, USA, in 1836, was really a basking shark. The illustrator interpreted the claspers as webbed feet. A sixteenth-century French woodcut of a sea monster (right).*

The Hawaiians recognized individual species of shark, collectively called *mano*, by giving them specific names, such as *kihikihi* for the hammerhead sharks, and *niuhi* for those that killed humans, such as the tiger shark. There was a great reverence for sharks among these people. A deceased member of a family could return in the form of a shark.

The reincarnated person became a guardian, or *'aumakua*, of its relatives and protected them and their resources on the reef. Sharks were believed to be capable of emerging from the sea as "shark men," or *mano kanaka*, and tricking swimmers or fishers by asking their destination so that they could later devour them.

## THE LORE OF RAYS

The sting of the rays also holds a prominent place in Greek and Roman myths. To kill his father, Odysseus (Ulysses), Telegonus tipped his spear with a large stingray spine. Pliny tells of the sting's remarkable ability to kill trees, and also to pierce armor with the strength of steel.

Contrary to some tales, the stingray cannot shoot the spine from its tail into its victims; the spine is thrust in during direct contact. Stings are almost always the result of stepping on an unseen animal, or of handling a threatened or wounded ray. But the stingray spine was used by natives in many Pacific islands, Australia, and Central America as part of their weaponry.

## CONTROVERSY

Even today, it is easy to find examples of honest misinterpretations of the truth.

**CULTURAL MORES**

*In Hawaiian belief, all sharks (even the human-eating tiger shark [left]) are accorded respect in legend, religion, and daily life. The spines of southern stingrays (below) were believed to be able to kill plants and trees. They were often used to make weapons.*

In the fall of 1808, a large sea monster was washed up on the Isle of Stronsa in the northernmost British Isles. It was measured and described by a number of quite reputable individuals as a sea snake that was 55 feet (17 m) long and about 4 feet (1.2 m) thick. It had a mane like a horse and six separate feet.

The possibility of it being a whale was quickly discounted because it had a long thin neck and tail. A detailed analysis of its skull, neck, shoulders, paws, and toes was made. After considerable inquisition by the local authorities, it was decided that the Stronsa beast was not a hoax, and in 1811 a paper was published on the find, and a new genus *Halsydrus* (sea-water snake) was noted.

The following year, the paper was noticed by Everard Home, a London physician and naturalist. Home had studied the local sharks and realized from the description that the Stronsa beast was really the carcass of a large basking shark (*Cetorhinus maximus*, then known as *Squalus maximus*). He thought that the "mane" was probably the fibers of the fins, and that the third pair of "feet" were probably the claspers.

For more than a century, scientists disagreed on the nature of the beast. The controversy was finally put to rest in 1933, when Professor James Ritchie, of the Royal Scottish Museum, published a paper supporting Home's conclusion and showing that the vertebral centrum exactly matched that of the basking shark.

# WHAT IS *a* SHARK?

*Sharks share most of the general features of the other fishes,*

*but are distinguished by some unique characteristics.*

Sharks comprise only about 1 percent of all living fishes, and share nearly all the major features of their finned relatives. Like all fishes, sharks use gills to extract oxygen from the water in which they live. The body of most species is designed for hydrodynamic efficiency and usually has three types of unpaired fins (dorsal, anal and caudal) and two sets of paired fins (pelvic and pectoral).

Swimming is achieved by side-to-side undulations of the tail, which creates forward propulsion. The vertebral column, or backbone, is composed of a series of individual vertebrae held together by connective tissue, cartilage and surrounding tissues. Sharks also share with other fishes nearly all the same general features of their internal anatomy, including circulatory, digestive, reproductive and nervous systems.

But there are a number of features that separate the

elasmobranchs from the other fishes. Externally, all of the shark's five to seven gill slits are visible, while the gills of most other fishes are protected by a bony plate known as a gill cover or operculum. The shark's fins are thick and relatively stiff, and lack the

delicate bony spines that are found in the fins of most bony fishes. The shark's skin has a layer of tiny, but tough, dermal denticles, as opposed to the much larger flattened scales in most other fishes.

### THE SKELETON

Internally, the body is supported by a cartilaginous skeletal frame, complete with a protective cartilage skull, while most other fishes have a hard, more dense skeleton made of true bone. Sharks do not have an internal swim bladder to help achieve neutral buoyancy but instead rely upon their low-density cartilage, liver oils, and hydrodynamic planing to keep from sinking.

Some of the most notable

**ALL RELATED**

*While the silvertip shark (above) in Papua New Guinea looks very different from the Pacific angelshark (left) in California, and the hammerhead shark (top of opposite page), they all share many distinctive characteristics.*

**NO MISTAKE** *A great hammerhead shark is one of the easiest to identify.*

differences in the anatomy of sharks and most bony fishes are found in the construction of the jaw, the method of its suspension from the head, and the organization of the teeth.

The upper jaw of the shark bears a full set of teeth, and is derived directly from the palatoquadrate cartilages that form during development from the upper mandibular arch. In the more recently derived bony fishes, this structure also supports the upper jaw, but the major tooth-bearing elements develop from special bones derived from the skin.

Similarly, the lower jaw in sharks, known as Meckel's cartilage, is formed from the lower portion of the mandibular arch during development and also bears a full set of teeth in the adult. This structure is greatly reduced in bony fishes, and forms the joint in the corner of the jaw. The teeth develop from other specialized dermal bones.

In most living sharks and rays, the upper jaw is seated on the underside of the skull where it is loosely attached by ligaments and connective tissue. It is suspended from the skull by the hyoid cartilage, which attaches near the back corner of the jaw. This arrangement permits the upper jaw to be thrust out from the skull during feeding, and this is an important means by which many sharks are able to take large, powerful bites from relatively large prey.

## GROUPINGS

Like all living organisms, sharks are classified by the characteristics they share—sharks with more shared characteristics are thought to be more closely related. The differences that can separate major groups of sharks are usually apparent to casual observers. For example, hammerhead sharks are easily distinguished from all other sharks by the broad lateral extensions of the head that give them their name. However, among the different species of hammerheads, characteristics as subtle as the number of lobes on the leading edge, or the presence of a central notch on the head may be a key feature. Other detailed differences of their internal anatomy or their skeleton are usually used by scientists to identify species.

## ARISTOTLE'S EARLY OBSERVATIONS OF SHARKS AND RAYS

The first critical look at shark biology in the Western world was by Aristotle (right) in his work entitled *Historia Animalium*, which appeared in 350 BC. Aristotle was a great observer and logician, and made many insightful observations on their anatomy, reproduction and behavior. For example, he recognized that sharks differed from other fishes in the construction of their uncovered and exposed gill slits. He wrote: "And of those fish that are provided with gills, some have coverings for this organ, whereas all the selachians [sharks and rays] have the organ unprotected by a cover."

He also understood the differences in the swimming mode of the sharks and rays: "Of the shark-kind some have no fins, such as those that are flat and long-tailed, as the ray and the stingray, but these fishes swim actually by the undulatory motion of their flat bodies."

And he formally recognized the sexual difference between male and female sharks: "Again, in cartilaginous fishes the male, in some species, differs from the female in the fact that he is furnished with two appendages hanging down from about the exit of the residuum, and that the female is not so furnished; and this distinction between the sexes is observed in all the species of the sharks and dogfish."

# WHAT IS *a* RAY?

*The ray lives in an almost two-dimensional body yet continues to thrive in a three-dimensional world.*

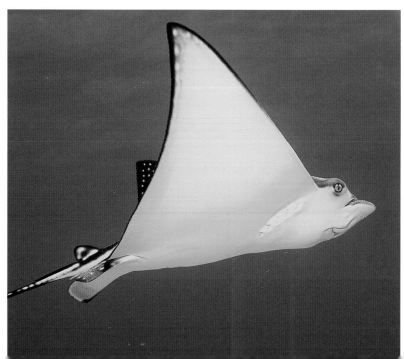

Rays and skates, known collectively as batoid elasmobranchs, are closely allied with the sharks. This remarkable group is represented globally by nearly 500 species and accounts for more than half of all living elasmobranch fishes. They are widespread in almost all bottom-dwelling communities of the oceans, inhabit offshore pelagic environments, and also extend into many inland freshwater habitats.

Batoids made a relatively recent appearance in evolutionary history, appearing some 200 million years after the first sharks. The first rays, relatives of present-day guitar-fishes, are thought to have been derived from flattened sharks

**SOCIABLE ANIMALS** *The spotted eagle ray (right) and the thornback skate (above) both belong to groups that engage in complex social behaviors. The whole family has a well-developed sensory system.*

around the time of the dinosaurs.

Living rays and skates have some important features that separate them from the sharks. The main body is highly flattened, both on the top and bottom. Unlike most sharks, which have short and stout pectoral fins that extend from the body below and behind the head, the pectoral fins of the batoids are attached at the back of the skull, and are greatly enlarged to form a body disc. The tail of most rays is usually reduced in size and not used for swimming. Instead, locomotion comes from the undulation of the tips of the pectoral fins.

The majority of species either lack dorsal and caudal fins on the tail, or have small ones. The eyes, positioned on

the top of the body rather than on the sides, provide a good view of the bottom around the animal, the distant horizon, and the waters above, but batoids are blind to their lower surface. Objects, such as prey items, under the animal are detected and located by a well-developed olfactory system in front of the mouth, and lateral line and electro-receptor systems that span much of the body's underside.

## BREATHING EQUIPMENT

Another major difference is the positioning of the gill slits. In batoids they are located on the bottom surface of the body, whereas in sharks they are found along the sides. Like several bottom-dwelling sharks, the batoids have well-developed spiracles behind the eyes, and these serve to take in water for breathing when

muscular shark-like tail with well-developed dorsal and tail fins. A remarkable convergence can be seen between the batoid sawfishes (Pristidae) and the sawsharks (Pristiophoridae) in which the body shape is much like that of the guitarfishes, with the addition of an elongated rostrum in the shape of a toothed sword that is used to capture prey.

the ray is at rest on the bottom or the mouth is being used for feeding.

Many batoids, such as whiptail stingrays, stingarees, eagle rays, some devilrays, and others, have sharp spines on the tail. These venomous weapons are used defensively against large shark predators and also during social interactions among their own species.

Rays and skates show a wide range of body forms and sizes. Skates are characterized by a round or diamond-shaped body with a small muscular tail that bears two small dorsal fins, and a tiny caudal fin. They are common inhabitants of deep waters around the world but also occur in near-shore areas.

Skates have weak electrogenic organs along both sides of the tail, that may be used in social interactions in the wild. Electric rays usually have a rounded disc, well-developed dorsal and tail fins, and modified muscles in the pectoral fins that in some species can produce electric discharges of hundreds of volts for capture of prey and defense. Whiptail stingrays and stingarees are common inhabitants

of inshore reef areas, and are major predators of small invertebrates in the soft bottom sediments, and also small fishes. Eagle and cow-nose rays actively swim near the bottom or up in the water column around reefs or open coastal waters, and have broad dental plates used to crush hard-shelled mollusks, such as snails and bivalves.

The large pelagic mantas and other devilrays inhabit waters of the open ocean and are distinguished by the presence of cephalic fins on either side of the mouth, which are used to channel water into the mouth while the manta feeds on plankton or small fishes.

The body shape of some batoids seems to be midway between that of a shark and ray. A good example is the guitarfishes, which have a flattened ray-like head and a

## SIZABLE BRAINS

The rays have the largest of the elasmobranch brains, and are highly complex animals that use their exquisite sensory systems for intricate social behaviors. For example, researchers have recently shown that male stingrays in wild populations use their electroreception system to find buried mates.

Other species form large schools that can be seen making long migrations along the coastline. Divers often encounter large aggregations of rays or skates engaged in social interaction or mating activity near the bottom. These animals are easy to watch and can usually be followed for an extended period of time. From simple observations, much can be learned about the behavior of these remarkable creatures.

23

# RELATIVES *of* SHARKS *and* RAYS

*The closest living relatives of the sharks and rays are the chimaeras,*

*thought to be descended from the same direct evolutionary lineage.*

Sharks and rays are members of the taxonomic class known as Chondrichthyes, and are separated from most other living fishes by having a cartilaginous skeleton. They have a long evolutionary history dating back more than 400 million years. During this long time period, they have coexisted with many different forms of fishes, many of which are still living today.

Also within the class Chondrichthyes are the chimaeras, sometimes referred to as ratfish, elephantfish, or ghostsharks, which are the closest living relatives of the sharks and rays. There are approximately 35 species of chimaera worldwide and all are marine creatures. Recent work by paleontologists has shown that the chimaeras first appeared about 340 million years ago during the Devonian, when they are thought to have split off from the early sharks. Some of the extinct species that lived during this time looked much like their living descendants, reinforcing the long history of these fishes.

The body plan of living chimaeras is quite different from that of the sharks or rays. The head is large, with prominent eyes, and the

**CLOSE RELATIVES** *Ratfish (above) occur mainly in deep offshore waters. They have compressed, cartilaginous bodies and rodent-like teeth.*

mouth is located on the ventral surface. The skin of the body is smooth and without scales, and a network of electrosensory pores and lateral line canals is evident on the head and body. Most species have elongate bodies that taper to a small and sometimes whip-like tail.

The first dorsal fin is movable and positioned above the pectoral fins, while the second dorsal is smaller and fixed. There is a long, sharp spine on the leading edge of the first dorsal fin that often bears a venom gland for defense. These fishes swim either by rapid movements of their pectoral fins, or by slow lateral movements of their tails. They are found in cold-water habitats on deep continental shelves and slopes but

some species frequent cold shallow waters in the higher latitudes.

## THE BASIC DIFFERENCES

Like sharks and rays, the chimaera skeleton is formed of cartilage with only slight calcification in some parts. They have a spiral valve intestine and possess no swim bladder. The palatoquadrate cartilage that forms the upper jaw is fused to the bottom of the skull, and does not move during feeding as in most sharks and rays. This type of jaw suspension, termed "holocephaly" or "holostyly," is a major reason for their separation from the elasmo-branch fishes, and the source for their scientific name "holocephalans."

In addition, the four gill arches on each side of the head are shielded by a gill cover with a single opening behind it. The ratfish gill apparatus is located below the skull, as opposed to behind and to the side in the sharks, and there is no spiracle. Water for breathing is taken in through the large nostrils rather than the mouth. The teeth are usually arranged into grinding plates that are beak-like or knobby, compared to the numerous, small, cutting teeth found in many sharks.

These are used by most species of ratfish for feeding on small fishes, hard-shelled invertebrates, or cephalopods.

Like the elasmobranchs, all male chimaeras have pelvic claspers, which are used during mating for sperm transfer from the male to the female. However, male holocephalans also have a secondary clasper located on the head known as a frontal or head clasper. This auxiliary structure is used by males to grasp the rear portion of the female's pectoral fin while the pelvic clasper is inserted into her cloaca. This sexual difference may explain why most male chimaeras are smaller than the females. A set of prepelvic claspers is also found in the male chimaera, but its function is still enigmatic. Female chimaeras lay large, tough, flask- or tadpole-shaped egg cases on the ocean bottom where the young later hatch.

## THE LIVING CHIMAERAS

There are three families of living chimaeras distributed in tropical and temperate seas of the world. The shortnose chimaeras, also called ratfishes or ghostsharks, (family Chimaeridae) consist of the two genera *Hydrolagus* and *Chimaera*, and about 21 species distributed widely across the Pacific and Atlantic oceans. These have a large head, a short, usually round snout, and a body that tapers to a thin, pointed tail, often with a filament extending beyond. The ratfishes occur in deep offshore waters but sometimes move into shallow waters along the coastline.

The plownose chimaeras, also known as elephantfishes, (family Callorhynchidae) occur in the southern hemisphere, mainly off the coasts of Africa, South America, New Zealand, and Australia. This family has one genus (*Callorhynchus*) and four species, which occur in shallow to deep waters. The plownose chimaeras are easily recognized by their elongate snout, which is down-turned directly in front of the mouth. They have a small tail with an elongate upper lobe, like that seen in many sharks.

The longnose chimaeras, also known as the spookfishes (family Rhinochimaeridae), are named for the long, straight, and pointed extension of the snout. There are three genera (*Rhinochimaera*, *Harriotta*, and *Neoharriotta*) and about six species. They occur in deep waters of continental slopes and the bottom of most oceans of the world.

# WHERE *in the* WORLD?

*Sharks and rays are found in nearly all geographic regions of the world,*

*and there are few boundaries that can restrict their movements.*

A human's view of the Earth differs considerably from that of a shark or ray. Marine organisms are free to roam at will, restricted only by the availability of resources, such as food, shelter, mating grounds, and nursery habitats.

The polar regions of the world are characterized by cold waters, relatively long annual periods of darkness, and seasonal productivity. The ice-capped Arctic regions are further limited by weak surface currents that do not promote high biological productivity. As a result of seasonal productivity, year-round food chains that can support sharks and their prey are meager.

Only a few species of shark are found in polar waters, and usually this represents an extreme of their range. Best known examples of polar sharks are the sleeper sharks of the genus *Somniosus*. The Greenland shark, *S. microcephalus*, extends its range into shallow Arctic waters to about 80 degrees north in the cold winter months, but retreats to deeper waters in the summer. Similarly, the Pacific sleeper, *S. pacificus*, extends its northerly range into the Bering Sea. The primary batoid elasmobranchs that occur in polar regions of the world are the skates, which are usually found on the outer region of continental shelves down to abyssal depths.

FOOD ABUNDANCE
As one moves away from the polar regions of the Earth, there is a dramatic increase in primary productivity and complexity of the marine food webs. The subpolar and temperate coastal regions of the Earth are rich in inorganic nutrients where spring and summer light levels produce large phytoplankton blooms. This extra light triggers a seasonal explosion of zooplankton and the small bony fishes that feed upon them.

Basking sharks take direct advantage of this seasonal productivity and make migrations into higher latitudes near almost all large

**CHOICE OF HABITAT** *Pacific cownose rays (above) schooling in a quiet lagoon on the Galapagos Islands. A southern stingray (right) prefers tropical shallows, such as around the Cayman Islands.*

islands and continents during summer months. Here, a basking shark may filter a half million gallons (2 million L) of water per hour to collect large numbers of the abundant zooplankton, such as larval crustaceans, small copepods, and fishes and fish eggs.

Blue and mako sharks make seasonal migrations to higher latitudes to feed upon small zooplanktivores and large species, such as mackerel and small tuna. Other species, such as the porbeagle and thresher sharks, may also leave their normal epipelagic habitat to come to inshore waters during the summer to feed on the abundance of small fishes.

Similar trophic links to the distribution of sharks and rays are seen in coastal areas of

temperate seas. In coastal temperate habitats, a high amount of photosynthetic energy is captured during the summer by both populations of phytoplankton and also by large expanses of macroalgae that grow on the bottom.

Numerous species of horn-sharks, catsharks, houndsharks, and small requiem sharks are prominent members of temperate rocky reef habitats around the world, where they feed heavily upon herbivorous invertebrates and smaller fishes. Because of their relatively small size, most of these species do not make long seasonal migrations to other areas, and can be observed year-round.

## TEMPERATE ZONES

Many species of stingray and bat ray are found in shallow temperate regions where they feed mainly on large bottom-dwelling mollusks and crusta-ceans. Larger shark species, such as many requiem sharks, are regular inhabitants of these areas and feed upon larger predatory fishes including other small sharks and rays.

The distribution of sharks and rays in the warm waters of the tropics is often related to the features of a particular region. For example, many large sharks, such as the whitetip reef, gray reef, and blacktip reef sharks, live almost exclusively on coral reefs of the Indo-Pacific. Among these sharks one may see eagle rays swimming up in the water column, or whiptail stingrays feeding on invertebrates on the sandy bottom.

Usually found on the coral bottom are wobbegongs, catsharks, or nurse sharks, which coexist with round stingrays, torpedo rays, or guitarfishes. Up off the bottom are the whale sharks and mantas, which feed upon plankton and small fishes in nearshore waters or lagoons. Other species, such as many hound and weasel sharks, bat rays, and some whiptail stingrays, congregate near river mouths and on continental shelves in tropical regions.

Unlike many species that are associated with a particular area, most pelagic sharks and rays are circumglobal in distribution. This includes the epipelagic blue, oceanic whitetip, thresher, and mako sharks; the mesopelagic crocodile sharks; and the bathypelagic cookiecutter and pygmy sharks. Similarly, pelagic rays, such as the manta ray, are also widely distributed in oceanic waters of the world.

27

# THE DANGERS *of* OBSERVATION

*Sharks and rays have few ways with which to express their intentions, so patience and common sense can be a diver's most valuable protection.*

To generalize about the behavior of all sharks and rays would be an impossible task. Each species lives in a particular habitat, feeds on slightly different prey and responds to a different set of conditions in its respective environment. So it is easy to understand why their behavior is hard to predict.

## BODY LANGUAGE

The mental state of a dog can be predicted reliably by observing the position of the ears, the exposure of the teeth, and the wagging of the tail. We are less familiar with the body language and movements of most sharks and rays. Rather than to advertise their presence or give conspicuous signals about their motivational state, shark bodies are designed for hydrodynamic efficiency and to be as unobtrusive as possible. To understand the behavior of a particular shark or ray species,

one must spend hours observing their natural movements and interactions with other organisms.

Small bottom-dwelling sharks and rays in coastal temperate waters or on tropical coral reefs are the easiest to observe. Many sharks, such as catsharks and hornsharks, spend much of their time at rest or probing in crevices and cracks on the reef for food. Other small coastal sharks, such as houndsharks, swim over the sandy bottom where their feeding or social behaviors can be observed by a snorkeler. When watching the behavior of small shallow-water species, it is important to stay well clear. Moving in close to a small shark will usually upset the animal and it will swim rapidly away. The observer must avoid inadvertently influencing its behavior.

**KEEP YOUR DISTANCE**
*A great white shark (left) goes after tuna bait set to attract it. Observing a southern stingray (above), Grand Cayman Island.*

## THE BOTTOM DWELLERS

Most bottom-dwelling species of ray make excellent subjects for observation. Unlike most species of shark, which are constantly on the move, many whiptail and round stingrays will forage in the sandy bottom or probe the reef bottom for hours within a small area. Often divers will encounter small groups of rays inspecting one another or interacting in some interesting way. These ray behaviors can be watched for hours from the surface while snorkeling, or up close using scuba gear. Rays can often be closely approached by prone divers.

Many of the larger sharks and rays are rather shy of the scuba diver, and require special attention in order to get close enough to watch. Most are fast swimmers and afford only a brief glimpse or snapshot from the camera as they swim by on their regular daily rounds.

If the diver is suspended in the water column, many sharks, such as the tiger shark, will often circle the diver just at the limit of visibility, and occasionally approach for a closer look. One technique in watching large sharks within an area is to sit quietly on the reef bottom hidden from view, and use slow, controlled breathing. The noise from the diver's regulator is noisy and distracting to the shark.

Larger requiem sharks, such as the Galapagos or gray reef sharks, can be unnerving to the novice as they approach to inspect the diver. In these cases, experienced divers stress that it is essential to stay calm.

One prominent exception to the general lack of known behaviors in large sharks, is the well-documented agonistic display of the gray reef shark of the Indo-Pacific.

Gray reef sharks will exhibit this behavior (see p. 108) when they are threatened by an approaching diver, and will often attack if further pressed. However, the risk can be greatly reduced by under-standing the nature and meaning of the agonistic display, and also by making allowance for a path by which to exit, if necessary.

## SENSIBLE PRECAUTIONS

Although sharks are clearly not the ravenous killers of the oceans so often portrayed in films and stories, they must be respected and not provoked. Many divers directly provoke resting nurse sharks by pulling them by the tail, and end up with serious bites.

In other cases, provocation may be something as simple as one's presence in the personal space of a gray reef shark. Some divers are bitten when sharks are artificially baited. In these circumstances, the diver has set the sharks in a feeding situation and their excitement increases. This can only heighten the chance of a diver being bitten, whether by accident or intent. Common sense is the diver's best tool.

## VIEWING SHARKS IN BAITED SITUATIONS

With increased interest in sharks by the public, and more people taking up diving, tours that view sharks underwater in the wild are becoming popular. Many of these operations put out bait, as in the picture above, to attract sharks into the area of a reef and also to keep them around for viewing. In some areas, this practice is highly controversial. Some feel that chumming is unnatural and potentially unhealthy for the sharks, and that it may make them dependent on humans for food. Such baiting activity may also increase the number of sharks in areas used for other water sports, putting people at risk. Others argue that the sharks will stop feeding on natural prey, and this will ultimately affect the health of the local reef. Much remains to be learned about the interactions between humans and sharks, and how best to arrange our meetings.

**FAMILY VIEWING** *Neal Watson with his two sons (left), watching a Caribbean reef shark in the Bahamas. Observation of the behavior of various species adds to our overall knowledge and helps us to understand how all organisms interact.*

... *all at last returns to the sea—to Oceanus, the ocean river, like the ever-flowing stream of time, the beginning and the end.*

*The Sea Around Us,*
RACHEL CARSON (1907–64), American writer and biologist

# SHARKS *and* RAYS *in* HISTORY

*Historically and geographically, not everyone has the same perception of sharks and rays.*

The better we know a place and the animals that inhabit it, the richer and more complex are our relationships with them. These associations are often reflected in the legends and historical accounts that make up our cultural fabrics.

## VARYING VIEWS OF SHARKS AND RAYS

The cultures, ancient and modern, of peoples who rely on the sea for their livelihood and recreation are rich in lore and knowledge about the animals that live within it. The Haida and Klingit people of Pacific Northwest America,

for example, featured dogfish sharks (as well as killer whales, salmon and other creatures) in their art. Clan hats, screens, and tall, carved wooden poles sometimes include dogfish sharks, with their typical spines before the dorsal fins being clearly visible.

Polynesian cultures viewed diverse kinds of sharks in a variety of ways, from utility to

reverence. On the other hand, continental cultures have had starker perspectives of sharks and a shallow tradition about marine creatures. A well-known story in the Judeo-Christian tradition involves the prophet Jonah, thrown overboard by fearful sailors and swallowed by an ocean monster. Biblical scholars and biologists still speculate whether it was a great white shark, a baleen whale or some other species.

**CULTURAL ICONS** *The Haida screen (above) features dogfish faces. The early sixteenth-century painting (below) depicts the story of Jonah and the whale.*

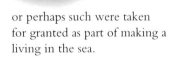

For the most part, the cultural histories of western industrialized nations, such as the United States, have been dominated by cultures not familiar with the diversity of life in the ocean. European mythology is more keyed to terrestrial animals. The fearsome predator is likely to be a bear or a wolf, certainly not a shark. But in oceanic cultures, legendary animals are more often sea creatures. The werewolves of European tales have their shark counterparts in the legends of Polynesia.

## EARLY RECORDINGS

Aristotle (384–322 BC) spent several years on the island of Lesbos, where he observed sea life and talked to sponge divers, fishermen and sailors. He wrote in detail on the biology, anatomy, and behavior of sharks and rays. In *Historia Animalium*, he recognized the relationship of the group and the cartilaginous nature of their skeletons. He noted the differences from fishes in gill anatomy, and recognized their universally carnivorous habits.

Aristotle also noted the startling behavior of what modern divers and fishermen call the electric ray (*Torpedo torpedo*): "The torpedo narcotizes the creatures it wants to catch, overpowering them by the power of shock that is resident in the body; and feeds upon them; it also hides in the sand and mud and catches all the creatures

**SHOCK TACTICS** *Aristotle knew that the ray* Torpedo torpedo *(right) could deliver a severe shock.*

that swim its way and come under its narcotizing influence. This phenomenon has actually been observed in operation … the torpedo is known to cause a numbness even in human beings."

Despite his interest and keen reporting about sharks and rays, Aristotle's accounts contain very little about shark threats to humans. Perhaps the Mediterranean of ancient times offered few encounters between humans and sharks,

## THE LEGEND OF KAPA'AHEO

Long ago, young local girls enjoyed swimming in a lovely cove in Kohala on the Big Island (Hawaii). Often a swimmer would disappear and never be seen again. The people were very afraid and wanted to learn what had happened to the girls. A fisherman noticed that when a swimmer disappeared, a mysterious stranger named Kapa'aheo could be seen sitting on the shore nearby. This fisherman then gathered all of the fishermen together so that they were on hand when the girls went swimming again.

As before, the stranger was sitting on the rocks overlooking the cove. When he vanished, the leader of the fishermen ordered them all to dive into the water and form a protective circle around the girls. A shark swam toward the group and a huge fight began. Many times the shark was wounded by the spears of the fishermen. Finally the shark swam away. When the men swam back to shore, they found the stranger dying from many wounds that looked as if they had been made by fishing spears. When the man died from the wounds, he was transformed into the stone found near the edge of the cliff by the ocean.

or perhaps such were taken for granted as part of making a living in the sea.

## HAWAIIAN LEGEND

In contrast, the oral tradition of ancient Hawaii features many particulars about interactions with sharks, including species implicated in human attack in modern times. Various interpreters of Hawaiian legends have called the large dangerous sharks of Hawaii *niuhi*. However, it is seldom clear which of the larger species is intended. It is likely to be the tiger shark, but it is also possible that the name refers to the great white. Based on the behavioral and anatomical differences in the two animals, however, we can make some educated guesses about which species is involved in a particular legend. Kapa'aheo, the Kohala shark god, seems almost certain to be a great white shark. In this legend, Kapa'aheo is transformed into a stone— a long, shark-sized reclining lava column (seen above)—which has been transported from its original site to rest in a secluded garden in the Bishop Museum in Honolulu.

# SHARK FISHING

*Although some traditional cultures have shown respect and even reverence for sharks and rays, humans have, for the most part, considered them as creatures to be at the least exploited, or at the most exterminated.*

Even cultures with great respect for sharks have fished for them. It is likely that humans have caught sharks since pre-historic times. Ancient graves of the Chumash people of what is now the coastal area of Santa Barbara County in California contain nasal cartilages of mako sharks.

The purpose for which these cartilages were used is unknown, but they were probably associated with rituals of some sort.

Cultures of Melanesia, Micronesia, and Polynesia have long traditions of shark fishing. The hooks they crafted especially for shark fishing can be large and elaborate. They used shark skin in drum heads, shark teeth in weapons and tools, and shark flesh for food as well as for ritual purposes.

### THERE'S ALWAYS A CATCH

*A wooden hook with rope attached (above left), used by islanders in the South Pacific to catch sharks. Shark teeth are embedded in these swords (right) from Wuvulu Island, Bismarck Archipelago. The pile of shark carcasses (below) was discarded after a sportfishing tournament.*

## WHO IS THE MORE FEARSOME PREDATOR?

From 1990 through 1996, sharks attacked 344 people worldwide and killed 44, an average "take" of about 6 humans per year. Although there are remote areas of the world where a shark attack might go unreported, death by shark is sensational enough to come to wide attention, so we have some confidence in this estimate.

According to the United Nations Fishery and Agriculture Organization (UN/FAO), humans landed at least 633,600 metric tonnes of sharks in a single year, 1991. Most fishery biologists believe that this is only a fraction of the real catch. Many countries do not report their catch to UN/FAO, and unlanded bycatch is not included. In any case, even if this number is low, humans catch many sharks every year. If the average shark caught is estimated to weigh 110 pounds (50 kg), the UN/FAO figure indicates that humans killed at least 12 million sharks in 1991 alone. And we have every reason to believe that shark fishing has increased in the past five years.

For every human killed by a shark, two million sharks are killed by humans. In other words, 12,000,000 sharks are killed by humans per year compared to 6 humans killed by sharks. If we express these statistics as the score of a sports competition, it is obvious that sharks are losing disastrously. And so, in fact, are we humans, because by fishing at this rate we are jeopardizing world populations of top predators that are essential to the health of marine communities.

## EXPLOITATION

Modern fisheries continue to exploit a wide diversity of sharks, from small (spiny dogfish) to large (giant whale sharks), from coastal to pelagic, and from tropical to temperate seas. There is strong evidence that all shark fisheries are over-exploiting their resources. Because of their small litter size and slow rate of reproduction, sharks are particularly vulnerable to overfishing.

A wide selection of shark products (see pp. 36–7) is sold in modern marketplaces. These include fins and flesh for food, liver oil as a source for pharmaceuticals and vitamins, hides for leather, skin for abrasive sheets and for surgical skin implants, teeth and skeletal parts for jewelry, and blood components and cartilage for health-food supplements (reputed to diminish the risk of cancer). Demand for these products has varied over time, in part because of techno-logical and cultural changes.

## FISHERIES

Since the mid-1980s, demand for shark products has greatly increased. As swordfish and tuna catches have fallen, fishers have, increasingly, turned to sharks. Because of demand for shark meat and for the fins used in shark fin soup, many species of sharks have come under heavy harvesting pressure in North American waters. Historically, with a few regional excep-tions, there have been few commercial shark fisheries in these waters.

A significant harpoon fishery for whale sharks is now underway in the western Pacific. Scientists have plans to see whether the whale sharks of Ningaloo Reef, Western Australia, may travel to the area of this extensive fishery.

Information on the inter-national shark trade is limited, but it is estimated that world trade of shark products exceeds $240 million. True numbers are unknown because many foreign markets do not reveal catch or trade statistics.

## PROTECTING SPECIES

Recently, the United States published plans to protect 39 species of shark. This Fishery Management Plan aims to reduce commercial and recreational fishing of sharks through quotas and licensing requirements. The plan also bans the practice of stripping the fins from sharks and dumping the maimed sharks back into the ocean.

Major environmental groups are also becoming increasingly concerned about overfishing of sharks and other species. In the United States, the Ocean Wildlife Campaign was launched recently as a collaborative effort involving the National Audubon Society, the National Coalition for Marine Conservation, the World Wildlife Fund, and other interested organizations. The effort is intended to increase public understanding of giant ocean fishes (sharks, tunas, and billfish) and to facilitate management measures that are appropriate.

Conservation of sharks is gaining support in many quarters. Some species, including great white sharks (*Carcharodon carcharias*), are protected in California and in Australia. Perhaps in the twenty-first century, the exploitation of the twentieth century will turn toward the reverence held for sharks by coastal cultures of long ago.

# THE USE
## *of* SHARKS *and* RAYS

*Sharks and rays are a valuable resource, but their harvesting will have to be carefully monitored and regulated if they are to be used and yet conserved.*

The use of sharks and rays for meat and other products predates recorded history. Every part of these creatures has been used by humans for some purpose. As a result, their conservation is a serious problem (see pp. 44–5). In a traditional fishery in northern Australia, Aborigines continue to catch sharks and rays to prepare *buunhdhaarr*, in which the liver and flesh are boiled separately, then minced and mixed for food. They also use the stinging spines of stingrays as tips for spears.

### ARTIFACTS
Shark teeth have traditionally been used in many cultures for making functional and ceremonial objects. The Maoris of New Zealand used the teeth of the broadnose sevengill shark (*Notorynchus cepedianus*) to make war weapons, and prized the teeth of the mako shark (*Isurus oxyrinchus*) as ear ornaments. Inuit people made knives from the teeth of the Greenland sleeper shark (*Somniosus microcephalus*). Today, the teeth and jaws of this shark are widely used in local curio trades, and are eagerly sought after by trophy hunters.

When Europeans first settled Australia in 1788, as well as eating shark meat, they began to extract oil from shark livers for lighting and medicinal purposes. This practice continued through the first half of the nineteenth century. Later, between 1875 and the early 1920s, sharks were used as fertilizer for Tasmanian orchards. Today, in other regions, sharks and rays are still processed into fertilizer and fishmeal to

**CURIOS** *The shagreen-covered box c. 1932 (above) was probably used for cigarettes. Scrimshaw of a sailing galleon on the tooth of a great white shark (left). Shark fins for sale (below) in Hong Kong.*

feed domestic animals.

During the 1930s and 1940s, shark liver was in demand as a source of vitamin A, but this market collapsed during the 1950s when synthetic vitamin A became available. Recently, there has been a demand for squalene oil, extracted from the livers of several species of shark, particularly deep-sea dogfishes. Rapid development of fisheries was triggered by demand for the soupfin shark (*Galeorhinus galeus*) in several parts of the world. Considered an aphrodisiac in parts of Asia, shark fin soup has been regarded as a delicacy by the Chinese for more than 2,000 years—it became an essential part of formal banquets during the Ming Dynasty (1368–1644). The fins of many species of shark and ray are currently among the world's most expensive fishery products, with Hong Kong the acknowledged world capital for shark fin cuisine.

## VARIED USES

Because it is embedded with enamel-tipped scales, the skin of sharks and rays is quite rough. Dried but untanned skin, called shagreen, is often used like fine sandpaper for polishing wood. In Sumatra, the stretched shagreen of the cowtail stingray (*Pastinachus sephen*) is used for the skins of drums and tambourines, and in Japan, it was used to bind the hilts of swords to provide a non-slip grip. During the seventeenth century, European artisans began imitating the Oriental practice of binding books with shagreen and also used it to cover personal articles, such as jewelry

## LIVER OIL

The oil (or lipid) content of shark liver varies from nil to more than 90 percent, depending on the species and the maturity of the shark. The lipid contains vitamin A and squalene. Vitamin A is essential for the formation of visual pigments within the retinal cells of the eye; people lacking this vitamin are likely to suffer from night blindness. Squalene, which is synthesized by sharks, has many commercial applications. It is used as a fine, high-grade machine oil in high-technology industries; as a skin rejuvenator in the cosmetics industry; and for pharmaceutical products requiring a non-oily base. Oils rich in squalene are low in cholesterol. They may also be rich in the polyunsaturated fatty acids that act as anticoagulants and keep the blood moving freely.

boxes, spectacle cases and silverware cases.

Today, boroso leather, made from the shagreen of small sharks by lightly polishing the scales to a high gloss, is expensive and in demand in specialty markets. Shark leather, made by chemically removing the enamel tips, has higher tensile strength than leather made from cattle hides.

Although it is traditionally consumed dried, salted, and smoked by coastal communities around the world, shark meat today forms a significant part of the fresh fish trade. Marketing campaigns have been introduced to overcome consumer resistance to shark meat for human consumption, and shark has often been sold under market names designed to disguise its true identity. For example, piked dogfish (*Squalus acanthias*) has been marketed in the United States as grayfish. Various shark organs are eaten in some areas, too. In the Solomon Islands, for example, all tissue other than the intestine is consumed. Elsewhere, consumption of intestine, stomach, heart, and even the skin is common. The rough

scales are first removed, then the skin is prepared for the table by bleaching.

Interest in sharks and rays for medicinal purposes is also growing rapidly. In the United States, shark corneas have been transplanted to humans. Many scientists believe that extracts from shark cartilage suppress the development of tumors and now use these extracts in the treatment of cancer. Chondroiten, derived from cartilage, is used as artificial skin for burn victims, and extracts of shark bile have been found effective for treating acne. Anticoagulant bloodclotting agents have also been extracted and may be beneficial in the treatment of some cases of cardiac arrest.

**THE EYE OF THE SHARK** *In the US, shark corneas are proving successful as transplants for human eyes.*

# DECLINE *in* SHARK *and* RAY POPULATIONS

*Fishing practices, habitat modification, and programs designed to reduce the risk of shark attack to bathers have all contributed to the decline in shark and ray populations.*

All around the world, shark and ray populations are falling as harvesting continues by traditional, artisanal (which includes small-scale commercial and subsistence fishers), and industrial fishing. Game fishers, divers, and other recreational fishers also play a significant part in the harvesting process. This raises serious ethical questions about the conservation of sharks and rays (see pp. 44–5).

## INDUSTRIAL FISHERIES

Reported landings of cartilaginous fishes currently exceeds 700,000 tons a year. A small part of this consists of chimaeras, with the rest fairly evenly divided between sharks in one category and skates and rays in another. Although cartilaginous fishes comprise less than 1 percent of the

**RAYS** *Spotted eagle rays (above) with their white markings and whip-like tails. A large manta ray (below) caught in the Sea of Cortez, Mexico.*

world's fish catch, commercial fishing is having a major impact on shark and ray populations.

The catch has been rising steadily since the 1920s, but several fisheries began much earlier than that. One fishery off the west coast of Ireland caught basking sharks (*Cetorhinus maximus*) for some 60 years from 1770 until the species became scarce. As stocks subsequently became re-established, the fishery renewed its activities during the 1940s, but the catch had peaked and then declined to a low level again by the end of the 1950s.

A similar pattern occurred in the Norwegian fishery for porbeagle sharks (*Lamna nasus*), where

the catch peaked in the 1940s and 1960s but declined to a low level by the mid-1980s.

Demand for shark liver oil during the 1930s and 1940s stimulated rapid growth of fisheries for the soupfin shark (*Galeorhinus galeus*) on the continental shelves off California, New Zealand, southern Australia, South Africa, the east coast of South America in southern Brazil, Uruguay, and northern Argentina. While profits fell during the 1950s because of a drop in demand for liver oil, the fishery had already collapsed in California during the 1940s because of a decline in the population of mature females.

In southern Australia and New Zealand, where this species was persistently targeted for the production of shark meat, catches have fallen steadily. More recently, similar trends have occurred for the piked dogfish (*Squalus acanthias*) taken in trawl fisheries off North America and in the eastern Atlantic, and for some of the larger species of shark taken off the east coast of the United States.

In addition to such specialized fisheries, trawl and tuna fisheries operating over wide areas take significant numbers of cartilaginous fishes as

**HUNTERS AND HUNTED** *A diver inspects the carcass of a scalloped hammerhead shark (left) caught in an illegally set net. Anglers A. Dean and B. Rogers with a great white shark (below) caught in Australian waters. One-time attack victims Rod Fox and Henri Bource look on.*

bycatch. Much of this accidental catch from bottom trawling on the continental shelves and continental slopes of the world is not adequately reported, or is discarded dead at sea. The widespread practice of removing the fins (finning) and discarding the rest of the carcasses, often while the animal is still alive, raises huge ethical questions.

## INSHORE FISHERIES

Many of the world's unregulated artisanal and recreational fisheries for bottom-living sharks and pelagic sharks have large numbers of small fishing boats in coastal waters. This results in the overfishing of many species of shark and ray in these waters. The effects of this vary considerably among species, because many of the species harvested are distributed widely inshore and offshore, and the boats are restricted to a much smaller range, generally only a few miles from shore. The falling catch rates in these areas probably reflect falling numbers of sharks in the local area rather than a major decline in overall population.

Traditional fisheries are wide and varied but, like the artisanal and recreational fisheries, have been confined to inshore and coastal waters. Catches have been small compared with those from the industrial and artisanal fisheries and for most species have had negligible impact on populations of sharks and rays.

## HABITAT MODIFICATION

The stock of juvenile soupfin sharks in Port Phillip Bay, Australia, has been depleted over the years, probably permanently. As a result of intensive fishing of juveniles, the catch from the bay increased threefold between 1942 and 1944, and then fell rapidly until the early 1950s, when small sharks of the species became protected by the introduction of a legal minimum length. At this time, the western region of Port Phillip Bay, known as the Geelong Arm, was identified as an important nursery area for the soupfin shark. Given the high movement rates of adult sharks, it is surprising that this inshore area has not been replenished. It now seems likely that the reduced use of this formerly important nursery by soupfin sharks is a result of habitat modification in the now highly industrialized area of the Geelong Arm.

## SHARK-ATTACK STRATEGY

The trend of initial decline in catch rates followed by stable numbers is a common one for most species detected in shark-fishing programs designed to reduce the risk of attack. These are in place at such centers as KwaZulu-Natal, South Africa, and in Queensland and New South Wales, Australia. Some of the trends seem to be caused by a fall in local numbers rather than by stock depletion. This theory is supported by the general pattern where catch rates are higher when fishing begins at a new site than at neighboring sites that have been fished for long periods.

# CHANGING HABITATS

*The close links between sharks and rays and their habitat mean that any disturbance to that habitat has the potential to change their distribution and abundance.*

Changes to a habitat can be natural or induced by humans. Cyclones and typhoons are natural events that can damage reef and inshore habitats. Large swells can cause structural change to shorelines, and storm tides can flood inshore areas and upset the balance in areas not accustomed to heavy wave action. Large, sudden influxes of abnormally warm, cold, fresh, or saline water into an area have been known to cause fish kills, and may even affect the survival of sharks and rays, particularly if the area is a nursery for newborn or young animals. But in general, sharks and rays have been living with these natural cycles of habitat change for millions of years, and are well adapted to cope.

They are not well adapted to cope with more permanent habitat changes induced by human activity. This sort of modification is most conspicuous in freshwater habitats with the construction of physical barriers, such as dam walls, and the collection of water for heavy industry and agricultural irrigation. Land clearing and poor land-use practices in a river catchment can affect shark habitat within the river, the estuary, and offshore. Sediment carried down rivers will muddy the water and may smother reefs and sea grass. Such changes can lead to infestations of noxious plants and animals that disturb a species' habitat.

Fishing activities also impact on fish habitat. Methods such as deep-sea trawling and scallop dredging can modify the seabed and affect the plants and animals living on it. While occasionally a change to habitat might be beneficial to a species, it is more likely that it will not.

## FISHING

The habitats and behavior of sharks and rays can be affected by various fishing practices. Fishers in the industrial shark fishery off southern Australia who target the soupfin sharks (*Galeorhinus galeus*) and

**HUMAN INTRUSIONS** *Satellite map (left) shows the hole in the ozone layer over Antarctica. A highway across the Florida Keys (above). Sign (below) on a California beach warns of contamination.*

gummy sharks (*Mustelus antarcticus*) believe that the presence of sharks captured in bottom-set gill nets repels free-swimming sharks temporarily from an area. The noise and disturbance to the habitat caused by trawl fishing also seems to have the effect of keeping sharks away.

Fish and other wildlife can become entangled in lost or discarded fish netting and plastic bait wrapping that often pollute their habitat. New laws and codes of practice in various parts of the world are being implemented to discourage people from discarding unwanted plastic and fishing gear at sea.

Gill nets can continue fishing ("ghostfishing") after being lost, until eventually

**DANGER**
**CONTAMINATED WATER KEEP OUT**

**PELIGRO**
**AGUA CONTAMINADA ALEJESE**

they roll up into a ball. This is not such a problem in areas of strong tidal flow where they roll up fairly quickly. Gill nets are rarely lost by experienced fishers equipped with modern position-fixing instruments and reliable equipment for retrieving the gill nets.

## ECOTOURISM

Growing interest in viewing and filming sharks, particularly white sharks (*Carcharodon carcharias*), from boats on the surface and from underwater cages is giving rise to a new form of ecotourism. Development of ecotourism based on sharks, however, depends on attracting the sharks to an area by spreading chum (a type of bait) made up of mammal or fish blood and oil. With the development of such an industry, there is an urgent need to answer such questions as: What are the effects of chumming sharks to an area? Does chumming impact on seals and other marine life, either directly by fouling an area, or indirectly by

concentrating sharks in that area? What do sharks do after chumming ceases? Does chumming in an area increase the risk of shark attack on humans in nearby areas?

## OZONE DEPLETION

Ozone thinning, through its effect on whole ecosystems, has the potential to alter shark habitats. An increase in the ultraviolet radiation that penetrates surface waters has the potential to alter phytoplankton which, through the process of photosynthesis, provide the primary source of food in marine waters. Any changes at this primary level of the food chain have flow-on effects farther up the chain.

## GLOBAL WARMING

At the global level, climate change also has the potential to alter shark habitats in the future. Long-term effects of climate change could include alterations in sea level, water temperatures, tidal and current patterns, coastal erosion, and storm patterns.

**INSIDIOUS DAMAGE** *Sand is eroded relentlessly by wave action in the Maldives (above); and a coastal settlement in Cairns, northern Australia, (below) inevitably causes pollution.*

Ecologists do not wholly understand what controls the distribution of species. Many factors, including climate, food supply, and the ability to compete with other species, are involved, and all of these factors affect the others in a complex web of interactions. Changes in climate can affect interactions between species within an ecosystem. A species that is successful in today's climate might be ousted by invaders better suited to a new climate.

Most important, global warming will vary from place to place. For example, changes are likely to be much greater at the poles than at the equator. Changing patterns in climate could impact first on migratory species of shark where migration is timed to fit in with food supplies along the route, or to take advantage of conditions suitable for the survival of large numbers of offspring. If events get out of phase, the effects on the migratory species could be catastrophic.

41

# OCEANS *under* THREAT

*Pollution of the oceans occurs worldwide, and whether deliberate or not, it has devastating and far-reaching effects on the marine environment.*

Dumping chemical, animal, and plant waste products into the oceans must be closely monitored. The shipping and oil industries must be tightly controlled to minimize their impact on marine ecosystems. And rapidly developing aquaculture practices—the cultivation of marine plants and animals for human consumption—must be regulated.

## POLLUTION

Physical disturbances and pollutants can affect whole ecosystems. Some of the more obvious pollutants are sewage effluent, plastics, chemicals, and pesticides. Extra amounts of the nutrients nitrogen, phosphorus, and silicon can find their way into the marine environment, causing an increase in phytoplankton and other plant growth. An abundance of nutrients often promotes or contributes to

algal blooms (some of which are toxic), leading to clogged rivers, channels and bays, or overgrowth of corals and reefs.

Some pollutants, such as heavy metals and organic chemicals—for example, PCBs (polychlorinated biphenyls)— take a long time to break down. When these materials persist in the environment, they can adversely affect aquatic organisms and ecosystems in general. Some are absorbed from the sea water into the tissues of organisms that feed on polluted materials. Individual organisms can accumulate

some of these pollutants to concentrations much higher than background levels ("bioaccumulation"). When these organisms are in turn eaten, the concentration of pollutants increases again, and so on, up the food chain ("bioamplification").

The heavy metal mercury is one pollutant that reaches high levels in sharks and rays. Mercury accumulates naturally in these organisms in the course of feeding, but when its background levels are further elevated from human sources, concentrations can become markedly increased. Very low levels of some organic pollutants ("environmental estrogens") can suppress the number of male fish produced.

## OIL AND SHIPPING

More than two million tons of oil escape into the marine environment each year, and only about 15 percent of this comes from natural seepage. The remainder comes from discharges by tankers and other shipping, discharges from storage facilities and refineries, and accidental events

**POLLUTION** *Underwater sewer outlets (above) and industries, such as this paper mill (left) in New Brunswick, Canada, pollute the oceans mercilessly.*

**CLEAN-UP** *An oil spill in Prince William Sound, Alaska, is a nightmare to rectify.*

such as oil spills and ruptured pipelines. Recent wars resulted in major oil contamination in the Middle East.

Although less of a problem in open waters, hydrocarbons and other toxicants in oil can contaminate fish flesh either through direct contact or via the food chain. Impact from oil spills is most likely through damage to vulnerable coastal sea grass, mangrove, salt marsh, coral reef, rocky reef, and polar habitats. Nurseries and shallow waters where sharks and rays gather are prone to harm from oil spills.

Dredging harbors and shipping channels can stir up mud and silt that may settle in sensitive coastal ecosystems. Replenishing sand on beaches for recreational purposes can have similar localized effects.

## SPREAD OF MARINE ORGANISMS

Biological invasion of marine areas by foreign organisms is a major threat to the natural communities of plants and animals. Organisms that become attached to the hulls of ships and to oil rigs are transported with them. Ships draw sea water into ballast tanks and floodable holds for stability. This water is later discharged while the ship is underway or in various ports. Water taken aboard may contain planktonic organisms and sediments. In this way, plankton groups are spread over long distances. Surveys show that all major taxonomic groups are being introduced to new areas in this way.

These transported organisms occur at all levels of the food chain, but some of the species that keep the system in balance may be missing. Without these natural controls, certain species may proliferate to levels that swamp the new site and replace indigenous species.

Many of the inshore and coastal waters receiving ballast water are already disturbed by the effects of urbanization around ports. This makes them particularly vulnerable to invasions that further alter community structure and function. Invasion by exotic species is a very serious threat to marine habitats, and the ecological impacts cannot be fully predicted by knowing the biology of the introduced organisms and ecology in their original habitat. Inshore areas used by sharks and rays as nurseries are particularly sensitive.

## FARMING COASTAL WATERS

As catches from wild fishery stocks decline, one way to supply an increasing demand for fish is by aquaculture. But such operations have many drawbacks. Aquaculture requires pollution-free waters but its practice alters and pollutes mangroves, marshlands, and other inshore habitats. Some species, such as shrimp, are farmed in such huge numbers that disease is a constant threat. When a site becomes contaminated, the industry tends to move on to a fresh location, devastating whole stretches of mangrove coastline. Escape of cultured exotic species and genetically altered strains is another worrying factor.

The most rewarding targets for aquaculture are high-value species such as prawns, shrimp, scallops, abalone, oysters, pearl oysters, salmon, and tuna. So far, there is no interest in farming sharks and rays. Their relatively low value and the small number of young produced by individuals make them poor prospects.

# CHANGING ATTITUDES

*Our attitudes toward sharks have always been—and probably always will be—colored by the fact that some species kill humans.*

The primal fear of being devoured by a predator is deeply rooted in our psyche. But too often that fear has been used, at least in part, to justify our wasteful killing and overfishing of such creatures, especially sharks.

Yet as each of us has learned more about the complexities of sharks and their behavior, our collective attitude is becoming far more enlightened. Certainly mixed into every personal point of view is a healthy respect and fundamental fear, but it can be ventured that our feelings toward sharks today are very different from the attitudes prevailing among the generations of the past.

## STUNNING IMAGES

Less than 40 years ago, there were few opportunities for general readers (or, for that matter, even scientists) to see even mediocre photographs of living sharks and rays. Today, books, magazines, and television afford a treasure house of sharp color images of an abundance of marine animals. Almost every reader of this book will probably have seen breathtaking images of even some of the largest species, whale sharks and manta rays. Many readers have seen or plan to see and photograph them firsthand.

**LEGENDARY ADVENTURERS**
*Using a bathyscaphe, naturalist William Beebe (right) stirred imaginations with investigations of the deep. Photographer Hans Hass (below), an early pioneer of underwater photo techniques, lifted the veil on ocean mysteries.*

A generation ago, to swim with sharks was to engage in the pursuits of a lunatic, or at least of a bold adventurer whose accounts were the stuff of sensational tales. But our current attention and enlightening interest is based on the foundation of such mad adventures. It is useful to review some of these accounts and realize the changes in our perspective and to appreciate the wealth of opportunity now available to us.

One of the earliest adventurers to look living sharks in the eye and to popularize his exploits was the American naturalist William Beebe. In addition to traveling to great depths in a bathyscaphe in the 1930s, a swim-suited Beebe made shallower dives on coral reefs in the Caribbean and the Pacific with compressed air supplied through a brass helmet. He viewed sharks firsthand, with the perspective of a biologist. Still, his account of harpooning a whale shark near Cabo San Lucas, Baja California, Mexico, in 1938, strikes us today as particularly brutal. But we must remember that at the time he thought he was collecting a rare species.

Many a present-day marine biologist was brought up on the adventuring tales of diving photographer Hans Hass, who

**CLEAN-UP** *An oil spill in Prince William Sound, Alaska, is a nightmare to rectify.*

such as oil spills and ruptured pipelines. Recent wars resulted in major oil contamination in the Middle East.

Although less of a problem in open waters, hydrocarbons and other toxicants in oil can contaminate fish flesh either through direct contact or via the food chain. Impact from oil spills is most likely through damage to vulnerable coastal sea grass, mangrove, salt marsh, coral reef, rocky reef, and polar habitats. Nurseries and shallow waters where sharks and rays gather are prone to harm from oil spills.

Dredging harbors and shipping channels can stir up mud and silt that may settle in sensitive coastal ecosystems. Replenishing sand on beaches for recreational purposes can have similar localized effects.

## SPREAD OF MARINE ORGANISMS

Biological invasion of marine areas by foreign organisms is a major threat to the natural communities of plants and animals. Organisms that become attached to the hulls of ships and to oil rigs are transported with them. Ships draw sea water into ballast tanks and floodable holds for stability. This water is later discharged while the ship is underway or in various ports. Water taken aboard may contain planktonic organisms and sediments. In this way, plankton groups are spread over long distances. Surveys show that all major taxonomic groups are being introduced to new areas in this way.

These transported organisms occur at all levels of the food chain, but some of the species that keep the system in balance may be missing. Without these natural controls, certain species may proliferate to levels that swamp the new site and replace indigenous species.

Many of the inshore and coastal waters receiving ballast water are already disturbed by the effects of urbanization around ports. This makes them particularly vulnerable to invasions that further alter community structure and function. Invasion by exotic species is a very serious threat to marine habitats, and the ecological impacts cannot be fully predicted by knowing the biology of the introduced organisms and ecology in their original habitat. Inshore areas used by sharks and rays as nurseries are particularly sensitive.

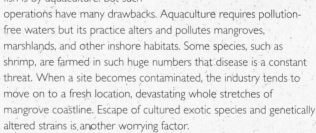

## FARMING COASTAL WATERS

As catches from wild fishery stocks decline, one way to supply an increasing demand for fish is by aquaculture. But such operations have many drawbacks. Aquaculture requires pollution-free waters but its practice alters and pollutes mangroves, marshlands, and other inshore habitats. Some species, such as shrimp, are farmed in such huge numbers that disease is a constant threat. When a site becomes contaminated, the industry tends to move on to a fresh location, devastating whole stretches of mangrove coastline. Escape of cultured exotic species and genetically altered strains is another worrying factor.

The most rewarding targets for aquaculture are high-value species such as prawns, shrimp, scallops, abalone, oysters, pearl oysters, salmon, and tuna. So far, there is no interest in farming sharks and rays. Their relatively low value and the small number of young produced by individuals make them poor prospects.

# SHOULD *the* FISHING *be* REDUCED?

*Sharks are valued as a food resource and for other products by many communities, but there are signs that current usage levels are not sustainable.*

Declining catch rates from many of the world's fisheries indicate that if we continue to harvest the oceans as we are now doing, populations of many species will continue to collapse. Sharks and rays tend to be longer-lived than other types of fish, and produce fewer offspring.

After the early stages of life, when all animals are most vulnerable, sharks and rays tend to have low natural mortality. Harvesting populations of such long-lived animals that produce only small numbers of young requires special care. It is usually safer to harvest

**THREATENED SPECIES** *The sand tiger shark (above) and the great white shark (below) now have protected status in certain parts of the world.*

short-lived animals that produce large numbers of young.

SUSTAINABILITY
Only a small proportion of the shark and ray populations can be taken sustainably each year. In southern Australia, it is estimated that with gummy sharks (*Mustelus antarcticus*), about 5 to 6 percent of the population can be taken each year without threat to the population. That means no more than 5 to 6 percent of the combined weight of all the gummy sharks in the population before fishing began. This species has a maximum lifespan of about 16 years.

For the soupfin shark (*Galeorhinus galeus*), which is known to have individuals

older than 50 years, no more than about 2 to 3 percent of the population can be taken sustainably. Continued harvesting of these species at greater than the above rates will inevitably lead to collapse of their stocks. Abundant species, such as the gummy shark, can continue to be harvested sustainably at present levels of fishing. But for some other species, fishing must be stopped, or markedly reduced. For example, populations of the great white

## WHAT IS SUSTAINABLE FISHING?

The low natural mortality rate and well-developed young of sharks and rays provide for remarkably stable populations compared with many short-lived bony fishes where the populations can vary greatly from year to year. In a fishery where the population size and the catch remain fairly constant over time, the population is said to be in equilibrium and harvested sustainably. Here, there is a rough balance between the number of fish recruited to the population from reproduction each year, and the number dying from natural causes and from fishing.

*Mullet (left) netted by professional fishermen.*

Fishing can be sustainable at many levels. Low levels result in small sustainable catches, and the population remains large. High levels can result in a similarly small sustainable catch, but the population becomes smaller, and the fishers have to work much harder to take the catch. The highest sustainable catches are obtained somewhere in between low and high levels of fishing. If the level of fishing is very high, such that total mortality is too high for recruitment to keep up, the population will continue to decline until it is either uneconomic to continue fishing, or the population collapses.

(*Carcharodon carcharias*) have been severely reduced in most regions where it occurs. As a relatively long-lived, top-level predator, producing very few young in a lifetime, it cannot replace losses quickly. In most areas, fishing for this species needs to cease immediately if the populations are to be allowed to build up again.

### THREATENED SPECIES

Several species of shark that gather in coastal waters to feed or breed are regarded as vulnerable. Notably, large, maturing or mature great whites are easily caught when feeding around seal-breeding colonies. The decline in abundance of the great white has led to its being protected in South Africa and several states of the United States and Australia. The sand tiger shark (*Carcharias taurus*), vulnerable to spearfishing, is protected in New South Wales, Australia.

Dogfishes and chimaeras inhabiting the continental slopes are taken as bycatch in several bottom trawl fisheries. Much of the catch of these species is either discarded dead, or not recorded. Like many of the bony fishes studied from these deeper and colder waters, the dogfishes are likely to be particularly long-lived and to have relatively few young. Given the limited areas occupied by these species, and the intensity of fishing, some of the species of dogfish and chimaera are at risk of severe depletion in some regions.

Some of the most "at risk" species of shark and ray are those occurring in freshwater habitats. These species are more vulnerable than those inhabiting marine waters, first because the

**VANISHING ACT** *The sawfish (right), a type of ray, is now becoming much less common.*

amount of fresh water in rivers and lakes is small compared with the amount of sea water on Earth. Second, tropical rivers and lakes where freshwater species occur are mostly in developing countries with large and expanding human populations. Such areas are much more vulnerable to exploitation than marine waters.

At least three species of "river shark" are now extremely rare. The Ganges shark (*Glyphis gangeticus*) is known only from the Ganges–Hooghly River system of the Indian subcontinent, although it is possible that more than one species of *Glyphis* occurs in the region of New Guinea, northern Australia and Borneo. The giant freshwater whipray (*Himantura chaophraya*) is considered endangered throughout its range and, as a result of fishing and river-habitat changes, it is critically endangered in Thailand. Sawfishes (family Pristidae), which to varying degrees occur in fresh and estuarine waters, seem to be much less common today than they were 50 to 60 years ago.

# MYTHS *and* FACTS

*Knowledge of their biology, lifestyle and environment is the key to understanding and demystifying the behavior of sharks and rays.*

The more we know, the better equipped we are to deal with rays and sharks rationally and responsibly. Reliable information is reaching more people through books, films, magazines, and aquariums, but myths still abound.

There are two kinds of myth about sharks and rays in contemporary lore. First, those stories that are grand representations of conflicts between good and evil, with the shark or ray always embodying the face of evil rather than good. Some of these, such as those from Hawaii related on page 33, come to us from other cultures.

Others have very recent origins in our modern folkways. Peter Benchley's novel *Jaws* and the resulting films, for example, created a substantial mythology about great white sharks (*Carcharodon carcharias*). Ian Fleming, in his novella *The Hildebrand Rarity*, tells of master spy James Bond's stalking and spearing a large stingray while skin-diving in the Seychelles Islands. The stingray had done nothing to Agent 007 other than reveal its evil nature as a relative of those useless devils, the sharks. Bond kills it as a good deed.

## MISCONCEPTIONS

While sensational accounts make exciting reading, we can recognize them as exaggerations. More insidious effects on our thinking are rooted in the second kind of myth—those of misconception. These once appeared widely in older books, but even now we can find such statements as: "the shark is a swimming nose;" "sharks are color blind;" "the shark is a living fossil;" "sharks have a rigid upper jaw and must turn on their backs to bite."

Although some of these misconceptions have a basis in fact, they are at best misleading, and at worst completely wrong. "The shark is a swimming nose" implies that all sharks rely principally on their sense of smell. It is true that all sharks that have been studied have

**SWITCHTAIL** *The southern stingray (Dasyatis americana) of the Cayman Islands is found in the offshore shallows.*

well-developed olfactory organs in their paired nostrils, the size and location of which vary with the species. But sharks use a variety of sensory systems to find prey and to survive in their world.

Most sharks have a well-developed sense of vision. Sharks active in low-light environments (such as the deep sea or the nocturnal reef) have special structures in their eyes called tapeta. These reflective layers under the retina reflect light back to the light receptors to boost the low signal. Some species, such as the great white shark, have been shown to have color vision. Although they did not have the instrumentation to confirm color vision, ancient

Wildlife Fund (WWF) launched a three-year effort known as the Endangered Seas Campaign to promote the conservation and sustainable use of marine fisheries worldwide. WWF will invest millions of dollars to reverse the effects of unsustainable fishing on sharks and other marine creatures, and the ocean ecosystems on which they depend.

The campaign will work all around the world to build the political will to end chronic overfishing, restore devastated fisheries, improve management schemes, and reduce the use of destructive fishing practices. WWF knows that it won't be easy: "fish neither 'sing' like whales nor look like pandas." Yet anyone who has seen a free-swimming shark or ray can attest that they have value beyond flesh, and beauty beyond danger.

used a modified military re-breather air-supply to explore the Caribbean in the late 1930s and the Red Sea in the late 1940s. His classic *MANTA, Under the Red Sea with Spear and Camera*, was for many readers an introduction to the phlegmatic and graceful plankton feeders we still hold in high esteem. In Hass's day however, these unfamiliar giant "devil-fish", as they were called, were considered ominous creatures—a perception reflected in his writings.

## GREATER ACCESS

When Jacques Cousteau's co-invention of the scuba regulator made it easier for more people to swim with sharks and rays, and to share their views with others, readers gained a wider knowledge of the sea. Interest increased with books such as Rachel Carson's *The Sea Around Us*, Cousteau and Dumas' *Silent World* (1953), and Eugenie Clark's *Lady and the Sharks* (1969).

As a result of these and many other vivid descriptions and filmed adventures and observations, we have come to have a better understanding

of the sea and its creatures, including its predators.

Despite these changes in attitudes, the world is still hungry for fish and profit. Many fisheries are unregulated or regulations go unenforced. Fisheries management has been reactive rather than planned. New fisheries are outpacing the managers and their rules. In central Indonesia, observers report that whales, manta rays, billfish, and sharks are newly jeopardized. In the Lembeh Straits, migrating sea mammals and large fishes enter the strait to feed and take a shorter passage around the island of Lembeh. Here, a Taiwan fishing company has set up a huge, permanent fish trap with an opening almost half a mile (0.8 km) wide. Set strategically in the middle of the migration path, it can catch everything that comes down the North Sulawesi coast, including dozens of giant manta rays.

Changed attitudes have coalesced into advocacy. In 1995, to help alleviate a recognized global crisis in overfishing, the World

**HUNTER AND PREY** *Setting a modern bottom-fishing net in Indonesian waters (above), a very efficient catch-all method of fishing. The huge manta ray (top) once seemed more terrible than it is.*

# THE NATURE *of* SHARK ATTACK

*Sharks are beautiful; they are graceful; their biology and behavior are complex and fascinating. But the fact remains: some of them have bitten and killed people.*

From a statistical point of view, shark attack is a very rare event. On average between 1990–6, 50 attacks per year were recorded worldwide, and fewer than 15 percent of these were fatal. To a victim, however, small statistical probability becomes total certainty. Interestingly, some survivors of even severe attacks have expressed philosophical attitudes. At least one Australian survivor, Rodney Fox, has made a career of helping people appreciate and understand the value of living sharks. Other survivors have continued their enjoyment of ocean sports and activities, declaring themselves guests in the sea, and assigning no hint of blame to the sharks.

Knowledge and good judgment are the best protection against shark attack. Good judgment means understanding the behavior of the kind of large shark that has been implicated in attack. In some cases, judgment may dictate that one avoids swimming or diving in an area known to abound with sharks.

## WHY DO SHARKS ATTACK HUMANS?

Most shark attacks on humans are prompted by two basic situations. First, there are those attacks related to threat and aggression. This kind of attack has been likened to a watchdog biting a mail carrier who enters a yard the dog is protecting. Second, there are attacks related to feeding, in which the shark approaches the victim as a meal.

Attacks in the first group can be subdivided into provoked attacks and unprovoked attacks. Provoked attacks involve the very poor judgment of divers who may, for example, pull the tail of a whitetip reef shark as it rests in an underwater cave, or attempt to hand-feed it. In the same way, any fisher who is bitten by a landed shark is considered to have provoked the "attack."

Unprovoked attacks are those in which victims blunder into the behavioral sphere of a shark and seem to threaten it with harm. For example, a surfer or windsurfer may speed into an area where a reef shark is swimming. If the surfer falls from the board near the shark, the shark will lash out to meet the perceived "threat."

Attacks motivated by feeding are most frequently

**NATURAL BEHAVIOR** *Tiger sharks in Hawaiian waters often take the green sea turtle (above) for food and may attack humans by mistake. Since surviving a shark attack in 1963, Australian Rodney Fox (right) has made it his mission to work for their welfare.*

associated with large species, such as the tropical tiger shark and the temperate great white shark. It is these attacks that can result in fatalities. Tropical tiger sharks have a diverse diet but are known to feed on large sea turtles. It is probably good judgment to avoid swimming in areas where sea turtles abound. Tiger sharks are also known to feed on floating carcasses of whales. Off Maui, Hawaii, in 1995, the body of a male humpback whale killed in courtship activities attracted at least five large tiger sharks. This would have been an area to avoid!

At smaller sizes, great white sharks feed on fishes. As they mature to a larger size they change their diet to seals and sea lions. It would be advisable to avoid swimming in areas of seal rookeries.

Even smaller species of shark may be confused by stimuli that are associated with prey behavior, for example, flashing of shiny surfaces such as jewelry, bleeding, and distressed swimming motions.

## SHARK BITE

Any injury from a shark should be considered a significant medical problem. Such injuries can range from slight abrasions to deep punctures, tissue damage or loss, and severe bleeding. In many coastal areas influenced by human activity, puncture or abrasion of the skin can result in severe infection. In some tropical areas, serious bacterial invasions are almost certain.

Abrasions from rough shark skin can result in many tiny cuts caused by the sharp streamlining edges of the denticles on the skin of the shark. Tissue damage from

## RARITY OF ATTACK

Risk of human death by shark attack is far down the list compared to other causes of death. Below are selected statistics for Hawaii, an area where shark attack is likely to be higher than many other places, yet where disease and accident rates are "near-normal." In Hawaii, millions of people engage in ocean activity, fatal shark attacks have occurred, and both great white sharks and tiger sharks (shown above) have been implicated in attacks.

### Selected Causes of Death in Hawaii, 1996

| | |
|---|---|
| Total deaths, all causes | 7,206 |
| Heart disease | 2,178 |
| Cancer | 1,713 |
| HIV | 145 |
| Motor vehicles | 124 |
| Falls | 58 |
| Homicide and legal intervention | 44 |
| Poisoning | 40 |
| Drowning | 40 |
| Shark attack | 0 |

*(Two non-fatal attacks were recorded in Hawaii in 1996)*

shark teeth is a far more serious matter, and medical attention should always be sought. First-aid measures include staunching the bleeding by pressure and covering the wound with cloth or rubber.

Medical treatment of shark bites involves treatment for shock; careful cleaning, debriding, and closure of the injury; treatment of broken bones crushed by the shark's jaws; removal of any tooth fragments; antibiotic regimens

to fight infection; and the restoration of fluids.

Some people have survived very serious shark attacks because of the initial control of blood loss. When Rodney Fox was severely bitten by a great white shark in Australia, his rubber wetsuit undoubtedly helped control the loss of blood. Joe Thompson, a surfer attacked in Hawaii by a tiger shark, lost one hand in the attack but managed to control blood loss with the other.

## FIRST AID

The Natal Sharks Board of South Africa reports a decrease in fatal injuries through the development of a treatment procedure and the widespread availability of a specially designed first-aid kit, known as the Shark Attack Pack. The key to treatment lies in stabilizing the victim before transfer to hospital.

**LUCKY ESCAPE** *Surfer Rick Grunzinski shows the chunk bitten from his board during a shark attack off Hawaii.*

# THE REALITY *of* SHARK ATTACK

*Although the chance of being attacked by a shark is statistically small, to each observer entering their watery world, it is a very real possibility.*

For peace of mind when diving, it helps to have an intellectual understanding of shark behavior and the low probability of attack. It also helps to appreciate that you are entering a world that is wild, natural, and not totally predictable. Knowing that sharks share the same waters with you yet, one hopes, keep their distance, adds to the thrill of any ocean experience.

## KNOWING THE ODDS
Any gambler, whether card player or swimmer, likes to know the odds. To estimate the chance of an event, a statistician needs to know at least two numbers: the observed number of "hits" (in this case, shark attacks) and the number of opportunities,

that is, how many people were in the water where dangerous sharks occur. Thanks to the International Shark Attack File and the biologists who maintain it, there is fairly good information on the first figure, although the estimate might be slightly low because not all attacks are reported.

Estimating total human exposure is more difficult. It is less than the world population

**IN TROUBLE** *Snorkelers (left) should swim in groups so they have less chance of being attacked by a shark. A hammerhead (below right) hopelessly entangled in a mesh beach net in Queensland, Australia.*

because not everyone enters the ocean. One thing is certain: as human populations continue to increase, and as more people enter the sea for their livelihood and recreation, more people are exposed to attack.

There is also a third important figure to estimate: how many sharks of the kinds implicated in human attack are there in the sea? We don't know but, given increased fishing catches, there is little doubt that there are fewer than there were a decade ago.

In the panel at left are statistics for the seven-year period 1990–6 for selected coastal areas with significant human activity in the sea. Note that death from a great white shark and a nip on the hand from a small reef shark are both considered to be shark attacks in this summary.

## BETTER CHANCES
Regardless of the estimated chances of shark attack in an area, humans can attempt to influence them, individually and collectively. Of course, individuals can greatly change the odds in their favor by staying out of the water—but

### SHARK ATTACK NUMBERS

| Area | average number attacks/year | average number fatal attacks/year |
|------|------|------|
| World | 50 | 6 |
| Australia | 6 | 1 |
| New Zealand | 1 | 0 |
| Brazil | 5 | <1 |
| South Africa | 4 | <0.5 |
| Hong Kong | 1 | 1 |
| Japan | 1 | <0.5 |
| Florida, USA | 15 | 0 |
| California, USA | 3 | <0.2 |
| Hawaii, USA | 3 | <0.5 |
| Other Areas | 10 | <3 |

**MISTAKEN IDENTITY** *From a shark's viewpoint, a surfer on a board looks like a turtle or a seal.*

that's no fun. In the panel at the right, there are some suggestions for swimming safely with sharks and rays.

GROUP ACTION
Groups of people have acted collectively to reduce the likelihood of shark attack. The best known of these measures is the netting of beaches to separate the activities of people and sharks, and in many cases to catch and remove sharks from the entire area. Netting of beaches is practiced most notably in Australia and South Africa.

In South Africa, as early as 1904, the Durban City Council ordered the installation of a semicircular enclosure, about 320 feet (100 m) in diameter, to protect swimmers. By 1928, the successful barrier had deteriorated and was removed. Few attacks were recorded in the next 20 years, but between 1945 and 1951, Durban recorded 21 attacks, 7 of them fatal. Desperate city authorities adopted an Australian system first used in 1937 when large-meshed gill nets were anchored seaward

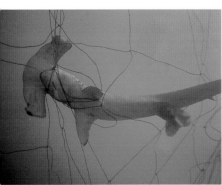

of the breaker zone at many Sydney beaches. The nets trapped large sharks and greatly reduced the incidence of shark attack. In 1952, 7 gill nets, each 400 feet (130 m) long, were stretched along the Durban beachfront. In the first year, 552 sharks were caught in these nets and they were judged successful in reducing serious injuries from shark attack on local beaches.

CLUSTER OF ATTACKS
A series of shark attacks at seaside resorts without nets south of Durban between December 1957 (since known as Black December) and Easter 1958 claimed the lives of 5 people in 107 days. After trying such ad hoc methods as depth-charging and the hasty construction of temporary barriers, authorities decided to expand Durban's netting operations. Soon after, the government established the Natal Anti-Shark Measures Board, now called the

Natal Sharks Board, and charged it with "the duty of approving, controlling and initiating measures for safeguarding bathers against shark attacks." By March 1966, 15 beaches had protective nets, maintained either by commercial fishers or municipal employees. In 1974, the Sharks Board assumed the servicing and maintenance of net installations, and since 1982, it is solely responsible for all shark netting in the province.

Barrier netting has not been used in the United States because the practice also catches and kills significant numbers of sharks. Changed attitudes now argue against such wholesale "fishing."

**AVOIDING ATTACK**

• When visiting a new area, seek local advice
• Be cautious, especially when spearfishing
• Don't swim at dawn, dusk, or at night, when sharks are most active
• Avoid swimming near flooding rivers or in murky or polluted waters
• Avoid swimming with an open wound or while menstruating; sharks are attracted by blood and other body fluids
• Don't wear shiny jewelry; reflections can resemble the sheen of fish scales
• Swim in groups, not alone
• Just because porpoises are in an area does not indicate that sharks are absent; both are predators, often feeding on the same prey
If you are attacked, report the incident to the International Shark Attack File.

# LIVING SAFELY *with* SHARKS *and* RAYS

*It seems that people's attitudes toward sharks are changing. Twenty years ago, sharks were widely feared and assigned little value.*

Today, people may still be apprehensive, but they are beginning to view sharks as interesting, even beautiful creatures, that deserve their place in the ocean. More than one shark attack survivor has said, in essence, "I regret the attack, but it wasn't the shark's fault. The sea is the shark's home, and I am only a visitor there."

### KEEPING SHARKS AWAY FROM PEOPLE

Around the world, people have attempted to lessen the chance of shark attack by controlling sharks in two ways: physically excluding them from places of human activity, and killing and removing them from such areas. Both methods have their own sets of problems. Physically excluding sharks usually involves stretching long nets across the mouths of bays with swimming beaches. This is the method of choice in Australia and South Africa, but netting is labor intensive, nets need repair and even reinstallation after storms, and sharks that become entangled in them must be removed.

In South Africa, the Natal Sharks Board provides protection against shark attack at some 60 beaches. It services more than 25 miles (40 km) of netting, spread at intervals along 200 miles (325 km) of coastline in KwaZulu-Natal.

Beach-netting is also maintained in Australia. There, as in South Africa, nets occasionally entrap other kinds of marine animals, including whales. Recently, authorities in Queensland have begun trials with acoustic

**DEVICES** *The US Navy Shark Chasers (above) were widely used during WWII. In an anti-shark bag (below) the navy diver is safe from the nearby tiger shark.*

signals to warn away baleen whales that may become entangled in shark nets.

Fishing programs to reduce shark numbers, in attempts to reduce the threat of shark attack, were in notable use in Hawaii in the 1950s, '60s and early '70s. Such fishing programs are ecologically questionable, expensive, and probably doomed to failure. Extermination of any species, especially a top predator, is inadvisable at best, and probably not practically possible.

### PROTECTING AND REPELLING

The best kind of repellent against shark attack is to avoid attracting or confusing sharks. Always avoid murky water, areas

filled with prey, waters polluted by a dead or bleeding animal, and waters over drop-offs.

Choice of activity can make a difference, too. An analysis of shark attacks indicates that scuba divers are attacked more rarely than swimmers and snorkelers on the surface. In the few recorded attacks, the scuba divers have either been at the surface rather than at depth, or have been associated with unusual activity that may have excited the shark. For example, in an attack on a scuba diver in July 1995, off Monterey, California, at a midwater depth of 40 feet (12 m), the diver was driving a submarine scooter with a battery-powered electric motor. It has been suggested that the electrical activity of the motor may have confused or even attracted the shark.

The quest for a chemical repellent was ambitiously pursued by the United States Navy and cooperating biologists during and after World War II in order to protect downed fliers and ship-accident victims awaiting rescue from the sea. Various substances were tested. A chemical preparation named "Shark Chaser" was routinely attached to life jackets. It consisted of a copper-based chemical packaged in combination with a brightly colored dye. Behavioral tests with sharks indicated that the repellent was ineffective, but it may have comforted many a survivor by its visual effect.

A physical barrier was also

developed by the United States Navy to protect crash survivors from sharks. The Johnson Shark Bag was essentially a surface flotation device with a long, closed tube extending downward. The survivor filled the sleeping-bag-sized tube with water and climbed into it. The tube retained any blood or other olfactory cues. Studies showed that the bag was effective, except that sharks would still approach and investigate if stimulated by bait in the water around it.

## SAFETY FIRST

Although scuba divers are rarely attacked, some divers wear protective suits or carry protective devices (see p. 76) if they are exposed to sharks in the course of their work. Steel mesh suits and gloves are worn by divers filming sharks in feeding situations, and by guide-divers who feed sharks for diving shark-watchers.

Photographers and researchers also use stainless-steel and aluminum cages to protect themselves from large species. Australian abalone divers have adapted cages into mobile bottom-vehicles for protection from sharks while prying abalone from the bottom. Pole spears with explosive heads have been used to kill sharks as they approach divers. But interest in repellents and defensive devices seemed to be higher in the past decade than now.

Recently, the Natal Sharks Board of South Africa has developed a battery-powered electrical repellent called a POD (Protective Oceanic Device) (see p. 77). This is intended to protect against attack from the three species considered "most dangerous" in the Natal region, the great white, tiger, and bull sharks.

Most scientific divers and scientists are cynical about the promise of repellents. As one diving scientist has said, "The best repellent for shark attack is dry desert sand. Lie down in it and you will be safe."

# UNVEILING *the* MYSTERIES *of the* OCEANS

*Aquariums allow everyone a glimpse of this fascinating realm and a chance to see sharks and rays that most divers would never encounter.*

Sharks and rays have always had the ability to inspire our imaginations, but we are only beginning to understand the role they play in our environment. They are often feared as vicious predators, or revered as powerful adversaries to the human race. With the advances made in scientific research and education, however, these attitudes are starting to change.

Much of this recent change in attitude can be attributed to the direct access people now have to sharks and rays through scuba diving. Researchers, cinematographers, conservationists, and many others, now have incredible access to sharks and rays and can observe them in their natural environment.

Unfortunately, not everyone has the opportunity to scuba dive. For those people who feel a need to get close to sea creatures, the public aquarium is the next-best alternative. In fact, it is the only place you can get close to animals such as sharks and rays in absolute safety.

### AQUARIUMS

There are many public aquariums throughout the world, and the number is growing rapidly. This is due to an increased interest in our

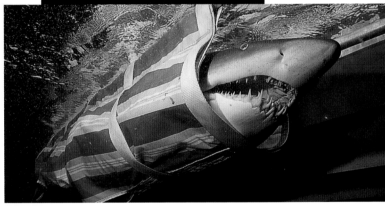

**HANDLED WITH CARE**
*Capturing a shark or ray in the wild is a delicate operation. A lasso (left) inflicts little damage; the animal is constrained in a sling (below), and sedated for transporting (bottom).*

aquatic environments. One of the major displays in most aquariums is often the shark and ray enclosure—it seems that most people are fascinated by these large predators. The Aquarium of the Americas and the Monterey Bay Aquarium, both in the United States, and Osaka Aquarium in Japan all have outstanding shark exhibits. These aquariums excel because of the care and attention to detail taken in creating natural environments for the animals.

On a global scale, there are approximately 100 species of shark and more than 50 species of ray on display. There are several species of shark that are arguably the

best for display in aquariums. They are the sand tiger (*Carcharias taurus*), bull shark (*Carcharhinus leucas*), sandbar shark (*Carcharhinus plumbeus*), blacktip reef shark (*Carcharhinus melanopterus*) and the

whitetip shark (*Triaenodon obesus*), all of which adapt to captivity very well. With the greatly increased size of modern aquarium tanks, better husbandry techniques, and greater knowledge of shark biology, aquarists have begun to display many species not previously kept. Most notable among these new attractions are whale sharks (*Rhincodon typus*). So far, they have only been displayed in Japanese aquariums.

These types of shark tend to be the drawcard animals for the institutions that display them. Surprisingly, they make up only a very small percentage of the sharks that are housed in public aquariums. Many of the sharks in public aquariums are small—less than 3 feet (1 m) in length—or bottom-dwelling species, and are often viewed as oddities or curios, as they exhibit rather strange and unusual biology or behaviors. Horn sharks (Heterodontidae), for example, are widely displayed in aquariums because their body shape is prehistoric and because the cases in which they lay their eggs are threaded like a carpenter's screw.

## STOCKING AQUARIUMS

Public aquariums have several methods for acquiring their sharks and rays—by donation, by breeding, and by collecting. Donation and breeding are the most common means with the smaller sharks, which means that their population in aquariums is stable and even increasing. The larger sharks tend to be more difficult to breed and harder to acquire through donation, so they are usually collected from the wild.

## A WINDOW ON THE BAY

Financed by the family foundation of philanthropist David Packard, a group of dedicated marine biologists, divers, and enthusiasts is busy creating an aquarium that fires the imaginations of some two million visitors a year from all around the world. In the former Hovden fish cannery beside Monterey Bay, California, people can now experience the world that divers visit, including getting close to sharks, in absolute comfort and safety. There's a great kelp forest (above) that sways in an artificially created tidal surge and teems with nutrients for the creatures that hide among its branches, as well as habitat exhibits for all manner of aquatic animals.

The aquarium focuses on the creatures and rich ecosystems of Monterey Bay, including its beaches, estuaries, offshore waters, and its deep, natural canyon that drops eventually to an incredible 12,000 feet (3,700 m). The opening of the aquarium in 1984 was soon followed by the establishment of MBARI (the Monterey Bay Aquarium Research Institute) in 1987. Staff from both institutions work together to develop new collection and husbandry techniques in order to display and keep animals never before seen by most people. They also generously share their success with other aquariums so that a wide public can learn about the ocean world.

When a public aquarium needs to collect a large shark, there is one rule that must always be adhered to—the shark must be kept in the best condition possible. This has led to the development of several different ways of catching the animal.

The most popular method is to use a barbless hook and line, either with a diver hand-feeding the shark or by fishing directly from a boat. Another often-used method is to have a diver lasso the shark and have the boat crew haul the animal to the side of the boat. With both of these methods, the shark is then maneuvered into a sling, brought on board the boat, and lowered into a transport container where it may be sedated for the trip to the aquarium.

Rays are treated with the same amount of respect and are generally carefully caught in nets or with barbless hooks on a line.

# SHARKS *and* RAYS *behind* GLASS

*Zoos and aquariums in the past were often categorized as simple menageries, merely catering to the curious observer.*

If you satisfy people's curiosity, you have the opportunity to educate them about the animals they are viewing. Millions of school children around the world visit public zoos and aquariums annually. Most of these children are simply curious. Their exposure to live, display animals, such as sharks and rays, will help them to develop not only a better understanding of wild animals but also, with supporting educational programs, a strong conservation ethic.

## ANIMALS IN CAPTIVITY

Most zoos and aquariums now have education, conservation, and research programs. In fact, much of what we know about sharks and rays

**VICARIOUS DANGER** *Part of the aquarium experience in many places is to see divers actually feeding sharks.*

has come directly from public aquariums. They also assist indirectly, by allowing fisheries and other research organizations the use of their facilities and space to house their research animals.

The downside to keeping animals in captivity is often their lack of ability to adjust to the artificial environment. This can be due to inadequate or inappropriate management, or poor selection of the species to be kept. Great white sharks (*Carcharodon carcharias*), for example, have been displayed at several

aquariums around the world with little success. A great deal of research is needed on the quality of the food provided for great whites and the design of a facility that can house them successfully. Fortunately, inappropriate management is becoming less of a problem as we become more aware of the needs of captive animals, and because of government regulation of zoological institutions.

When sharks and rays are kept in aquariums, it is always a balancing act to keep the animals at a healthy weight. Most sharks and rays, when well maintained in a low-stress environment, grow larger than their wild counterparts. In most species of animal, one finds a physical difference between the wild and the captive creature. In captivity, the problem is often trying to keep an animal's weight down, whereas in the wild it is quite often the opposite. This is because in captivity an animal has more food available, and needs to expend less energy to catch its prey. After a few weeks in captivity, the sand tiger (*Carcharias taurus*), for example, which is often collected in a very lean state, can dramatically increase in weight. Most sand tigers will

feed the day they are brought into a captive environment, which is a good indicator of their ability to adapt.

SHARKS IN AQUARIUMS
Most species of shark can be kept in aquariums, and with adequate husbandry they will prosper, reproducing as regularly as they would in the wild. In fact, with a few notable exceptions, sharks and rays in aquariums live longer than those in the wild. Whale sharks (*Rhincodon typus*) and basking sharks (*Cetorhinus maximus*) both feed on large quantities of plankton and are difficult to hold for any period of time because this food is difficult and expensive to supply. Being very large, these animals also require gigantic aquariums to give them adequate space for a healthy lifestyle. The king of sea beasts, the great white shark, is also difficult to display for reasons of size. Some smaller sharks, such as angelsharks (Squatinidae), need a deep, sandy or muddy bottom so that they can bury themselves.

Most sharks in aquariums are housed in multi-species exhibits, so they need to be able to survive within a mixed community. There may be as many as 20 different species of

shark within one communal exhibit, as well as an assortment of rays and bony fish. If the correct species are housed together, the end result can be a spectacular exhibit with little or no aggression among its inhabitants. The ability of most sharks to live together makes them one of the most suitable large aquatic animals for display. Their ferocious reputation adds to the mystique surrounding them, and makes them the most popular of all the aquarium animals.

RAYS IN AQUARIUMS
Rays are one of the most intriguing of all the animals that aquariums display. They do not usually have obvious fins, their mouth generally faces the ground, and they have a reputation of being dangerous to humans. They are also one of the hardiest marine creatures kept in aquariums. All of which makes them particularly desirable as display animals.

Of all the rays, there are only a few that present any problems in captivity. Devil-rays (Mobulidae) are by far

**TUNNEL VISION** *Displays are often set up so that sharks pass within a few feet of viewers walking through a tunnel, as at Sydney Aquarium (above); divers in the tank at feeding time (below).*

the most difficult to display. They need a constant supply of plankton and a very large aquarium because of their size. Torpedo rays (Torpedinidae) and shorttailed electric rays (Hypnidae) can be a handful for aquarium keepers, as they

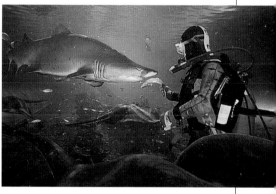

can deliver an electric shock capable of stunning a human. These animals are not often kept in aquariums for that reason. The main environmental requirement for most rays is a soft, deep substrate in which to bury themselves.

As with sharks, rays that are given the right conditions in aquariums will reproduce and prosper just as well as they would in the wild.

# WHAT'S HAPPENING TODAY

*Research on sharks and rays is being conducted in centers all over the world. In just about every country with a coastline, biologists are investigating sharks and rays.*

Much of what we know about shark and ray biology has been learned from dead specimens, caught by fishermen or in active research-fishery programs. Scientists once felt that the way to learn was by "sacrificing" animals.

## CHANGING PERSPECTIVE

We can still learn from dead specimens and in experimental situations, but refreshingly, more and more researchers are studying living animals in the wild. The scientific museums of the world are well stocked with specimens of sharks and rays that are available for study.

Scientists around the world are studying living sharks and rays. For example, at the Department of Biological Sciences, Florida Institute of Technology, Dr. Timothy C. Tricas and his students are studying the neurobiology and behavior of stingrays.

Tricas has also investigated the biting mechanics of the jaws of great white sharks and the wanderings of tiger sharks in Hawaii.

Current research focuses on how information from biological sources is processed by the brain, and especially how rays use their electrosensory system. This work combines watching stingrays in their native haunts, studying natural bioelectrical stimuli encountered by rays and skates in the wild, and studying the neural responses of the electrosensory system to these natural stimuli.

Florida's Mote Marine Laboratory Center for Shark Research (MML/CSR) was established in 1992 as an outgrowth of the

**ON SHOW** *A diver with rays (above) at Stingray City in the Cayman Islands. A shark encounter exhibit (below) at Sea World, San Diego, California.*

Laboratory's Shark Biology Program. It is now an international center for scientific cooperation, research, education, and public information on sharks and the related skates and rays.

CSR research includes basic and applied studies of shark biology, from anatomy and physiology to ecology and fisheries science. In contrast to the MML Biomedical Research Program, which concentrates on sharks and skates as laboratory models for studies of disease-resistance, the CSR research program has a broader focus on field and laboratory studies of these animals. CSR scientists

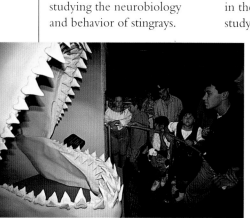

investigate various biological adaptations that sharks have made to their marine environment, with an emphasis on the role of sharks as an important marine resource.

## STUDYING WILD SHARKS

Watching a wide-ranging shark or ray go about its life day after day, 24 hours a day, would be enlightening, but it is not practicable. However, intrepid field biologists do spend many sunny hours and dark nights watching and following sharks. Some researchers have developed ways to tag sharks with battery-powered transmitters that can record or transmit

## ACCIDENTAL CATCH

In 1976, some United States Navy acoustic researchers off Oahu, Hawaii, made an unusual discovery. Entangled in their equipment was a large, adult male shark. Unfortunately, the shark could not be saved, but the researchers realized that it was unusual and invited scientists to inspect it. Preliminary inspection by Leighton Taylor and other scientists confirmed that it represented a very distinct, undescribed species. The so-called megamouth shark (*Megachasma pelagios*), pictured above, is now known from less than a dozen specimens. Who knows how many earlier megamouth specimens were discarded by accident?

selected information about the tagged animal. Tags can relay location, depth, compass heading, temperature of the water, temperature of the muscle tissue, and so forth.

At the Hawaii Institute of Marine Biology, University of Hawaii, Kaneohe Bay, Dr. Kim Holland and his students are tagging and studying scalloped hammerhead sharks and tiger sharks. Dr. Samuel Gruber, University of Miami, Florida, continues his research program and tagging studies of lemon sharks in the vast sand flats and shoals of Bimini, in the Bahamas. He and his students are building on more than 20 years of data collected from living lemon sharks. Gruber's program admits volunteers and seasonal students to help in the research.

Scientists from Scripps Institution of Oceanography and Hubbs-Sea World Institute in San Diego are designing programs to tag western Pacific whale sharks with radio tags. These transmitters will send signals via satellites, and help us to learn whether these largest of all fish migrate, and if so, to where.

## ANGLERS CAN HELP

The need for shark fishery management and depletion of shark populations worldwide are changing attitudes toward sharks by sports anglers. Mote Marine Laboratory, Florida, has organized an annual fishing tournament since 1988. Not a single shark is needlessly killed. Instead, all sharks caught are identified and measured, tagged when possible, and released. The collected data are used to track local shark populations, to gauge catch-and-release mortality, and to provide migratory and age/growth information. Fishers compete for prizes, and the event publicizes the state of the sharks and the importance of management measures.

## CLUBS, SOCIETIES, AND WEBSITES

The Resources Directory (page 272) provides a list of some of the larger clubs, societies and websites that are involved in the research and conservation of sharks and rays. It also lists universities and museums that curate excellent collections for study.

# GETTING INVOLVED *in* SHARK CONSERVATION

*The oceans of the world need our help. The human race is harming the habitats of marine creatures and it is up to us to stop the damage.*

Knowledge and awareness are the keys to living in harmony with the diversity of life on Earth. As we learn more about sharks, we begin to appreciate their important ecological roles and to understand the consequences of our predation on them and of our disturbance, and destruction of their habitats.

Faced with drastically changed environments or catastrophically reduced population sizes, many species may change and evolve, become rare, or even go extinct. The changes humans continue to make, through the effects of our technology and our sheer numbers, gravely affect many habitats and species, including most sharks and rays.

Overfishing of sharks, especially those caught as bycatch, is of growing international concern. Few shark fisheries have any kind of enforced management controls in place. Combined with the longevity and low reproductive rates of sharks, overfishing is certain to result in rapid declines in populations.

Biologists and conservation groups recommend immediate measures to reduce fishing to sustainable levels, to stop wasteful fishing practices, and to protect fragile habitats, such as inshore breeding grounds.

### PEOPLE POWER

Humans have the power to change the world. Of course, so do many other species. Birds transport seeds to newly created islands and forests are born. Corals and algae build reefs and islands. But the power humans possess is in many ways unique. We can make changes by accident or by design. We can try to understand the consequences of our acts or we can act in ignorance and carelessness.

Like every species, Homo sapiens interacts with and depends upon the multitude of other species with which we share the land and ocean. But unlike other species, our power to change is greatly magnified by our technology and by our overwhelming

**GOOD AND BAD MANAGEMENT**
*Responsible control of Australia's Great Barrier Reef Marine Park (above) means that it will survive in good order for future generations to enjoy. Poor local government practices result in rubbish on beaches (below). Cleaning up after oil spills (below right) is a recurring problem.*

numbers. Many of the changes we have made and continue to make are careless or heedless of consequences, motivated by greed and selfishness. Every environmental change we make, oil spills, silting of reefs, forest clearcutting, even flushing a toilet, eventually affects the seas.

Each of us can choose to act in ways that do not harm the ocean. We can act in ways that cause the least disturbance to the species around us, realizing that every action will still have some effect. We can assure that, for example, the flushed toilet goes to an environmentally sound treatment plant; that land-grading for our house lots does not send mud into coastal waters.

One of the best ways to help is to see that our children and our fellows recognize the power we have to change the environment, but we risk our credibility if we oversimplify or preach stridently. Sharks and rays and all other creatures are in jeopardy unless we truly understand how nature works and modify our acts to have minimal consequences.

## THE PUBLIC FORUM

We can act individually, and in concert. Consider joining one of the societies or conservation groups

## GREENPEACE: A FORCE TO BE RECKONED WITH

An international action group, Greenpeace has been a visible force for change in the way we treat our environment for the past 25 years. Formed by a group of Americans and Canadians, it has since attracted a growing band of activists and supporters worldwide. It accepts no government or corporate funding, financing its campaigns solely from donations and member support. Some of its abiding concerns are the ecology of the oceans, and how to prevent them from becoming a barren dumping ground for waste. It is often Greenpeace that blows the whistle on dubious activities taking place unobserved far out to sea.

Greenpeace works in a non-violent way by studying problems and suggesting viable solutions, by lobbying governments and businesses to change bad practices, such as drift-net fishing, and by making people aware of irresponsible activities, such as unsustainable levels of fishing and the dumping of toxic pollutants. Sometimes, Greenpeace intervenes directly. Pictured above, supporters protest about whaling activities in Icelandic waters. Contact a Greenpeace office in your nearest major city to find out how to offer your support.

listed in our Resources Directory (see p. 272). Work toward having effective marine park areas and no-take zones declared. Subscribe to natural history and diving magazines and add your vote to campaigns they orchestrate for the protection of the environment. Work with the public aquarium in your area to learn about local and global marine issues and ways to act. The Internet and the World

Wide Web are also great tools for learning and for sharing your observations and ideas for solving problems. If you dive regularly, record shark sightings to help to add to our knowledge about various species. Make notes while your memories are fresh and send them off with photos, if possible, to magazines, or groups such as the American Elasmobranch Society (see p. 275). Report any unusual objects or dramatic changes in numbers of marine creatures in areas you visit regularly. Such changes may indicate a problem that can be fixed by prompt local action.

Your every act affects the natural world in some way. Strive to know what these effects may be and work to make them helpful to land and sea. Live so that your effect on the world enhances its diversity and wonder.

*When once [the ocean deep] has been seen, it will remain forever the most vivid memory in life, solely because of its cosmic chill and isolation, the eternal and absolute darkness and the indescribable beauty of its inhabitants.*

*Half Mile Down*,
CHARLES WILLIAM BEEBE (1877–1962), American scientist

# PLANNING *a* FIELD TRIP VACATION

*Careful planning is essential to ensure that your encounters with sharks and rays are safe, environmentally sound, exciting, and memorable—for all the right reasons.*

Sharks and rays can be found in all the world's oceans, but because they occur in smaller numbers than other species of fish, they can sometimes be hard to locate. In some areas, access to sharks and rays may be fairly easily gained, and little planning is required. Caribbean reef sharks in the Bahamas or stingrays at Grand Cayman, for example, can be found there all year round, and day trips provided by local dive centers or dive resorts will virtually guarantee sightings. If you are fortunate enough to live near an ocean environment that sharks or rays inhabit, perhaps all you need do to see them is to don mask, fins, and snorkel, and wade in off the local beach.

Many species are not only unique to certain countries, but they may congregate in an area for only limited seasons. The whale sharks at Ningaloo Reef in Western Australia are an excellent example of this— they congregate there only during late March, April and May. To meet up with them may involve traveling long distances, and proper timing of your trip is critical.

Some sharks and rays are found in remote locations. For example, to see the silvertip sharks in Papua New Guinea or the sharks and rays in the Galapagos Islands, you may have to take a trip on a live-aboard dive boat for 7 to 10 days to reach the area.

When planning your trip, contact a dive-travel specialist experienced in dive-vacation packages. Some vacation

**ERODED BY TIME** *The Natural Arch near Darwin Island in the Galapagos. A great white shark (above) glides past.*

*I must go down to the seas again, to the lonely sea and the sky.*

Sea Fever,
JOHN MASEFIELD
(1878–1976), British poet

packages provide encounters with just one species, but because some of the congregations are seasonal, you may be able to combine several in the one trip. For example, if you were to take a trip to Australia during March or April, it would be possible to see gray nurse sharks in New South Wales and great white sharks in South Australia when the weather is favorable, before pursuing sightings of whale sharks at Ningaloo Reef from March to May.

## FIELD GUIDES AND BOOKS

The best way to find out what options are available for shark and ray encounters is to study reference books and a well-respected field guide dedicated to this subject. The Field Guide section in this book (page 132) provides an introduction to 68 species of shark and 20 species of ray. The appearance, behavior, and habitat of each species is discussed. *Encounters with Sharks and Rays* (page 226) features 21 sites worldwide where you are likely to view specific sharks and rays.

**BIODIVERSITY** *Tropical coral reefs (above) and temperate zone kelp forests (left) are famously diverse communities. In both, sharks and rays are dominant predators.*

## SURFING THE NET

Another good source of information is the Internet. Many operators, dive-travel agencies, and divers with experience of shark and ray sightings communicate on the Net. Be aware that some of the information may not be accurate, and further research will be necessary to maximize your chances of an encounter. Animal behavior can vary, weather can be unreliable and even the best dive operator can experience problems that affect the normal operation of the tour. Nevertheless, the Internet is a good place to get ideas, information, and many contacts that can be checked out directly with the dive operators on the Internet.

# PREPARATION

*The best preparation for a field trip is to gather as much background information as possible and to be aware of the hazards such a trip may involve.*

Gathering information prior to going on a field trip is a time-consuming, but rewarding, task. Many avenues are open to the intending traveler.

## DIVE MAGAZINES

The national dive magazines of various countries are an excellent source of information about special-interest marine animal encounters. These magazines place accuracy above all other concerns. They will be first with news of discoveries and carry updates on existing informa-tion. Many of the advertisers in these magazines are dive operators and dive travel agencies.

## BROCHURES

Although travel brochures can provide good information about some of the facilities and features of a destination, they are never comprehensive and not always accurate. Such brochures might feature photographs of rarely seen shark or ray species. In other instances, the photograph may have been taken at a different location entirely. Always follow up on the information

**EXOTIC LOCATIONS** *Scuba diving at Ihuru, in the Maldives (above), and on the reef off Belize, in the Caribbean (left).*

offered in brochures and check details carefully with your dive-travel consultant.

## PLAN AHEAD

Prepare yourself by studying up-to-date site maps of the area. These can be obtained from your dive-travel consultant. As your departure date nears, it is important to consult accurate short-term

and long-term weather reports for the area from recognized agencies.

## DIVE-TRAVEL HAZARDS

With any foreign travel, it's wise to check if a "travel advisory" has been issued by your government. For United States travelers, the US State Department oper-ates a 24-hour hotline (see p. 272) that you can call for the latest word on political instability, epidemics, war, or terrorism. Another source is the World Wide Web at http://www.stolaf.edu/network/travel-advisories.html.

Some of the most exciting destinations where sharks and rays can be found are in tropical areas where the dive traveler may be exposed to certain health hazards. One of the most serious is malaria, a virus carried by the anopheles mosquito and passed into the bloodstream of the host when the mosquito feeds.

Travelers must be prepared for a number of minor illnesses that can arise from a change to their regular environment. Ask your doctor to prescribe a range of drugs to deal with diarrhea, nausea, pain and insomnia. Do not expect to find these drugs readily at your destination.

Always dive conservatively, do not exceed the recommended dive times, and follow proper procedures. If you don't, bubbles can form in the bloodstream and you may fall victim to decompression sickness. This can lead to irreversible brain damage or paralysis if treatment in a recompression chamber is not begun quickly.

Many travelers underestimate the power of the tropical Sun, which burns quickly regardless of the time of day. If you are severely burnt on the first day of your vacation, it may spoil the rest of your trip. The tropical Sun will burn you within 15 minutes. Cover up, stay in the shade, use plenty of sunscreen, keep your dive-suit on in open boats, and wear a hat.

Never ignore coral cuts and scrapes,

**THE BENDS** *A diver receives oxygen treatment (right) for decompression sickness before being transferred to a recompression chamber.*

which can become severely infected. Dive staff are experienced at treating these wounds, and you should seek their immediate help.

Learn to identify marine species that can cause harm and discomfort. These include fire corals, stinging hydroids, sea jellies, coralliomorphs and venomous fish, snakes or shells. While these species do not attack people, ignorance can result in accidents.

## PREVENTING MALARIA

Prevention is better than cure, and it is important to defend yourself against this disease when you travel in regions where malaria may be present.

• Obtain preventative drugs prescribed by a doctor who has up-to-date knowledge of the latest malarial prevention for the areas you wish to visit.
• Check with the doctor that these drugs are compatible with diving.
• Make sure that you commence the prescription prior to entering the malarial area. Most important, continue to take the drugs for the required time after leaving the area as the virus can survive, dormant, in your bloodstream for up to four weeks.
• Avoid being bitten. The anopheles mosquito is most active at dusk and dawn, so cover up with light-colored clothing and use plenty of repellent. Stay out of the jungle and stay on the water as much as possible.
• If you have a choice, keep in mind that live-aboard boats will expose you to far fewer mosquitos and other bugs than shore-based accommodation.
• Learn to recognize the signs of malaria and report any symptoms immediately. People living in malarial areas are experienced at treating an outbreak.
• If symptoms appear after your trip, tell your doctor that you have been in a malarial area and insist on complete testing.

### TRAVEL INSURANCE
Once you book your trip, it is wise to take out travel insurance. This inexpensive option will provide you with compensation for the loss of your trip should you have an accident before or during travel, and offers other benefits, such as cover for medical expenses and lost baggage. Take out a policy recommended by your dive-travel consultant as it is more likely to be tailored to diving-related considerations.

### DAN INSURANCE
Divers Alert Network (DAN) is an American-based diving insurance and diving accident management service. DAN membership may be secured by paying an inexpensive annual membership fee (see Resources Directory pages 272–3). Members receive automatic emergency evacuation to the nearest suitable medical facility. This may include transfer to another country where a recompression chamber is available.

American residents also have access to other DAN insurance, including cover for travel, medical, disability and accidental death.

# GETTING CLOSER

*A good dive-travel agency will take the time to determine
your expectations and level of experience before helping you
plan a trip to your chosen destination.*

Choose your dive-travel agency carefully. Try to ensure that the consultants are reputable and experienced, as well as environmentally responsible.

### DIVE OPERATORS

Enthusiasts who want to encounter sharks and rays will find they need the services of a dive operator to organize air and scuba equipment, a dive boat, accommodation, and shark cages or other specialized equipment or support. These dive operators also know the best dive sites, the species and behavior of sharks and rays in their area, and other marine life of interest to the dive traveler.

Operators who are skilled in the field soon make a name for themselves that becomes respected worldwide.

### DIVE-TRAVEL AGENTS

Dive operators are represented worldwide by specialist dive-travel agents. These consult directly with dive travelers wishing to plan a vacation or excursion that can include encounters with marine life. Dive-travel agents have first-hand experience of the area you wish to visit. They also have video promotional tapes, brochures and photographic material that provide infor-mation about the destination, the dive operator, and any special features of the area.

It is very important to make your expectations known to your consultant. A good dive-travel consultant will always try to ensure your expectations are met. If it is important to you, always ask about weather patterns and seasons. If you don't, your consultant may assume this is not an issue for you. Some shark and ray enthusiasts are unconcerned that it is cyclone season in a particular area if that is the best time for them to see sharks and rays.

Once you have agreed on the trip you want, the dive-travel agency will put together a package that will include all flights; transfers; accommo-dation; and a diving package that includes boats, divemaster services, scuba cylinders and weights. If you do not have your own diving equipment, check if it is cheaper to take a hire package from your local dive center or to hire at your chosen location.

If your trip involves a live-aboard dive boat, meals will be included. This is rarely the case if you are staying at a shore-based resort.

### DIVE CENTERS

Today's dive center provides a much wider range of service than just

**SCUBA SCHOOL** *Last-minute briefing (right) from the divemaster. A dive vessel at Roach Island, off the north-east coast of Australia.*

scuba training and gear sales. The modern dive center offers specialized training; scuba equipment sales, hire and service; and underwater photographic equipment and photography training. Most important, it offers group trips guided by an experienced tour leader/divemaster. Many dive centers have a travel consultant on the staff who will understand your needs and expectations. The dive operators also have trained and experienced staff at the dive destinations who can provide information to clients through their local dive centers.

## GROUP TRAVEL

There are many advantages to participating in a group diving vacation. The solo dive traveler cannot take advantage of the experience of a tour leader who has local knowledge of the area, and the ability to smooth out occasional difficulties during the trip. Dive-tour leaders are often qualified divemasters or instructors who have an intimate knowledge of unique marine life and shark or ray behavior. They are skilled in helping group members

improve their diving skills during the trip. Group trips are also very social, and new divers will soon feel welcomed into the group.

## LIVE-ABOARD VERSUS SHORE-BASED DIVING

At many locations that are known as "hot spots" for sharks and rays, there is a choice of staying at a shore-based resort or participating in a 7 to 10 day trip on a live-aboard dive boat.

The main advantage of shore-based facilities is a greater variety of other interests that may suit non-diving partners and children. Also, there is usually the option of a shorter stay and fewer dives, which makes a budget vacation possible.

Live-aboards, however, provide the best value for money. Your trip aboard will

**UNLIMITED GEAR** *is available from dive centers such as this (left). Live-aboard dive boats, like the Telita (below), offer divers every comfort.*

include unlimited diving, all meals and refreshments, a greater range of dive sites, and much more opportunity to meet special creatures—such as sharks and rays. Going diving on a live-aboard trip is much simpler and more comfortable. The vessel is often at the dive site for many hours, so divers can choose their own dive times. Equipment is carried on board, and showers and food are readily available. Live-aboard dive groups are smaller and more intimate.

Keep in mind that the quality and performance of the various dive operators can often differ greatly. Ask for recommendations from your dive center or dive-travel agency, or from friends who have already experienced enjoyable trips. In the highly competitive world of the diving industry, if one deal is cheaper than another, be wary. There is always a very good reason for it.

# EXPANDING *the* KNOWLEDGE

*Sharks and rays provide an opportunity for divers and snorkelers to enjoy an encounter with some of the world's most graceful and magnificent creatures.*

A most important aspect of any shark or ray encounter is your behavior, so you must understand and "read" the behavior of the species of sharks or rays you are likely to meet.

## APPROACHING SHARKS AND RAYS

If you wish to get close to a shark or ray, keep in mind some simple guidelines. Always dive in a small group. When you see a shark or ray, stay still, or move very slowly. The creature will be less intimidated and will probably approach you. Slow your breathing to minimize the noise of your exhaust bubbles. If you need to swim close, take an indirect path to the animal, swimming on a converging course.

Manta rays are exceptional among sharks and rays in that they sometimes seem to enjoy human contact. Some have been known to instigate contact and return to a dive group repeatedly. However, such encounters are rare, and divers should not encourage them. You should never initiate contact with any wild animal. To do so could adversely affect its health and behavior. Whale sharks are often greatly stressed by divers attempting to touch them.

**GIANTS OF THE DEEP** *The whale shark (above) grows to at least 40 feet (12 m). A marbled ribbontail ray (below right) grows to more than 5 feet (1.5 m).*

## PERSONAL DIVING EQUIPMENT

Dive travelers should ensure that their equipment is complete and in perfect order. Check your diving skills and proficiency, and all your gear, by having a practice dive before a trip. Should this not be possible before the trip, do it as a check-out dive with the divemaster as soon as you are at the location. The sea floor or the confines of a shark cage surrounded by sharks is a very unpleasant place to discover that your regulator or mask is leaking, your air is low, your battery has gone flat in your dive computer, or your weight belt is slipping.

Pack your certification card and dive log with your equipment. All dive operators require proof of certification, and some will demand a record of dive experience before taking you on an advanced dive. This is a legal necessity in some countries.

## KEEPING A RECORD OF OBSERVATIONS

Divers or snorkelers can contribute a great deal to marine science or conservation if they are willing to record their observations. Sharks and rays are hard to study in their own habitat, and too few scientists and

**LIQUID SPACE** *Diving from a fishing trawler (right) in the Maldives. As well as a dive logbook (below right), keep records of your observations.*

marine biologists are available to monitor the behavior, health or movements of rays and sharks adequately. Often it is the casual observer or the dive operators and staff who are in the best position to observe special behavior, new discoveries, or any critical changes.

Your observations are valuable only if you record the data properly and take great care to be accurate and objective. Do not jump to any conclusions that might bias your ability to observe accurately. Simply write exactly what you witness, and let the experts do the interpreting. An important point to remember is to carry a waterproof slate and pen, and to record everything immediately—it's surprising what you can forget during the time span of a dive. Remember to note any conspicuous markings or shapes. These can help to

identify a species or even a known individual.

Try to record the date, time, depth, and water temperature. Include any details of tides, currents, weather, or moon phase. These can be important clues to mating or movement patterns. Also, take note of the surrounding habitat in which the behavior took place—for example, the ocean surface, mid-water, on a reef, among kelp, or on a shipwreck. It was observations such as these that established that sand tigers congregate to mate during a certain month every year on the wreck of

the US submarine *Tarpon*, in the Atlantic Ocean near North Carolina in the United States.

Avoid disturbing the animals' natural behavior by your presence on the scene. Try to stay still, breathe slowly, and don't get too close. Include observations of injury, improper or illegal fishing activities, or evidence of stress on the animals. Keep in mind that what you don't see can also be important. If the sharks are supposed to be there and they are missing, record it. Provide copies of your observations to the dive operator, shark and ray conservation groups, and marine science authorities.

Photographic flash units do not disturb marine life, so if you are a photographer, so much the better. Send photographs with your recordings to one of the natural history or recreational diving magazines. Other readers may have a similar story to tell.

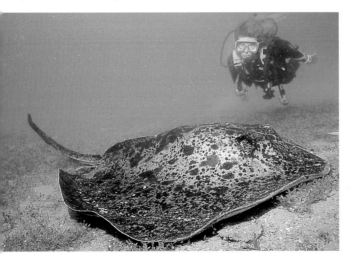

# ENCOUNTERS
## *with* SHARKS *and* RAYS

*For the most part, sharks and rays do not pose a threat to humans. They are not aggressive animals—they are usually prepared to live and let live.*

Having swum among sharks for generations, indigenous people of Polynesia and Melanesia are well aware of their behavior. Yet they do not live in fear of them, and shark attacks among these people are very rare. They have a spiritual relationship with these sea creatures and will not kill them. In some cases, they believe that sharks are the reincarnated souls of their deceased family members.

Most other cultures do not share this attitude toward sharks and rays, being, at the very least, wary of these creatures. Indeed, if you are snorkeling or diving in areas where you are likely to encounter sharks and rays, you should be especially careful. There are a number of precautions you should take, and guidelines to follow.

**KNOWING THE QUARRY** *People of Papua New Guinea (right) are on good terms with sharks. The silvertip shark (below) is territorial and not to be trifled with. This giant black stingray (far right) was seen in Queensland, Australia, and the zebra shark (top right) in the Red Sea.*

## GUIDELINES FOR SHARK AND RAY ENCOUNTERS

Never panic. Most approaches by sharks and rays are motivated by simple curiosity. Do not assume that you are in trouble.

Maintain eye contact. If you want to retreat, do it in a slow, controlled manner.

Don't be afraid to move toward these creatures. Move slowly so as not to intimidate them. They are wary of other large predators, and they will often swim away rapidly. The exception to this is a reef shark defending its territory. Do not approach any reef shark that is swimming with an exaggerated side-to-side motion with its back hunched, and its pectoral fins down. Instead, calmly and quickly leave the area.

Avoid periods of low light (dawn or dusk) and low visibility. At these times, a shark could mistake you for its natural prey.

On the surface, avoid excess splashing. To a shark, you will appear to be a disabled animal and you will attract the wrong kind of interest. Underwater, swim with slow, deliberate strokes so that you will appear to be another healthy predator, and sharks will be wary.

Avoid areas where people are spearfishing. A struggling fish transmits distress signals that sharks are able to pick up from miles away.

If baits are used to attract sharks into the area, pay careful attention to the ocean current and make certain you are always up-current of the bait. Any object in the odor corridor carried along by the current will attract sharks.

Make sure the dive boat is up-current and not far away.

Beware of any small, light-colored object that contrasts with your equipment, especially if it is hanging loosely. Sharks can mistake white fins, gloves, a white underwater slate, or torch for a piece of bait.

Diving in a group can be safer. When you are finished, leave the site as a group because sharks will become bolder as numbers reduce.

Never touch, surround or try to contain a shark or ray. They must always be allowed plenty of room to retreat, or they may panic and rush you in a frantic attempt to escape.

If a shark becomes overly curious and approaches too close for comfort, a hard punch on the nose will usually cause it to retreat rapidly. Some divers carry a shark billy (any short, blunt rod) for just this purpose.

Always remember, although they are not aggressive, there is no such thing as a harmless shark or ray. Each can and will defend itself if threatened, and this is the natural response.

# PROTECTIVE EQUIPMENT

*Over the years there have been many attempts to provide effective protection for those professionals who must work with sharks and rays.*

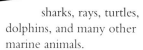

During the past 60 years, many strategies designed to protect swimmers and divers from sharks have been developed and tested (see pp. 54–5). Until very recently, all have failed.

## PROTECTING THE PROFESSIONAL

During the Second World War, the United States Navy put its faith in a chemical shark repellent. The sharks swam right through it. They also kept swimming through other repellents, such as air bubble curtains, sound wave barriers and dyes. Mesh netting has been installed at a number of beaches to create a safety barrier for bathers. But, unfortunately, these nets kill a great number of harmless sharks, rays, turtles, dolphins, and many other marine animals.

Divers developed a number of strange, and unsuccessful, devices. Dressing a diver as a black-and-white sea snake was one unusual strategy put to the test—until it was realized that some sharks eat sea snakes. Weapons with a detonating device were developed to shoot any aggressive shark. But, since most shark-attack victims never see the shark coming, these weapons were directed at sharks that were mostly harmless. A hypodermic gas device called a "shark dart" was also developed. This killed the shark, after first inflating it and rendering it harmless. However, because the dart had to be fired into the shark's stomach, it was effective only on sharks swimming by rather than ones that were attacking.

A very effective device— a stainless-steel suit of chain-mail—was finally developed by Australian underwater photographers and shark

**TESTING TIMES** *Developing the protective stainless-steel chain-mail suit involved close contact (above) and trying to get a shark to bite it (left).*

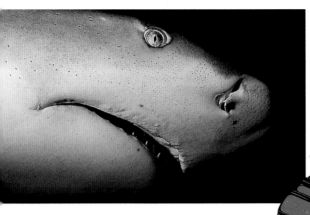

**PROTECTIVE DEVICE** *The POD (below) disrupts signals picked up by a shark's natural detectors, the ampullae of Lorenzini, situated along its face.*

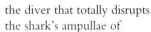

experts, Ron and Valerie Taylor. This suit has become standard equipment for film makers, dive guides, and scientists who work with sharks. However, it does have some disadvantages, and must be used only by experienced specialists trained in its use. It can restrict movement, and its weight prevents it from being discarded easily in an emergency. It is also possible that a very large shark could crush or tear the garment.

A recent major breakthrough, however, promises to provide the ultimate protection from accidental shark attack for all divers, snorkelers, and water sport enthusiasts. It is a device called the shark POD (or Protective Oceanic Device). It has been rigorously tested by the South African Natal Sharks Board and by Ron and Valerie Taylor.

The shark POD is a compact accessory that fits onto a diver's scuba cylinder. It is connected to a wire that runs from the POD to a small plate attached to the diver's fin. A switch is provided to enable the diver to turn it on before entering the water, and a warning light reveals that the unit is on and working. The unit can be switched off in the water should the diver want to get closer to sharks or

rays. A red light display indicates the remaining battery life, giving the diver time to surface and replenish both battery and air supply.

The POD repels sharks at close quarters by creating an electrical force field around

the diver that totally disrupts the shark's ampullae of Lorenzini. These are the natural electrical detectors situated along a shark's face that it uses to detect minute electronic signals emitted by potential prey. This disruption cannot be tolerated by sharks.

Tests have shown that the shark POD is very effective, does not injure sharks or rays and has no effect on other marine life, as these creatures do not have ampullae of Lorenzini.

The Natal Sharks Board is currently developing a version that can provide a complete screen for a beach or bathing area. Once this has been perfected, the meshing of our beaches against sharks would become unnecessary. This would relieve the community of a major annual expense, and much innocent marine life would be spared.

## SHARK PARTNERS

Both Australian-born, Ron (b. 1934) and Valerie (b. 1935) Taylor originally shared a common interest in spearfishing, at which they both excelled, and underwater photography. Working independently and together, they have notched up a list of extraordinary films and TV documentaries, including *Playing with Sharks*, *Shark Hunters*, *Blue Water, White Death*, and *Inner Space*. The Taylors' focus of interest has altered over the years to one of committed conservation of all marine creatures, no matter how fearsome. They now work tirelessly for better understanding of the denizens of the deep, especially the much-maligned and misunderstood shark. Valerie and her husband pioneered the use of a protective mesh diving suit made of stainless steel, which made possible photographic work among sharks without the photographer being confined to a shark cage. More recently, the Taylors have been helping to test the POD.

# UNDERWATER PHOTOGRAPHY

*Capturing encounters with sharks and rays on film can be a thrilling and satisfying exercise for many dive travelers.*

Fortunately for both the amateur and professional photographer, great advances in technology mean that successful underwater photography is now possible.

## CAMERA EQUIPMENT

The complete beginner might choose a disposable camera in a waterproof housing. This is an inexpensive system that calls for no technical knowledge of photography. Such cameras produce a good result, particularly in shallow, clear, sunlit, tropical waters.

More serious photographers prefer amphibious 35 mm cameras with interchangeable lenses, underwater strobe lighting, variable focus, and exposure control. Such features allow a much wider range of photographic composition and the means to deal with low light levels or limited visibility.

Advanced or professional photographers should consider combining a current model auto focus 35 mm SLR (single lens reflex) land camera with one of the many excellent waterproof camera housings that are now available. These systems provide a very wide choice of lens options that allow photography of small, medium, or very large

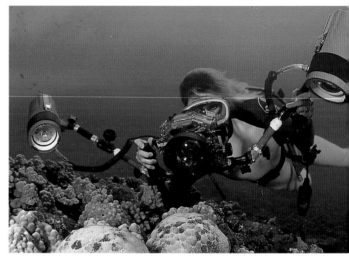

**RECORDING THE COLORS** *of sea stars and coral in Hawaii (above); and a special amphibious camera (above left).*

sharks and rays. Auto focus, auto exposure, and motor drive film transport features are invaluable for action shots of fast-moving subjects.

## TYPE OF FILM

Sharks and rays are often encountered near the water surface where light levels are good, so

any slide or print film with a medium sensitivity rating of ISO 50 or 100 is suitable. In deeper water, below 30 feet (10 m), the photographer can use a strobe (flash unit) to provide extra light and restore natural colors. Films with sensitivity ratings of ISO 200 are often used for fast-action subjects photographed in available light situations. Choose a film that favors the blacks, whites, and subtle shades of color common among shark and ray species.

## TECHNICAL CONSIDERATIONS

Photographing sharks and rays frequently involves the use of available natural light, so it is very important to be aware of the position of the

**FINGERTIP CONTROL** *Strobe units and cameras are securely mounted on a bracket for maximum flexibility.*

## PRACTICAL CONSIDERATIONS

A dive buddy willing to act as a rear guard can be very valuable—particularly when the photographer is pre-occupied with composing pictures of one shark while other sharks are about. Since chum is often used to attract sharks, and baits are provided to overcome their natural caution, the sharks will often become very excited and curious. It is not unusual for several sharks to approach at once. A second set of human eyes is useful at this point.

Photographers may sometimes find it necessary to extend their camera and upper body through the windows of shark cages to obtain a good angle. The shark you can see is not a problem, but another shark approaching from the side could be. Once again, a vigilant companion is vital.

The diver needs to exercise care whenever making a close approach to any large shark or ray, even if it is a harmless species. A whale shark, for example, can break bones or knock a diver unconscious with its tail. Be particularly careful always to leave space for a shark or ray to retreat and remember that they all have some method of defense, such as biting, ramming, or a powerful tail slap.

Sun. To ensure that details of the shark or ray are revealed, try to position yourself so that the Sun is always coming at an angle over your shoulders. Avoid photography around midday when the Sun is directly above you.

When a strobe is used to provide light, the angle of the Sun in relation to the subject is not so critical, but beware of suspended matter in the water that may be emphasized by the strobe light and spoil the image. This effect is termed "backscatter" and it can be avoided by using low power settings on the strobe and longer strobe arms. Some common sources of back-scatter in shark photography are chum—a mixture of products used to attract sharks; particles of shark bait used for feeding sharks once they arrive; and plankton—a natural food source of whale sharks and manta rays. Also a problem are the small bubbles constantly created by the movement of shark cages, the dive boat, or the wake from other snorkelers' fins.

To ensure clear, sharp images underwater, avoid shooting until you are less than a few yards from the subject. If the subject is a very large shark or ray, you will need a 15 mm or 20 mm wide-angle lens to capture the whole creature. Lenses of the 60 mm, 35 mm or 28 mm variety are useful for portrait shots of the face, details of the body, or for complete images of smaller species.

Because many sharks and rays are dark in color, the camera's light meter may be less accurate than normal and may tend to give an over-exposed image. You can compensate for the dark color by overriding the camera's automatic exposure functions and setting them manually.

# UNDERWATER FILMING

*Words seem inadequate when you describe diving with sharks and rays to others, but underwater videos convey all the wonder and excitement.*

The variety of compact video camcorders and well-designed watertight housings on the market today makes it possible for anyone to capture all the underwater action and drama of shark and ray encounters.

## CAMERA EQUIPMENT

Video cameras, or camcorders, are the world's most user-friendly cameras. They are effective in low light, fully automatic, and simple to operate. Not only do they provide more than one hour of continuous recording time, but the results can be viewed almost at once. This means that any missing or poorly recorded images can sometimes be re-shot before you leave the site.

A compact model is the best choice of camcorder and the most popular format is Video 8 or High 8. The size of these compact camcorders makes them ideal for use in an underwater housing.

The best watertight housings are made of aluminum and feature magnetic switches, water alarm, interchangeable lens optics, and many controls. Basic acrylic housings are also available and are sometimes cheaper. Although they have certain limitations, if you are on a restricted budget, it is still possible to get good underwater images with cameras in these housings.

## TECHNICAL CONSIDERATIONS

To capture good images of sharks and rays you will need a housing with wide-angle lens optics to encompass large species, and a zoom control that enables you to use a telephoto option to capture small or shy species.

**WATERTIGHT HOUSINGS** *(above) are specially designed to make video equipment feel lighter under the water.*

Filters are also available to offset the excessive blue of tropical water or the predominant green cast of temperate water. They work well, but should not be used in shallow water less than 10 feet (3 m) deep, as the filter color will dominate and distort the natural color.

Because video camcorders respond even in very low light, underwater lighting will not be necessary. There will be a lack of bright colors at greater depths, but few sharks

**UP CLOSE** *It is possible to video the most intimate life happenings of reef creatures and the fascinating reef itself.*

and rays are colorful. The added feature of movement and action will compensate for any lack of color, but the enthusiast keen on recording faithful color could consider adding underwater lighting to shoot more colorful species. Although flash and strobe units do not disturb marine life, stronger lighting may. Check with local operators to see if any lighting restrictions apply in a particular area.

## PRACTICAL CONSIDERATIONS

Since the camcorders are automatic, most problems are caused by the operator. To ensure quality footage, the camera must be held steady to prevent wobble. Keep the action in the center of the viewfinder so that the automatic focus does not need to hunt for focus, and shoot in sequences of wide shots,

medium shots, and close-ups.

Beware of air bubbles on the lens—these bubbles are created by snorkelers' fins, scuba exhaust, dive-boat propellers, shark-cage movement, and breaking waves. The bubbles cling to the camcorder lens port and become very pronounced once the image is reviewed on the television screen. Wipe your hand regularly over the port to remove them.

**THE HUGE MANTA RAY** *(below), with long, gray remoras attached, presents an exciting scene. A photographer's buddy must keep a vigilant watch (right).*

## EDITING

Do as the professionals do and plan a "shot list" of everything you think you will need to make an interesting and cohesive short story. Shoot everything on the shot list, including any unexpected encounters, before you return home. Finally, edit the useful shots into an action-packed short story by dubbing across from your camcorder to your home video cassette recorder.

# LEARNING *to* SCUBA DIVE

*Scuba diving is a sport that must be taken seriously. Training with a qualified instructor is essential before you will be accredited as a diver.*

**DIVING TECHNIQUES** must be mastered in a pool (left) before those who qualify for certificates venture into the ocean. Below are two divers with a school of colorful milletseed butterflyfish.

Swimming with scuba is simple and relatively non-strenuous. Any healthy person aged more than 12 years can learn to scuba dive. It is essential, and, in fact, mandatory, to complete a training course before you attempt any scuba dive. Any lack of knowledge of such topics as pressure changes and decompression, and a lack of training in the correct assembly and use of the equipment can lead to serious injury and death.

Dive centers offering scuba courses can be found in most cities and towns, or at most tropical resorts around the world. The Open Water Diving course is the one most likely to suit your needs.

It is essential to learn from a qualified instructor who is a current member of one of the instructor agencies with worldwide recognition and credibility. Participants who qualify at the end of the course receive a certification card that enables the holder to purchase or hire diving equipment, and participate in diving activities. Without this qualification, participants will now find it almost impossible to dive anywhere in the world.

## GETTING STARTED

The best source of dive centers in your area is the telephone directory. Contact several centers and carefully compare the inclusions of their training programs. Most will offer a full-time or part-time training schedule. A full-time course should consist of at least four or five days' training. Part-time courses should provide a minimum of two complete weekends for the practical training, plus night lectures. Be wary of shorter courses, and check to see if all of the following are provided: diving equipment, air fills, textbook, logbook, dive tables, pool fees, boat diving, certification card, and any necessary accommodation.

Check the student-to-instructor ratio. Instructional agencies usually insist on a maximum of eight students for every one instructor. If the agency assigns assistant instructors or divemasters to a class, this does not necessarily mean they can increase student numbers.

The practical training component of your course must include five pool sessions and a minimum of four ocean dives, utilizing the best part of four cylinders of air.

Find out what you can about the dive center and its instructors. Keep in mind that the instruction you get is only as good as their experience, ethics, and professionalism, regardless of any affiliation they may have with any particular instructor agency.

## COMMENCING YOUR TRAINING

A medical examination is required before the start of your course to determine that you are fit to dive. A diving medical form must be completed, which identifies key medical considerations unique to diving, such as asthma, diabetes, heart conditions, and sinus and ear cavity conditions.

You will be issued a training text with self-study guides and quizzes, which should be studied before the commencement of the appropriate lectures or diving sessions.

Initially, you will be introduced to all the skills and drills of equipment assembly and use in a swimming pool, or a very shallow dive site that provides calm, sheltered water. Once you are competent at these skills, you will progress to open-ocean diving. Do not allow yourself to be rushed into the ocean if you are not proficient with these skills. If you have chosen a good program, there will be time for the instructors to provide extra instruction.

## RESORT COURSES

Many dive resorts also have instructors on staff to provide training. This is a good option if you do not have time to learn at a local dive center. The classroom, pool, and training dives will, however, cut into the opportunity to fully explore the area. If the resort course is your preferred

**BASIC TRAINING** *consists of classroom lectures (right) and practical work in a pool or shallow water. A small group of divers (below) sets out on a great adventure.*

option, try to schedule a longer stay so that you can pursue good diving opportunities in the area after the completion of your scuba course.

## INTRODUCTORY DIVES

For the beginner who just wants to dip a big toe in the water, many resorts or dive centers offer introductory dives. These are a single-day diving experience with a minimum of training, which allow potential enthusiasts to give the sport a try.

Such introductory dives do not count towards certification, but they can provide special experiences, unique encounters with marine life, and kick-start you into the fascinating world of divers.

## ADVANCED SKILLS

Should you wish to continue your diving training, there are many programs with advanced and specialty courses available. Check with your local dive center.

The Advanced Open Water diver program will introduce you to better navigation and orientation skills, deep diving and night diving. This should be completed as soon as possible after your Open Water Diving course.

Other courses to consider are those in rescue diving, deep diving, wreck diving, underwater photography, and even shark diving. All these diving programs will improve your knowledge and skills in these specialized areas.

# SCUBA—
# WHAT YOU NEED *to* KNOW

*Once you are feeling confident that scuba diving is the right sport for you, it is a good idea to start purchasing your own gear.*

When diving, you will feel more comfortable if you wear good-quality diving equipment that has been selected just for you. Your instructors will provide valuable advice on equipment selection, and instruct you on the fine points of using, maintaining, and servicing your equipment. Keep in mind that the advice they give is more important than the price of the equipment. Your instructors will place your welfare and future enjoyment above anything else, so it is often a false economy to shop around elsewhere to try to find a cheaper deal.

**REEF DIVING** *from a yacht (below) in Fijian waters. A diver in the South Pacific (bottom right) studies a gorgonian fan. The dive computer (above left) is an important piece of gear.*

## SCUBA DIVING

The basic rules of safe scuba diving can be summarized as follows:
• Never dive without obtaining adequate professional training.
• Always evaluate the conditions carefully before diving.
• In an emergency, do not panic.
• Never drink alcohol before diving.
• Never dive beyond your limits.
• Never hold your breath during an ascent. This can cause severe damage to your lungs.
• A good guide is never to surface faster than your smallest exhaust bubbles.
• Do not dive to the limits of your dive tables, and do not dive deeper than the depths for which you have been trained.
• To reduce the risk of decompression sickness, always do the deepest dive of the day first, the deepest part of any dive first, and take a safety stop at 12–15 feet (4–5 m) for three minutes after each dive.
• Do not attempt specialized dives without specialized training. Examples of specialized dives are deep diving, cave diving, wreck diving, night diving, and penetration diving (the deep penetration of wrecks and caves).
• Never dive with equipment that is faulty, obsolete, or in need of service.
• Never succumb to peer pressure, or be afraid to call off a dive.
• Local knowledge is invaluable, so always seek it before diving in an area or dive site that is new to you.
• Avoid airplane travel for 24 hours after a dive.

## SCUBA EQUIPMENT

Currently, equipment that is considered mandatory for the modern diver includes:

- A face mask that is low-volume, and has a nose pocket (with the option of prescription lenses for divers requiring corrected vision; alternatively, contact lenses can be used inside the face mask).
- A snorkel that is contoured, and has an exhaust valve and a water deflector.
- Boots with zippers and reinforced soles.
- Fins with an open heel and adjustable quick-release straps.
- Gloves that are flexible and close fitting, with reinforced fingers and palms.
- A small, stainless-steel dive knife with a serrated edge and a quick-release sheath.
- An exposure suit with ankle-to-wrist coverage (anything less is not a dive suit). It should be of a thickness suited to deal with the local water temperatures.
- A comfortable weight belt.
- A regulator. This delivers air to the diver in two stages. It should have a balanced twin-stage function—a good-performance first stage and simple second stage. It should also feature effective exhaust deflectors.
- An "octopus" regulator. This is a back-up second stage, specially designed for the purpose of dive-buddy rescue.
- A pressure gauge that indicates the air remaining with color-coded low-air calibration.
- A depth gauge.
- A dive cylinder. This is optional for the traveling diver, who will probably use a dive cylinder supplied by the tour operator rather than taking this item.
- A Buoyancy Control Device (BCD), which consists of secure tank bands to hold the dive cylinder, and a secure adjustable harness. It should, if possible, be weight integrated, so that the diver has the option of wearing dive weights in the BCD instead of on a weight belt.
- A dive computer. This is a multi-level computer that indicates the dive time remaining, ascent rates, decompression information, and options for the amount of time you can spend on the bottom during your next dive. It also records information from up to 10 completed dives in its user-retrievable memory.
- A dive watch that is waterproof to about 650 feet (200 m).
- A compact dive light with a powerful beam for night diving, or a large dive light with a wide beam for cave and wreck diving.
- Accessories. These should include a whistle, a compass, an underwater slate and pencil, a safety buoy, a chemical light stick, a strobe light, and waterproof dive tables.
- A dive-gear bag. This should be large, water resistant, and have compartment pockets and strong nylon straps.

# SNORKELING— WHAT YOU NEED *to* KNOW

*Snorkeling is easy. Almost anyone of any age can participate, and even beginners can enjoy the experience.*

Snorkel divers should never feel compromised by any lack of scuba diving skills or equipment. The world's most beautiful coral reefs are accessible to the snorkeler and, indeed, snorkeling is considered the best way to encounter some species of sharks and rays (such as stingrays at Stingray City in the Caymans or reef sharks and stingrays at Lord Howe Island, off the east coast of Australia).

## SELECTING SNORKELING EQUIPMENT

Your enjoyment of snorkeling can be heightened by making use of modern equipment and learning some snorkeling skills. Take the time to select a good-quality, low-volume face mask that will provide excellent vision, and allow the option of prescription lenses for optical correction if required. Select a high-quality snorkel with a water deflector to prevent much water from entering, and a purge valve to expel the excess if it does.

Spend a little extra on high-performance fins. They are far more comfortable, and if you are following sharks or rays, you will need plenty of power. Consider a lightweight exposure suit that will cover you from wrist to ankle. Some excellent Lycra ones that are non-restrictive

**A WORLD HERITAGE AREA** *Lord Howe Island (above) lies off the east coast of Australia. Snorkeling amid schooling hussar (below).*

are available, and these will retain some body heat while also protecting you from coral, stingers, and sunburn.

Check with your local dive center for snorkel classes. There are quite a few skills that instructors can show you.

**SEA STARS** *at Manado, Indonesia
(left). The coral reefs surrounding the
many small islands there teem with life.*

person on the surface keeping
a sharp watch.
• Tow a buoy with a dive flag
in areas where other boats are
likely to be.
• Take a course in CPR
(cardiopulmonary resuscitation)
and basic lifesaving skills.
• Always respect marine life
and avoid touching and
damaging reefs.

Don't be embarrassed to go to
your local pool and practice
until you feel confident about
your skills and equipment.

Practice slow, but steady,
controlled swimming with a
minimum of splash and
maximum thrust. Practice
duck diving to the bottom
and equalizing pressure on
your eardrums by holding
your nose and very gently
forcing some air into your
inner ears as you descend.
You should not force yourself
deeper if you feel any pain.
This procedure equalizes
pressure on the eardrums, and
prevents pain and possible
injury to the inner ear.

Learn to extend your time
underwater by deep breathing
before a dive to expel excess
carbon dioxide. Never
take any more than five or
six deep breaths, or you may
hyperventilate and lose
consciousness while you
are underwater.

## SNORKEL DIVING
• Before you go snorkeling,
practice in a pool or confined
water until you are confident

in and competent with
your equipment.
• Before the excursion,
obtain local knowledge
from dive centers or
dive operators.
• Evaluate currents,
waves, visibility and
ocean conditions prior
to diving. Choose safe
entry and exit points.
• Do not descend if
you are suffering from
nasal congestion or
sinus problems.
• Never hyperventilate.
Avoid deep, rapid
breathing beyond
6 to 10 deep breaths.
• Avoid any excessive
surface splashing.
• Always dive in pairs.
Have one person
down, and the other

## JACQUES-YVES COUSTEAU

The growing popularity of the
sport of snorkeling has largely
been made possible by innovation
and improvement in the gear
available. Until comparatively
recently, exploration of ocean life
was restricted to the surface close
to land or to what could be seen
from the confines of a diving suit.
More than anyone else, French-
born Jacques-Yves Cousteau
(1910–97) has liberated observers
in this so-called "inner space". For
many years, he pioneered dramatic
improvements in diving techniques, and
captained the research vessel, *Calypso*,
which sails the oceans of the world
collecting data. By co-inventing the
aqualung, he released divers to move as
freely in water as they did on land.

Cousteau won great renown as a
dedicated oceanographer, film-maker
and writer. His books, translated into
many languages, include *The Silent World*
(1953), *The Living Sea* (1962), and
*Cousteau's Amazon Journey* (1984). A
widely screened TV series, *The
Undersea World of Jacques Cousteau*,
successfully raised awareness about the
need for research into and conservation
of ocean life. His films include an Oscar-
winner, *The Golden Fish*, and *Cousteau:
The First 75 Years*. His remarkable work
awakened a sense of wonderment
in people all over the world to the
compelling marvels of ocean life.

# BOATING *and* FISHING

*Many sharks and rays are killed each year because of ignorance or lack of understanding on the part of boating and fishing enthusiasts.*

Today, the waterways and oceans off our coasts are busy with a continual stream of traffic consisting of ships, power-craft, yachts, and jet-skis. These craft all take a toll on the many species of sharks and rays that spend much of their time on the surface—some of which may already be close to being classified as endangered species. It is not uncommon to see whale sharks, the largest and most gentle of all sharks, displaying the scars of encounters with watercraft. Some have had an entire fin torn off by a propeller blade.

Today's conservation-minded boaters and sailors should keep a careful watch for any creatures just beneath the surface so that the injuries to marine animals can be reduced. People on watch

should wear polarized sunglasses that allow a much improved view through any glare on the water surface.

### UNINTENDED CATCH

It is not unusual for fishing enthusiasts to find they have accidentally caught a shark or ray. The correct management of the problem can go a long way toward preventing the death of an innocent creature.

Take great care—it is very important to avoid injuring

**ACCIDENTAL DAMAGE** *The whitetip reef shark (above) may have escaped being caught, but a hook remains lodged in its jaw. The whale shark (below) has probably had its dorsal fin and tail tip amputated by a boat propeller.*

**UNNATURAL HAZARDS**
*A discarded fishing net snares some angelsharks and Port Jackson sharks (left). This shark's mouth (below) was damaged by a hook and line.*

yourself. Bring the creature as close as possible, but not so close that you are at risk from its teeth or barbs. Do not use a gaff or any instrument that will injure the animal. Cut the line as close to the hook as safety permits. Avoid the temptation to remove the

hook. To do so is hazardous to you, and the creature will struggle so much that it will probably be injured, or die later from the stress.

Consider fishing with hooks made of regular, rather than stainless, steel. Such hooks will rust away

reasonably quickly if they are left in the mouth of the fish. A shark or ray that is encumbered by a hook and attached wire leader could become tangled in the wire and either suffocate, or starve slowly to death.

PROTECTED SPECIES
AND PROTECTED AREAS
Ignorance is no excuse. It is the responsibility of fishing enthusiasts to make themselves aware of which shark and ray species are protected, and of restrictions to fishing areas. They should also know about prohibited fishing practices.

Sharks, rays, and other forms of marine life are now under a great deal of pressure from overfishing, loss of habitat due to development, diminishing fish stocks, accidental by-catch, and pollution of all kinds, so our acts of conservation are vital.

## APPROACHING SHARKS OR RAYS WITH BOATS

An informed skipper can contribute greatly toward a worthwhile shark or ray encounter that is safe for all involved. The boat operator should be aware of certain procedures.

• Never drive the vessel directly toward the creature.
• Steer a parallel course. Move approximately 100 yards (90 m) ahead, then turn across the animal's course and drop the divers in its probable path.
• If the passengers are non-divers, stop the vessel in the animal's path and turn off the motor.
• When divers or snorkelers are in the water, have a lookout on watch at all times and be ready for an urgent pick-up.

89

There is, one knows not what sweet mystery about this
sea, whose gently awful stirrings seem to speak of some
hidden soul beneath.

*Moby Dick*,
HERMAN MELVILLE (1819–91), American novelist

# CHAPTER FOUR
# SHARKS

# IDENTIFYING *and* CLASSIFYING SHARKS

*To recognize a shark, you need a good understanding of its external features, and sometimes a quick eye and a keen memory.*

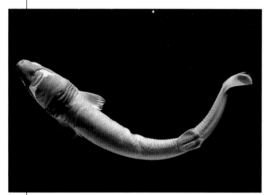

Classification and description of the 350 or so species of living shark is based on the science of taxonomy, in which the morphological characteristics are used to group closely related species. Early modern taxonomists, such as Carolus Linnaeus (1707–78), did not fully understand evolutionary relationships among organisms and often used superficial features to form these groups.

**ANATOMY OF A SHARK** *The diagram below shows the key external characteristics of a typical shark. The pygmy or dwarf shark (above) reaches a maximum size of 10 inches (25 cm).*

Modern shark taxonomists use shared character-istics that have appeared in species throughout evolutionary history, such as the way the upper jaw is attached to the skull, how the skeletal structures are arranged, and the shape of the teeth. Since such features cannot be readily observed in living animals, the keys we have for the identification of most organisms are still based largely on external features that can be observed or measured with relative ease. These are not necessarily im-portant evolutionary markers.

## THROUGH THE AGES

The basic body plan of sharks has been conserved for hundreds of millions of years. The features of extinct fossil sharks, such as *Cladoselache*, are found today among living species, such as the whale

shark, *Rhincodon typus*, which can be more than 43 feet (13 m) in length, and also the unrelated spined pygmy shark, *Squaliolus laticaudus*, which reaches only about 10 inches (25 cm). The identification of different shark species usually involves information on relative sizes of the animals, placement and shape of fins, and detailed anatomical features, such as tooth shape.

Sharks can be separated into the higher taxonomic level of order by observation of basic anatomical features. For example, the angelsharks (Squatiniformes), sawsharks (Pristiophoriformes), and dogfish sharks (Squaliformes) can be identified by their lack of an anal fin. Once this feature is known, it is relatively easy to differentiate among the three orders by the shape of the body and head. Some other important identifying features at the order level are the number of gill slits, the presence or absence of dorsal fin spines, the position of the

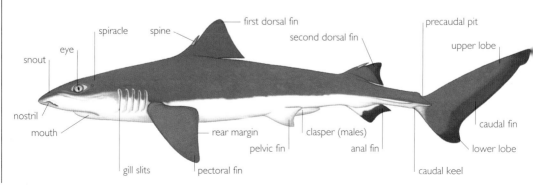

first dorsal fin
second dorsal fin
spiracle — spine
precaudal pit
upper lobe
eye
snout
nostril
mouth
caudal fin
rear margin — clasper (males)
pelvic fin
anal fin
lower lobe
gill slits — pectoral fin
caudal keel

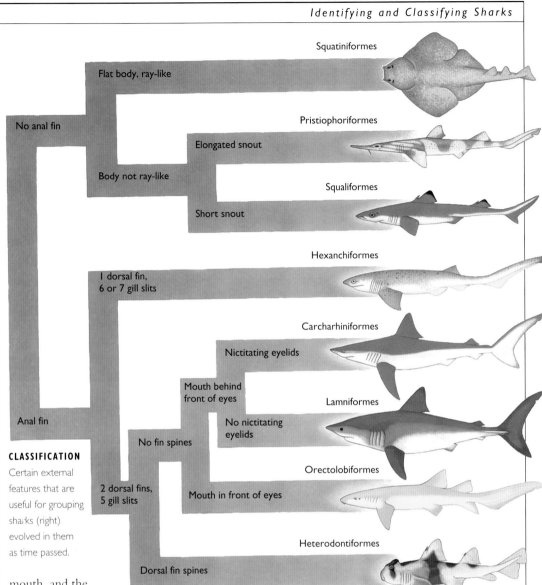

Squatiniformes

Flat body, ray-like

No anal fin

Pristiophoriformes

Elongated snout

Body not ray-like

Squaliformes

Short snout

Hexanchiformes

1 dorsal fin,
6 or 7 gill slits

Carcharhiniformes

Nictitating eyelids

Mouth behind
front of eyes

Lamniformes

Anal fin

No nictitating
eyelids

No fin spines

**CLASSIFICATION**

Certain external
features that are
useful for grouping
sharks (right)
evolved in them
as time passed.

Orectolobiformes

2 dorsal fins,
5 gill slits

Mouth in front of eyes

Heterodontiformes

Dorsal fin spines

mouth, and the
presence or absence
of a nictitating eyelid.

To identify species, shark
taxonomists have developed
a list of external features and
standard measurements.
These include descriptive
features such as the presence
or absence of spiracles, dorsal
fin spines, an anal fin, a lower
lobe on the caudal fin, an
interdorsal ridge, caudal keels,
and nictitating membranes.
Total body length, interdorsal
distance, head length and
width, fin length and height,
or size and number of teeth,
must also be measured or
counted. Collectively, these
features usually provide the
investigator with enough
information to make a
positive identification.

UNFAMILIAR SHARKS
To identify an unfamiliar
species of adult shark, first
examine the basic features,
body size, location of fins, and
shape of head. If, for example,
the shark is greater than about
16 feet (5 m) in total length,
the list of potential species
shrinks to only a handful that
includes the whale, basking,
great white, tiger, sleeper,
thresher, megamouth, and
great hammerhead sharks.
While a few species are very
small, less than 1 foot (30 cm),
most adult sharks range from
about 3–10 feet (1–3 m). In
these cases, shape of body,
color pattern, and fin placement may confirm the species.

While scientists using preserved specimens can spend
weeks making a tedious
examination of the external
features, internal anatomy,
and teeth, divers may
encounter a shark on a reef
for only a few seconds. When
trying to identify an unknown
species, a good knowledge of
distribution, habits, and
ecology may help to narrow
the field. For example, if a
6½ foot (2 m) requiem shark
was observed in the waters
off Hawaii, the choice can
be narrowed to about a dozen
possibilities. If it was observed
in blue oceanic water, the
candidates could be further
reduced by about half.

# THE BODY FORM
## *and* FUNCTION *of* SHARKS

*The shark's body is beautifully attuned to life in an
unforgiving watery world. It provides the ultimate biological
example of hydrodynamic efficiency and power.*

Many features of the shark's body have evolved in response to the physical constraints of its dense aquatic environment. The internal skeleton of sharks and rays is composed of cartilage, an elastic tissue much higher in water content than bone. A skeleton of cartilage allows a high degree of body flexibility, provides protection and support for organs, and reduces total body mass. Skeletal parts that experience physical stress, such as vertebrae, jaws, and parts of the skull, are often stiffened by secondary calcification rather than by heavier bone. It is unlikely that large, modern sharks would be capable of such quick, agile movement had they evolved bony skeletons.

### BIOLOGICAL TORPEDOES
A species that swims actively in the water column, such as the blue shark, usually has a fusiform (cigar-shaped) body.

**Blue shark,** a graceful swimmer

**Mako,** a powerful swimmer

**Angelshark,** a sluggish bottom dweller

The diameter of the body is greatest at about a third of the way back from the snout, and tapers off toward the tail. This shape lets water flow smoothly over the body as the shark swims and reduces turbulence along the skin.

Swimming power and stability are provided by the shark's well-developed fins. In most sharks, the tail, or caudal fin, creates forward thrust by wide side-to-side movements that produce an undulation of the body. Special helically wound connective tissue fibers under the skin transfer much of the body's power directly to the tail. The unpaired dorsal and anal fins keep the body from rolling to either side during forward motion. The pectoral and pelvic fins, paired and displaced off the body midline, are used for lift and control of movements.

The fastest sharks, such as the mako, are perhaps the

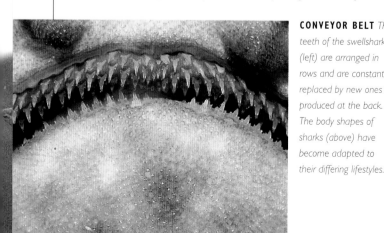

**CONVEYOR BELT** *The teeth of the swellshark (left) are arranged in rows and are constantly replaced by new ones produced at the back. The body shapes of sharks (above) have become adapted to their differing lifestyles.*

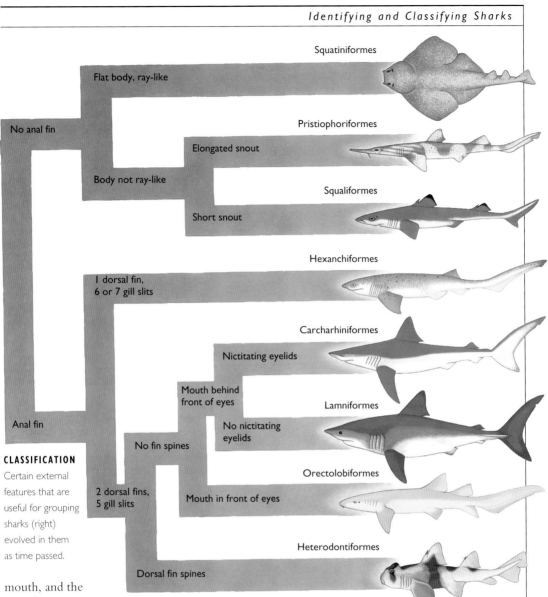

Squatiniformes

Flat body, ray-like

No anal fin

Pristiophoriformes

Elongated snout

Body not ray-like

Squaliformes

Short snout

Hexanchiformes

1 dorsal fin,
6 or 7 gill slits

Carcharhiniformes

Nictitating eyelids

Mouth behind
front of eyes

Lamniformes

Anal fin

No nictitating
eyelids

No fin spines

**CLASSIFICATION**

Certain external
features that are
useful for grouping
sharks (right)
evolved in them
as time passed.

2 dorsal fins,
5 gill slits

Orectolobiformes

Mouth in front of eyes

Heterodontiformes

Dorsal fin spines

mouth, and the
presence or absence
of a nictitating eyelid.

To identify species, shark
taxonomists have developed
a list of external features and
standard measurements.
These include descriptive
features such as the presence
or absence of spiracles, dorsal
fin spines, an anal fin, a lower
lobe on the caudal fin, an
interdorsal ridge, caudal keels,
and nictitating membranes.
Total body length, interdorsal
distance, head length and
width, fin length and height,
or size and number of teeth,
must also be measured or
counted. Collectively, these
features usually provide the
investigator with enough
information to make a
positive identification.

UNFAMILIAR SHARKS
To identify an unfamiliar
species of adult shark, first
examine the basic features,
body size, location of fins, and
shape of head. If, for example,
the shark is greater than about
16 feet (5 m) in total length,
the list of potential species
shrinks to only a handful that
includes the whale, basking,
great white, tiger, sleeper,
thresher, megamouth, and
great hammerhead sharks.
While a few species are very
small, less than 1 foot (30 cm),
most adult sharks range from
about 3–10 feet (1–3 m). In
these cases, shape of body,
color pattern, and fin placement may confirm the species.

While scientists using preserved specimens can spend
weeks making a tedious
examination of the external
features, internal anatomy,
and teeth, divers may
encounter a shark on a reef
for only a few seconds. When
trying to identify an unknown
species, a good knowledge of
distribution, habits, and
ecology may help to narrow
the field. For example, if a
6½ foot (2 m) requiem shark
was observed in the waters
off Hawaii, the choice can
be narrowed to about a dozen
possibilities. If it was observed
in blue oceanic water, the
candidates could be further
reduced by about half.

# THE EVOLUTION *and* RADIATION *of* SHARKS

*Sharks have dominated the oceans for more than 400 million years, yet the sharks of today still look much like their ancestors.*

The sharks, rays and chimaeras are all "cartilaginous fish," members of the taxonomic class Chondrichthyes. As the name implies, the skeletons have no true bone but are composed of cartilage, a soft, firm tissue with little, if any, calcification (similar to tissue supporting our nose and ears).

## TWO MAJOR GROUPS

Living cartilaginous fishes fall into two groups. The Elasmobranchii (sharks and rays) are characterized by five to seven external gill slits on each side of the head, placoid skin scales known as denticles, teeth that are replaced regularly, and an upper jaw that is not firmly attached to the skull as it is in mammals, birds, reptiles, and amphibians. The chimaeras, or ratfishes (Holocephalii), differ from sharks in that the gills are covered by a flap with only one opening. They also lack scales and have plate-like teeth for eating hard-shelled invertebrates. The upper jaw is firmly attached to the skull.

As a result of the lack of a hard skeleton, fossils of complete sharks (and ratfishes) are rare, and paleontologists must rely instead on finds of fossilized teeth, small dermal scales, and calcified vertebrae to piece together their evolutionary history.

Sharks appeared in the fossil record more than 400 million years ago in the Silurian and Devonian Periods. At this time, the early insects had appeared in primitive plant forests. Early amphibians had emerged from their aquatic habitat to invade terrestrial environments, but the dinosaurs would not arrive for nearly 200 million years.

Similarly, the oceans were teeming with small planktonic life and the marine benthos was rich with widely varied forms of shelled invertebrate animals. This seemingly primitive era marked the beginning of the Age of Fishes, when many diverse groups of jawless and jawed fishes evolved to inhabit the wide marine oceans and fresh waters of the planet. Prominent among these were the ancestors of today's sharks.

## EVOLVING FEATURES

The best known shark ancestors of the Devonian Period were members of the genus *Cladoselache*, which shared many of the features of modern sharks. Cladodonts had five external gill slits, two well-developed dorsal fins with spines, pectoral and pelvic fins, and a powerful symmetrical tail. The upper

**DENTAL RECORDS** *A fossil tooth (above, extinct* Carcharodon megalodon *shown b a tooth of the great white shark. The fossil hybodont (below),* Hybodus hauffianus.

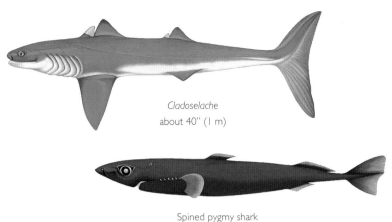

Cladoselache
about 40" (1 m)

## THE SHAPE OF SHARKS

*Long before the dinosaurs ruled the world, sharks had already evolved their basic powerful, streamlined body shape, and little modification has occurred since the Devonian Period.*

Spined pygmy shark
about 10" (25 cm)

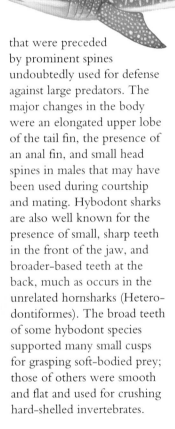

Whale shark
about 43' (13 m)

jaw was loosely attached to the skull, and the lower jaw was large, with many sharp teeth, each equipped with a single prominent central point and smaller lateral cusps (*clado* = branched, *dont* = tooth). These features made *Cladoselache* a swift predator, well adapted for feeding on fast-swimming fishes. This is verified by impressions of large fish prey found in the stomachs of fossilized sharks. Fossils of later species show that, over time, the teeth underwent a wide range of changes in size and number of cusps per tooth, which probably reflected the expansion of the shark's feeding habits in different ecological niches.

About 150 million years later in the Triassic and Jurassic Periods, when dinosaurs ruled the terrestrial reaches of the Earth, the hybodont sharks (*hybo* = hump) were the dominant fish predators in the oceans. Like its *Cladoselache* ancestor, *Hybodus* had two dorsal fins

that were preceded by prominent spines undoubtedly used for defense against large predators. The major changes in the body were an elongated upper lobe of the tail fin, the presence of an anal fin, and small head spines in males that may have been used during courtship and mating. Hybodont sharks are also well known for the presence of small, sharp teeth in the front of the jaw, and broader-based teeth at the back, much as occurs in the unrelated hornsharks (Heterodontiformes). The broad teeth of some hybodont species supported many small cusps for grasping soft-bodied prey; those of others were smooth and flat and used for crushing hard-shelled invertebrates.

## DIVERSIFICATION
The expansion of the hybodont sharks was quickly followed by the appearance of most modern forms. The sixgill and sevengill sharks (cowsharks) were among the earliest to appear in the fossil record and are distinguished by the presence of a single dorsal fin rather than two. With their upper jaw bearing sharp, pointed teeth and those

in the lower jaw being broad and saw-like, they can efficiently remove pieces of flesh from a large fish prey. During this time, most of the other modern shark families also evolved, but the order in which they appeared and the evolutionary forces that drove their rapid diversification remain unclear.

Perhaps the most intriguing fossil shark of all is *Carcharodon megalodon*, the largest shark ever to have lived and a close relative of the living great white shark, *Carcharodon carcharias*. Fossil teeth of *C. megalodon* are routinely found from excavations dating back 3 to 25 million years. Reconstructions of the jaw indicate that this shark reached total lengths of at least 45 feet (15 m) and had a mouth gape of about 6½ feet (2 m). Using data on the great white, we can assume that a large megalodon weighed more than 25 tons (25,000 kg). This mammoth carnivore probably fed on large marine animals, such as marine mammals, other sharks, and dead whales, as does its living relative.

# THE BODY FORM
## *and* FUNCTION *of* SHARKS

*The shark's body is beautifully attuned to life in an unforgiving watery world. It provides the ultimate biological example of hydrodynamic efficiency and power.*

Many features of the shark's body have evolved in response to the physical constraints of its dense aquatic environment. The internal skeleton of sharks and rays is composed of cartilage, an elastic tissue much higher in water content than bone. A skeleton of cartilage allows a high degree of body flexibility, provides protection and support for organs, and reduces total body mass. Skeletal parts that experience physical stress, such as vertebrae, jaws, and parts of the skull, are often stiffened by secondary calcification rather than by heavier bone. It is unlikely that large, modern sharks would be capable of such quick, agile movement had they evolved bony skeletons.

### BIOLOGICAL TORPEDOES
A species that swims actively in the water column, such as the blue shark, usually has a fusiform (cigar-shaped) body.

**Blue shark,** a graceful swimmer

**Mako,** a powerful swimmer

**Angelshark,** a sluggish bottom dweller

The diameter of the body is greatest at about a third of the way back from the snout, and tapers off toward the tail. This shape lets water flow smoothly over the body as the shark swims and reduces turbulence along the skin.

Swimming power and stability are provided by the shark's well-developed fins. In most sharks, the tail, or caudal fin, creates forward thrust by wide side-to-side movements that produce an undulation of the body. Special helically wound connective tissue fibers under the skin transfer much of the body's power directly to the tail. The unpaired dorsal and anal fins keep the body from rolling to either side during forward motion. The pectoral and pelvic fins, paired and displaced off the body midline, are used for lift and control of movements.

The fastest sharks, such as the mako, are perhaps the

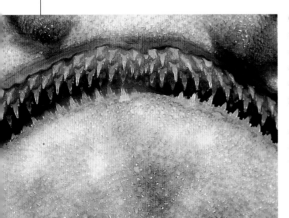

**CONVEYOR BELT** *The teeth of the swellshark (left) are arranged in rows and are constantly replaced by new ones produced at the back. The body shapes of sharks (above) have become adapted to their differing lifestyles.*

**BODY SHAPE** *The bottom-dwelling angelshark (left) disappears on the ocean floor.*

ultimate biological example of hydrodynamic efficiency and power. The snout and head are fused into a missile-like nose cone, and the stream-lined body is stout, and massive. Thrust is derived almost exclusively from quick lateral motions of the symmetrical tail with only minimal flexing of the body. The pectoral fins are short with a small surface area to reduce drag. Their stiffness helps the fish to maneuver at high speed. The claspers of males are retracted into special grooves behind the pelvic fins. Well-developed lateral keels on the caudal peduncle act as horizontal stabilizers. These swift, biological torpedoes are capable of bursts of speed of 22 miles per hour (36 km/h).

## BOTTOM DWELLERS

In contrast to species that are constantly on the move, some are adapted for a life near the sea bottom. One extreme example is the angelshark, which has a flattened, ray-like body and spends much of the day buried in the sandy bottom waiting to ambush passing fish

prey. Sawsharks have a broad, flattened surface under the head that helps to detect and capture benthic inverte-brates. They retain the powerful tail for long-distance move-ment across their marine habitat.

The outer skin is composed of many tiny placoid scales, known as denticles, which are usually about 1/32 inch (less than 1 mm) wide. These are formed in the dermal layer of the skin. The surface of the denticles consists of hard enamel that covers a dentine layer and pulp cavity. The enamel crowns have multiple sharp ridges that reduce drag during swimming as well as protect-ing the animal from injury.

The jaw is beneath the skull so the opening of the mouth is usually behind the snout on the underside of the head. In large, predatory sharks, the jaw is highly adapted for grasping or cutting prey. The upper jaw (palatoquadrate cartilage) is loosely suspended under the skull by ligaments and connective tissue. The lower jaw (Meckel's cartilage) is connected to the upper jaw at the corners of the mouth and is covered by massive muscles used for biting. This entire mechanism is suspended from the skull by the hyoid cartilage.

The attachment of rela-tively small muscles between the jaw, skull, and adjacent cartilages results in a powerful, highly protrusible mechanism that can be decoupled from

the skull and thrown forward from the head during a bite. This enables predators, such as great whites and reef sharks, to bite off parts of prey that are too large to swallow whole.

## THE TEETH

The teeth, formed from skin tissue, are arranged in ordered rows on both jaws. An enamel crown forms the primary cutting edge of the tooth, which in many species has additional lateral cusps or serrations. New rows of teeth form along the rear margins of the jaws, migrating forward as they become enlarged. This constant supply of sharp teeth emerges from the gums to replace those that are dulled or lost during use.

### JAW ATTACHMENT

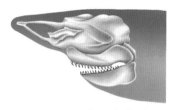

Like ancestral form, the jaw is normally positioned below the skull.

Like ancestral form, upper jaw remains close to skull as mouth opens.

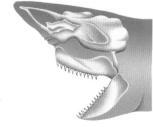

Modern shark's upper jaw can detach from skull.

# THE INTERNAL ENVIRONMENT *of* SHARKS

*Beneath the denticled skin of the shark lies a well-organized and coordinated biological factory that is designed for maximum efficiency.*

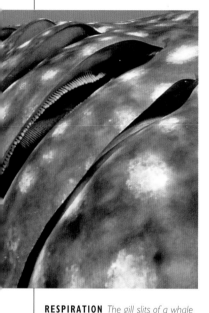

**RESPIRATION** *The gill slits of a whale shark (above). The illustration (below) shows the heart, gill arches and direction of water flow. Water enters the mouth (and spiracles), passes over the gills and out the gill slits. Diagram (right) shows detail of water flowing counter to blood.*

As well as being a superb hydrodynamic vehicle, a shark's body also controls many biological processes. Its internal organs share many features that are common in other fishes, but also show a number of special-izations unique to vertebrates.

## RESPIRATION

Sharks and rays extract oxygen from the water to metabolize their food. The gills are found on five to seven vertical arches that form the walls of the external gill slits. In a separate chamber beneath the gills, the heart pumps oxygen-depleted blood to capillary beds in the arches. Water is pumped into the mouth and out across the gills counter to the direction of blood flow. This exchange system greatly enhances the rate and efficiency of oxygen diffusion into the blood. In fast-swimming species, water flows into the open mouth as the animal swims. In bottom-dwelling species, such as sawsharks and spiny dogfish, there are well-developed spiracles that serve as auxiliary water inlets when the animal is resting or using the mouth to feed.

## DIGESTION

When prey is captured in the mouth, it is usually swallowed whole or cut into large pieces.

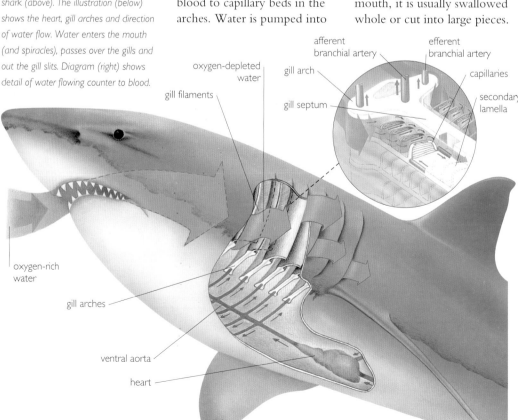

afferent branchial artery

efferent branchial artery

oxygen-depleted water

gill arch

capillaries

gill filaments

gill septum

secondary lamella

oxygen-rich water

gill arches

ventral aorta

heart

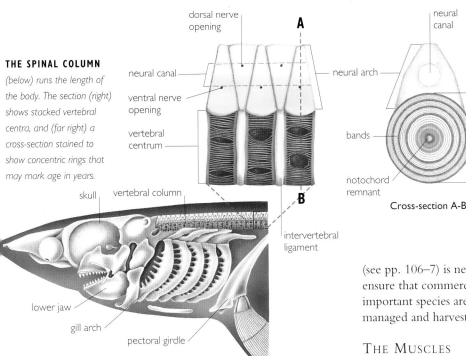

**THE SPINAL COLUMN**
*(below) runs the length of the body. The section (right) shows stacked vertebral centra, and (far right) a cross-section stained to show concentric rings that may mark age in years.*

dorsal nerve opening

A

neural canal

neural canal

neural arch

ventral nerve opening

vertebral centrum

B

bands

notochord remnant

vertebral centrum

intervertebral ligament

Cross-section A-B

skull

vertebral column

lower jaw

gill arch

pectoral girdle

The stomach produces strong acid and digestive enzyme secretions that, eventually, emulsify the food to a thin, soup-like consistency. Large bones and other indigestible material in the stomach are blocked from entering the intestine by a very small pyloric opening and regurgitated later. The absorptive surface area of the intestine is greatly increased by internal coils that are wound like a spiral staircase (spiral valve intestine) or, in some species, like a long, rolled up sheet of paper (scroll valve intestine).

## WATER BALANCE

The concentration of minerals in the body tissues of sharks is maintained by remarkable physiological processes. In marine fishes, the concentration of salt is about three times greater in the water than in the body, so there is a constant tendency for dehydration by loss of water across the gills. Sharks greatly reduce this loss by retaining urea, derived from the digestion of protein. They also produce an organic compound, TMAO

(trimethylamine oxide), which helps to maintain osmotic balance. When excess sodium chloride enters the body after the animal swallows sea water or ingests prey, it is removed by secretions from a specialized organ called the rectal gland.

## GROWTH

Lack of bony body parts in sharks and rays makes it hard to estimate age and growth rate of individual species. The vertebrae, which are partly calcified, can be stained to reveal concentric rings much like those seen in tree trunks, but we do not know if each ring represents a single year's growth. Additional research is necessary to confirm the meaning of each ring.

Tagging and recapture methods are another means of determining growth rates. Some species, such as the sandbar and dusky sharks, grow very slowly and may not reach sexual maturity for 15 years or more. Other smaller species, such as the sharpnose shark, reach maturity in three to four years. Information on growth rates and reproduction

(see pp. 106–7) is necessary to ensure that commercially important species are reliably managed and harvested.

## THE MUSCLES

Most body muscle consists of white muscle fibers with relatively poor vascularization. These are an excellent source of power for brief bursts of speed. Normal swimming activity is produced by contractions of relatively small bands of highly vascularized red muscle along the sides of the body. Red muscle can be used almost indefinitely for sustained swimming.

The fast-swimming lamnid sharks (great white, mako, and porbeagle) have developed a counter-current vascular system ("rete mirable") in the red body muscle and viscera. Heat that would be lost in blood leaving the muscle is retained locally by warming the cooler, oxygen-rich blood as it enters. In this way, the muscle maintains a temperature 9 to 15 degrees Fahrenheit (5–8° C) above that of the surrounding water and produces more power when burning oxygen. This provides faster cruising and bursts of speed useful for following large prey, such as tuna and mackerel, and also when diving to deep, cold waters in search of prey.

# VISION, SMELL, TASTE, *and* TOUCH

*Sharks have at least eight well-developed sensory systems and a large brain, which makes it rather illogical to think of them as primitive.*

Even today, sharks are often presented as sluggish, instinctive, and uncalculating predators that possess poorly developed sensory systems and rudimentary brains. This view stems from their long fossil history, and the assumption that they are less advanced than the more recently evolved vertebrates. Nothing could be further from the truth.

## VISION
The location of the shark's eyes on the sides of the head provides it with an excellent field of vision, in almost all directions. The eyeball is elliptical with a clear central cornea, and the globe wall is made of a white fibrous sclera. The amount of light entering the eye is regulated by a well-developed iris, which contracts and expands to change the size of the opening, called the pupil.

A clear, nearly spherical lens behind the pupil can be moved to focus images on the retina which lines the inner surface at the back of the eye. Within the retina are photoreceptors, called cones. These provide color vision and good detail in daylight.

Images seen during twilight and at night are mediated primarily by rod photoreceptors. Compared to cones, the rods provide relatively poor detail, but they

**THE SENSES OF THE SHARK** *The diagrams (below) show the components of the various sensory systems and their location on the body. For an explanation of how they function, see the text on this and the following three pages.*

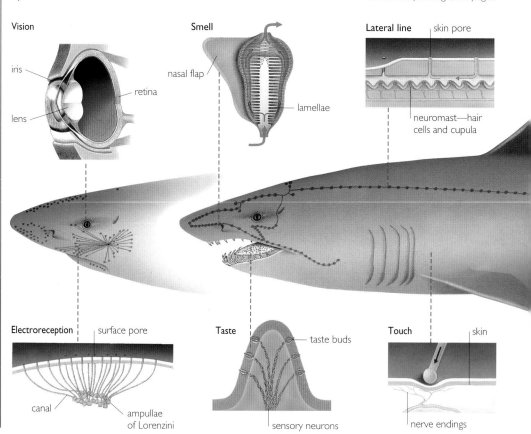

Vision
- iris
- retina
- lens

Smell
- nasal flap
- lamellae

Lateral line — skin pore
- neuromast—hair cells and cupula

Electroreception — surface pore
- canal
- ampullae of Lorenzini

Taste — taste buds
- sensory neurons

Touch — skin
- nerve endings

are highly sensitive in low-light conditions and excellent discriminators between light and dark objects.

Another such adaptation to low-light conditions is the tapetum lucidum, which is located behind the retina. This structure is a layer of minute mirror-like crystal plates that functions as a biological photomultiplier, reflecting any light that passes through the retina back again onto the photoreceptors. Sharks and rays feed during the periods of dusk, night, and dawn, so this is an especially useful adaptation for them.

## SMELL

The sense organs for smell are found within the two olfactory sacs under the snout. Each sac is covered by a flap of skin that channels water into the chamber and across the sensory lamellae. Water, along with any dissolved molecules or suspended particles, flows through the series of small valleys between the lamellae, which are lined with olfactory receptor cells.

Molecules such as amino acids, the building blocks of proteins, bind to the surface of the receptor cells and evoke neural discharges that are carried to the brain for processing. Researchers have reported a neural response to solutions of glycine, and also behavioral responses to fish extracts at concentrations of about 1 part per 10 billion parts of water.

## THE SHARK BRAIN

Contrary to popular belief, the relative size of the brain in sharks and rays rivals that of some birds and mammals. Like the brains of all vertebrate animals, the shark brain consists of hundreds of thousands of specialized cells known as neurons. Neurons receive electrical impulses from the various sensory systems of the body, process information in different regions of the brain, and send control commands to the muscles of the body.

The hindbrain processes information from many sensory systems, controls movements of the head and jaw, and is also a relay station between the higher brain centers and the spinal cord. The cerebellum coordinates body movements and may even be capable of motor learning. The tectum receives and integrates visual, electrosensory, lateral line, and other sensory information (see main text and pp. 102–3).

Below the midbrain is the diencephalon, which regulates the production of hormones, controls behaviors and activity patterns, and acts as a relay station for information passing to the forebrain. Finally, the forebrain, which is especially well developed in stingrays and mantas, receives information from the olfactory, electrosensory, and lateral line systems (see also pp. 102–3). Much work remains to be done to determine how the forebrain controls the behavior of sharks and rays.

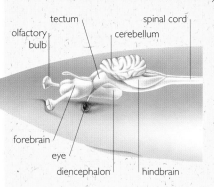

tectum
olfactory bulb
spinal cord
cerebellum
forebrain
eye
diencephalon
hindbrain

## TASTE

Like the olfactory system, the sense of taste is specialized to detect biological compounds. There are taste receptor cells on small taste buds that cover small bumps inside the mouth. They are best stimulated by direct contact with items such as food. The shark normally uses this sense to decide whether the food item it has captured is palatable.

**SUPERSENSITIVE** *With its elaborate nostrils, the hornshark (above) is able to detect minute amounts of chemicals.*

## TOUCH

Tactile sense in elasmobranchs is mediated by a network of nerve endings beneath the surface of the skin. Free nerve endings are simple, unspecialized touch receptors near the skin surface. They discharge impulses briefly when the overlying skin is depressed by as little as 0.0008 inch (20 μm). In Wunderer corpuscles, a more defined organization is seen, with the nerve endings tightly coiled into small capsules lying deeper in the skin layer. These structures respond both to direct touch and to the fin or body bending.

Finally, the Polou-mordwinoff endings are thought to be stretch receptors for muscle fibers of the fins of rays, providing information on muscle length and contraction rate.

# Balance, Hearing, Lateral Line, *and the* Electrosense

*Signals relayed through a system of amazingly sophisticated sensory organs keep the shark fully informed about what is going on within and around it.*

Sharks and rays have exquisite sensory organs for balance (vestibular system), hearing (auditory system), and detecting prey (lateral line and electrosensory systems). In all these sensory systems are hair cells—small receptors that excite sensory neurons when a physical force is applied to them. The hair cell is ubiquitous among vertebrates, including the organs of balance and hearing within our own ears.

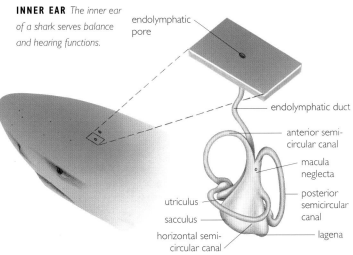

**INNER EAR** *The inner ear of a shark serves balance and hearing functions.*

- endolymphatic pore
- endolymphatic duct
- anterior semicircular canal
- macula neglecta
- posterior semicircular canal
- lagena
- horizontal semicircular canal
- sacculus
- utriculus

## The Vestibular System

The vestibular system is a complex of fine membranous organs designed to maintain the shark's orientation, balance, and control of body movements. Inside each ear are three fluid-filled semi-circular canals, at right angles to each other and firmly embedded in the otic capsules of the skull. As the shark turns its body, or moves its head from side to side during swimming, the fluid in the canals that are within the plane of rotation presses against a vane of hair cells, and stimulates nerve impulses to the brain.

Attached directly below the semicircular canals are the three otolith organs. The hair cells of each of these organs are arranged in a carpet-like layer known as the maculae, suspended vertically (the sacculus and lagena) or horizontally (the utricle) within the inner ear.

A conglomeration of hard calcium granules, known as otoconia, rests on each macula and, depending on the orientation of the body, will produce a shearing tug on the hair cells due to the force of gravity. Signals from these organs let the brain know about the position of the body relative to gravity and also tell it in which direction the body is moving.

## Hearing

Although sharks and rays lack any external evidence of well-developed ears, their hearing is very acute. In field studies, many sharks are regularly attracted to sounds like those made by struggling fish played through underwater speakers. Recent work suggests that the macula neglecta

**SENSORS** *Along the lateral line, which runs down the shark's head and sides, are special hair-cell receptors that provide the animal with an amazing fund of information. Ampullae of Lorenzini are visible on the nurse shark (right).*

**HYPERSENSITIVE** *The whale shark (right) uses its extraordinary electrosense to locate the fish on which it preys.*

is probably the organ of hearing. These tiny, paired hair-cell organs, located near the top of the skull above the semicircular canals, lack otoconia. It is currently proposed that sound-pressure waves traveling through the water, such as those produced by the movements of fishes or unusual acoustic disturbances on a reef, are channeled down tiny cartilaginous tubes in the top of the skull where they enter the inner ear to stimulate the macula neglecta.

## LATERAL LINE

The lateral line of sharks and rays is an important means for detecting water movements made by prey and potential predators. Sensory hair cells are arranged in tiny clusters less than 1/50 inch (0.5 mm) long, known as neuromasts (see p. 100). On the surface of the skin there are superficial neuromasts, often referred to as pit organs, that detect water movements (velocity) relative to the surface of the body. These organs are distributed across the shark's body, and are especially well positioned along the tail of the stingray for detecting an approach from the rear by a foraging hammerhead or bull shark.

The lateral line canal neuromasts are also found within an extensive network of small, water-filled canals immediately below the surface of the skin on the head and sides of the body. Neuromasts among the skin pores are stimulated by water movements within the canal that result from differences in pressures at the pores. This

makes them sensitive to water acceleration. Much of the canal system on the head lacks surface pores altogether, which means that these neuromasts are relatively insensitive to water disturbances on the skin. Laboratory research indicates that, when stimulated, the unpored lateral line system in the stingray probably functions as a specialized touch receptor for use when handling prey.

## ELECTROSENSORY SYSTEM

The electrosense is perhaps the most intriguing and mysterious sensory system of the elasmobranch fishes. This sense is used to detect and locate prey, and in stingrays also to locate mates during the reproductive season.

Each of the electrosensory organs, known as ampullae of Lorenzini (see p. 100), consists of a small chamber (the ampulla) lined with hair cells, and attached to an insulated tube filled with a

conductive jelly. Many ampullae are grouped, like small grapes, in three to five clusters on each side of the head and lower jaw. From these, the tubes radiate to pores at separate locations on the skin, so that these small "biological cables" can sample voltage potentials at different locations.

The weak bioelectric stimuli produced by prey originate primarily from their biological membranes, and appear to the shark or ray as a weak electrical aura around them, even when the prey is buried in the sand. Sharks and rays use the electrosensory system to detect voltage gradients as low as 5 nano-volts/cm, or 5 billionths of a volt measured across a distance of only about 1/2 inch (1 cm). The strength of the bioelectric fields produced by small organisms falls off rapidly with distance from the source, so the effective range of the electrosense is usually less than 1 foot (20–30 cm).

# THE SHARK'S LAIR

*Each species of shark is exquisitely adapted for life in
one of the many vast realms of the world's oceans.*

Sharks inhabit almost
every marine ecosystem
on Earth. Nearly all
coastal regions of the world
have large populations of
small, bottom-dwelling sharks
that are almost always an
important component of the
local marine ecosystem.
Temperate latitudes are
usually dominated by small
requiem sharks, hornsharks,
catsharks, houndsharks, spiny
dogfish sharks, and sometimes
angelsharks. These species
frequent rocky algae-laden
reefs, muddy bottoms of bays,
and open sandy habitats.
Their major food source is a
rich abundance of small fishes,
and a selection of bottom-
dwelling invertebrates, such as
crabs, shrimp, and mollusks.

The most common sharks
associated with the bottom
on tropical reefs include
the collared carpetsharks,
catsharks, nurse sharks, zebra
sharks, and wobbegongs,
although not all may be
present on any single reef.
Like their counterparts in
temperate zones, most small
tropical reef sharks feed
heavily on bottom-dwelling
invertebrates and small fishes.

## LARGE SHARKS

The larger sharks are also
commonly found near coastal
areas, but differ from most
smaller sharks by swimming
constantly over large ranges.
In temperate latitudes, these
include the large sevengill
sharks, which are common
visitors to shallow waters
along the shoreline and the
deeper continental shelves.

Great white sharks are
seasonal visitors to many
temperate coastal waters near
rookeries and haul-out sites
for seals and sea lions. Other
large species, such as sand
tigers and many requiem
sharks, frequent coastal areas
adjacent to their normal
distribution ranges above
the continental shelves.

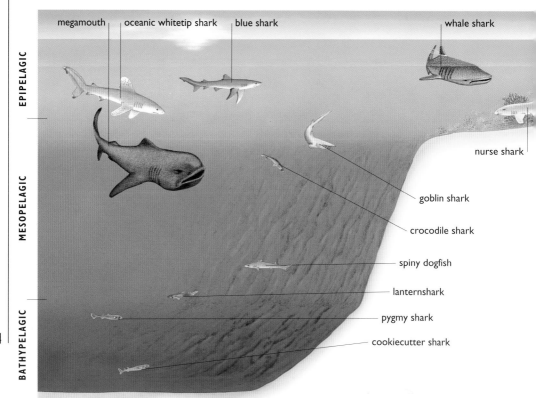

megamouth | oceanic whitetip shark | blue shark | whale shark

EPIPELAGIC

nurse shark

MESOPELAGIC

goblin shark

crocodile shark

spiny dogfish

lanternshark

pygmy shark

cookiecutter shark

BATHYPELAGIC

In tropical reef habitats we find relatively large, mobile species of requiem sharks, including many well-known species, such as the gray reef, Queensland, whitetip reef and silvertip sharks of the Indo-Pacific, the Caribbean reef shark, and lemon sharks. The largest members of circum-global tropical reef sharks include the tiger shark, great hammerhead, and bull shark.

## FINDING FOOD

Many species live in the open ocean. Blue sharks are quite common in temperate pelagic waters both near and far from land. Other oceanic visitors to coastal areas are the mako, salmon, and porbeagle sharks, which often follow coastal migrations of their fish prey. In tropical oceans, blue sharks avoid the warm surface temperatures and swim at greater depths where the water is cooler. Mako sharks are commonly found among tuna schools in tropical seas. The most common open-ocean requiem shark is the oceanic whitetip, which feeds on fishes and cephalopods.

There are three families of very large sharks that are known to filter feed on small oceanic plankton. The most commonly encountered planktivore in temperate waters is the basking shark, which has extremely long gill slits and reaches a length of about 30 feet (10 m). These sharks feed on tiny zooplankton in coastal areas with a rich upwelling of nutrients.

Another planktivore found in tropical and subtropical coastal seas is the whale shark, which reaches a length of 39 feet (12 m). The diet of the recently discovered megamouth shark (see p. 154) probably includes plankton, small crustaceans, copepods, and jellyfish.

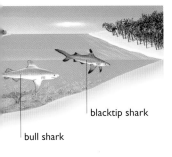

blacktip shark

bull shark

## THE WONDERS OF THE DEEP

The least-known realms of the shark are the deep mesopelagic waters of the open ocean, the slopes of continental shelves, and the abyss of deep oceans. The large and sluggish bramble sharks range from shallow shelf waters to the upper continental slopes. Velvet dogfish and gulper sharks are regularly collected at bottom depths of 2 miles (3,500 m).

The world's smallest sharks, including pygmy sharks and lanternsharks, inhabit the mesopelagic and bathypelagic regions. They show special adaptations to their gloomy environment, such as well-developed luminescent photophores that are probably used for visual communication in these dark depths.

Many of the most unusual species, such as goblin sharks and roughsharks, are found on continental shelves and on their upper slopes.

# SHARK REPRODUCTION

*The reproductive strategies of sharks, which in many ways are more like those of birds and mammals than other fishes, serve to enhance the survival of their relatively few precious offspring.*

Females of most fishes eject thousands (or millions) of small eggs to be fertilized outside the body by males. Female sharks, on the other hand, produce a relatively few large eggs that are fertilized inside the body by males. The gestation period, inside the female, may be as long as almost two years. So in many ways, a shark's reproductive system is more like that of mammals (including our own) and birds than that of other fishes.

### THE JOURNEY BEGINS
Before or during the mating season, sperm is produced by male sharks within their testes, paired organs found in the body cavity just below the backbone. Mature sperm are transported down a series of small ducts and, in some species, assembled into packets known as spermatophores. Sperm is then stored in the collecting ducts or specialized sperm sacs near the cloaca.

Mating in sharks is facilitated by the clasper organs of males, which develop from medial folds of the pelvic fins. During courtship a single clasper is rotated, inserted into the female's cloaca, and then flared. In many species it is anchored by spines or hooks. Sperm is then forced through the folds of the clasper into the female.

On the female side, small germ cells within the ovaries grow and develop into large, yolked eggs up to 1½ inches (4 cm) in diameter. After ovulation, the eggs pass through the ostium and enter the reproductive tract. They are usually fertilized one by one in the shell gland, and are encased in either a horny protective shell in egg-laying species (such as swellsharks and hornsharks), or a thin membranous covering in livebearers (such as requiem and hammerhead sharks). The fertilized egg

**Female**

pelvic fins

cloaca

ostium | shell gland | ovary | uterus with pups

**Male**

pelvic fins

clasper

testis | ductus deferens | seminal vesicle | cloaca

**THE NEXT GENERATION** *The diagram (left) shows the bottom view of male and female reproductive organs of a typical shark. In the two egg cases (right) the almost fully developed embryos of the lesser spotted dogfish are clearly visible.*

**BIRTHDAYS** *The pup of a lemon shark emerges from its mother's uterus (right); and a whitespotted bambooshark hatches from its egg case (left).*

then descends the oviduct and passes to the uterus, where the embryo develops. Nutrients pass from the egg yolk by means of the yolk stalk.

## MOTHERCARE

Egg-laying, or oviparous, species deposit their eggs on the bottom substrate where the embryos develop, receiving nourishment entirely from the egg yolk. The egg case of hornsharks is soft when first laid, and a female often picks it up in her mouth and deposits it in a crevice so that when it hardens, it becomes wedged. Catsharks have purse-like egg cases with long tendrils that twist around objects on the bottom. In zebra, bamboo, and epaulette sharks, there are sticky filaments instead of tendrils.

The majority of sharks are viviparous, livebearers, and the embryo develops entirely within the uterus. Most species show aplacental viviparity in which the embryo is nourished entirely by the yolk but is not released by the mother until fully developed. In others, the embryo remains in the mother's uterus even after the yolk sac has been fully absorbed. In the tiger shark, the uterus provides additional nutrient-rich secretions that are thought to be absorbed directly by the embryo. Embryonic sand tiger sharks receive supplemental nutrition through sibling cannibalism. The first-born consumes its siblings, then continues to feed upon hundreds of unfertilized eggs produced by the mother.

In species with placental viviparity, the spent yolk sac forms a connection with the uterine wall and absorbs nutrients from the mother. These are passed to the embryo via the yolk stalk umbilicus. In other species, the yolk stalk shows leaf-like elaborations that absorb nutrients directly from the surrounding rich uterine fluid.

Sharks and rays do not guard eggs or newborn young. The young are small versions of their parents, active swimmers, and begin to feed almost immediately.

## THE MATING GAME

Most oviparous sharks mate for a brief period each year and lay eggs that hatch 3 to 15 months later. The reproductive cycle for viviparous sharks is often limited by the gestation period. Small species may mate annually and give birth to live young from a few months to about a year later.

For example, sharpnose sharks, which reach a maximum size of about 40 inches (1 m), carry 1 to 7 young for 10 to 12 months. At the other extreme is the spiny dogfish shark, which takes nearly 2 years for up to 20 young to develop to a viable size.

Larger sharks, such as the blue shark, may have litters of more than 100 pups after a gestation period of 9 to 12 months. In the other large requiem sharks, such as the blacktip, the gestation period is 10 to 12 months, and they are thought to give birth only in alternate years, but this is by no means certain.

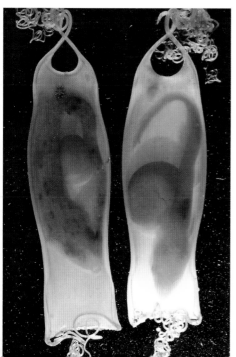

# SHARK BEHAVIOR

*Most sharks have a diversity of often complex behaviors related to feeding, mating, and social interactions that we still don't fully understand.*

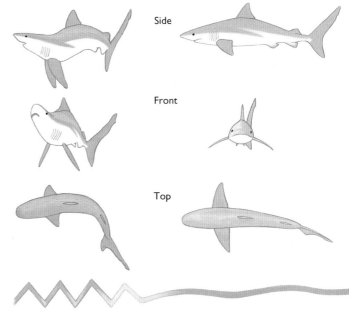

Side

Front

Top

Aggressive behavior      Non-aggressive behavior

Although inhospitable to humans, the ocean realm has very few boundaries that can contain the movements of sharks. Scientist divers are able to spend only a few hours at a time in the water, and are limited in their movements to relatively short distances and shallow depths. In contrast, the streamlined bodies of large sharks are designed to carry them over great distances each day, and they are also capable of rapid, deep dives. As a result of the shark's wide-ranging journeys in the ocean, information on their behavior is usually limited to brief snapshots of their daily lives.

Activity patterns are often closely tied in with a shark's daily feeding. The blue shark, whitetip reef shark, catsharks

**SIGN LANGUAGE** *The agonistic display (above) of the gray reef shark. Hammerheads (below) schooling with Pacific creole fishes, Galapagos Islands.*

and many other species feed primarily at night, but only a few species are known to feed mainly during daylight hours. These include the bonnethead shark, which takes crabs, shrimp, and small fishes in bays and along sandy beaches. Lemon sharks are especially

active around dusk and dawn, but these are only the times of major activity. Like most predators, sharks feed when-ever there is an opportunity.

SAFETY IN NUMBERS
Sharks are known to occur both as solitary individuals and

in various groupings. For example, tropical reef species, such as blacktip reef, gray reef and lemon sharks, are often observed by divers as solitary individuals in search of food. At other times, these same species are seen swimming together in small groups, apparently engaged in hunting or social activities.

Research in the Sea of Cortez has identified a large population of scalloped hammerhead sharks that forms schools on seamounts during the day, then moves off at night to feed on fishes and squid. Some species, such as the pelagic blue shark and bottom-dwelling bonnethead sharks, often form large, single-sex schools or schools of similar-sized individuals. There may be biological reasons for these aggregations, including the avoidance of larger predators, habitats that have preferred food items, and optional birthing grounds for females, to name only a few.

## PECKING ORDER

Many social interactions are observed within schools or groups of sharks. While feeding on whale carcasses, large white sharks will often aggressively chase away or even severely bite smaller individuals of the same species, and will ultimately do most of the feeding. Dominance hierarchies between species over food are also common, such as the interaction between reef whitetip sharks (low dominance), gray reef (middle dominance), and silvertip (high dominance). Similar hierarchies also clearly exist for many species in non-feeding situations. For example, male bonnethead

sharks will display a threat posture known as a "hunch" toward others in the group, and physically bump and bite females or smaller males.

Perhaps the most spectacular and well-documented of the shark's social behavior is the agonistic (ready for combat) display demonstrated by the gray reef shark of tropical Pacific reefs. When approached by a diver at rapid speed or cornered against the reef, the shark will exhibit a threat display in which it arches its back, depresses the pectoral fins, and moves in an exaggerated swimming motion. This is a graded behavioral display in which the intensity of the display increases with the level of the shark's agitation.

If a shark in an intense display is further pressed, it will probably attack the source of the threat. Because the agonistic display of the gray reef shark occurs in non-feeding contexts, it may be a form of territorial defense, but it seems to be unrelated to defense of any specific site, so it may represent some defense of personal space or be anti-predator behavior.

## COURTSHIP

All species of shark yet studied engage in some form of complex social reproductive behavior because the male must copulate to fertilize the female's eggs. In many species, a male closely follows a female during the mating season with its nose near the female's vent, which is probably a way of obtaining chemical information about her reproductive condition. During courtship, a male may aggressively bite the back,

**COURTSHIP AND MATING** *A diver observes a group of Port Jackson sharks mating (below). It is hard to gather data for species living in some remote habitats.*

flanks, and fins of the female, inflicting severe wounds, but this seems to stimulate her willingness to copulate.

Near the end of courtship, the male usually grasps the female's pectoral fin in his mouth, flexes a single clasper and rolls on his side to insert the clasper into the female's cloaca. In most large reef species, the pair will rest together for a few minutes on the bottom during sperm transfer, but some large species continue to swim while they copulate.

In smaller species, such as catsharks, which are more flexible, a male will often coil its body around the female during copulation without biting her fins. While nearly all of our information on shark mating comes from reef-dwelling species, almost nothing is known about the sex lives of the large pelagics because of their inaccessible environment and wide range.

# FOOD *and* FEEDING

*Each species of shark occupies a specific feeding niche within its habitat, and provides an important link in the flow of energy through the Earth's oceans.*

Contrary to popular myths, sharks are not scavengers of the deep, feeding indiscriminately on garbage or anything that crosses their path. They are carnivores occupying nearly all feeding levels of all marine food webs. Most small sharks associated with reef systems or bays are major predators of large invertebrates, such as crabs, shrimp, worms, squid, and small bony fishes. Snails and sea urchins, which are primary grazers on fields of benthic algae, are also important prey for hornsharks and some other small species.

The diet of the wide-ranging requiem sharks of reef habitats includes larger bony fishes, squid, cuttlefish, and octopus. Large tiger sharks, usually found in the deeper regions of tropical reef systems, consume a wide variety of vertebrates,

**MODIFICATIONS** *The teeth of sharks (above) show adaptations to cope with their various diets. Stages in the biting action of the great white shark (below): the mouth begins to open; the snout lifts as the upper jaw protrudes; the lower jaw slips forward; and closes again on the prey.*

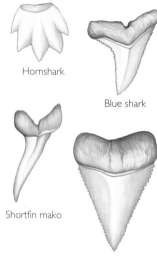

Hornshark

Blue shark

Shortfin mako

Great white shark

including large fishes, turtles and sea birds. Even large marine mammals, such as seals, sea lions, and dolphins, are preyed on by adult great whites and other large sharks.

## HUNTING STRATEGIES

Each species of shark usually hunts in a certain way. Many small reef sharks, such as hornsharks and smooth-hounds, are benthic foragers that move over wide areas of the reef or open sand bottom

in search of invertebrates. Other benthic species, such as the wobbegongs and angel-sharks, are ambush predators. Their bodies are camouflaged by cryptic colors and patterns that match their background. They lie concealed on the bottom until an unsuspecting small fish or crustacean comes close enough for a strike.

Many ambush predators also use trickery. For example, the wobbegong mimics benthic algae, and the nurse shark rolls its pectoral fins under the body to mimic a small reef crevice. Both of these strategies are designed to lure unsuspecting small reef fishes into what looks like a safe shelter. Other sharks are pursuit predators that actively chase down their fleeing prey. Blacktip reef sharks move in groups over coral reef flats during the day in search of surgeonfishes and mullet. Gray reef sharks cruise the edges of coral reefs at dawn and dusk, pursuing prey fishes.

Hammerhead sharks commonly roam the sandy

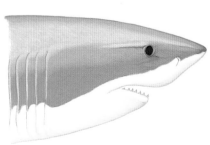

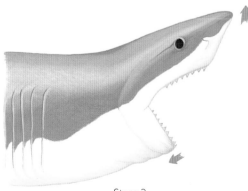

Stage 1

Stage 2

reef flats in search of stingrays, which they pin to the bottom with their head and devour. One of the most unusual predatory behaviors is that of reef interior hunters, such as reef whitetip, nurse, and epaulette sharks. The bodies of these species are so attenuated and flexible that they can swim into small holes in search of hidden crustaceans and fish prey, only to emerge from another hole on the other side of the reef.

## "BITE AND SPIT" THEORY

Adult great white sharks are the major predator of elephant seals and sea lions, such as the group at right. These animals bask at the surface in many temperate coastal waters of the world. Surfers and skin divers are also sometimes attacked at the surface by great whites in these areas.

One similarity between encounters with both humans and marine pinnipeds is that the initial attack frequently involves a single, massive bite that inflicts a major, often fatal injury. Usually no flesh is removed until the subsequent bites.

This predatory behavior, unique to the great white shark, has led researchers to propose the "Bite and Spit" hypothesis. The prey is released after the first quick and powerful killing bite, aimed to incapacitate the victim. This behavior is thought to reduce the chance of injury to the shark during, for example, prolonged contact with a large, struggling elephant seal. Such a formidable opponent usually has dangerous teeth and nails and could weigh more than 1,000 pounds (500 kg).

## LETHAL WEAPONS

Sharks show many anatomical and behavioral adaptations for feeding, with the dentition of the jaw being particularly efficient. Species, such as the hornsharks and bonnethead sharks, that consume armored invertebrates, have small, sharp teeth at the front of the jaw for grasping their prey, and flat, molariform teeth at the back to crush the hard shell before swallowing. Larger requiem sharks have flat, triangular teeth with serrated edges to cut large fish and cephalopods into pieces before swallowing.

This tooth design reaches its climax with the large, triangular and serrated teeth of the lamnid great white shark, which can easily cut a 22 pound (10 kg) chunk of blubber from a whale body in a single bite.

Other species, such as the mako and sand tiger sharks, have long, thin, needle-like teeth that have become adapted for grasping large fish. The jaw and associated muscles form a highly efficient mechanism for the rapid capture, processing, and manipulation of many types of prey.

In the great white shark, the feeding action begins when the head and snout are lifted, and the lower jaw is simultaneously depressed. Once the jaw is fully open, muscle contractions force the forward rotation of the upper jaw, which detaches from the skull and comes completely out of the mouth. This action creates this predator's powerful and awesome bite.

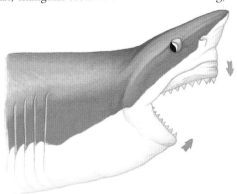

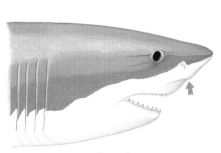

Stage 3

Stage 4

# DAILY MOVEMENTS
## *and* MIGRATIONS

*As advanced technologies tap into the ocean's secrets, we are gradually*

*building up a picture of the way sharks use their environment.*

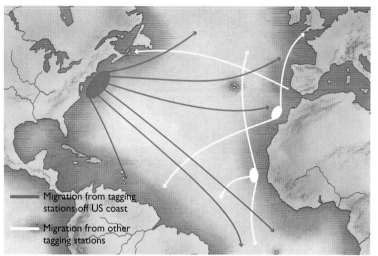

Migration from tagging
stations off US coast

Migration from other
tagging stations

**EPIC JOURNEYS** *The map (left)
shows the migratory patterns of
the blue shark around the Atlantic
Ocean, as revealed by an
extensive tagging program.
Individual animals may travel
incredible distances each year.*

Cooperative Shark
Tagging Program, is
sponsored by the United
States National Marine
Fisheries Service and has
been in operation since
1962. To date, more
than 87,000 sharks of
46 species have been tagged
by scientists and fishers off
the eastern seaboard of North
America. Of these, there have
been nearly 4,000 returns
covering 30 species.

Sharks are classified in
three categories based on their
migratory patterns. Local
sharks are non-migratory
species, such as the bull shark,
nurse shark, and bonnethead
shark. These sharks are
found near the shore or above
reefs, and seem to range
within an area of only a few
hundred miles.

Coastal pelagic sharks
occur in deep waters above
continental shelves. These
include large species, such
as the dusky, sandbar, tiger,
and blacktip sharks, that are
capable of migration distances
in excess of 1,000 miles
(1,600 km). The sandbar
shark, for example, is known

Spanning vast distances
between continents, the
world's oceans provide
highways for the global migrations of many pelagic sharks.
Other species never venture
far from major landmasses,
but travel long distances
parallel to the shoreline or
adjacent continental shelf.

Many such migrations are
to follow movements of their
prey while others are related
to mating activities or
pupping of the young. Much
of our current understanding
about shark movements
comes as a result of
tremendous human effort,
and with the advent of new
technologies, knowledge
continues to expand.

## MAJOR MIGRATIONS
Because of seasonal changes
in many local shark numbers,
fishers and researchers realized

long ago that sharks make
large-scale migrations.
Much of the relevant data
about these movements
comes from long-term tagging
programs supported primarily
by government agencies,
researchers, and sport and
commercial fishers.

The main tool is the dart
tag—a numbered, labeled
plastic streamer attached to
a nylon or stainless-steel barb.
Sharks are captured by hook
and line, identified to species,
sexed and, if possible,
measured. The dart, attached
to an applicator pole, is
inserted under the skin
usually near the first dorsal
fin. The shark is then released
unharmed to continue with its
normal movements. If it is
later recaptured, data on size,
date of capture, and location
are sent to the tagging agency.

The largest of these, the

to migrate from the northeastern seaboard of North America to southern Mexico. Highly pelagic sharks, such as the mako and blue shark, make long, often transoceanic migrations across the deep basins of the Atlantic.

The longest linear movement by an individual was recorded for a blue shark tagged off the coast of the northeast United States and recaptured 300 miles (500 km) south of the Equator, a travel distance of 3,740 miles (6,000 km). Multiple recaptures of tagged blue sharks indicate regular transatlantic migrations over distances greater than 10,000 miles (16,000 km). Although shark tag and recapture data are relatively scarce in the Pacific, it is probable that blue sharks make similar long migrations between the coast of North America and Asia. While dart tagging is still valuable, it will be new technologies, such as satellite telemetry, that will eventually unravel the mystery of the global movements of sharks.

## DAILY MOVEMENTS

New technology has emerged that is helping to record shark movements in their everyday environment, too. In recent years, many scientists have used ultrasonic telemetry transmitters, which are attached to the shark and tracked with a hydrophone from a boat or by a diver. These devices can be fitted with sensors to monitor depth, swimming speed, body or water temperature, or even stomach pH. Telemetry studies of the blue sharks off Santa Catalina Island, California, show that at certain times of year, individuals spend daylight hours not far offshore. After dark, they move in closer, presumably to feed.

Other studies show that tiger sharks associated with Pacific reefs move over a home range as large as 14 square miles (40 sq km) each day and make frequent vertical dives along the reef slopes at night, probably to feed. Other tropical reef species, such as the gray reef shark, may cover areas of about 11 square miles (30 sq km) each day. Within a given species, smaller sharks generally have smaller home ranges than do larger adults. For example, juvenile lemon sharks, which live in shallow reef flats near mangrove habitats, have a home range of less than ½ square mile (1 sq km), while adults use 20 square miles (50 sq km) or more.

Sharks also seem to pay visits to particular areas at regular times. For example, hornsharks found on temperate rocky reefs were observed to forage in the same area of the reef each day, rest in the same area of the rocky reef in the afternoon, and return to shelter in a single cave each night. Similarly, telemetered large gray reef sharks visit specific regions of the reef each day.

**BUILDING THE PICTURE**
*A lemon shark swims past a monitor (top) that picks up a signal from an ultrasonic transmitter implanted in its body. A numbered tag from the University of Miami (above) carries instructions and a return address. A tiger shark (right) being tagged.*

# CHAPTER FIVE

# RAYS

*The secret pit of the ocean holds a universe of*
*tangled infinities.*

JOSEPH MACINNIS (b.1937), Canadian ocean explorer

# IDENTIFYING *and* CLASSIFYING RAYS

*Rays are among the most distinctive of the cartilaginous fishes but their classification is difficult and the subject of spirited ongoing scientific debate.*

There are almost 600 living species of rays from some 18 families. Their body shapes have become highly modified and specialized. They are flattened in various ways and the pectoral fins and part of the body are joined to form a distinctive structure known as the "disc." This is typically wider than deep and may be wedge-shaped, oval, circular, or triangular. Members of major families are easy to recognize, but species can be confusingly similar in form.

### DISTINCTIVE FEATURES
Some shark groups, such as angelsharks and sawsharks, also have enlarged pectoral fins that resemble a small disc, but their gills are on the sides of the head. Rays, on the other hand, have five (or six) pairs of gill slits on the under-surface. In many ray groups, the head forms part of the disc and when the head is separate, the pectoral fins join the head

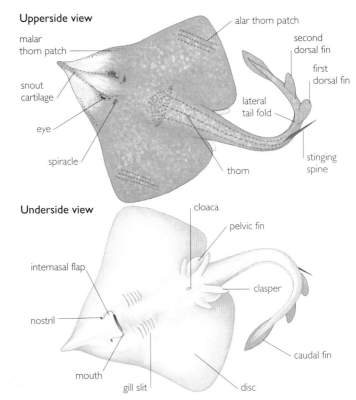

**Upperside view**

alar thorn patch

malar thorn patch

second dorsal fin

first dorsal fin

snout cartilage

lateral tail fold

eye

spiracle

thorn

stinging spine

**Underside view**

cloaca

pelvic fin

internasal flap

clasper

nostril

mouth

gill slit

caudal fin

disc

in front of the gill slits. In bottom-dwellers, the eyes and spiracles are usually on top of the head. In a few blind electric rays, the eyes are covered with skin and difficult to see.

Some ray charactersistics are very useful for identification, for example, snouts that resemble saws, electric organs, enlarged pelvic fins that are joined to form discs, and lobe or horn-like projections on the snouts. The sexes can be distinguished at an early age. Male claspers are important in distinguishing species, because their shape and structure varies not only among families but also within them. They have been used extensively to

distinguish close relatives and also to assess evolutionary relationships between genera and species. The skin, thick in many rays, is either smooth with a coating of slimy mucus or may have a protective armor of strong bony tubercles or thorns. Size, shape, and location of these special types of denticle varies from species to species, which is important in identification.

## WHAT SIZE TELLS US

With more than half of the species exceeding 20 inches (50 cm) in length, rays are among the largest fishes. The tail, which is often damaged, varies greatly in length from one specimen to another, so scientists prefer to express size in width. The gigantic manta ray may exceed 22 feet (6.7 m) in width and weigh several tons. The smallest, the short-nose electric ray, is less than 4 inches (10 cm) wide and weighs less than 1 pound (500 g). The average adult size varies greatly from family to family. While all numb-fishes are smaller than 3 feet (90 cm), the range for sawfish species is from 5–25 feet (1.4–7.6 m), and the highly diverse skates, with more than 280 species, vary from 8 inches to 8 feet (20 cm to 2.5 m).

Our knowledge of ray taxonomy is increasing only slowly. Unknown species lurk in the ocean depths, particularly in the Indo-Pacific where more than 50 new species have been discovered in the past decade. Inshore species are often mistakenly identified and need further study. Large adults can be bulky and heavy, making them difficult to collect, transport, and store,

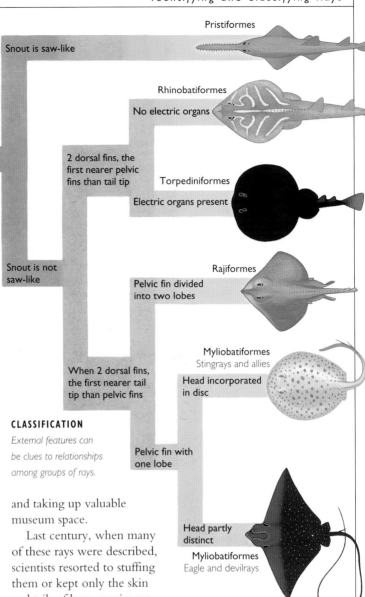

Pristiformes

Snout is saw-like

Rhinobatiformes

No electric organs

2 dorsal fins, the first nearer pelvic fins than tail tip

Torpediniformes

Electric organs present

Snout is not saw-like

Rajiformes

Pelvic fin divided into two lobes

Myliobatiformes
Stingrays and allies

Head incorporated in disc

When 2 dorsal fins, the first nearer tail tip than pelvic fins

### CLASSIFICATION

*External features can be clues to relationships among groups of rays.*

Pelvic fin with one lobe

Head partly distinct

Myliobatiformes
Eagle and devilrays

and taking up valuable museum space.

Last century, when many of these rays were described, scientists resorted to stuffing them or kept only the skin and tails of large specimens. Many such specimens are now lost or in poor condition.

## GATHERING CLUES

Male and female rays can differ in shape and color, as can the young. To identify features that distinguish one species from another, taxonomists need to examine several specimens, including juveniles and mature males and females. For many species, this simply has not been possible.

When trying to identify a ray, it is important to note its external features. Is the disc large or small compared to the tail? Is the head separate from the disc? Is the tail broad and muscular, long and whip-like,

or short and narrow? Does the tail have dorsal and caudal fins and where are they? All these important initial observations are needed to identify the ray's family group.

Beyond this point, the identification becomes more difficult and a knowledge of the species occurring within the area is usually needed. Each region has a unique ray fauna, with the species often having narrow distributional ranges. If you know where the ray was caught, the number of options can be reduced. Details of color, denticles, and placement of thorns are also vital clues.

# THE EVOLUTION *and* RADIATION *of* RAYS

*Given the difficulties in studying these interesting animals, it may be some time yet before the ray's evolutionary history is fully unraveled.*

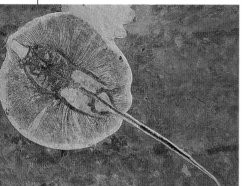

Rays evolved from sharks but there has been much debate about which groups are the oldest, and the sequence of their evolution. They belong to a major group of cartilaginous fishes called Squalea, which includes dogfishes, sixgill and sevengill sharks, angelsharks, and sawsharks. Ancestral rays may have resembled sawfishes and probably evolved during the age of the dinosaurs.

Guitarfishes and their relatives are thought to be among the oldest ray groups, and eagle rays, devilrays, and stingrays are the most recently evolved. Skates may be the immediate recent ancestors of either shovelnose rays or electric rays. Some ichthyologists believe that electric rays

**ANCIENT AND MODERN** *The white-spotted guitarfish (right) shares many characteristics with its fossilized ancestor Heliobatis (above) taken from Eocene deposits more than 35 million years old.*

evolved before sawfishes. Yet another theory says that electric ray groups may have evolved from an ancestral guitarfish. The picture is unclear, so several classes of batoids have been proposed.

### THE FOSSIL RECORD

The earliest known fossil rays date back to the Jurassic Period, more than 150 million years ago (mya). Most species are known from only a few teeth, denticles, and spines, but well-preserved whole bodies of ancient guitarfishes have been found. The appearance of these rays has changed little with time.

Sadly, the fossil record of many groups is incomplete. We know from examining the distributions of living rays and from Earth's geological history that several groups

roamed those ancient seas for even longer than the fossil evidence suggests. While ray fossils of the Cretaceous (65–145 mya) are comparatively rare, they are common throughout Tertiary sediments (25–60 mya). Many such fossils are represented only by teeth, but whole fossil animals, including the stingray *Heliobatis*, trapped in coastal lakes when sea levels fell and the oceans receded, have been found in shales from the Green River, Wyoming, USA.

The oldest known fossil skates were found in sediments of a prehistoric sea dated to the late Cretaceous, some 70 mya. It has been suggested that these rays colonized the Pacific and Atlantic via an ancient marine pathway, the Tethyan Sea. But it is also probable that an old group of skates had an ancestor in the

seas around Gondwana-land, the ancient southern supercontinent. This group, which includes the rough skate, *Raja nasuta*, has species still living in the coastal seas of South America, New Zealand, and southern Australia. These three regions were connected to Antarctica in the Cretaceous Period, but later drifted apart. Since skates do not migrate across open oceans, they must have lived there before the breakup of Gondwanaland (about 80 mya). The oldest Antarctic fossils date from 50 mya.

## WIDE DISTRIBUTION

Living rays, very successful fishes, are found in all oceans and seas on Earth. They are valuable in determining the evolutionary structure of the world's fish faunas because some of the groups contain species that are closely related but which have very restricted distributions. The eggs of many bony pelagic fishes drift in the open sea and are often transported to areas far from where they were laid. Young rays, on the other hand, are born alive or hatch from eggs laid on the bottom. Dispersal beyond their existing range depends almost entirely on the movements of the mother.

Unlike bony fishes, which produce eggs numbering millions in some species, rays have very few young at the end of quite a long gestation period. This limits how rapidly their populations can increase, so they rely instead on the survival of the few young they produce. If their numbers are affected by external influences, such as overfishing or loss of habitat, the survival of the species could be threatened.

Ray distributions also vary greatly from group to group. Sharkfin guitarfishes, devil-rays, and sawfishes occur throughout the tropics but seldom visit cooler temperate waters. The ubiquitous skates live around the shelves and slopes of oceanic islands and all continents but have never been found near the coral islands of the Pacific. These are the dominant rays in cool waters but they are mostly confined to deeper waters in the tropics. Few of the

**DISTANTLY RELATED GROUPS**
*The thornback skate (top), and the widely distributed sparsely spotted stingaree (above), probably have similar body forms because of the similarity of their lifestyles.*

families have restricted distributions, although the shorttailed electric rays (Hypnidae) are confined to Australian seas, and the river rays (Potamotrygonidae) are native to the South American rivers and lakes that drain into the Atlantic Ocean.

## RICH DIVERSITY

The shortnose electric rays (Narkidae) have an unusual distribution that includes the Indo-West Pacific (from Indonesia to Japan) and New Zealand, but not Australia. Within some families, genera may be quite restricted. Stingarees (Urolophidae) and whip-rays (*Himantura*) have groups of species that occur in the Indo-West Pacific and off Central America but are quite distantly related to each other. Other groups have diversified greatly in some regions but less in others. Stingrays are much more diverse in the Indian Ocean than in the Atlantic.

The richest ray faunas are in the Indo-Pacific, from South Africa to Japan and Australia. About a third of all species occur off Australia and Indonesia. Atlantic faunas are smaller but still contain endemic species.

# THE ANATOMY *and* BIOLOGY *of* RAYS

*The secret lives of rays can be glimpsed by studying their anatomy and, in many cases, this is the best evidence we have.*

We know details of the biology and ecology of only a small number of ray species. For example, while we are aware that most species live and feed on or near the bottom, we generally have a poor understanding of the more intimate aspects of their lives. Fortunately, a basic profile of a ray's life can be gleaned by examining its body features, such as shape, color, size, mouth structure, fin details, and internal anatomy. This field of study, known as ecomorphology, is becoming increasingly useful in predicting the lifestyles of many species of fish, including rays.

## BODY SHAPE

Ray families vary greatly in shape, which makes them ideal subjects for eco-morphological studies. Their discs are well adapted for either a bottom-dwelling life or for swimming almost continuously above the bottom. The extent of flattening of the disc, its musculature, and its overall shape reflect the animal's preferred lifestyle. The tail,

which is separate from the disc, is variably developed. The shorttailed electric rays (Hypnidae) have probably the shortest tails of all fishes. In contrast, the long, skinny whip-like tails of some stingrays, often several yards long, are among the longest found in fishes. In guitarfishes, the tail is comparatively broad, muscled, and powerful.

The dorsal and caudal fins vary greatly in shape, size and position among species. In some sawfishes and guitar-fishes they are tall and shark-like, but in most other rays they are small. In the stingrays and eagle rays they are absent or rudimentary. One or more

venomous stinging spines on the tail of many stingrays and stingarees are used to repel attacks by predatory sharks. Some eagle rays and butterfly rays also have stinging spines.

## INTERNAL FEATURES

Ray skeletons, made almost entirely of cartilage, are highly modified, with the strong skull very flattened and a chain of small vertebrae that extends to the tip of the tail. The snout of guitarfishes and many skates is kept rigid by cartilage that extends from the front of the skull. This cartilage is absent in some species, such as the stingarees and stingrays, which need

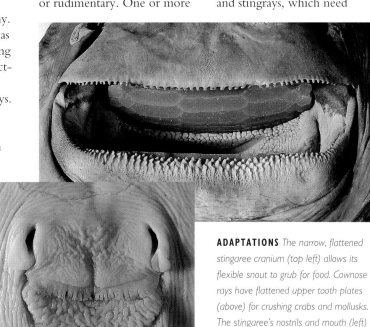

**ADAPTATIONS** *The narrow, flattened stingaree cranium (top left) allows its flexible snout to grub for food. Cownose rays have flattened upper tooth plates (above) for crushing crabs and mollusks. The stingaree's nostrils and mouth (left) house a well-developed sensory system for locating prey. A bat ray (right) consuming squid eggs.*

highly flexible snouts to grub for food. An animal's skeleton stops the body from flopping and provides attachment points for its muscles. The ray's disc is supported by numerous thin, pectoral-fin cartilages. These cartilages are flattened, densely packed and extend over most of the disc.

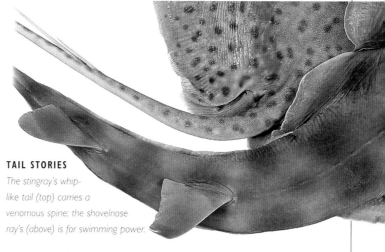

**TAIL STORIES**
*The stingray's whip-like tail (top) carries a venomous spine; the shovelnose ray's (above) is for swimming power.*

The brain of a ray is small and simple compared to that of a dolphin or a seal, but in ratio to body weight it is surprisingly large. In fact, this ratio is similar to that found in marsupials and birds. Of the cartilaginous fishes, rays are among the best endowed brainwise, with the manta ray having the largest brain of all.

All rays are carnivorous but most occupy a level below that of sharks in the food chain hierarchy. Where sharks are important predators on reefs and in open water, rays play a more significant role as predators on soft substrates. Large rays, including several torpedo rays, stingrays, and skates, are known to feed on fishes. However, small mobile invertebrates, such as sand worms, crustaceans, and mollusks, are more important dietary items. Algae and sedentary invertebrates, such as sea tulips, anemones, corals, and sponges, are rarely eaten.

## FEEDING STRATEGIES

As the majority of rays are bottom dwellers, the mouth is located on the undersurface. Most rays feed by trapping prey against the substrate with their disc. Food is directed to the mouth by maneuvering the disc over the prey, or by manipulating the victim by means of the flexible disc flaps. Rays can be quite selective feeders and the various shapes of their mouth and teeth are an indication of their food preferences.

The bowmouth guitarfish, for example, has a contoured mouth with small, tightly packed, flattened teeth for crushing hard-shelled inverte-brates. Eagle and cownose rays have a series of flattened tooth plates, rather like beaks, to crush crabs and mollusks. Torpedo rays have a very arched lower jaw studded with small spiny teeth. This can be thrust forward to suck up small fishes from the sub-strate. The cavernous mouth of the plankton-feeding manta ray is at the front of the snout. The teeth, which are not important in feeding, are minute and covered in skin in the lower jaw and totally absent in the upper jaw. Skates and most stingrays have compact rows of strong, pointed teeth in both jaws for simultaneously holding and crushing struggling prey.

The part of the sensory system used to find and gather food is well developed in rays. Sawfishes and most guitarfish have long, slit-like nostrils just forward of the mouth. The nostrils of other rays are partly covered with a broad, fleshy lobe, known as the internasal flap. This is covered in sensory pores and usually reaches the mouth. The pores form part of the ampullae of Lorenzini—an electroreceptor system for detecting electric fields produced by the nerves and muscles of other animals. Rays use them to detect predators, prey, and other members of the same species.

# THE HABITAT *of the* RAY

*These highly successful animals have adapted to all kinds of*
*habitat and have found niches in oceans and seas all around the globe.*

The majority of rays live exclusively in the sea, but some spend part of their lives in estuaries. A few have even invaded fresh water, living in rivers thousands of miles from the coast. Rays are important in marine communities, playing an integral part in the day-to-day life of the sea. Each has a discrete role—the common perception of a particular ray being just another ray is quite wrong.

For example, the lives of rays found in estuaries differ markedly from those living on outer continental shelves. Similarly, species living together in one area are biologically distinct from each other in some way. They may eat the same food, but they will have different seasonal distributions, reproductive methods, or prefer to live on different types of bottom. Most rays are highly efficient, and in some regions appear to have ousted bottom-dwelling

**GLASS WALLS** *This ray likes to rest on the smooth wall of its aquarium tank at Underwater World in Perth, Australia.*

## BALANCING SALINITY

Rays living in estuaries must be able to overcome potentially severe ionic stresses from fluctuating salinity. In high-salinity environments, such as the sea, water diffuses out through permeable membranes of living cells in a process known as osmosis, and salts are gained. In fresh water, the reverse occurs, water diffuses into the animal, and salts are lost. Animals living in either environment need to balance their salt and water concentrations to survive. In brackish estuaries, this is made more difficult because the salinity of the water is changing continuously as river water mixes with the sea.

To achieve a balance, the ray adjusts its internal osmotic pressure to minimize the transfer of water through its membranes. In the sea, rays supplement chloride levels in the blood and tissue with nitrogen compounds, such as urea. Apart from some water taken up through the membranes of the gills and mouth, their bodies are almost impermeable, so rays can live in estuaries for short periods without the osmotic stresses experienced by bony fishes. Rays that live full-time in fresh water, such as the ocellate river ray below, have more difficulty. These rays need to reduce their osmotic concentration. To compensate, they have very well-developed kidneys and endlessly excrete large quantities of weak urine to remove excess water and minimize ionic losses.

bony fishes such as soles and flounders.

DIFFERING LIFESTYLES
Rays occupy a variety of habitats in the sea. They are found inshore in very shallow water but extend offshore down into the abyss to depths exceeding 10,000 feet (3,000 m). Some rays are predominately pelagic, swimming tirelessly in midwater and rarely resting on the bottom. Others lie on or bury themselves in the substrate, only swimming off the bottom to browse for food, reproduce, or escape from predators. However, unlike some bottom-dwelling bony fishes, none of the rays live in burrows.

The habitat needs of rays are evident from their body

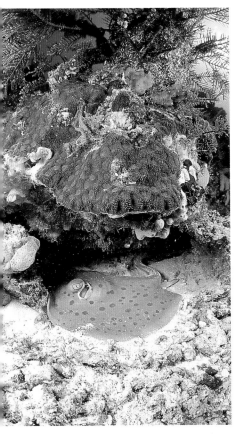

reefs seek refuge on sandy patches among corals or under ledges.

## SEASONAL CHANGES

Some habitats are used seasonally or for only part of the day. Estuaries, tidal flats, and mangrove swamps are very important feeding areas for many tropical rays but few live there permanently. Instead, they move into these areas on the incoming tide and retreat as it recedes. Others move into some particular habitat for part of the year, perhaps to breed, and such seasonal migrations can be highly consistent from year to year.

Beyond the continental shelf break, demarcated by the 655 foot (200 m) isobath, lies the open ocean. Much of the deep-sea floor is muddy ooze. Some deep-water skates use their long, firm snouts, covered in sensory pores, to grub around in the soft upper layers. The equally long, but softer and more flexible snout of the sixgill stingrays (Hexatrygonidae) appears to be used like a finger to probe more deeply into the sediments for food.

## OCEANIC MYSTERIES

Devilrays live throughout tropical seas and migrate across the open oceans in water many miles deep. Their activities when far from shore are not well understood, but we believe they remain quite close to the surface.

One species of stingray is primarily oceanic and may venture into deep water. Unlike coastal rays, which typically have pale bellies, the pelagic stingray (*Pteryoplaty-trygon violacea*) is black all over. Our knowledge of its distribution in the open seas is based on specimens hooked accidentally by longline fishers catching tuna.

**HABITAT PREFERENCES** *A blue-spotted ribbontail ray (top left) shelters under a ledge near Bunaken Island, Indonesia, while the stingray (below) is more at home swimming near the sandy sea floor surrounding the Bahamas.*

shapes and may be quite specific. A rounded, flattened body is ideally adapted to burying itself in the substrate. The disc is amazingly flexible near its margin, which is important for swimming, burying, and feeding. The pectoral fins of pelagic ray groups, such as eagle rays and mantas, are pointed and have strong lateral muscles for prolonged swimming. Most species prefer sandy and muddy bottoms, but a few live mainly on rocky reefs, sea grasses and coral. The mangrove whipray, *Himantura granulata*, wraps its disc around the tops of small coral heads (bombies) with its tail hanging out sideways. Adults, which may be more than 5 feet (1.5 m) wide and 10 feet (3 m) long, make an impressive sight in this pose.

In aquariums, skates often prefer to rest on the smooth, vertical glass walls, rather than on coarse rubble or rocky bottoms. Other rays living on

# LIFE CYCLE *and* REPRODUCTION

*Nature has equipped these creatures with marvelous ways to handle the hazards that arise during the dangerous time of conception and birth.*

Rays use two types of reproductive strategy, egg laying (oviparity) or a form of livebearing (ovoviviparity) in which there is no placental attachment of the embryo to the mother. In all species, male rays, like sharks, fertilize females internally using their claspers, the modified inner edges of the pelvic fin. Claspers are present as a pair of minute lobes near the cloaca in young males at birth. They expand greatly in late adolescence and become firm with the development of internal cartilage when the male reaches sexual maturity. They are made up of many small cartilages, but their anatomy varies greatly among the ray families and even within certain genera.

The end of the clasper, known as the glans, carries many tiny structures, which may include hooks, spines, discs, plates, spongy tissue, and grooves. When the glans opens during copulation, these structures are responsible for maintaining contact within the female, as well as holding and transferring the semen. Lubricating fluid is produced in secretory glands at the base of each clasper. In some rays, this fluid may also block the female's oviduct, to prevent her from being fertilized again by another male.

## COURTSHIP AND DEVELOPMENT

Copulation can appear violent and takes place in a variety of positions, either belly to belly, or back to belly with the

**PROPAGATION** *A giant black stingray with its pup (top). Detail of a pair of male claspers (above) belonging to the eastern shovelnose stingaree. The ends are modified to hold the male in position while the sperm is delivered.*

claspers greatly twisted. The male often initially follows the female with his acutely sensitive snout close to her cloaca in search of chemical "green lights." Courtship usually includes some degree of nibbling or biting of the disc. The teeth of mature male skates are more slender and pointed than those of females, and probably help them to grasp the female during copulation.

Eagle rays use their flattened tooth plates to gouge the female's fins during courtship. Copulation can last just a few minutes or go on for hours, depending on the species. The act may take place on the bottom or in midwater. In each case, the teeth and body spines are important in helping the male maintain his position. In some skates, the male moves beneath the female and holds himself in place by the retractable alar thorns on top of the pectoral fins. Females may mate with several males in succession.

Skates are the only rays that do not give birth to live young. They lay leathery egg cases that are anchored or attached to the bottom. These are rectangular with long tendrils at each corner. Part of the egg case is usually sticky and shell bits and sand become attached,

## THE MATING GAME

The breeding strategies of rays, which vary considerably among groups, are known for only a few of the more common species, such as the mating fiddler rays below. Round stingrays are segregated by sex outside the breeding season, with females occupying deeper parts of the continental shelf. Both sexes reunite inshore in late winter and spring to breed. In the morning, patrolling males locate

receptive females, who make themselves obvious by resting on the substrate in harems, their bodies often in stacks. Groups of sexually inactive females, those we think may have already mated or are not reproductively active, remain buried in the shallows. During the afternoon, these females emerge to feed among sea grasses and the males become inactive. This daily cycle continues over a fortnight or so.

weighting the egg case to the bottom. Embryos may take more than six months to develop so the cases have to be tough enough to avoid being eaten by predatory invertebrates and fishes. Some marine snails use their horny, rasping tongue to bore holes in the case and siphon out the contents.

In the ovoviviparous rays, the developing embryos either swallow nutrients secreted from the mother's uterus (as in torpedo rays), or absorb nutrients via string-like extensions of the uterus that reach the gut through the spiracles (typical of stingrays, eagle rays and butterfly rays). A newborn pup is sometimes more than 50 times heavier than the unfertilized egg.

PROTECTIVE MEASURES
Sharp parts of young rays are likely to damage the mother at birth and in the uterus. Young sawfishes have a snout like the adult's, so the entire saw and its teeth are soft, flexible and covered with a membranous sheath at birth. The snout straightens and the teeth harden soon after. Similarly, the stinging spines of venomous rays are soft at

birth. Some skates and stingrays that are very thorny as adults are born almost devoid of denticles. On the other hand, some mothers, for example, female electric rays, must avoid stunning and possibly killing their young. It has been found that torpedoes stop producing shocks in the presence of their pups and can be safely handled by humans. After the young are born, the rays

revert to their usual habit of delivering shocks.

Rays have long gestation periods and produce relatively small litters, which makes them highly vulnerable to population collapses from over-fishing and habitat degradation. Many species also have a restricted range of distribution.

These two factors make the group more fragile than most other marine animals, including bony fishes. Despite their obvious vulnerability, we have been slow to recognize their plight and their numbers continue to decline. Rays play an important role in the sea and the implications of their loss on the ecosystem are unknown.

**BIRTH PANGS** *A sparsley spotted stingaree (left) in the process of giving birth, and a newborn stingaree pup (above) with umbilical cord still attached.*

# SURVIVAL and DEFENSE

*All animals face risks and rays have developed a powerful and*
*surprising armory to defend themselves in the battle to survive.*

The ray's ability to avoid and ward off predators is vital to its survival. Although they are relatively large fishes, they still have enemies and are a major food item for some species of shark. The ray's defensive armory includes electric organs, venomous spines, and hard bony thorns, also known as scutes. They can also make themselves difficult to detect by lying concealed in the silty or sandy substrate.

## ON THE DEFENSIVE

The stinging spines (or stings) of rays, which are modified dorsal-fin spines, lie on top of the tail. The nearer the sting is to the tip, the more useful it becomes as a defensive weapon. It is a hard, flattened structure that tapers to a sharp point. The edges are serrated so that once driven into a victim, the sting either remains or tears the adjacent tissue when withdrawn.

Venom is produced and delivered in two narrow grooves running lengthways along the undersurface of the sting. The whole structure is covered by a thin skin which, when ruptured, releases its venom into the victim. Humans are frequent victims of ray stings but injuries are usually less severe than in shark attacks.

Longtailed rays, such as whiprays (*Himantura*), can use the tail to lash out when startled. The tail's effectiveness as a whip is lessened by the resistance of water, but this is partly compensated for by a covering of short sharp thorns that can severely lacerate unprotected skin. Despite this capability, these rays seem to use their tails on humans only in defense.

Sawfishes have been observed using the top of the snout as a bat to knock fishes away and laterally as a saw to lacerate. Large sawfishes can stun or kill fish as big as a grouper.

The shock-generating organs of the electric rays are

## TREATMENT OF RAY STINGS

The sting of a ray can be mildly painful to fatal, depending on the extent of the wound, its location, and the species of ray involved. The victim usually experiences immediate pain that increases in intensity over an hour or two. In most instances, the pain will abate within 6 to 12 hours. Victims of severe ray stings may experience breathing problems, nausea and vomiting, muscle cramping, and partial paralysis. Mechanical damage from the attack can also be fatal if the spine, pictured above, penetrates a vital organ.

Professional medical attention should be sought immediately. Meanwhile, any venom remaining on the surface of the wound should be washed away (fresh water is best, but salt water will do), and spine fragments removed. If the sting is on a limb, raise the limb higher than the victim's heart. The venom contains a large water-soluble protein that is destroyed by heat, so the wound should be washed in hot water (about 120 degrees Fahrenheit [50° C]) until the pain abates. Secondary infections can result if foreign bodies remain, so wounds are often X-rayed.

among the most powerful found in fishes. Large torpedo rays can produce shocks of more than 200 volts. This is sufficient to knock humans off their feet or to stun an unsuspecting diver. Apart from defense against sharks, these organs are probably used to communicate, and to locate and stun prey. A kidney-shaped electric organ

**NON-SLIP GRIPPERS** *The small teeth (above) of a shovelnose ray hold its prey firmly while it is crushed before swallowing.*

**DEFENSIVE ARMORY** *A porcupine ray (right) has a very rough upper surface consisting of plate-like denticles and sharp thorns (also present on the outer disc). The green sawfish (below) uses its saw both to cut and as a bat.*

is located lengthways near the middle of each side of the disc. Shocks can be delivered at will but quickly weaken in intensity. Some electric rays are known to rush at intruders to deliver a shock, but prey and predators alike are usually shocked accidentally when they wander over a concealed ray or strike it on the back.

## SURVIVAL TACTICS

Rays rarely use their teeth to retaliate. Eagle rays can bite if distressed, but are not likely to do so to deter predators, although surf fishers have had fingers crushed when removing hooks from a ray's mouth. Humans have also been bitten on the fingers when feeding stingrays. Recently, an oceanarium attendant who was wearing only scuba gear and swimsuit when hand-feeding a group of large whiprays, was severely lacerated by an overexuberant ray.

The sensory capabilities of rays, such as sight, smell, vibration, touch, and electrical and magnetic impulses, are very well developed. The animal uses them in combination to survive. Signals to the brain supply the ray with a full picture of its surroundings. Rays are known to detect and use magnetic fields to locate prey, and they are also thought to use this sense to move along compass headings and detect ocean currents. Large rays migrating across open ocean, where senses such as sight and smell are of little use, probably use these capabilities to navigate.

Rays have their share of parasites. Particular species of rays become infected with adult tapeworms when they eat a smaller fish with a dormant cyst of the worm in its flesh. Digestive juices in the ray's stomach enable the cyst to hatch and the tapeworm grows to adulthood in the alimentary canal of its host. These worms, which may eventually grow to several yards in length, lay eggs that are passed into the sea with the ray's feces. These, in turn, may infect the ray's prey, thus continuing the life cycle.

Sometimes, small flattened crustaceans (copepods) and worms (monogeneans) are seen crawling on the skin within the ray's mucus, particularly on the head, near the cloaca, and on the tail. Unless present in large numbers, these parasites are rarely injurious to the ray.

# MOVEMENT
## *and* PROPULSION

*The acrobatic gliding and rolling maneuvers of manta rays are well known
to divers, but all rays ripple and glide with seemingly effortless grace.*

Because they move in ways that vary greatly from group to group, the body shape and fins of rays are highly adapted to a pelagic existence or, more typically, to a life on the bottom.

## POWER AND GRACE
To understand the role of fins in movement, let us compare a ray with a glider. The pectoral and pelvic fins of the ray are equivalent to the wings, elevators, and ailerons of the glider, controlling horizontal stability and up-and-down movements. The tail fin and rudders (dorsal and caudal fins of the ray) are often more responsible for

**EFFORTLESS MOTION** *Startled by something on the floor of the Coral Sea, a mangrove stingray (top) stirs up a great flurry of sand. A smoothtail mobula leaps out of the water (below).*

vertical stability, sideways movements, and steering.

Propulsion is mainly achieved either from the tail, by horizontal or lateral movement, or the pectoral fins, by vertical movement. Strongly built guitarfishes and sawfishes have powerful tails and relatively small pectoral fins compared with other rays. The tail muscles are arranged more as in sharks, and they move by laterally undulating the entire back half of the body. The pectoral fins are rather stiff and, rather than

being flapped, are used to provide vertical control and stability. These rays also have well-developed dorsal and caudal fins, as do sharks, which enhance the swimming efficiency of the tail. The long lower lobe of the sharkfin guitarfishes provides lift.

Most rays have a well-developed disc, formed mostly from the pectoral fins. The tails vary from very short to several times longer than the discs. Except in some electric rays, the musculature is weak and plays a lesser role in propulsion. Skates and stingrays move by vertical undulations of the disc, either by flapping or sending ripple-like waves along the flexible disc edge. These ripples flow either from front to back to move the ray forward, or in reverse.

If only one side of the disc is moved independently, the

**FLYING PROGRESS** *Ripple-like waves along the edge of the disc enable the stingray (top) to move. A bat ray (right) changes direction by moving only one side of its disc.*

denticles make the body stiffer, so electric rays and stingarees with smooth skins generally have highly flexible discs capable of extremely delicate movements.

Rays lack the swim bladder of bony fishes and large oily liver that most sharks have to maintain neutral buoyancy, so unless they swim, they sink to the bottom. However, their enlarged pectoral fins give them one advantage over sharks. The flattened disc enables a ray to glide for long distances between active movements, which provides obvious benefits in conserving energy and may be useful in surprising prey. With their huge, lightweight discs, butterfly rays glide silently over the bottom searching for food and looking like stealth bombers.

effect is like using oars on one side of a boat: the ray rotates. Movements of parts of the disc also enable the ray to dive, climb, turn, bank, or stop. Low-speed, finely controlled movements, not achievable by other bottom fishes, make rays incredibly maneuverable. This gives them a great advantage in seeking prey, enabling them to move around in the mud while still partly buried.

Some electric rays, such as numbfishes, use both disc and tail to move. On the bottom, delicate movements of the edge of its round disc allow the animal to forage around slowly. Above the bottom, it uses its well-developed tail and vertical fins to swim.

## DISTANCE SWIMMING
Mantas, cownose rays, and eagle rays are well adapted to a life that involves extended periods of swimming in open water. Most have long whip-like tails that serve no purpose in propulsion. Their powerful pectoral-fin muscles enable the stiff outer disc to flap like the wings of a bird. The

center of the head and body are raised slightly on the downstroke and lowered on the upstroke. Unlike birds, they can flap one wing at a time to turn rapidly or beat a swift retreat by zigzagging away at great speed. This ability is used to foil predatory charges by sharks.

Unlike some bony fishes that drift passively in water currents or attach themselves to larger fish, rays are active continuously in open water. Some whiprays may seem passive at times when they ride on the backs of larger individuals, but apart from brief periods when copulating, they do not stay attached, as do lampreys and remoras.

Many rays are covered with a thick, slimy mucous coating to reduce drag. The mucus smooths out irregularities on the body surface and reduces surface tension. Apart from some stingrays and skates, rays seldom have large denticles and many are entirely smooth. The skin

## BEATING A RETREAT
Rays are surprisingly good at retreating quickly from their resting position in the substrate if disturbed by a predator. They can turn quickly and accelerate rapidly at right angles to their original position. Others, including eagle rays and guitarfishes, prop on the tips of their pectoral fins in a racing start.

These animals differ in the way they retreat—eagle rays bear off by flapping one pectoral fin before accelerating, while guitarfishes twist the body and accelerate by using the tail. The powerful pectoral discs of eagle and manta rays enable them to move at great speed. Some species have been observed skipping along the surface, often leaping several yards clear of the water.

# BEHAVIOR *and* CONSERVATION

*With new technologies, studies of less accessible marine creatures, such as rays, are now possible, and we are slowly gaining an understanding of their place in the ecosystems of the sea.*

The ecological role and behavioral complexity of rays have never been fully appreciated by humans. Because of their more fearsome reputation, sharks have generally stolen the limelight. Rays were once thought of as simple animals with uncomplex behaviors, but we now know them to be complicated animals with rather large brains and very well-developed sensory systems.

Knowledge of their behavior is still based largely on observations made by underwater divers and photographers, and studies of captive rays in oceanariums. Unfortunately, few of the species have been studied—they are generally less visible than terrestrial predators of a similar size and, among our marine fauna, they are considered less glamorous than seals and dolphins.

## SOCIABILITY

Rays are basically sociable animals, often occurring in large groups of hundreds or even thousands of individuals. By sheer weight of numbers, schooling eagle rays may pose a nuisance to shellfish farms and they can decimate oyster beds. Farm managers place protective net fences around sites to keep them away, or sometimes try to entangle them in mesh nets. Rays resting in confined spaces, such as sand patches among reefs, will often rest on top of each other. Their skin is sensitive to touch and it has been observed that they seem to go into a trance if stroked.

Solitary rays are commonly seen among bony fishes at cleaning stations on coral reefs. They swim slowly above the bottom with gills and jaws open so that small wrasses can access the mouth cavities and spiracles to remove waste tissue and mucus. Parasites are also removed from the body.

They also share symbiotic relationships with other bony fishes, such as trevally, pilot fish, cobia, and remoras, which either swim together with the ray or attach themselves to its skin. These fish feed on food rejected by

**SYMBIOSIS** *Cleaner fish at work inside a manta ray's open mouth (top), and southern stingrays (right) hitching a ride by swimming on top of each other.*

**CONSTANT COMPANY**

**CONSTANT COMPANY**
*The Pacific manta ray is usually accompanied by cleaner fish, in this case orange clarion angelfish, and often has remoras attached to its body.*

Experiments on rays have shown that their strong instincts are supplemented by a reasonable learning capacity. Round stingrays (*Urobatis halleri*) have been conditioned to move to specific sites within a circular tank to obtain food. Correct strikes were rewarded with a herring meal, incorrect movements were given a solid prod. Using a reward system, bat rays have been taught to fetch little floats on their snouts.

## VARIETY OF USES

Humans have used rays for many purposes through the ages. Japanese Samurai warriors used rough stingray skin covered in large denticles on the handles of their swords to provide grip. The tails have been used to make clubs and necklaces, the stings for spear tips, the skin for leather, and the flesh for food.

Large tonnages of rays are still being caught around the globe with little regard to their long-term sustainability as a resource. Catches are being monitored in only a few regions, so ray survival is becoming quite a serious conservation issue.

the ray or disturbed from the bottom by the beating of the ray's wings. Some rays live alone, presumably only socializing to mate. Like sharks, they sometimes occur in single-sex groups outside the breeding season.

## CURIOSITY

Rays also differ greatly in their response to humans in their natural environment. Large stingrays are often inquisitive and will approach a diver cautiously. Sometimes they will threaten divers by quickly raising the tail over the back in a scorpion-like manner. The raising of the tail in a fixed upright pose by small stingarees is thought to be a territorial response.

Some whiprays swim in circles in front of an intruder with their long tails raised and trailing in an ominous display of defiance. Eagle rays and smaller stingrays tend to be shy and will depart rapidly if approached. Giant mantas are gentle and seem to be unafraid of humans in the sea.

## RAYS IN MYTH AND MEDICINE

The venomous barbs of rays, such as that of the southern stingray at right, earned notoriety long ago. Aristotle described rays as dangerous, and the Greeks noted that rays retained their venomous properties well after

death. These powers were considered so great that plants and trees were expected to wither and die if a sting was scraped along their bark. It was believed that the flesh was also poisonous—native tribes in parts of the Indo-Pacific placed a taboo on eating it. Even today, artisanal fishermen of the region are reluctant to eat rays, and cut off the tails to avoid being stung. In Malaysian folklore, there are tales of a leviathan ray that lived beneath a gigantic sea mushroom.

The ray's sting is also thought to have magical properties. Malaysian witch doctors produced a magical potion, consisting of burnt and powdered spines mixed with fruit and needle-shaped crystals (calcium oxalate) derived from plants. Powdered and blended with the Christmas rose (hellebore), ray stings were used as an anesthetic in dentistry by the ancient Greeks. (Interestingly, alkaloids removed from hellebore are used today in the treatment of heart disease.) The Greeks also used the sting as a charm—when removed from a live ray and attached immediately to a pregnant woman's navel, it was thought to promote an easy labor.

In a world older and more complete than ours they move
more finished and complete, gifted with extensions of
senses we have lost or never attained, living by voices
we shall never hear.

*The Outermost House,*
HENRY BESTON (1888–1968), American writer

CHAPTER SIX

# SHARKS FIELD GUIDE

# USING *the* SHARKS GUIDE

*Knowing as much as possible about sharks and their appearance can only enhance your explorations of the watery world below the surface.*

The accounts and illustrations in this field guide will help you to appreciate a wide range of sharks. Some are familiar sights over reefs and sand flats around the world. Others are much more infrequently seen. Using the guide, you may be able to confirm the rarity or perhaps novelty of a shark you see, photograph, or find as part of a catch. You might even discover a little-known shark, and your observations could help to advance scientific knowledge of these extraordinary creatures. To this end, some rarely seen species have been included in the guide in the hope of enlisting your assistance in the search for new information, to help unlock the secrets of the sea.

The **main photograph** shows as much of the species as possible, given the constraints of photographing such wild creatures in circumstances and conditions that can be difficult.

The **common** and **scientific names** of each species. The species are grouped according to taxonomy.

The **text** provides information on the appearance of the shark, its common names, habitat, and where and what to look for when you want to find it. It also gives clues on how to differentiate between similar species, and supplies information, where known, about the shark's migratory habits and methods of reproduction.

Triakidae: Houndsharks

## Soupfin Shark
*Galeorhinus galeus*

### FIELD NOTES
■ Widespread: west coast of North America, east coast of South America, northeast Atlantic, South Africa, southern Australia, New Zealand
■ Varies throughout the world, but up to 6½' (2 m)
■ Not encountered by divers
■ Abundant

The soupfin shark is also known as the school shark or tope. It is a moderately slender shark, bronzy gray on the upper side and pale underneath. It has an unusually large subterminal lobe on the caudal fin. The small second dorsal fin is about the same size as the anal fin.

The soupfin shark is usually found on continental shelves and continental slopes in temperate waters. It feeds mainly on fish, squid, and octopus near the seabed or in the water column. Often preferring to congregate in schools, it lives to be more than 50 years old.

Although considered harmless, it is a very shy creature and encounters are unlikely. It will flee long before a diver arrives in its vicinity. Large numbers of new-born pups are sometimes caught inshore by anglers.

This species migrates long distances so pregnant females can give birth in cooler waters. Sharks tagged in England and Ireland have traveled to Ic... (1,530 miles [2,460 km]) Canary Islands (1,570 mi... [2,525 km]). Sharks from... Californian region have... recaptured off British C... (1,000 miles [1,610 km...

The soupfin shark is ovoviviparous. sizes vary—a litter of 52 pups is the la... known. After a gestation of 12 month... pups are born, 12–14" (30–35 cm) in... Discrete, inshore nursery areas have... in Australia, Argentina, and South... Female sharks reach ma... 8 to 10 years and... every second... This low re... rate, con... soupfin... made i... to ove... meat, t...

Close-up of the eye of the soupfin shark, showing the free

166

Secondary photographs show details of particular features or amplify some aspect of the shark's habitat or behavior.

This *illustrated banding* at the top of the page is a visual pointer to indicate that the page is about a shark species.

This **panel** refers to the family of sharks that the species belongs to.

Triakidae: Houndsharks

Triakidae: Houndsharks

Carcharhinidae: Requiem Sharks

## Gummy Shark

Mustelus antarcticus

**FIELD NOTES**
- Southern Australia
- Females to 5¾' (1.77 m); males to 4¾' (1.45 m)
- Harmless
- During the day, year-round
- Abundant

The gummy shark takes its name from its teeth. They are flat, and arranged in a pavement-like pattern, ideal for crushing rather than cutting its prey. This includes a wide variety of octopus, squid, crustaceans, and fish found on the sandy and rocky bottoms where it dwells.

The gummy is a slender, bronzy gray shark with numerous white spots and sometimes black spots on its back and sides. A thin ridge runs along its back.

The dusky smoothhound (*Mustelus canis*) of the western Atlantic is another of the 20 or so species of the genus *Mustelus*. It is a slender shark, uniformly gray in color, and similar in biology and diet to the gummy shark.

Both species occur mainly in temperate waters on the continental shelf from the shore down. Some also dwell on the continental slope: the gummy shark to depths of 1,150' (350 m), the dusky smoothhound to 1,900' (580 m). They are abundant, and divers will often see them lying on the seabed in shallow coastal waters. Since they are harmless, they can be approached quite safely.

Tagging has shown that a small number of female gummy sharks make long migrations

across the ocean off southern Australia—the longest known journey is about 1,140 miles (1,840 km). Most travel only relatively short distances.

The gummy shark is ovoviviparous. After a gestation of about 12 months, pups of about 12–14½" (30–36 cm) long are born in coastal areas. There are between 1 and 38 pups in a litter, with 15 being the average. They live for about 16 years. In the past there was concern about declining stocks, but these days they are fished sustainably—for their meat, which is popularly known as "flake."

teeth of the lower jaw

167

## Silvertip Shark

Carcharhinus albimarginatus

**FIELD NOTES**
- Widespread in tropics from East Africa to Panama; not in the Atlantic
- 10' (3 m)
- Aggressive, but not a significant risk
- During the day, year-round
- Common

[...] large and [...] gray in [...]on name [...]ctive [...] all their [...]narrow [...]orsal [...]t [...]like [...]n sharks that are [...]e reef edge in [...]ar to those of [...]nus

[...] ideal [...]ey feed [...] water, [...]al [...]er [...]ive

dorsal fin

Silvertip sharks are viviparous; females usually have 5 or 6 pups to a litter, but there can be as many as 11. The young hatch after 12 months.

Experiments conducted using underwater sound have shown that silvertips are attracted to low-frequency sounds, probably because these frequencies mimic the sound made by an injured fish, potentially an easy meal.

169

Quick-reference Field Notes panel
- Distribution range of the shark
- Size
- Possible risks when encountering the shark
- Best time of day or year to observe the species
- Information on population numbers

Color illustrations supplement the text by showing some basic features of the shark.

# Frilled Shark

Chlamydoselachus anguineus

The frilled shark, or eel shark, has a long, slender body with an elongate tail fin, which gives it an almost eel-like appearance and one of its common names. A single small dorsal fin is located well back on its dark chocolate brown body, directly above the large anal fin. The pectoral fins are short and rounded. This shark has six pairs of large gill slits—most sharks have five—the first pair of which joins under the throat. The gills are surrounded by frilly margins of skin—hence the common name of frilled shark. Its snout is short, while the lower jaw is long, with the mouth almost at the tip of the snout rather than under the head.

The frilled shark's teeth have broad bases with three sharp cusps separated by two small intermediate cusps. Little is known about its diet, but with such teeth, it probably feeds on small deep-water fishes and squid.

Very little is known about the biology and ecology of this shark, the only living member of the frilled shark family. It is found on the bottom shelves and upper slopes around continents and large islands. Occasionally, it is seen near the surface in open waters, but it usually lives at a depth of 330–4,260' (100–1,300 m), so the only chance of observing it is from a deep-water submersible. It is sometimes collected as bycatch during bottom trawling.

Female frilled sharks bear 8 to 12 live young, about 16" (40 cm) long. Gestation is probably one to two years.

Thoughts on this shark's evolution are contentious. Some think it is a direct descendant of the primitive cladoselache sharks (see p. 94), but others say it is closer to modern forms.

**FIELD NOTES**

- Eastern Atlantic, western Indian Ocean, western and eastern Pacific
- Up to 6½' (2 m)
- Harmless
- Occasionally seen at the surface
- Not uncommon

snout with distinctive teeth and frilled gill margins

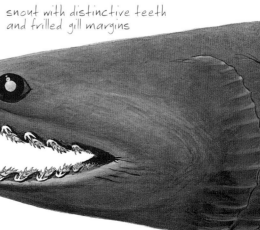

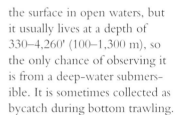

# Broadnose Sevengill Shark

Notorynchus cepedianus

The broadnose sevengill shark is immediately recognizable because of its seven pairs of gill slits—most shark species only have five pairs. Its other unusual feature is a single, small dorsal fin. It has a wide head with a short, blunt snout and small eyes. It is a large and powerful shark. Its silvery gray to brownish back and sides are speckled with numerous small dark and white spots, while the underside is pale. Juveniles have white margins on their rear fins.

**FIELD NOTES**

- Temperate regions of the South Atlantic, Pacific, and Indian Oceans
- To about 10' (3 m)
- Potentially dangerous
- Not usually seen by divers
- Not abundant

The seven gills and distinctive spots of a broadnose sevengill shark.

(135 m). Although the species is widespread, it is not particularly abundant. It will often come close inshore in shallow bays and inlets, but does not rest on the seabed. This might explain why it is not commonly seen by divers. There are no records of it attacking people (except for divers in aquariums), but it will scavenge on human corpses. It is potentially dangerous. In captivity, it is aggressive when attacked, and it struggles vigorously to escape when captured.

The teeth of the broadnose sevengill shark are very effective for cutting. The teeth of the upper jaw are jagged with cusps, except for a single middle tooth; the teeth of the bottom jaw are comb-shaped. The shark's diet includes other sharks, rays, bony fishes, seals, and carrion. It bites pieces of flesh from other sharks caught by gill nets and hooks.

The shark lives in temperate waters on continental shelves, at depths down to 450'

Males mature at about 5' (1.5 m), and females at about 7' (2.2 m). They bear live young in shallow bays. Litter sizes vary, and can be as large as 82 pups. The pups are about 16–18" (40–45 cm) when born.

137

# Bluntnose Sixgill Shark

Hexanchus griseus

The bluntnose sixgill shark has a massive body, with a long and powerful tail, which it uses to swim in a strong, constant motion. A single dorsal fin is located to the rear of the body, slightly in front of the anal fin below. The eyes are small, and set on the side of the wide, short-snouted head.

The shark has six pairs of gill slits. Only two other shark species have six: the frilled shark (see p. 136) and the bigeyed sixgill shark (*Hexanchus vitulus*). The latter belongs to the same family as the bluntnose sixgill shark, and can be distinguished from it by its more slender body and large eyes. It has five rows of saw-like teeth on each side of its lower jaw, whereas the bluntnose sixgill shark has six rows of similar teeth. Its upper jaw has smaller recurved teeth with a single cusp.

This large shark is a voracious predator of other large fishes, such as

### FIELD NOTES

■ Worldwide in northern and cold temperate to tropical seas

■ 5–16½' (1.5–5 m)

■ Not dangerous unless provoked

■ Most likely seen at night, year-round

■ Common

sharks, billfishes, dolphin, cod, and flounder, which it can quickly cut into bite-sized chunks with its teeth. It also takes smaller prey, such as herring, squid, crab, and shrimp.

The bluntnose sixgill shark is found both near the bottom and in the water column above continental and island shelves, at depths of 650–5,400' (200–1,800 m). It prefers dimly lit or dark waters, and is seen at night near the surface of the open ocean. Small sixgills move close inshore and forage near the bottom, but in coastal waters adults usually stay below 330' (100 m).

Females reach sexual maturity at about 14' (4.5 m). They produce up to 100 live young, about 28" (70 cm) long. Little is known about this shark's biology other than data from commercial fisheries—it is fished in many parts of the world for both its meat and its oil.

The broad, rounded snout of the bluntnose sixgill shark.

138

# Prickly Shark

Echinorhinus cookei

The prickly shark is a spiny-skinned dogfish, one of two species of the bramble shark family. The bodies of both species are short and stout, the heads slightly flattened. There is a small spiracle behind each eye and in front of the first of five pairs of gill slits. Two spineless dorsal fins are located well back on the body above the pelvic fins. Anal fins are absent.

The prickly shark is grayish brown with white around the mouth and underneath the snout, and black along its relatively large fin margins. Its denticles, usually about ⅕" (5 mm) wide at the base, are all over its body.

Little is known about the ecology and habits of this shark. It is primarily a deep-water species, dwelling in cold temperate to tropical seas on continental and island shelves and upper slopes at depths of from 36–1,390' (11–424 m). Individuals are seen occasionally in shallow waters. This slow-moving species is probably a suction-feeder of crabs and cephalopods near the bottom. It also takes fishes such as juvenile sixgill sharks, flatfishes, and herring. Females reach maturity at about 8–10' (2.5–3 m)

**FIELD NOTES**

■ Pacific, from the Americas to Hawaii, New Zealand, and Asia

■ 13' (4 m)

■ Harmless

■ Rarely seen, except when taken by commercial fisheries

■ Fairly common

long. They bear up to 24 live young, 16–18" (40–45 cm) long.

The related bramble shark (*Echinorhinus brucus*) gets its name from its much larger and very prominent spine-like denticles, about ⅗" (15 mm) in diameter at their base. They are scattered over the shark's body as well as on the underside of the snout in adults, and are sometimes fused into plates. The bramble shark is brown to dark gray above, with a lighter belly. It is most commonly encountered in the Mediterranean Sea and along the west coast of Europe and Africa.

skin and denticles of the bramble shark

139

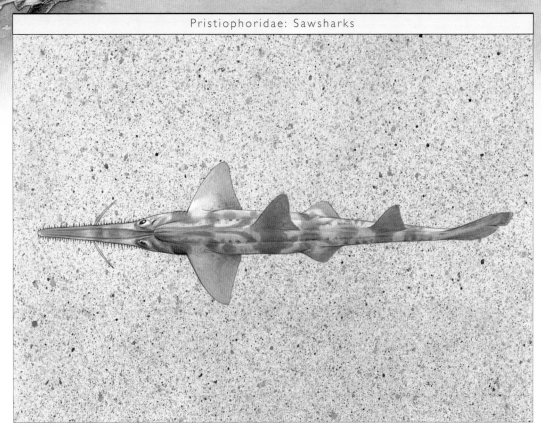

# Common Sawshark

Pristiophorus cirratus

The common sawshark is also known as the longnose sawshark. Like all the sawshark family, it is immediately recognizable from its saw-like snout with a pair of barbels. Because of this snout, it can sometimes be confused with sawfishes (see p. 204). However, the sawshark's five pairs of gills are on the side of its head, while the sawfish's gills are underneath. Also, the sawfish does not have a pair of barbels.

The common sawshark is a slender shark with a slightly depressed and flattened body. It has an attractive patterning of darker bands and brownish spots and blotches on a pale yellowish brown background. This shark is found only in

**FIELD NOTES**

■ Southern Australia, from southern New South Wales to mid-Western Australia

■ Females to 5' (1.5 m); males to 4⅓' (1.3 m)

■ Harmless unless provoked

■ Year-round

■ Common

temperate waters in southern Australia. The southern, or shortnose, sawshark (*Pristiophorus nudipinnis*), also endemic to Australia, is found in a similar area. This brownish gray shark prefers to dwell on the inner continental shelf to depths of 230' (90 m); the common sawshark seems to prefer deeper water, on continental shelves and slopes to depths of about 1,015' (310 m).

Divers may find sawsharks lying on the sandy bottoms. They are timid and harmless, but will strike with their snout if handled. They feed by trailing their barbels along the bottom to locate the small bony fish that they eat. The teeth on the snout are probably then used for stirring up sediment to rouse the prey and strike it.

The common sawshark lives for more than 15 years. Like all sawsharks, it is ovoviviparous. Mature females appear to breed every 1 to 2 years, carrying from 3 to 22 young, with about 10 being the average. After about 12 months' gestation, the pups are born in shallow coastal areas. They are about 11–14½" (27–37 cm) long at birth.

snout of the southern sawshark

140

# Pacific Angelshark

### Squatina californica

A ngelsharks are unusual, flattened sharks that are often mistaken for rays. They used to be called monkfish because the strange shape of their heads resembles the hood on a monk's cloak. The dozen species range along temperate coasts from shallow waters to more than 4,265' (1,320 m) deep. They are unique in having a blunt nose; the leading edge of their pectoral fins is free from the body; and the lower caudal fin lobe is longer than the upper.

The Pacific angelshark is easily identified by its large eyes, a conspicuous spiracle, and a generally brown-gray coloration. During the day, it remains buried in sand on the bottom with only its eyes and head exposed, ready to burst upward out of the sand and ambush a fish or squid with its protruding, trap-like jaws and numerous spiky teeth. Occasionally, divers may encounter a Pacific angelshark swimming over sandy bottoms near kelp beds at depths of about 10' (3 m) and

**FIELD NOTES**

▦ Eastern Pacific, from southeast Alaska, USA, to Baja California, Mexico, and from Ecuador to southern Chile

▦ To about 5' (1.5 m)

▦ Can bite if surprised or harassed

▦ Best seen at night

▦ Once common, now reduced due to heavy fishing pressure

more. It can become aggressive if harassed—a diver or angler who foolishly grabs the tail of an angelshark soon discovers how quickly the shark can bite and how painful the bite can be.

Males and females are mature at about 3' (90 cm), and the female is ovoviviparous, producing eggs that are retained within her body. There are about 8 to 13 pups in each litter.

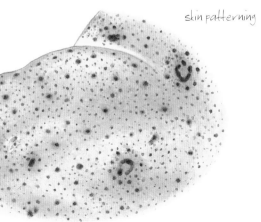

skin patterning

141

# California Hornshark

### Heterodontus francisci

Named for the spine in front of each dorsal fin, the California hornshark is one of nine living species of the family known as bullhead, horn, or Port Jackson sharks. The sharks of this family are unmistakable, with their blunt foreheads, pig-like snouts, and broad eye ridges. Their taxonomic name (from Greek for "mixed-tooth") refers to the small, pointed teeth at the front of the jaw and the blunt teeth at the rear. With these, they can grab soft-bodied fish and crustaceans, and crush sea urchins and the shellfish that they prefer.

California hornsharks have small dark spots on their bodies and fins. They live in cool, shallow waters, and lay curious, fist-sized, screw-shaped egg cases (always with a right-hand thread). The egg case is wedged into a rock crevice, and hatches after 6 to 10 months, depending on water

**FIELD NOTES**

- Central California, USA, to the Gulf of California
- To 4' (1.2 m), but most adults less than 3' (90 cm)
- Generally sedentary; not dangerous
- Day and night, year-round
- Not uncommon; neither direct nor indirect sport or commercial fishing of species

The egg case of a California hornshark.

dorsal fin with horn spine

temperature. During the day, divers find the sharks, as well as their egg cases, resting among large rocks in shallow-water kelp beds and at the base of boulders. At night, the sharks patrol for food out in the open.

California hornsharks are very popular in public aquariums. There, while sitting placidly on the bottom, they defy the commonly held belief that all sharks must swim in order to be able to breathe.

# Port Jackson Shark

Heterodontus portusjacksoni

The Port Jackson shark, also called the oyster crusher or tabbigaw, is very similar to the related California hornshark (see opposite). It is brownish gray, with conspicuous, dark, narrow stripes in a harness-type pattern across the shoulders. Two other Australian bullheads, the crested hornshark (*Heterodontus galeatus*) and the zebra hornshark (*Heterodontus zebra*), have large crests above the eyes and a dark striped livery respectively. Port Jackson sharks are abundant and survive well in aquariums.

Although individuals may range over considerable distances, they favor certain reefs or caves, and usually return to this favored spot to rest during the day. Divers frequently encounter them in shallow water, in caves, and near rocks and at the base of seaweeds. Groups of adults move in and out of shallow water according to water temperature and breeding conditions.

*The distinctive pig-like snout and pointy front teeth of the Port Jackson shark.*

### FIELD NOTES

- Southern Australia, from Queensland to mid-Western Australia, including Tasmania; rare in New Zealand
- To 5½' (1.7 m), but rarely larger than 4½' (1.4 m)
- Generally sedentary; harmless unless handled
- Mostly sighted at night, all year
- Not uncommon

This species segregates by sex and maturity. In Australia, females and some males in the Sydney area move into shallow water in summer to mate. In August and September, females lay two eggs every 8 to 17 days among rocks in 16–100' (5–30 m) of water, often in a communal nursery. The female will wedge the pointed edge and flanges of the screw-shaped egg case into a rocky crevice using her mouth. The young hatch 9 to 12 months later and move into bays and estuaries. After a decade, they will have grown to 20–30" (50–75 cm) and have reached adolescence.

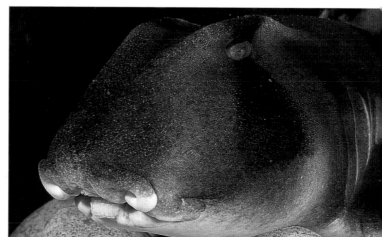

# Necklace Carpetshark

*Parascyllium variolatum*

With its long, slender, and slightly flattened body, and its long but almost indistinct tail, the necklace carpetshark has a quite eel-like appearance. It is easily identifiable by its dark gray-brown body scattered with numerous white spots and the large black blotches on the edges of the fins. Most striking is the dark band, or collar, studded with small bright white spots that encircles the head like a necklace, hence its common name. It is also known as the varied carpetshark. Its spiracles are small, and its nostrils bear short barbels (probably for chemo-sensory purposes) and grooves that connect to the mouth.

Collared carpetsharks are closely related to nurse sharks and wobbegongs but are often mistaken for catsharks, which they resemble only superficially. Collared carpetsharks are distinguished by their mouth being located well in front of the eyes. The family has two genera: the *Cirrhoscyllium*, which have barbels on the throat, and the *Parascyllium*, which do not.

**FIELD NOTES**

- Southern Australia
- Less than 3⅓' (1 m)
- Harmless
- At night, year-round
- Common

The necklace carpetshark is common on shallow rocky reefs along the southern temperate coast of Australia. It feeds and is active at night, and is often encountered by divers after dark. During the day it is difficult to spot because it rests either in caves or on the bottom, where it is perfectly camouflaged among the algae.

Little is known about this carpetshark's diet, but it probably feeds on invertebrates and small fishes. It is oviparous, laying egg cases with curled tendrils that anchor the cases to the substrate.

*This necklace carpetshark, one of seven collared carpetsharks, is being attacked by a voracious 11-armed sea star.*

# Blind Shark

### Brachaelurus waddi

**B**lind sharks get their name from their habit of closing their eyes when caught by fishers. The blind shark, along with the blue-gray carpetshark (*Brachaelurus colcloughi*), make up the blind shark family. They are closely related to bamboosharks, nurse sharks, and collared carpetsharks. Although often referred to as catsharks, they are related only distantly to them.

The blind shark has a stout, cylindrical, brown body, usually dotted with pale spots. Its two spineless dorsal fins are close together, with the first originating above the pelvic fins. It has very large spiracles positioned behind and to the side of the eyes. Its nostrils are well developed, with a pair of long, smooth nasal barbels, which are connected to the mouth by a groove that permits water that has passed over the olfactory organs to flow into the mouth. The blind shark

**FIELD NOTES**

- Northern and eastern Australia
- Up to 4¼' (1.3 m)
- Harmless
- Secretive; most likely seen at night
- Common

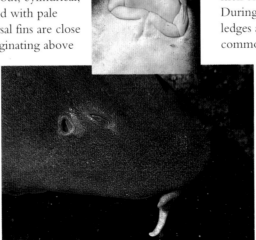

*Snout and barbels from below (top) and from the side (above).*

can be distinguished from the blue-gray carpetshark by the presence of a small (symphyseal) groove in the middle of the chin, which the blue-gray carpetshark lacks.

This shark inhabits shallow, warm temperate and tropical waters—it can occur in water just deep enough to cover it. It is also found on the continental shelf to about 490' (150 m). During the day, it shelters under ledges and in caves, and it is commonly observed by divers under ledges but is rarely seen out in the open. It emerges after dark to forage on the reef and the adjacent sandy areas for anemones, cuttlefish, and crustaceans.

Females reach sexual maturity when about 26" (65 cm) long, and give birth during summer to as many as eight young. 145

# Tasselled Wobbegong

### Eucrossorhinus dasypogon

**FIELD NOTES**

- Western Pacific
- 10–13' (3–4 m)
- Dangerous when provoked, captured, or disturbed
- Year-round in many areas
- Common

Wobbegongs share many of the basic features of nurse sharks, blind sharks, bamboosharks, and collared carpetsharks. They have elongated bodies that are flattened, especially in the head region, and the two dorsal fins of similar size are set far back on the body. The broad, short pectoral fins are well adapted for a life on the reef bottom.

Tasselled wobbegongs are patterned with small, reticulated markings on a drab gray or brown background; the underside is white. These unusual sharks are distinguished by a very broad, flat head. The upper jaw is surrounded by many finely branched dermal lobes that appear as fleshy flaps hanging down over the mouth. The chin and sides of the lower jaw are also decorated with small, reticulated fleshy tassels. Within this mass of tassels are branched nasal barbels and grooves that channel the water leaving the nostrils to the mouth. The mouth

*A tasselled wobbegong's jaw, with branched, fleshy tassels.*

is studded with sharp, narrow teeth, perfect for capturing the fish on which this shark preys.

Living in warm temperate to tropical seas, the tasselled wobbegong is a common member of tropical reefs of New Guinea, the north Australian coast, and Indonesia. During the day, it is commonly found in caves on the reef, where it feeds on sheltering fish. At night, it emerges to feed on small fishes and invertebrates. Females are believed to bear live young, about 8½" (22 cm) long.

Divers are most likely to encounter smaller individuals, about 3⅓' (1 m) long. Because of their markings, tasselled wobbegongs are difficult to see against the sea floor. There have been many reports of attacks on divers. Most are provoked by divers pulling the shark's tail or accidentally stepping on it. But in some cases, the attacks were apparently unprovoked.

# Ornate Wobbegong

Orectolobus ornatus

The ornate, or banded, wobbegong has large, black-bordered, saddle-shaped markings on the back. The body is flattened and wide from the head to the back of the trunk, where it quickly tapers to the tail. On each side of the head there are five or six dermal lobes. Each nostril bears a single barbel and there is a groove from the back of each nostril to the mouth. The teeth are long and slender, well adapted for grasping small fish prey.

This is one of four wobbegong species in the genus *Orectolobus*. While the relative position of these wobbegongs' fins is similar to that of the tasselled wobbegong (opposite), the fin lobes in *Orectolobus* are smaller in comparison to the body. *Orectolobus* also differs in having no dermal lobes or tassels on the chin or lower jaw. The back is smooth, which distinguishes sharks of this genus from the heavily tubercled cobbler wobbegong (*Sutorectus tentaculatus*), common on the southwest coast of Australia.

The ornate wobbegong is a large, common inshore inhabitant of temperate rocky and tropical reefs. During the day it rests in the open on rocky bottoms or table coral, or it sometimes hides under reef ledges. It becomes active at night, searching the reef for invertebrates and fishes to eat. Divers should be cautious because this species can easily camouflage itself against the sea floor, and it is considered dangerous—numerous provoked and unprovoked attacks have been documented. Females produce litters of up to 12 pups, each about 8" (20 cm) long.

### FIELD NOTES

- Western Pacific
- 10' (3 m)
- Dangerous, particularly when provoked, captured, or stepped on
- Almost year-round
- Common

*Close-up of an ornate wobbegong's coloring.* 147

# Epaulette Shark

Hemiscyllium ocellatum

The 13 species of longtailed carpetsharks are subdivided into the epaulette sharks (*Hemiscyllium*) and bamboosharks (*Chiloscyllium*). These usually small fish have thin, slightly flattened, elongated bodies. The two relatively large, spineless dorsal fins are about the same size. The anal fin is far back on the underside, immediately in front of the caudal fin, from which it is separated by a notch. These short, stubby, paired fins are used by many species for "walking" across the bottom. Most juvenile longtailed carpetsharks have

**FIELD NOTES**

- Indo-West Pacific
- 3⅓' (1 m)
- Harmless
- Day or night, year-round
- Common

broad contrasting bands of color on the body. In adult epaulette sharks these bands become spotted, and a prominent black spot develops above the pectoral fins. The yellowish or brownish body of *Hemiscyllium ocellatum* is covered with dark brown spots, and the characteristic large black spot has a white ring around it. Its nostrils and mouth are almost at the tip of the snout, which is short and rounded like all the epaulette sharks.

The solid bands of color of the juvenile carpetsharks fade or disappear altogether in adult bamboosharks such as the brownbanded bambooshark (*Chiloscyllium punctatum*). It is a uniform brown as an adult. However, the adult slender bambooshark (*Chiloscyllium indicum*) is covered with small dark spots and bars, and has small side ridges. It has rounded dorsal fins and the pointed snout typical of the bamboosharks.

Longtailed carpetsharks are common inshore on coral and rocky reefs and in tide pools. Divers often encounter adults, but juveniles are rarely seen because they hide within the reef. These nocturnally active sharks feed on small benthic invertebrates and fishes. Many species lay eggs.

*Adult brownbanded bamboosharks congregating on the bottom.*

# Nurse Shark

Ginglymostoma cirratum

No one is sure how the nurse shark got its name, perhaps from the sucking noise made by a feeding nurse shark, which sounds like a nursing baby. This fairly large bottom dweller is uniformly brown to gray-brown and has large, rounded fins. Noticeable barbels protrude from the nasal openings in front of the corners of its small mouth. A small spiracle behind and below each eye allows it to take in water over the gills when breathing.

Common over inshore coral reefs in tropical waters, it is probably the shark that snorkelers and divers in the Caribbean see most often. Although sluggish during the day, it is active at night, when it feeds on bottom-dwelling invertebrates, such as lobsters and other crustaceans, as well as snails, clams, octopus, squid, and any fish slow enough to be caught by its great gulping

**FIELD NOTES**

- Eastern Pacific, from Mexico to Peru; western Atlantic, from Rhode Island, USA, to southern Brazil; tropical West Africa
- To 14' (4.25 m); rarely longer than 10' (3 m)
- Harmless unless provoked
- During the day, year-round
- Common, particularly in the Caribbean

and inhaling style of feeding.

Because they are abundant and easy to capture, handle, and transport, nurse sharks are common residents of public aquariums. Behaviorists have used them to study learning in sharks, and have demonstrated that nurse sharks can be taught to react to novel situations.

These ovoviviparous sharks conduct an interesting court-ship. Male and female swim in close synchrony, the male alongside or slightly behind and below the female. (Sometimes, a second male accompanies them to prevent the female from retreating.) When the male grabs the female's pectoral fin in his mouth, she rolls onto her back. He swims above her and inserts a clasper into her vent to deliver sperm.

*A nurse shark resting on a reef in the Bahamas.*

149

# Zebra Shark

### Stegostoma fasciatum

The zebra shark is a lovely creature, found over tropical coral reefs. Its very long, broad tail and its coloring make it quite distinctive. The juvenile shark has zebra-like stripes (yellow on black), which give the shark its common name. It takes on a yellowish brown color with dark brown spotting as it reaches adulthood. Because of this adult coloration, it is also known as the leopard shark. (It cannot be confused with the other shark known as a leopard shark, a very different, cold-water species of the eastern Pacific, from the houndshark family (see p. 168).)

**FIELD NOTES**

▨ Widespread in the tropical western Pacific and Indian Ocean

▨ To 11½' (3.5 m)

▨ Harmless

▨ More active at night, seen year-round

▨ Common

The zebra shark has small barbels on its snout, a small mouth, and small eyes. Its teeth are pointed, with each tooth having two smaller, lateral, flanking points. Prominent ridges run along its flanks.

This is a sluggish species. Divers occasionally find one resting on the bottom during the day, propped up on its pectoral fins with its open mouth facing into the current in order to obtain oxygen more easily from the water. It poses no danger to humans. Its slender, flexible body allows it to wriggle into narrow crevices in the reef, searching for the shellfish, crustaceans, and small fishes upon which it prefers to feed.

The zebra shark is oviparous. It lays large, brown or purplish black egg cases, from 5–7" (13–18 cm) in length, that have fibers for attaching to the seabed.

*Bunches of hair-like fibers secure the egg case of the zebra shark to the ocean floor.*

# Whale Shark

Rhincodon typus

The sole living member of its family, the whale shark is the world's largest living fish. Its massive, fusiform body reaches lengths in excess of 46' (14 m). It has alternating thin white vertical bars and columns of spots on a dark background, with long ridges along the upper side of the body and a prominent lateral keel. The narrow mouth extends across the full width of its flattened head. The eyes are small and far forward on the head. Each nostril has a small barbel and the gill slits are long and extend above the pectoral fins. Above the relatively small pelvic fins are the first of two dorsal fins. The powerful caudal fin is semicircular.

This shark swims slowly near the surface, consuming small crustacean plankton, small fishes, such as sardines and anchovies, and even larger fishes such as mackerel. It has well-developed internal spongy filters at the gill arches, which help to retain small prey within its huge mouth. This

**FIELD NOTES**

- Western Atlantic, eastern Atlantic, Indo-West, central, and eastern Pacific
- Up to 46' (14 m)
- Harmless
- Seasonally, day and night
- Common in some regions

mechanism may impede the flow of water through the mouth during swimming, which limits the amount of plankton the shark can strain. So, as well as filter feeding, it can also pump water into its mouth to feed on concentrated patches of plankton.

The whale shark is found in all tropical and subtropical oceans, along coastal regions, and enters lagoons on tropical islands. It is mostly seen on the surface, where divers and snorkelers can swim with this gentle, curious creature (see pp. 262–3).

The whale shark is a livebearer. Pregnant females were recently found to contain hundreds of young, up to about 2' (60 cm) long.

*A trevally disappears into the gaping mouth of the filter-feeding whale shark.*

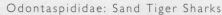

# Sand Tiger Shark

*Eugomphodus taurus*

**FIELD NOTES**

◼ *Western Atlantic, eastern Atlantic, western Indian Ocean, western Pacific*

◼ *10½' (3.2 m)*

◼ *Dangerous only when provoked*

◼ *Day and night; year-round in some regions, regional in others*

◼ *Common*

Depending on where you are in the world, the sand tiger shark may be known as the spotted raggedtooth or gray nurse shark. It is one of four species belonging to the sand tiger family, a group of large, fearsome-looking sharks that swim slowly with their mouths open, exposing long, narrow, needle-like teeth. Their bodies are stout, with two large dorsal fins. The elongated tails have a long upper lobe; there is a precaudal pit but no caudal keels.

The sand tiger shark has a short, flattened snout. Its dorsal fins are about equal in size, with the first located closer to the pelvic fins than to the pectoral fins. It is bronzy above, gradually becoming paler below. Juveniles have reddish or brownish spots scattered on the tail and rear of the body, which tend to fade with age. There are three rows of large teeth on each side of the midline of the upper jaw.

This shark is found in shallow bays, sandy coastal waters, and rocky or tropical reefs from shallow waters down to about 655' (200 m). Divers often find large numbers in aggregations around rocky outcroppings in offshore waters.

Essentially gentle sharks, they usually become aggressive only if provoked. Their diet consists of many species of large and small bony fishes, small sharks, rays, crustaceans, and squid.

The sand tiger shark is able to hover motionless in the water by swallowing surface air and holding it in its stomach, thus achieving near-neutral buoyancy. It is also known to make long coastal migrations for reproductive purposes. Reproduction is oviphagous. In each of the two uterine chambers, the first embryo to hatch, at about 6½" (17 cm), kills and devours the other developing siblings. The two embryos continue to feed on the other eggs inside the separate uterine chambers. After a gestation period of eight to nine months, the two live young are born, about 3⅓' (1 m) long.

*A male sand tiger shark swimming, mouth characteristically open.*

# Goblin Shark

Mitsukurina owstoni

Perhaps the most mysterious, and bizarre, of all sharks, the goblin shark is the only species of its family. Its light pink body is long but thin. The flesh has a soft, watery texture, which probably helps it to maintain neutral buoyancy, important in what is thought to be a slow-swimming species. The two dorsal fins are similar in size, while the anal fin is well developed. The tail consists almost entirely of a single long upper lobe.

This shark has an elongated snout flattened in the shape of a paddle. The nostrils are located immediately in front of the mouth. The teeth at the front of its narrow, pointed jaw are long and needle-like, ideal for grasping small fish. The teeth at the back of the mouth are small and form a crushing or grinding plate for processing captured prey. The goblin shark probably feeds mostly on small fishes, crustaceans, and squid, and its paddle-like snout is thought to aid the electrosensory

**FIELD NOTES**

■ Western and eastern Atlantic, western Indian Ocean, western Pacific

■ 11' (3.3 m)

■ Harmless

■ Not commonly seen

■ Probably common

upper and lower teeth

system in detecting and capturing a potential meal.

In addition, its jaw is highly specialized to project rapidly from the head. This makes the goblin shark a very efficient predator, capable of quickly grasping or sucking prey into its mouth in a single bite.

Very little is known about the biology and ecology of this shark. It occurs near the bottom on continental and island shelves and slopes, at depths of about 3,940' (1,200 m). Living in such deep waters, it is rarely seen or collected. However, it is occasionally found in shallow water near shore.

Until recently, no one had seen a living goblin shark. Early specimens had been preserved with the jaw in the extended position, which gave the shark a very weird appearance. However, we now know that when its jaws are closed, the very protrusible upper jaw fits tightly against the bottom of the skull.

153

# Megamouth Shark

Megachasma pelagios

The accidental capture of a large, black, blubbery shark off Hawaii in 1976 was the shark discovery of the century. The creature had become entangled in a deep-water net line. It had a large head, a huge distending mouth about 3⅓' (1 m) wide, and numerous small teeth. But other characteristics indicated a relationship with the ecologically disparate white sharks and makos. A new genus, species, and family of vertebrates was created, known as the megamouth shark. Its scientific name comes from the Greek to mean "giant yawner of the open sea."

Only nine more megamouth sharks have been found. The first six were all large males; more recently, a 12' (3.6 m) female, a 16½' (5 m) female, and a small, 6' (1.8 m) male have been observed.

Not surprisingly, we know very little about the megamouth. It lives in the open ocean, often at great depths, which may explain the rarity of encounters. It appears

**FIELD NOTES**

- Throughout the world's oceans
- To 17' (5.2 m)
- Harmless
- Not likely to be seen by divers
- Known from 10 specimens

to be a plankton feeder, like the whale shark (see p.151) and the basking shark (see p. 157). It swims slowly through the open ocean, filtering small shrimps and other prey from the water as it goes. It spends the day feeding in deep water and comes up to shallower water at night. The silvery lining of its mouth cavity is probably reflective, so that when shrimps and other luminous crustaceans enter the open, cavernous mouth, they may encourage others to enter.

*upper and lower teeth*

154

The great mouth filters huge amounts of water for tiny organisms.

# Pelagic Thresher

*Alopias pelagicus*

The pelagic thresher has a dark, countershaded body grading from gray above to white on the underbelly. It shares many of the features common to all the threshers (see p. 156), but the first dorsal fin of the pelagic thresher is closer to the pectoral fins. It has at least 30 rows of small teeth in each jaw; all the teeth bear a distinct cusplet in the tooth notch.

Widespread in tropical and subtropical Indo-Pacific seas, the pelagic thresher is commonly observed far from land, swimming at the surface. It also frequents the seaward edges of coral reefs and submarine seamounts. However, it is shy, and difficult for divers to approach. Occasionally, it makes excursions to depths as great as 490' (150 m). It feeds either near the surface or in deep waters on small fishes and squid, which it grasps and cuts with its small, sharp teeth.

The bigeye thresher (*Alopias superciliosus*) is known to reach 15' (4.6 m) in length. It is easily distinguished from the others by the deep grooves above its very large eyes, which are located almost on top of the head. It has large pelvic fins. Its pectoral fins are long, curved on the trailing margins and rounded at the tips. This species occurs in nearly all tropical and

**FIELD NOTES**

- Indo-Pacific
- Up to 11' (3.3 m); tail comprises half the total length
- Harmless and shy of divers
- Spring and summer
- Becoming less common in some areas because of heavy fishing

subtropical open oceans and coastal areas, from the surface to depths of about 1,640' (500 m). It is known to feed in the water column on pelagic mackerel, tuna, herring, and billfishes, as well as on bony fishes and squid near the bottom.

Female pelagic threshers reach reproductive maturity when about 8½' (2.6 m) in length. Embryos are cannibalistic in the uterus and only two live pups are born. These are almost 3⅓' (1 m) long. Bigeye threshers also bear cannibalistic pups, but litter sizes range from two to four, suggesting that some embryos coexist through gestation.

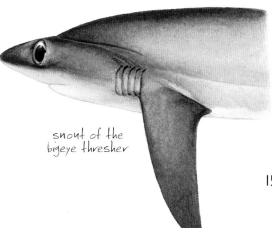

snout of the bigeye thresher

155

# Common Thresher Shark

*Alopias vulpinus*

The common thresher is one of three thresher sharks. These large, pelagic sharks are immediately recognizable by their long tails. They have a short, conical snout, large eyes placed well forward on the head, and a husky, spindle-shaped body. The first dorsal fin is much larger than the second. The broad pectoral fins provide lift when swimming—these strong, active sharks have enough power to leap out of the water.

The jaws are relatively small, with remarkably efficient small, sharp teeth for capturing cephalopods and schooling fishes. They use the long tail to slap the water surface, frightening prey into tight groups to make capture easier.

Common threshers can be distinguished from their relatives by the position of the first dorsal fin, with its leading edge above the trailing edge

**FIELD NOTES**

■ Western and eastern Atlantic, Indo-West Pacific, central Pacific

■ 16½–20' (5–6 m)

■ Not aggressive, but should be treated with caution

■ During the day, almost year-round

■ Becoming uncommon in many areas due to fishing pressure

of the pectoral fins. The pectoral fins are curved, with pointed tips. The body is dark blue-gray above, with a sharp, ragged break marking the edge of the white underside. There are prominent labial furrows at the sides of the jaws.

The common thresher shark is widespread in tropical and temperate waters. It is commonly seen swimming at the surface in coastal waters, but also occurs at depths of 1,150' (350 m) and more. It is best viewed from boats or by snorkelers in open water. While not aggressive toward humans, this is a large shark. Respect its power, and keep clear of its tail.

Females reach maturity at about 10' (3 m) long and produce four to six live young, about 5' (1.5 m) long. The thresher is targeted by fisheries for its fins and meat, and populations are diminishing in many coastal areas.

common thresher shark

156

# Basking Shark

Cetorhinus maximus

The basking shark is the second largest fish in the world, after the other plankton filter feeder, the whale shark (see p. 151). Its huge size makes it easy to identify, as do its very broad gill slits that extend around the top and bottom of the head. The grayish brown body is streamlined and stout, with a strong crescent-shaped tail fin and lateral keels. The short snout is narrow and conical, with huge jaws that expand laterally when the shark feeds.

Basking sharks are frequent visitors to cold and warm temperate waters, where they take advantage of plankton blooms in coastal regions. They often enter large bays to feed. You will see them close to shore, swimming slowly near the surface with mouth wide open to form a very wide "net" for capturing the plankton. Water passes into the mouth and across the specialized gill rakers, which strain out the plankton before the water

## FIELD NOTES

- Western and eastern Atlantic, western Indian Ocean, western and eastern Pacific
- 33' (10 m)
- Possibly dangerous when attacked
- Seasonal, according to region; during the day
- Common in some regions, but depleted in others

emerges through the gill slits. This feeding posture is in distinct contrast to the long but narrow mouth opening of a feeding whale shark.

Basking sharks are highly migratory, appearing seasonally in specific locations and supporting regional commercial fisheries—they are taken for their flesh and large liver.

Populations of basking sharks are often segregated by sex and size. Very little is known about their reproduction, but females reach maturity at about 13–16½' (4–5 m) long, and are thought to bear live young.

*A feeding basking shark reveals its gill arches, which strain plankton from the water passing over them.*

157

# Great White Shark

Carcharodon carcharias

**FIELD NOTES**

■ Worldwide, along continental margins of all temperate seas and entering tropics

■ Largest said to be 21¼' (6.6 m) and 7,300 lb (3,285 kg)

■ Dangerous

■ Africa: Dec–Feb; Australia: Jan–May; Mexico: Aug–Sept

■ Nowhere abundant; protected in South Africa, Australia, Maldives, and California, USA

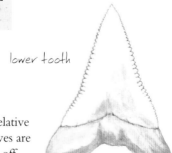

upper tooth

lower tooth

Also called the white shark, the white pointer, white death, and more, this is the largest flesh-eating shark. Star of film and literature, it strikes terror in many people, but little is known of its biology and behavior.

The great white shark is a robust, torpedo-shaped, conical-snouted species with a normal assortment of dorsal, anal, and paired fins. Unlike most sharks, but like other mackerel sharks, the upper and lower lobes of its tail are almost equal in size. This indicates that it swims constantly (because it must swim to breathe) and sometimes rapidly.

The great white differs from its relatives in having nearly symmetrical triangular teeth with serrated edges. It is also huge. It prefers shallow, cool, coastal oceanic waters, but is occasionally seen as close to the equator as Hawaii, USA. During the day, adults search for the seals and sea lions that are an important part of their diet.

Great white sharks are responsible for the majority of unprovoked attacks on people in cool waters and they can kill humans. However, the number of attacks is usually fewer than 10 a year. By diving inside a steel cage, it is possible to see them in relative safety. Dives are organized off Baja California, Mexico, southern Australia (see pp. 264–5), and South Africa (see pp. 250–1).

Females give birth to seven to nine live pups per litter, and are thought to produce only four to six litters in a lifetime. The young do not mature until about 10 to 12 years old, so the species is extremely vulnerable to overfishing.

# Shortfin Mako Shark

Isurus oxyrinchus

The shortfin mako shark is also called the bonito or mako shark. It is the most spindle-shaped shark of the mackerel family, with a long, conical snout, short pectoral fins, and a crescent-shaped caudal fin. Its back is indigo blue, and the belly white. Its teeth are visible even when its mouth is closed—long, slender, smooth-edged daggers. The less common longfin mako (*Isurus paucus*) has longer pectoral fins and a blunter snout.

The shortfin mako, the shark featured in Ernest Hemingway's novel *The Old Man and the Sea*, is well known as a sport fish, capable of spectacular leaps 20' (6 m) in the air when

**FIELD NOTES**

- Worldwide
- To 13' (3.95 m)
- Potentially dangerous
- During the day, year-round
- Not uncommon; however, reduced by developing fisheries

hooked and of achieving bursts of speed of more than 22 mph (35 km/h). It uses its speed to capture oceanic fish and squid. Large makos also catch billfish and cetaceans. One is known to have traveled 1,322 miles (2,128 km) in 37 days, an average of 36 miles (58 km) a day.

Shortfin makos live offshore in tropical and temperate waters, from the surface down to 490' (150 m). They are rarely encountered, but may be seen by open-water divers. They are dangerous and have attacked humans. However, attacks on fishing boats, when an angry mako leaps into a boat after being caught on the end of a fishing line, are more likely to occur.

Shortfin makos are viviparous, but lack a placental connection. Litters of 4 to 16 pups are common. Older embryos eat some of the eggs and smaller embryos while still in the uterus.

*The very obvious teeth of the shortfin mako shark.*

# Salmon Shark

*Lamna ditropis*

The salmon shark shares its generic name, *Lamna*, with the porbeagle (opposite). To the ancient Greeks, "Lamna" signified "a horrible monster of man-eating tendencies," and it was invoked to scare naughty children. The salmon shark and porbeagle are so similar that they were not recognized as two separate species until 1947. Generally speaking, if it lives in the North Pacific, it is a salmon shark; if in the Atlantic, it is a porbeagle.

The salmon shark shares the frightening appearance of all the mackerel sharks. However, it differs from the great white shark (see p. 158) in having smooth rather than serrated teeth, and from the mako sharks (see p. 159) in having a blue-gray rather than an indigo back. The feature that is found only in the salmon shark and the porbeagle is the secondary keel along the base of the tail.

Salmon sharks are heavy, torpedo-shaped predators. They have large, sharp, pointed teeth, and are well designed for chasing and capturing such fast-swimming oceanic prey as salmon and mackerel. Unlike most other mackerel sharks, they form schools of 20 to 30 individuals when feeding. They are not a threat to humans,

**FIELD NOTES**

■ Subarctic waters of North Pacific, from Alaska to California, USA, and from the Bering Sea to Japan

■ To 10' (3 m)

■ Potentially dangerous

■ Not seen by divers

■ Abundant within center of range

upper and lower teeth

mainly because they are not encountered by humans: salmon sharks inhabit the more frigid waters of the North Pacific, from the surface to depths of 500' (155 m), and they rarely come close to shore. They will consume the catch in fishing nets and sometimes become entangled in nets and lines.

Salmon sharks are viviparous, without a placental connection. As in related species, the embryos consume eggs and smaller embryos in the uterus. There are typically two to four young in each litter. They are born when they are about 26–28" (65–70 cm) in length.

# Porbeagle

Lamna nasus

T he porbeagle and its North Pacific relative, the salmon shark (opposite), are the smallest of the five mackerel sharks. They are still an impressive sight at 350–500 lb (158–225 kg). The porbeagle's stout body is dark blue-gray to brown dorsally and white underneath. It has a patch of white on the trailing edge of the first dorsal fin. The porbeagle and salmon shark are the only sharks with a secondary keel at the base of their crescent-shaped tails. This efficiently cuts the water in its side-to-side swimming movement.

This fast-swimming shark inhabits the continental shelves in cold waters, down to depths of 1,210' (370 m). With its sharp, slender teeth, it feeds on mackerel and squid when it ventures into open waters, and also on cod, hake, flounder, and other bottom-dwelling fish. Like all mackerel sharks, but unlike most sharks that live on the bottom, the porbeagle must swim continuously in order to breathe.

It reproduces viviparously, without a placental connection. As with other mackerel sharks, the older embryos feed on some of the eggs and smaller embryos in the uterus.

The mackerel sharks are unique among sharks for their heat-exchanging circulatory system, which makes them, functionally, warm-blooded. They can capture the heat generated by their swimming muscles and, through a complicated arrangement of microscopic arteries and veins, use it to heat the blood. This blood is directed throughout their body, to the muscles, internal organs, and brain. As a result, their body temperature is higher than that of the surrounding water.

This gives them increased muscle strength and allows more rapid nervous-system activity. The porbeagle has achieved the greatest body temperature elevation. Its body can be 20° F (11° C) warmer than the frigid North Atlantic Ocean that it inhabits.

**FIELD NOTES**

▪ Cold waters of North Atlantic, South Atlantic, and South Pacific

▪ To 12' (3.7 m)

▪ Potentially dangerous

▪ Not seen by divers

▪ Common

tail with double keel

# Coral Catshark

Atelomycterus marmoratus

The coral catshark is a rather small species with a striking body coloration of white spots on a dark background grading to a white underbelly. The dorsal fins, almost equal in size, have white spots on their tips. The tail fin is short.

Unique features include the short caudal fin, the long labial furrows at the corners of the mouth, and nasal flaps that extend to the front of the mouth. The eyes are set in front of large spiracles, which are used to move water into the gill chambers when

**FIELD NOTES**
- Indo-West Pacific, from Pakistan to Papua New Guinea
- 2' (60 cm)
- Harmless
- Seen mostly at night, almost year-round
- Common

the shark is at rest or feeding.

The Australian marbled catshark (*Atelomycterus macleayi*), which occurs in northern Australia, is similar in appearance to the coral catshark, but can be distinguished by the gray saddle-like markings along its back and small black spots over most of its body. With more than 100 species, the catshark family is the largest of the shark families. The name comes from the cat-like shape and color of the eyes.

Adult coral catsharks are commonly seen on shallow reefs in temperate and tropical waters. They live among coral branches and in the holes and tight crevices of the reef. With their very slender and flexible bodies, they can also be found swimming with sinuous movements near the bottom. They are more active during the night, when they feed on benthic invertebrates and small fishes.

Females reach sexual maturity when about 20" (50 cm) long. They lay purse-shaped egg cases, usually two at a time, with tendrils to anchor the cases to the bottom. The pups, about 4" (10 cm) long at birth, are rarely encountered. They probably spend their time sequestered within the reef, out of the way of predators.

**162**  *A coral catshark swimming over a reef in the Philippines.*

# Swellshark

### Cephaloscyllium ventriosum

The swellshark cannot be mistaken for any other shark. It has a broadly rounded snout and small dorsal fins on the rear half of the body, and is covered in large, spiky denticles. The patterning of dark brown blotches and saddle-like patterns on the yellow to brown background of its back, along with small dark spots on its belly and flanks, provides good camouflage for this sedentary shark. It has a wide, grinning maw laden with small, pointy teeth—very effective for capturing fish that carelessly swim by without noticing it.

Divers, too, frequently overlook swellsharks because of their camouflage. You will see them from 30' (10 m) to more than 200' (60 m) if you look carefully in caves and among shallow rocks and crevices around kelp forests. They are not

> **FIELD NOTES**
> - Temperate eastern Pacific, from central California, USA, to southern Mexico, and central Chile
> - To 3⅓' (1 m)
> - Harmless unless handled or provoked
> - Active at night, secretive during the day
> - Not uncommon

*A small swellshark pup emerging from its purse-shaped egg case.*

dangerous unless handled and provoked. Swellsharks swallow water when distressed. They balloon themselves up in this way when positioned in a rock crevice or other narrow hiding place, until they are wedged tightly inside and are safe from potential predators.

The female swellshark lays large, greenish amber eggs among seaweeds. These purse-shaped eggs hatch after 7 to 10 months, depending on the temperature of the water. The young are about 6" (15 cm) long. The unhatched juveniles use their enlarged dermal denticles to pry themselves free of the egg case.

163

# Striped Catshark

*Poroderma africanum*

The striped catshark is easily recognized by its pattern of solid horizontal stripes. Like the other two species that belong to the genus *Poroderma*, it has a stout, well-tapered body and a relatively short tail fin, and it lives off southern Africa. It also has barbels on the middle fold of the nasal flap, which extend back toward the front of the mouth. These barbels are short and usually end before the mouth. In contrast, the barbeled catshark (*Poroderma marleyi*) has relatively long nasal barbels; its body is covered with large, solid black spots. The leopard catshark (*Poroderma pantherinum*) also has longish barbels. It has a pattern of broken rings and small dark spots across its body.

The striped catshark inhabits temperate coastal waters, and is common on shallow inshore rocky reefs as well as in deeper waters to about 330' (100 m). This fish will hide in caves or rest in reef crevices during the day. At night, when it is most active, divers will see it moving about the bottom in search of food. Its diet is

**FIELD NOTES**

■ Eastern South Atlantic, western Indian Ocean off South Africa; possibly Madagascar and Mauritius

■ 3⅓' (1 m)

■ Harmless

■ Commonly seen at night

■ Common

quite varied and includes small bottom-dwelling crustaceans, such as shrimp and crabs, small bony fishes, cephalopods, and mollusks.

Females reach sexual maturity when about 27" (70 cm) long. During the mating season, they lay two tendril-bearing egg cases every few days. The young emerge after five to six months and are about 6" (15 cm) long.

*The tendrils on the egg case of the striped catshark anchor it to the reef or the bottom or, as here, to a convenient piece of kelp.*

# Smallspotted Catshark

Scyliorhinus canicula

The smallspotted catshark has a long, slender body and relatively short tail. Its head is slightly flattened and has large nasal flaps that project back to the edge of the mouth. There are neither labial furrows at the side of its mouth, nor barbels at its nostrils. The catshark's body is covered with small, usually dark, spots. Some sharks have an additional eight to nine dark, saddle-like shapes or blotches along their back. These markings are highly variable among individuals and in different locations.

This bottom-dwelling shark inhabits temperate waters. During the day, it can be found resting in open or sheltered areas on rocky reefs, sandy bays, and muddy bottoms. It also inhabits continental shelves in waters as deep as 330' (100 m). Like most catsharks, it is active at night, and divers may see it feeding on a wide variety of small fishes, mollusks, and crustaceans such as shrimp, crab, and lobster. Catsharks employ a quick biting

**FIELD NOTES**

■ Eastern North Atlantic

■ 2–3⅓' (60–100 cm); considerably smaller in the Mediterranean

■ Harmless

■ Day and night, almost year-round

■ Abundant

action that sucks water into the mouth along with prey items.

Aggregations of females are found inshore during winter, where they are joined by males in spring. In late summer, the adult population migrates to deeper offshore waters to mate. The male bites the female during courtship, then coils around her to transfer sperm. Females move into shallow water to deposit their egg cases with tendrils for attaching among the rocky reefs or algal patches. After about nine months, the young emerge, measuring about 3½" (9 cm).

This species is commercially important in Europe for meat, fishmeal, and oil.

*The slightly flattened head of the bottom-dwelling smallspotted catshark.*

# Soupfin Shark

*Galeorhinus galeus*

The soupfin shark is also known as the school shark or tope. It is a moderately slender shark, bronzy gray on the upper side and pale underneath. It has an unusually large subterminal lobe on the caudal fin. The small second dorsal fin is about the same size as the anal fin.

The soupfin shark is usually found on continental shelves and continental slopes in temperate waters. It feeds mainly on fish, squid, and octopus near the seabed or in the water column. Often preferring to congregate in schools, it lives to be more than 50 years old.

Although considered harmless, it is a very shy creature and encounters are unlikely. It will flee long before a diver arrives in its vicinity. Large numbers of new-born pups are sometimes caught inshore by anglers.

**FIELD NOTES**

- Widespread: west coast of North America, east coast of South America, northeast Atlantic, South Africa, southern Australia, New Zealand
- Varies throughout the world, but up to 6½' (2 m)
- Not encountered by divers
- Abundant

This species migrates long distances so pregnant females can give birth in cooler waters. Sharks tagged in England and Ireland have traveled to Iceland (1,530 miles [2,460 km]) and the Canary Islands (1,570 miles [2,525 km]). Sharks from the Californian region have been recaptured off British Columbia (1,000 miles [1,610 km]).

The soupfin shark is ovoviviparous. Litter sizes vary—a litter of 52 pups is the largest known. After a gestation of 12 months, the pups are born, 12–14" (30–35 cm) in length. Discrete, inshore nursery areas have been found in Australia, Argentina, and South Africa. Female sharks reach maturity at 8 to 10 years and breed only every second or third year. This low reproductive rate, combined with the soupfin's longevity, has made it vulnerable to overfishing for its meat, fins, and liver oil.

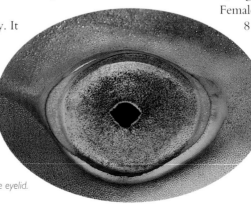

*Close-up of the eye of the soupfin shark, showing the free eyelid.*

# Gummy Shark

Mustelus antarcticus

The gummy shark takes its name from its teeth. They are flat, and arranged in a pavement-like pattern, ideal for crushing rather than cutting its prey. This includes a wide variety of octopus, squid, crustaceans, and fish found on the sandy and rocky bottoms where it dwells.

The gummy is a slender, bronzy gray shark with numerous white spots and sometimes black spots on its back and sides. A thin ridge runs along its back.

The dusky smoothhound (*Mustelus canis*) of the western Atlantic is another of the 20 or so species of the genus *Mustelus*. It is a slender shark, uniformly gray in color, and similar in biology and diet to the gummy shark.

Both species occur mainly in temperate waters on the continental shelf from the shore down. Some also dwell on the continental slope: the gummy shark to depths of 1,150' (350 m), the dusky smoothhound to 1,900' (580 m). They are abundant, and divers will often see them lying on the seabed in shallow coastal waters. Since they are harmless, they can be approached quite safely.

Tagging has shown that a small number of female gummy sharks make long migrations

**FIELD NOTES**
- Southern Australia
- Females to 5¾' (1.77 m); males to 4¾' (1.45 m)
- Harmless
- During the day, year-round
- Abundant

across the ocean off southern Australia—the longest known journey is about 1,140 miles (1,840 km). Most travel only relatively short distances.

The gummy shark is ovoviviparous. After a gestation of about 12 months, pups 12–14½" (30–36 cm) long are born in coastal areas. There are between 1 and 38 pups in a litter, with 15 being the average. They live for about 16 years. In the past there was concern about declining stocks, but these days they are fished sustainably—for their meat, which is popularly known as "flake."

teeth of the lower jaw

167

# Leopard Shark

### Triakis semifasciata

Leopard sharks are regular and conspicuous inhabitants of most bays along the coast of northern California, USA.

They have attractive and elongated bodies, with a series of black spots and saddle-shaped markings on a generally gray background. This makes them popular occupants of public aquariums. They possess all the fins typical of a modern shark, but they do not need to swim in order to breathe. In fact, they are usually quite sluggish. They have small, pointed teeth, which they use to capture a wide variety of food,

**FIELD NOTES**

■ Pacific coast from Oregon, USA, to Baja California, Mexico

■ To 6' (1.8 m)

■ Harmless

■ Usually seen during the day, year-round

■ Once extremely abundant, now becoming uncommon in places because of intensive sport and commercial fishing

including fish, fish eggs, shrimp, crabs, and clams.

Each year, leopard sharks migrate from the inner bays to the outer coast of the temperate Pacific Northwest. Divers and kayakers will see them there, above the sandy or muddy bottoms of bays and along the outer coast. They are harmless, but because they are social and travel in schools, they are often caught in large numbers.

At maturity, males are smaller than females, but they ultimately grow to be slightly larger. Females produce up to 24 young every spring.

*The striking markings (left) of the leopard shark; and its impressive array of small, pointed teeth (below).*

# Silvertip Shark

Carcharhinus albimarginatus

Silvertips are fairly large and slender sharks, dark gray in color. Their common name is derived from the distinctive white tips and margins on all their fins. The pectoral fins are narrow and pointed, and the first dorsal fin is narrowly rounded. Apart from these features, they look like many of the other gray requiem sharks that are commonly found out beyond the reef edge in warm tropical waters.

The teeth of silvertips are similar to those of other species that belong to the genus *Carcharhinus*. They are strongly serrated and narrowly pointed in the lower jaw, and sharp, serrated, and oblique in the upper jaw. They are ideal for catching and cutting the fish that they feed upon, such as reef wrasses and, in open water, tuna and flyingfish.

These sharks prefer offshore islands, coral reefs, and banks. However, they also enter lagoons, and it is here that you will encounter them often. Given their size and their aggressive behavior, you should always treat them with caution and respect. They have been known to harass divers, but reports of them actually attacking people are rare.

**FIELD NOTES**

- Widespread in tropics from East Africa to Panama; not in the Atlantic
- 10' (3 m)
- Aggressive, but not a significant risk
- During the day, year-round
- Common

*dorsal fin*

Silvertip sharks are viviparous; females usually have 5 or 6 pups to a litter, but there can be as many as 11. The young hatch after 12 months.

Experiments conducted using underwater sound have shown that silvertips are attracted to low-frequency sounds, probably because these frequencies mimic the sound made by an injured fish, potentially an easy meal.

169

# Gray Reef Shark

Carcharhinus amblyrhynchos

The gray reef shark, or longnose blacktail shark, is similar in shape and general appearance to the silvertip shark (see p. 169), although usually smaller. It has a black edge on its tail. Some specimens have a narrow white edging on the first dorsal fin, but they lack the bold white-edged margins of the silvertip's tail and pectoral fins.

The teeth of the gray reef shark are triangular with fine serrations. It feeds on small reef fish. It is one of the most common sharks on Indo-Pacific coral reefs, and is seen in the reef passes. An inquisitive animal, it is attracted to the low-frequency underwater sounds and commotion caused by a speared fish—there are many stories of a gray reef shark taking a fish off the end of an unsuspecting spearfisher's spear.

If you startle one or get too close, it will perform a contorted threat posture. This includes wagging its head from side to side, sweeping its tail, depressing its pectoral fins, and arching its back. That should be ample warning to any diver—such behavior often precedes an attack. Sharks have severely bitten and injured divers, to threaten them, not to eat them.

**FIELD NOTES**
- Central Pacific to Madagascar
- To 8' (2.5 m); rarely larger than 6' (1.8 m)
- Has attacked if threatened
- During the day, year-round
- Common

The gray reef shark is viviparous. Female sharks give birth to up to six pups after a year's gestation. Pups are about 20–24" (50–60 cm) at birth and reach maturity after about seven years, when they are about 4¼' (1.3 m) long.

tail with black edge

The scars on the female gray reef shark at right are mementos of encounters with males during mating.

# Bronze Whaler

*Carcharhinus brachyurus*

**FIELD NOTES**

- Southwest and eastern Atlantic, eastern Pacific, western Indian Ocean
- Up to 10' (3 m)
- Considered dangerous
- Seasonal in higher latitudes; during the day
- Very common

The bronze whaler, also known as the copper shark, gets both common names from its brownish red, sometimes grayish red, coloring, which shades to white on the underside. It has a short band of pale pigmentation, like a white stripe, that extends down the side of the body almost to the pelvic fins. Apart from darkened tips on the pectoral fins of some individuals, there are no noticeable markings on the relatively slender body. The narrow snout is rounded at the tip. The upper lobe of its tail fin is broad and used for its powerful swimming motion. While the first dorsal fin is large, the second is far smaller.

The bronze whaler is found in most warm temperate and subtropical waters of the world, except along the eastern coastline of North America and the northern Indian Ocean. It is usually seen close inshore along rocky reefs and shallow bays, as well as in the deeper waters of continental shelves and around islands. This species is considered dangerous when excited by the smell of food, and while searching for food, is known to attack swimmers and bathers, probably attracted by their splashing.

Like many other requiem sharks, some populations of bronze whalers are known to make spring and summer migrations to waters in higher latitudes, probably to follow prey. Their diet consists of a wide variety of fishes, such as anchovies, sardines, mullet, hake, and jacks. They also feed on small elasmobranchs, such as spiny dogfish, sawfish, stingrays, and electric rays. Sea snakes and squid are also sometimes taken. Their teeth are pointed with many small serrations; those of the upper jaw have a rounded leading edge.

Little is known about the biology of the bronze whaler. Females are mature when about 8' (2.4 m) long. They produce between 13 and 20 young in each litter.

*The claspers are visible on this male bronze whaler.*

171

# Silky Shark

Carcharhinus falciformis

This large, slender shark gets its name from the smooth, silky texture of its skin. Its body is nearly black to gray above, with no distinctive markings, and whitish underneath. There is a narrow interdorsal ridge on the back. The second dorsal fin is much smaller than the first, and has a trailing tip. The pectoral fins are long and narrow. The smoothly rounded snout is long and the upper teeth are tall, serrated, and nearly triangular in shape, while the lower teeth have a tall, narrow cusp that is only very weakly serrated.

The silky shark is widely distributed in nearly all tropical and warm temperate waters of the world. It is occasionally seen in waters close to shore, but is more common in oceanic waters, especially near large landmasses. A major

**FIELD NOTES**
- Worldwide
- More than 10' (3 m)
- Potentially dangerous
- Year-round, usually during the day
- Common

pelagic species, it occurs at depths from 60' (18 m) to at least 1,640' (500 m). It is known to form schools segregated by sex—juveniles group in waters relatively close to shore, while adults gather farther out to sea. It is not often encountered by divers, and while it is not responsible for many attacks, it should be treated with respect.

This shark is a fast swimmer and is capable of quick, darting movements. Its diet includes many small fishes, such as mackerel, tuna, mullet, and sea cats, and also invertebrates such as pelagic crabs and squid.

Females reach sexual maturity when nearly 7½' (2.3 m) in length, and give birth to 6 to 14 young per litter. The pups are about 29–31" (75–80 cm) long at birth. These sharks are commercially fished for their fins, meat, and liver.

*A silky shark "flying" overhead in tropical Atlantic waters.*

172

# Galapagos Shark

Carcharhinus galapagensis

The Galapagos shark is a large, grayish requiem shark without any distinctive markings. It looks similar to the gray reef shark (see p. 170) and the silvertip shark (see p. 169), except that it lacks their conspicuous white or black coloration on its fins. Its most distinctive feature is a ridge between its dorsal fins, but you would be wise not to get close enough to be able to make it out.

The Galapagos shark is generally not a threat to divers, and prefers to avoid them. However, although it has never attacked a diver, it can be aggressive and divers should always be cautious. Like the gray reef shark, it performs a seemingly awkward threat display before attacking a potential competitor or predator. It has attacked and eaten swimmers.

The shark was named in 1905 after specimens found in the waters of the Galapagos Islands.

**FIELD NOTES**

- Cosmopolitan in tropical seas, generally near oceanic islands
- To 12' (3.6 m)
- Potentially dangerous
- During the day, year-round
- Not uncommon in Hawaii, USA, and off Galapagos Islands, Ecuador

It has since been found around most tropical oceanic islands, ranging from inshore to well offshore. It prefers clear water, and can be seen beyond the deep reef edge, either near the surface or swimming in groups near the bottom. It feeds primarily on bottom-dwelling fish, squid, and octopus.

There are 6 to 16 young in a litter. They are born alive and remain in nursery areas, where the water is shallower than the area inhabited by the adults of the group. This is a not uncommon adaptation of a number of shark species to avoid cannibalism.

*The long, rounded snouts and streamlined bodies of two Galapagos sharks.*

# Bull Shark

Carcharhinus leucas

This large, stout, and sluggish gray shark is widespread along continental coasts. It also enters rivers and lakes, and is therefore known by such names as the Lake Nicaragua shark and the Zambezi shark. It was also thought to be the rare Ganges shark, but this is now known to be a separate, distinct species.

The bull shark can tolerate highly salty sea water and fresh water—it has been recorded as far as 1,750 miles (2,800 km) up the Mississippi River and 2,500 miles (4,000 km) up the Amazon in Peru. It has ample opportunity to encounter, attack, and consume people. Because it has been confused with other similar-looking requiem sharks, it seems likely that it is responsible for even more attacks than those with which it is credited. This makes it more dangerous than the great white or tiger sharks.

In the Americas, it is usually found close to shore in estuaries and shallow marine habitats from just a few feet deep to 100' (30 m). The famous Matawan Creek incident of 1916, when sharks killed four people and injured one along the New Jersey shore over a 12-day period, was

**FIELD NOTES**

- All tropical and subtropical seas; also inland in fresh water
- To 11½' (3.5 m)
- Dangerous
- Not encountered by divers
- Common

probably the work of bull sharks. It will eat almost anything it can capture, including other sharks, rays, fishes, turtles, birds, dolphins, mollusks, crustaceans, and things that fall overboard, such as cattle, dogs, rats, and people.

The bull shark has a unique appearance. It has a very blunt, rounded snout; small eyes; a pointed first dorsal fin; and dusky fin tips. It is viviparous, and selects estuaries as pupping grounds for litters of 1 to 13 pups, which are born after almost a year's gestation.

Because they live close to shore and in rivers and lakes, bull sharks are vulnerable to fisheries.

*The bull shark's blunt, rounded snout is shorter than its mouth width.*

# Blacktip Shark

### Carcharhinus limbatus

The blacktip shark takes its name from the black markings on the tips of the dorsal and pectoral fins and the lower lobe of the tail fin. The spinner shark (*Carcharhinus brevipinna*) has similar markings and a similar range, so the two species can be confused. The blacktip is a much stouter shark, however, and its well-developed first dorsal fin begins at about the middle of the pectoral fin. The spinner shark's first dorsal fin begins much farther back.

The blacktip is a large gray or gray-brown shark, grading along the sides to a white underbelly and a white anal fin. A subtle white band usually runs along the side of the body. The snout is long and parabolic; the eyes are on the side of the head near the mouth's leading edge.

Blacktip sharks are found in all tropical and temperate waters of the world. They live at the surface above continental and island shelves, but will also frequent shallows along sand beaches, bays, and rocky coastlines in warmer months. They migrate along continental coasts in large schools, possibly for food or pupping.

Divers regularly see blacktips inshore. As long as there is no food stimulus present, they do not generally present a hazard. The blacktip's diet includes small schooling fishes such as sardines, anchovies, and menhaden, which the sharks feed on in the water column. On the seabed, they also eat bottom-dwelling fishes, crustaceans, and squid. They are often seen near shore jumping out of the water during feeding.

Females reach maturity at about 5' (1.5 m) and produce 4 to 8 pups per litter, about 10" (25 cm) long, after a gestation of 10 to 11 months. South African blacktip populations appear to segregate, with mainly adult males and non-pregnant females grouped together.

**FIELD NOTES**
- Western and eastern Atlantic, Indo-West, central, and eastern Pacific
- 9' (2.8 m)
- Harmless unless provoked or feeding
- Day or night; year-round in many areas, seasonal in others
- Common

*Two blacktip sharks in Bahaman waters.*

175

# Oceanic Whitetip Shark

### Carcharhinus longimanus

The oceanic whitetip shark should not be confused with the sluggish, slender, and small-finned whitetip reef shark (see p. 186). The oceanic whitetip's enlarged first dorsal fin and long, paddle-shaped pectoral fins are unmistakable. These fins have conspicuous, mottled white tips; the fins of juveniles may also have black markings.

The oceanic whitetip is a large and stocky gray species, usually found far offshore, from the surface to depths of at least 500' (150 m). It prefers the open ocean, and can sometimes be seen from boats or encountered by divers in open water. Although it is generally slow moving, it is dangerous because it has powerful jaws, large teeth, and it will not hesitate to approach swimmers or small boats. It is probably responsible for many of the open-ocean attacks on people after air or sea disasters. It is most abundant in the tropics, but can also be found from coastal California, USA, to southern Australia, following the warm water masses.

**FIELD NOTES**

- All tropical and subtropical waters
- To 13' (4 m)
- Potentially dangerous
- Day or night
- Once abundant, now reduced by overfishing

Oceanic whitetips eat just about anything that they can catch in the open sea, including a variety of fishes and squid, whale carcasses, turtles, sea birds, and garbage disposed of at sea. They are aggressive and will dominate other shark species that are competing for food.

The litter size increases with the size of the mother—as many as 15 live pups are born after a gestation period of about a year.

*mottled tail and fin tips*

# Blacktip Reef Shark

Carcharhinus melanopterus

Blacktip reef sharks are the most common sharks in the shallow lagoons and coral reefs of the tropical Pacific and Indian Oceans, along with whitetip reef sharks (see p. 186) and gray reef sharks (see p. 170). They are different from blacktip sharks (see p. 175), larger sharks with thin black tips on most fins that live mainly in the open ocean.

Blacktip reef sharks are easily recognized by the very distinct black marks on their fins, particularly the first dorsal and caudal fins. They also have a conspicuous white slash along their flanks. They are small to medium in size, with a short, blunt snout. Their teeth are narrow, sharp, and strongly serrated, designed for eating the reef fish that comprise their main food.

Divers and snorkelers commonly see these sharks patrolling in shallow waters from about 1' (30 cm) deep. Divers will find them in reef passes, while waders and snorkelers will see them in lagoons, their dorsal and caudal fins above the surface. On rare occasions, they have bitten waders on the legs and ankles,

**FIELD NOTES**

- Indo-Australian Pacific to central Pacific
- To 6' (1.8 m)
- Potentially dangerous to waders; otherwise, not aggressive
- During the day, year-round
- Common

probably attracted by the splashing commotion made by the waders. They will attack speared fish, and are curious, but not aggressive, around divers.

Blacktip reef sharks are viviparous, with the yolk sac being attached by a placenta. Litters number from two to four. The pups are born after a gestation period of about 16 months. They are 13–20" (33–50 cm) long at birth.

In recent years, blacktip reef sharks have entered the eastern Mediterranean via the Suez Canal. Because they are a small, hardy species, a number of them have been captured in the central Pacific, off Christmas Island, and sent to public aquariums worldwide.

*Black fin tips, particularly on the first dorsal and caudal fins, make this shark instantly recognizable.*

177

# Dusky Shark

Carcharhinus obscurus

The long, streamlined body of the dusky shark is brown-gray to gray above and white below. A faint pale stripe extends along the side of the body to the pelvic fins. In juveniles, the tip of the lower caudal fin and the undersides of the pectoral fins are notably dark or dusky, but this is indistinct in adults. The snout is relatively short and broad. The upper lobe of the caudal fin is well developed, indicating that this species is a strong swimmer. Its pectoral fins are long and curved on the trailing edge. Its second dorsal fin is much smaller than the first, and an interdorsal ridge is present.

Although divers occasionally see dusky sharks close inshore, this species occurs primarily above coastal shelves in offshore waters adjacent to the open ocean. It is widely distributed in warm temperate and tropical waters. While few attacks on humans are attributed to it, this is not a shark to seek

**FIELD NOTES**

- Western and eastern North Atlantic, western Indian Ocean, western and eastern Pacific
- To 13' (4 m); normally about 10' (3 m)
- Considered dangerous
- Day or night; seasonal in many regions
- Numbers dwindling in many areas

out. Like many other large requiem sharks, it migrates into higher latitudes during warm months and more central latitudes during winter. The migratory pattern near South Africa appears to be complex and is at least partly related to pupping and nursery grounds.

The dusky shark has a varied diet that includes small schooling fishes such as sardines and anchovies, larger, fast-moving tuna and mackerel, and bottom-dwelling flatfishes and eels. It is also a significant predator of dogfishes, catsharks, smoothhound sharks, rays, and skates.

Females reach sexual maturity at about 9' (2.8 m). They mate in spring, and give birth after a 16-month gestation to litters of about 10 young that are up to 3' (95 cm) long.

Numbers of this species in the western Atlantic have fallen because of overfishing.

*Dusky sharks patrolling off the coast of Australia.*

# Caribbean Reef Shark

Carcharhinus perezi

The Caribbean reef shark has a relatively stout body, gray or gray-brown above grading to white underneath. The first dorsal fin has a sharp point and a short, trailing tip. The pectoral fins are relatively long and narrow. It has an interdorsal ridge, and a blunt, rounded snout. The well-serrated upper teeth have broad bases and narrow cusps. The lower teeth also have broad bases and small serrations, but are narrow and straight. Such teeth are probably designed for a diet of

**FIELD NOTES**

■ Western Atlantic and Caribbean, from Florida, USA, and Bermuda to southern Brazil, including parts of the Gulf of Mexico

■ Up to 10' (3 m)

■ Potentially dangerous

■ Day and night, year-round

■ Abundant

bony reef fishes, small sharks and rays, and cephalopods.

Large numbers of these sharks occur on island reefs throughout the Caribbean Sea. It is a fast swimmer, but is known to rest in caves and under ledges during the day. It has been called the sleeping shark, although there is no evidence that it is actually asleep when resting.

Divers encounter Caribbean reef sharks in surface waters near shore, cruising over the bottom of coral reefs, or swimming along the reef drop-offs down to depths of 100' (30 m). In the Bahamas, it is possible to dive with them after they have been attracted to "shark feeds" (see pp. 240–1). While they are not particularly aggressive, they have been responsible for attacks on divers, especially in situations involving bait or spearfishing.

Very little is known about the Caribbean reef shark's biology. Females bear four to six pups per litter; these range from 2–2½' (60–75 cm) in length at birth. This shark is targeted by local fisheries for its meat, hide, liver oil, and for fishmeal.

*A Caribbean reef shark, with another reef shark behind.*

179

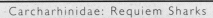

# Sandbar Shark

### Carcharhinus plumbeus

The most notable feature of this shark, also called the thickskin shark, is its strikingly tall first dorsal fin. It can be more than one-tenth of the length of this sizable shark, which usually reaches 6½' (2 m) and weighs 100 lb (45 kg), with some animals to 8' (2.4 m) and twice as heavy.

The broad head is flattened. The streamlined body is gray or brown above, while the belly is white and the dorsal and tail fins both have dusky upper edges. In this strong-swimming species, the upper lobe of the tail fin is well developed. There is a ridge between the first and the far smaller second dorsal fins.

With broad, serrated upper teeth to cut up prey, the sandbar shark eats many fishes, including menhaden, eels, flatfish, other sharks, goatfish, skates, octopus, squid, and crustaceans.

Sandbar sharks live in tropical and temperate waters around the globe. Large schools range over continental and island shelves, with the schools often being segregated by sex. They can be found behind the surf zone on sandy beaches or at depths as great as 1,310' (400 m). Sometimes, divers see them near sandy beaches or rocky reefs, but they are not particularly aggressive. They prefer to swim near the bottom, often in large bays and estuaries, but do not move into fresh water.

Off the Atlantic coast of north America, females reach maturity at about 16 years of age. Mating occurs from spring through early summer, and females carry the developing young for 9 to 12 months. They retreat to shallow nursery grounds to give birth to 8 to 12 young, depending on the size of the mother. Pups are about 8½" (22 cm) long at birth.

> **FIELD NOTES**
>
> ■ Western and eastern Atlantic, western Indian Ocean, western, eastern, and central Pacific
>
> ■ 6½–8' (2–2.4 m)
>
> ■ Not dangerous
>
> ■ Day and night; seasonally abundant in many coastal areas
>
> ■ Common, but declining in some regions because of overfishing

*The sandbar shark is heavily fished for its meat and fins.*

# Tiger Shark

Galeocerdo cuvier

This large, dangerous shark is to tropical waters what the great white shark (see p. 158) is to temperate waters. It is named for the dark stripes on its gray back, which are pronounced in juveniles (see above) but become pale or disappear in large adults. Its wide mouth, broad nose, barrel chest, and the slenderness at the base of its tail are distinctive. So, too, are its heavily serrated, cockscomb-shaped teeth. These, combined with its jaw strength, allow it to cut through the bodies of large sea turtles, as well as seals, sea lions, and cetaceans. It also has a liking for such spicy treats as venomous jellyfish, stingrays, and sea snakes. One of the few true shark scavengers, it has eaten cattle, pigs, donkeys, sheep, and humans that have fallen overboard.

Adult tiger sharks spend their days beyond the reef edge to depths of about 500' (150 m), except at

**FIELD NOTES**

- Worldwide in tropical waters
- To 18' (5.6 m); possibly to 24' (7.4 m)
- Dangerous
- Very rarely seen
- Not common

certain times of the year, when they also come inshore during the day. They are active at night, and enter shallow reefs and lagoons after dusk to feed. In certain areas, they migrate between island groups to take advantage of colonies of young birds learning to fly over water.

Generally, tiger sharks are sluggish, but they can move quickly when feeding, and should be treated carefully on the rare occasions they are sighted. If you see one while diving, calmly leave the water, keeping it in sight at all times.

The tiger shark is the only ovoviviparous requiem shark. It has between 10 and 82 pups after a year-long gestation. The young are 20–30" (50–75 cm) at birth. They mature after about 4 to 6 years, and live for about 12 years.

*The shark's powerful body makes it capable of bursts of speed.*

upper and lower teeth

181

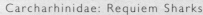

# Lemon Shark

Negaprion brevirostris

This large, stout-bodied reef shark has a pale yellow–brown body with no obvious markings and a broad, flattened head. It is easily identified by its large dorsal fins, which are about equal in size. The anal fin, immediately below the second dorsal fin, is also large. The pectoral fins are long and curve back on the trailing edge. There is no lateral keel, and unlike many requiem sharks, it has no interdorsal ridge.

The only other species in the genus is the sicklefin lemon shark (*Negaprion acutidens*), found in the Indo-Pacific. The trailing edges of its pectoral fins are more curved than the lemon shark's.

The lemon shark is abundant in tropical reef systems, especially those with sea grass and associated mangrove habitats. It has adapted to be highly tolerant of shallow waters

**FIELD NOTES**

■ Western Atlantic, from New Jersey, USA, to southern Brazil; the Caribbean; possibly the west coast of Africa; eastern Pacific from southern Baja California, Mexico, to Ecuador

■ 11' (3.4 m)

■ Harmless unless provoked

■ Day and night; year-round in tropical regions

■ Common

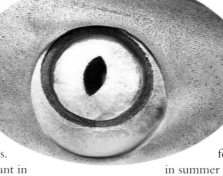

with low oxygen levels, such as warm–water mangrove swamps or bays, places where it is commonly observed. It has attacked humans, but is generally not considered aggressive, unless provoked.

Lemon sharks are active throughout the day and night. Among the Bimini Islands population, in the Bahamas, the level of activity seems to increase at dusk and dawn, possibly due to feeding. The diet consists of bony fishes, rays, crustaceans, guitar-fishes, and mollusks. Some populations probably undertake lengthy seasonal migrations in search of food, because they are found in summer along sandy beaches and continental shelves in waters of high latitudes.

Females reach maturity when they are about 8' (2.4 m) long, and mate in spring and summer. About one year later, 4 to 17 live young, about 2' (60 cm) in length, are born.

*The eye (above) of the lemon shark is an effective hunting tool.*

# Blue Shark

Prionace glauca

The blue shark, one of the most attractive sharks, is large and slender. Its upper body is indigo blue, the sides are bright blue, the belly markedly white. With its long, narrow, and pointed pectoral fins, long snout, and large eyes, it is unmistakable.

The blue shark is found in the open ocean throughout the tropics and into cooler seas. In the tropics, it often enters deeper, cooler water, while in temperate coastal waters it comes close to the edge of kelp beds, where divers may see it. It migrates regularly in the Atlantic, following the Gulf Stream to Europe, moving south along the African coast, then returning to the Caribbean.

Open-water divers may see these sharks, particularly if the sharks have been attracted by

**FIELD NOTES**

- Worldwide in open ocean
- To 12½' (3.8 m)
- Potentially dangerous
- During the day, year-round
- Previously very abundant, now reduced by heavy fishing

chum (berley). Dive operators offer tours using cages off southern California, USA (see p. 230–1), and elsewhere. Although attacks are unlikely, excited sharks have occasionally taken a nip at an unwary diver.

Blue sharks feed ravenously on large schools of squid, but are also very opportunistic and will decimate a floating whale or porpoise carcass. Fisheries consider them a menace because they attack nets and eat fish caught on lines. Once the most plentiful shark in the sea, they are now endangered through overfishing.

Although not yet observed, blue shark courtship is thought to be very lively. Males bite the females' shoulders; fortunately, their skin is three times as thick as that of the males. Females reach maturity when about five. They mate and store sperm for nearly a year, after which fertilization occurs. Litters of from 4 to 135 pups, depending on the size of the mother, are born alive the following year.

*A blue shark (left) feeds on a school of northern anchovies off the California coast.*

# Milk Shark

Rhizoprionodon acutus

O ne of the most common small requiem species in the western Pacific and Indian oceans is the milk shark, a brownish red to gray shark with a white underbelly. Like the other sharks in this genus, it has a long, slender body, a parabola-like snout when viewed from above, and relatively large eyes near the tip of the mouth. The first dorsal fin is much larger than the second dorsal fin. The pectoral fins are short and stout, and the pelvic fins are small.

Long labial folds at the corners of the mouth distinguish the milk shark from all other requiem sharks in its range. The similar gray sharpnose shark (*Rhizopriono-don oligolinx*) inhabits coastal areas from the west coast of Africa, east to New Guinea and north to Japan. The Australian sharpnose shark (*Rhizoprionodon taylori*) ranges across the northern half of Australia. Both of these closely related species have very short labial furrows at the edge of the mouth.

Milk sharks are found in large numbers in coastal areas and continental shelves to depths of

### FIELD NOTES

■ Eastern Atlantic, Indo-West Pacific

■ Up to 6' (1.8 m); smaller individuals about 3⅓' (1 m)

■ Harmless

■ Day and night, year-round

■ Common

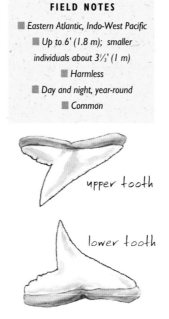

upper tooth

lower tooth

655' (200 m). They spend most of their time in small groups or large schools foraging for food near the bottom, where they may be encountered by divers. Their diet consists of small fishes (herring, sardines, croaker, mojarra, and flatfish) and invertebrates (squid, octopus, snails, shrimp, and crabs). They are a major food source for large sharks. With barrier nets removing large predator sharks from beaches in South Africa, swimmers and divers are seeing more milk sharks off beaches there. They are no threat to humans, being quite harmless.

Females reach sexual maturity when about two years old and about 2½' (75 cm) long. They produce litters of one to eight live young, about 10" (25 cm) long at birth, after about a year's gestation. This shark is commercially important as a food source in many parts of its range.

# Caribbean Sharpnose Shark

*Rhizoprionodon porosus*

The Caribbean sharpnose shark has a gray body that grades to white below. Like other *Rhizoprionodon* species, this small shark is slender, with a long, parabolic snout and relatively large eyes adjacent to the tip of the mouth. Its sides are sometimes scattered with white spots and the fins edged in white. The first dorsal fin is much larger than the second, and the pectoral and small pelvic fins are short.

Currently, there are thought to be six or seven species in the genus *Rhizoprionodon*. Although the taxonomic relationships among them are still under investigation, most species seem to have non-overlapping distributions in the tropical and subtropical latitudes of the world. The Caribbean sharpnose is similar to the Atlantic sharpnose shark (*Rhizoprionodon terraenovae*), which occurs in the Gulf of Mexico and also along the Atlantic coast of North America, but is

**FIELD NOTES**

- Western Atlantic and Caribbean islands, from Bahamas to Uruguay
- 3⅓' (1 m)
- Harmless
- Day or night; seasonal in some areas
- Usually common

distinguished from it by the number of vertebrae.

The Caribbean sharpnose is a common inhabitant of shallow inshore waters along continental and island shelves. It frequents sea-grass beds, coral reefs, and can tolerate the reduced salinity of estuaries. It is also collected at depths greater than 1,640' (500 m). Although common, this shy, harmless shark usually avoids contact with divers.

This species feeds on a variety of small fishes, and invertebrates such as snails and shrimp. It is a common prey for larger sharks. Gestation takes 10 to 11 months, with litters of 2 to 6 pups, about 1' (30 cm) in length, born in spring or early summer. This shark is taken for food and fishmeal by local and commercial fisheries.

*A sharpnose shark swimming in tropical Bahaman waters.*

# Whitetip Reef Shark

Triaenodon obesus

The whitetip reef shark should not be confused with the larger and more graceful oceanic whitetip shark (see p. 176). It is a sluggish, fairly slender, gray requiem shark with conspicuous white tips on its dorsal and caudal fins.

It has medium-sized, pointed teeth with smooth edges, which are flanked by small cusps. Unlike most requiem sharks, it is not an effective fish hunter in open water. It feeds mostly on the bottom, taking advantage of its tooth structure and its short, broad snout to pursue prey into reef crevices, where they cannot escape. Like most reef sharks, it too falls prey to other, larger sharks and large reef groupers.

Whitetip reef sharks live close to shore, at depths of 26–130' (8–40 m). During the day, divers and snorkelers predictably find them resting in caves, particularly in Hawaii and the Galapagos Islands, or under rock and coral ledges. They are active at night and during slack tides. They can become accustomed to the sounds of boats and to spearfishers, and are aroused by the presence of divers, approaching them out of curiosity. Although this is not an aggressive species, foolhardy divers have lost a hand when feeding members squid and fish.

Whitetips are viviparous and bear litters of one to five pups. They are born after a short gestation period of at least five months and are 20–24" (50–60 cm) long at birth.

The flesh and liver of whitetips are consumed by humans. It is unique among sharks in having caused ciguateratoxin poisoning, a type of food poisoning with severe gastrointestinal and neurological symptoms.

**FIELD NOTES**

- Red Sea, Indian Ocean, central Pacific, and tropical eastern Pacific
- Said to reach 7' (2.2 m), but rarely more than 5¼' (1.6 m)
- Potentially dangerous
- Year-round
- Common

*The whitetip reef shark uses its pointed, cusped teeth to grip and pull fish prey out of their hiding places in reef crevices.*

# Winghead Shark

Eusphyra blochii

The stout-bodied winghead shark is one of the smaller hammerhead sharks. The first dorsal fin is tall, and the second dorsal fin is set behind the anal fin. It is gray to brown above, grading to a white underside, with no conspicuous markings on the fins or body.

The winghead is easily identified by its broad wing-shaped head, the ultimate example of the cephalofoil, measuring about half the shark's total body length. The eyes are set far apart on the extremely broad head; this may have the effect of improving the shark's stereoscopic vision. The nares are located near the middle of the head, but the nasal grooves extend along almost its full width. These wide nasal grooves can sample a very large section of the water column, which may enhance the shark's ability to detect and locate odor sources. The electroreceptive ampullae of Lorenzini and

**FIELD NOTES**

- Indo-West Pacific
- Up to 5' (1.5 m); commonly reaching 3⅓' (1 m)
- Harmless
- Day or night, usually year-round
- Common

mechanoreceptive lateral line on the wings have an extended distribution across the head. This may be useful for detecting and localizing prey, such as crabs, shrimp, cephalopods, and small fishes, buried in the sediment.

This poorly studied species is widespread along the coast of southern Asia in the Indian Ocean, and around islands of the western Pacific. It is also common in shallow tropical waters on continental and island shelves. It is exploited commercially in Southeast Asia, but because the winghead population has a high natural mercury content, it is not generally marketed elsewhere.

Females reach sexual maturity when about 3⅓' (1 m) in length. They mate in spring and give birth to 6 to 20 young, about 13–18" (32–45 cm) long, after almost a year's gestation.

wing-shaped cephalofoil

187

# Scalloped Hammerhead

Sphyrna lewini

The scalloped hammerhead, also known as the kidney-headed shark, belongs to a family of eight sharks with a unique specialization—the front of the skull expands laterally like a hammer to form a head structure called a cephalofoil. This serves many biological functions. Its wide, flattened shape adds lift during swimming, improving hydrodynamic efficiency. The increased surface area allows for the expansion of many sensory systems important for feeding. The eyes and nares are at the tips of the head; the electroreceptors and lateral line are over a wider area. Thus these fast, active sharks can capture large or elusive prey.

**FIELD NOTES**

■ Western and eastern Atlantic, Indo-West, central, and eastern Pacific
■ 10–13' (3–4 m)
■ Not aggressive, but potentially dangerous
■ Day or night; year-round or seasonal, depending on region
■ The most abundant and widely distributed of the large hammerheads

Scalloped hammerheads can be distinguished by the broad leading edge on the head, which is arched toward the back. There is a prominent indentation in the center with two smaller lobes on either side, giving a scalloped look. These sharks are found in most warm temperate and tropical waters. They occur in coastal areas above continental and island shelves, and in adjacent offshore waters to depths of nearly 1,000' (300 m). They enter shallow bays and estuaries, and aggregate around seamounts. Here, divers see them interacting, chasing, thrusting, shaking their heads, and biting each other. This behavior needs further study, but may be for social reasons, migration to feeding areas, or reproduction. They are often indifferent to divers, but do make close passes.

Their diet consists of bony fishes and cephalopods. Females bear 15 to 30 pups, 17–22" (43–55 cm) long at birth.

*The unmistakable scalloped-looking head.*

# Great Hammerhead

Sphyrna mokarran

The great hammerhead is easily identified by its thick, broad head, which has an almost flat leading edge, except for an indentation in the center. It is a large, stout shark, gray-brown above, grading to a paler color below. The first dorsal fin is extremely high and pointed, with a curved rear margin. The base of the anal fin is much longer than that of the second dorsal fin.

This species is distributed in nearly all warm temperate and tropical waters. It occurs in coastal areas above continental and island shelves, and in adjacent offshore waters to depths of about 260' (80 m). Divers are likely to see it in shallow waters close to shore, especially near coral reef drop–offs and adjacent sand habitats. It makes long migrations to cooler waters during the summer months.

The great hammer–head has a very keen olfactory sense, and is

### FIELD NOTES

- Western and eastern North Atlantic, Indo-West and eastern Pacific
- Up to 11½' (3.5 m); individuals more than 20' (6 m) long have been reported
- Few attacks recorded, but considered dangerous
- Day and night, year-round
- Common

an impressive predator. Its diet consists of many mobile fishes associated with the water column, including sardines, herring, tarpon, and jacks, and benthic species such as grouper, sea cats, flatfish, and croaker. But this shark is best known for its preference for other elasmo-branchs, such as stingrays, skates, and other sharks. In its voracious and unique predatory behavior toward stingrays, the great hammerhead uses the side of its head to pin a fleeing ray to the bottom. It then rotates its head to the side and cleanly bites off a large chunk of the ray's wing. It continues to circle and feed on the incapaci-tated prey until it has been totally consumed.

*The very broad head allows for some unique feeding techniques.*

Females reach sexual maturity when about 10' (3 m) long. They usually produce 20 to 40 young per litter, and the pups are about 2¼' (70 cm) long at birth.

189

# Bonnethead Shark

*Sphyrna tiburo*

The bonnethead shark is a small hammerhead, and can be distinguished by its smooth, rounded, shovel-shaped head. Its body is plain gray-brown above, shading to a light color on the underside. The pectoral fins are short and straight along the rear margin. The anal fin is slightly concave but has no notch.

This shark frequents many different habitats within the temperate and tropical waters of its range. It is abundant in the surf zone, bays and estuaries, on coral and rocky reefs, and over sandy or muddy bottoms. It also inhabits waters of the continental shelf to depths of about 260' (80 m). Large schools migrate to warm latitudes in winter and to cooler latitudes during summer. Although harmless, it is timid and not easy to approach.

Bonnetheads have remarkable dentition, with small sharp teeth at the front of the jaw for grasping either its mate or a soft-bodied prey, and broad molar-like teeth at the back of the jaw for crushing hard-shelled invertebrates. It feeds

**FIELD NOTES**
- Western Atlantic, eastern Pacific
- About 3⅓' (1 m); individuals 5' (1.5 m) long are known
- Harmless
- Day or night; year-round in many areas
- Common

primarily on invertebrates, crabs, shrimp, mantis shrimp, bivalves, snails, and cephalopods, as well as small bony fishes.

The behavior of this species has been well studied. Individual sharks exhibit specific types of behavior toward other individuals, including patrolling, head-shaking, jaw-snapping, hitting, and hunching. The function of such behavior is to establish and maintain dominance hierarchies and other agonistic relationships.

Individual populations are sometimes segregated by sex. Females reach sexual maturity when about 2½' (75 cm) long. They retreat to shallow bays and estuaries to give birth, delivering litters of 8 to 16 pups about 14" (35 cm) long.

*The head of the bonnethead looks like a shovel.*

# Smooth Hammerhead

*Sphyrna zygaena*

The smooth hammerhead has a cephalofoil that is long and narrow, its leading margin shaped in a smooth arch without a notch in the middle. Its body is olive to gray-brown above, becoming light on the underside. The tips of the pectoral fins are dusky on the bottom. The first dorsal fin is high, with a slightly curved rear margin. The pectoral fins are short and straight along the rear margin, while the anal fin has a prominent notch.

The smooth hammerhead is found in nearly all warm temperate and tropical waters. And while its distribution overlaps that of the scalloped hammerhead (see p. 188) and great hammerhead (see p. 189), the smooth hammerhead is mostly concentrated in temperate waters. It seems to prefer shallow inshore waters less than 65'

### FIELD NOTES

- Western and eastern North Atlantic, western Indian Ocean, western, central, and eastern Pacific
- 8–13' (2.5–4 m)
- Possibly dangerous
- Day or night; year-round in many areas
- Common

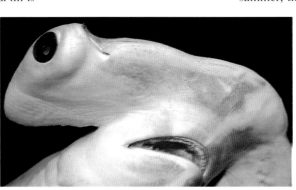

*The smoothly arched leading edge of the cephalofoil, or head, of a juvenile.*

(20 m) deep, and divers are especially likely to see it around rocky reefs. Divers need to take care, however, especially those who are spearfishing. It also occurs at the surface in the open ocean, and forms enormous schools to make long migrations to cooler latitudes during the summer, then returns to warmer waters for the winter months.

The smooth hammerhead feeds on small schooling bony fishes such as herring and menhaden, as well as porgies and sea bass from the reef, and stingrays, skates, and other small sharks. Large crustaceans and cephalopods round out the diet.

Females reach sexual maturity when about 7½' (2.3 m) long, giving birth to large numbers of live young, between 29 and 37 per litter. The pups are about 22" (55 cm) long at birth.

191

# SHARKS *of the* DEEP MIDWATERS

Below the euphotic zone, at depths of 650' (200 m), the sea is without the sun-driven photosynthesis that supports most life on Earth. Animals depend on dead and decaying plants and animals falling from above, or they venture to the surface to dine. Many small sharks from the dogfish family (Squalidae) ascend at dusk and return at dawn to the safety of the deep midwaters, relying on their large eyes and good vision in low light to detect prey. They also use their ventral bioluminescence to camouflage themselves from potential predators and prey.

## BLACKBELLY LANTERNSHARK
Etmopterus lucifer

This small, stocky shark has spines in front of each dorsal fin. Its dorsal side and flanks are brownish, the underbody black, and there is no anal fin. It has blade-like teeth and feeds on squid, lanternfish, and crustaceans. A variety of features distinguish blackbelly lanternsharks from the other lanternsharks. These include the arrangement and number of their denticles, and subtle differences in fin size and coloration. It is closely related to *Etmopterus perryi*, the dwarf dogshark, which is a mere 8" (20 cm) long, and probably the smallest living shark.

The blackbelly lanternshark, widespread on outer continental shelves, lives on or near the bottom at depths of 590–2,700' (180–835 m). Its mode of reproduction is presumed to be ovoviviparous, like that of most sharks.

The 17 or more species of lanternsharks have numerous minute, bio-luminescent (light-producing) photophores

### FIELD NOTES
■ Southern oceans, also the China Sea and off the Philippines
■ Males to 16" (40 cm); females to 13" (33 cm)
■ Harmless
■ Not encountered by divers
■ Not uncommon

along the underside of their bodies. The light from the photophores is a means of camouflage because it "counter-illuminates" the shark. The shark produces just enough weak light on the underside of its body to equal the amount of down-welling light between it and the ocean's surface. Because of this optical illusion, it merges with the ocean and cannot be seen by potential predators, nor by unsuspecting prey.

Lanternsharks produce their own light by mixing a luciferin-like substrate with a luciferase-like enzyme. This differs from the method many fishes use, which relies on a symbiotic relationship with certain bacteria.

## PYGMY SHARK
Euprotomicrus bispinatus

Although it is a member of the dogfish family, the pygmy shark lacks the spines that normally precede the dorsal fins of other dogfishes. Its dorsal fins are quite small and on the rear half of the body. It has a bulbous head and an underslung jaw. It is generally black, with contrasting pale fins.

Pygmy sharks live in the open ocean, usually in temperate and tropical waters. They probably spend their days in deep water and migrate after sunset to the surface, covering as much as 4,900' (1,520 m) in either direction. This has been compared to a person walking 7 miles (11 km) every day. They migrate to follow their food supply, the deep-water crustaceans, squids, and bony fishes that make this same journey to feed on surface plankton at night, when there is less risk of being seen.

Pygmy sharks have luminescent photophores on their underside. These help to camouflage the shark and perhaps help it to find a mate.

### FIELD NOTES
■ Oceanic, north and south of the Equator
■ Females to 10½" (27 cm); males to 8½" (22 cm)
■ Harmless
■ Not encountered by divers
■ Not uncommon

Pygmy sharks are ovoviviparous. They produce about eight young in a litter, and these are about 2½–4" (6–10 cm) long at birth.

## SPINY DOGFISH
Squalus acanthias

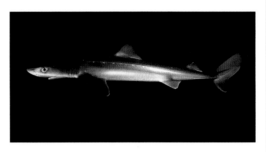

The spiny dogfish is also known as the piked dogfish or whitespotted spurdog. It is identified by a large spiracle behind each large eye, the presence of spines on the two dorsal fins, and the lack of an anal fin. It ranges from gray to brown in color, with small white spots above a light underside.

### FIELD NOTES
■ Temperate and cold waters of the Pacific and Atlantic Oceans, Mediterranean, Black Sea
■ Up to 4' (1.5 m)
■ Harmless
■ During spring and fall in temperate latitudes
■ Common, but stocks are nearly depleted in many areas

Spiny dogfish are cold-water sharks, preferring temperatures from 45–59° F (7–15° C). They are caught in waters down to about 2,600' (800 m) deep, but not exclusively in deep water. They form extremely large schools, routinely frequenting the shallow and coastal waters of higher latitudes in spring and fall, and migrating into deep waters during the cooler winter months.

The diet includes small fishes, such as cod, herring, menhaden, and haddock, as well as invertebrates such as krill, squid, scallops, and crustaceans. This species is extremely slow-growing and lives for up to 70 years. Females reach sexual maturity when 21 to 25 years old. They give birth to up to 20 live young, about 8–12" (20–30 cm) long, after a gestation of 18 to 24 months—the longest known for any of the elasmobranchs.

The spiny dogfish is of high commercial importance in many parts of the world. However, with its slow growth rate and low fecundity, it is very susceptible to overfishing, and has been overharvested in many regions.

# SHARKS *of the* DEEP BOTTOMS

S ome shark species live in the abyss, that portion of the ocean that is below the continental slope and covered by 13,000' (4 km) of sea water. This makes up two-thirds of the globe. For sharks such as some of the slow, lumbering sleeper sharks and gulper sharks, it is a cold place, usually 31° to 39° F (–0.6° to +4° C). It is almost completely dark, except for the light made by other animals. Pressure can be a thousand times that at the surface. Adaptation at such depths requires the ability to find and capture food, to avoid being eaten, and to find a mate—in the dark.

## GREENLAND SHARK
Somniosus microcephalus

The Greenland shark is also called the sleeper or gurry shark. This gigantic dogfish is the only polar shark of the Atlantic. It lives in deep water to 1,800' (550 m) at temperatures of

36 to 45° F (2 to 7° C), only coming up to shallow water during the colder months. At such temperatures, it will not be encountered by divers, although it may be caught by fishers. It is a sluggish beast, and provides little resistance when captured. Nevertheless, it should always be handled carefully.

There are four or five species of sleeper shark. All have a short and rounded snout, a caudal fin with a well-developed lower lobe, and two small, spineless dorsal fins; they lack an anal fin. They vary in color, some being mottled, while others, such as the Greenland shark, range from pinkish to brown, black, or purplish gray.

The teeth of the Greenland shark's upper jaw are long and pointed, very different from

### FIELD NOTES
◾ North Atlantic Ocean
◾ To 21' (6.5 m)
◾ Not encountered by divers
◾ Potentially harmful
◾ Not uncommon

those of its lower jaw, which are strongly oblique, sharp, and close set. These teeth allow it to gouge large chunks of flesh from dead cetaceans, and probably to remove the heads of seals and sea lions rapidly before dining on the carcasses. It also eats fish such as salmon, and a variety of bottom-dwelling fishes.

That this sluggish shark can capture such wily and fast-moving prey may be because of small copepods that attach themselves to the corneas of the shark's eyes. Brightly luminescent, these copepods are thought to attract curious and hungry prey, which soon end up in the shark's cavernous maw.

Little is known about the Greenland shark's reproductive behavior. It was recently discovered to be ovoviviparous, bearing about 10 pups, 15" (38 cm) long, in each litter.

## SPINED PYGMY SHARK
Squaliolus laticaudus

At 8" (20 cm) long, this deep-water dogfish rivals the dwarf dogfish (*Etmopterus perryi*) for the title of the world's smallest shark. At the moment, not enough specimens exist to make a final decision. The spined pygmy and its Australian relative, the smalleye pygmy shark (*Squaliolus aliae*), are unique in having a spine in front of the first dorsal fin but not the second. They are cigar-shaped, with a bulbous snout and a large spiracle behind the eye. Their upper jaw teeth are small and narrow; the lower teeth are larger and blade-like. Underneath, they have many luminous photophores, which serve to camouflage them from predators.

The spined pygmy dogfish lives in temperate and tropical waters, offshore near continental and island landmasses. Like other deep-water sharks, it makes a daily migration to feed. It ascends at dusk and feeds during the night on squid, shrimp, and midwater fishes, especially lanternfishes, then descends again at dawn.

### FIELD NOTES
- All oceans
- Females to 10" (25 cm); males to 9" (23 cm)
- Not encountered by divers
- Harmless
- Uncommon

Unlike other species, it stops within 650' (200 m) of the surface, before heading down to ocean depths as great as 6,560' (2,000 m).

Little is known about its reproductive biology, but it is likely to be ovoviviparous.

## PRICKLY DOGFISH
Oxynotus bruniensis

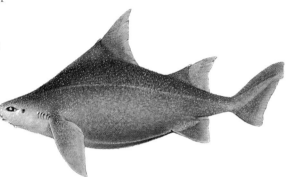

Among the most unusual looking sharks of the deep ocean bottom are the roughsharks (Oxynotidae). These small sharks have a stout body that is laterally compressed and bears a prominent ridge on the abdomen. Most notable are the high, spined dorsal fins with their forward extensions, which give the appearance of two sails. There is no anal fin. The head is slightly flattened, with large eyes, prominent spiracles, and small gill slits. The nostrils are placed relatively close together and the fleshy mouth is small and usually surrounded by labial furrows.

### FIELD NOTES
- Off southern Australia and New Zealand
- Up to 2⅓' (72 cm)
- Harmless
- Rarely seen
- Common

One of four roughshark species, the prickly dogfish is distinguished by its forward-pointing first dorsal spine and its skin, which is covered with rough, prickly denticles. The body is gray or brown with whitish margins on the tips of the dorsal fins and trailing margins on the pectoral and pelvic fins.

The prickly dogfish occurs in temperate waters, dwelling at depths of about 165–1,640' (50–500 m). Very little is known of its biology. The diet consists of benthic invertebrates, such as segmented worms.

About seven young hatch from eggs that are retained inside the mother. The pups are born live when about 4" (10 cm) long.

# TOOTHY MIDWATER HUNTERS

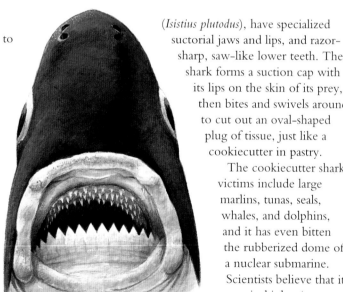

suction mouth
and teeth

The deep waters of the open ocean are home to many small predatory sharks. These sharks have developed special features and behaviors that enable them to prey on the many organisms that live in their habitat, and thus survive in the dim to dark waters of the world's oceans.

## COOKIECUTTER SHARK
Isistius brasiliensis

Before its feeding behavior was discovered, this species was known as the "cigar shark." It is a small, brown shark with a short snout. Its cigar-like appearance is enhanced by its small dorsal fins being displaced to the rear of its body and by the lack of an anal fin. It also has a black collar around the back of its head.

The cookiecutter shark and its close relative, the largetooth cookiecutter shark

(*Isistius plutodus*), have specialized suctorial jaws and lips, and razor-sharp, saw-like lower teeth. The shark forms a suction cap with its lips on the skin of its prey, then bites and swivels around to cut out an oval-shaped plug of tissue, just like a cookiecutter in pastry.

The cookiecutter shark's victims include large marlins, tunas, seals, whales, and dolphins, and it has even bitten the rubberized dome of a nuclear submarine. Scientists believe that it uses its bioluminescent light organs, which glow in the dark, to lure fast-swimming prey close, so that they can ambush them.

A tropical shark, it has been caught at the surface at

### FIELD NOTES
- Throughout the tropical oceans of the world
- To 20" (50 cm)
- Harmless
- Not seen by divers
- Probably not uncommon in deep oceanic waters

night, but it normally inhabits depths as great as 11,500' (3,570 m). It is ovoviviparous, but nothing is known about the size of its litters.

# CROCODILE SHARK
Pseudocarcharias kamoharai

also sometimes seen offshore. It is probably a fast-swimming predator that chases small prey, either near the surface at night or down to 1,000' (300 m) in the mesopelagic zone during the day. The shark has powerful jaws and long, thin, needle-like teeth, which

The crocodile shark, the only species of the family Pseudocarchariidae, is related to the sand tiger shark (see p. 152). Its muscular and highly streamlined body looks like a mini-torpedo. The first dorsal fin is about midway between the small pectoral and pelvic fins. The second dorsal fin is much smaller.

The body is dark brown above grading to lighter underneath, with dark blotches often scattered over the sides and bottom surfaces. The head is long, the snout conical, and the eyes large. The liver of this species contains squalene, a fine, low-density oil that increases the shark's buoyancy.

The crocodile shark is widespread through-out the open oceans of the world, from the surface to depths of about 1,970' (600 m). It is

*The characteristic wound inflicted by a cookiecutter shark shows clearly on the Pacific spotted dolphin at the top of this photo.*

are similar in shape to those found in the larger mako sharks (see p. 159). This combination of jaws and teeth is designed for the crocodile shark to grasp its small midwater prey, including shrimp, lanternfishes, and squid.

Although little is known about the shark's reproductive biology, there seem to be four young in each litter (two from each uterus). After exhausting their own yolk supply, the developing embryos apparently eat all but one sibling in each uterus. They continue to develop by feeding on eggs produced by the mother. It is unknown how or why two embryos coexist in this manner.

> **FIELD NOTES**
> ■ *Tropical oceans throughout the world*
> ■ *About 3⅓' (1 m)*
> ■ *Harmless*
> ■ *Near the surface at night, probably year-round*
> ■ *Common*

*graceful catshark*

# SOME UNFAMILIAR SHARKS

Sharks are members of marine bottom communities from the sunlit shallows of intertidal pools to the dark abyssal plains thousands of feet deep. While many of the species that live on or near the bottom belong to families that are familiar and well known, there are also species from smaller families about which little is understood. Among these are the finback catsharks, false catsharks, barbeled houndsharks, and weasel sharks.

## GRACEFUL CATSHARK
Proscyllium habereri

The graceful catshark is one of the finback catsharks (Proscylliidae), close relatives of the catshark family. Their first dorsal fin is above or in front of the pelvic fins, while in true catsharks, it is behind them. These small, bottom-dwelling sharks have slender, elongated bodies. The large, cat-like eyes have a nictitating membrane, usually reduced in size, and there is a prominent spiracle behind the eye, used for ventilation. The labial furrows in the corner of the mouth are small or absent, the teeth in the back of the mouth are comb-like, and there are no nasal barbels.

The graceful catshark is found above island and continental shelves in warm temperate and tropical waters at depths of between 165–330' (50–100 m). This species is distinguished by the pattern of dark spots that covers its fins and small body. The two spineless dorsal fins are of about equal size, with the second positioned above the anal fin.

The diet of the graceful catshark includes small bony fishes, crabs, and cephalopods. Little is known about this animal's biology, but the females are thought to lay eggs.

**FIELD NOTES**
- Western Atlantic, Indian Ocean, western Pacific
- About 26" (65 cm)
- Harmless
- Not often seen by divers
- Uncommon

## FALSE CATSHARK
Pseudotriakis microdon

The false catshark is thought to be the only species of the family Pseudotriakidae, which is closely related to the catshark family. Its body is long and slender, and its distinguishing feature is the long base and low height of the keel-like first dorsal fin. The eye is oval and cat-like, with the nictitating membrane reduced in size. There is a large spiracle. The jaw of the false catshark is large, and the back rows of its numerous rows of teeth are comb-like.

This is a deep-water shark that lives on shelf slopes from 660–4,920' (200–1,500 m). Its body is watery and soft, which may help to give it the neutral buoyancy that suits its somewhat sedentary lifestyle on or near the bottom. The false catshark probably feeds on deep-water fishes and invertebrates. Females are thought to reach sexual maturity when about 7¼' (2.2 m) long, and bear two to four live young.

**FIELD NOTES**
- North Atlantic, western Indian Ocean, central and western Pacific
- Up to about 9½' (2.9 m)
- Harmless
- Not seen by divers
- Common in certain areas

*false catshark*

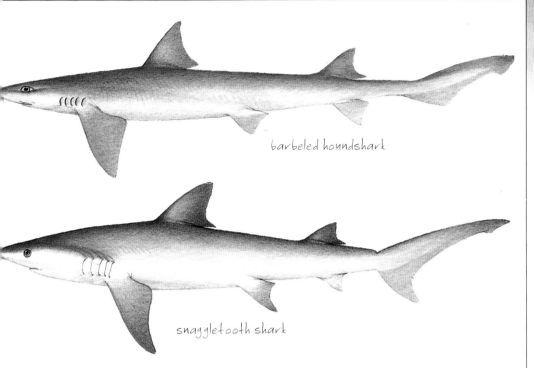

barbeled houndshark

snaggletooth shark

# BARBELED HOUNDSHARK
Leptocharias smithii

The barbeled houndshark is the only member of the unusual family Leptochariidae. While closely related to the requiem sharks and houndsharks, many of its characteristics are unique. It is a small species, with an elongated gray or brownish body. The first of two spineless dorsal fins is between the pectoral and pelvic fins, while the second is positioned above the anal fin. The head is small and the eyes are large and cat-like. The nasal flaps are modified into short, slender barbels. The corners of the mouth have long labial furrows, and the teeth of both jaws are small, with narrow cusps and cusplets.

The barbeled houndshark is usually found in coastal areas, both inshore in waters about 30' (10 m) deep, and also above the adjacent shelf at depths of about 245' (75 m). It prefers muddy bottom areas, especially near river mouths, where it feeds on crustaceans, small fishes, and cephalopods. It can be approached by divers.

Females mature when about 20" (50 cm) long. They have a gestation period of at least four months and give birth to litters of about seven live young, probably in October.

This shark is commercially fished by local fisheries for its meat and skin.

**FIELD NOTES**
- Eastern Atlantic coast of Africa
- Up to about 2¼' (84 cm)
- Harmless
- Day or night, most of the year
- Common

# SNAGGLETOOTH SHARK
Hemipristis elongatus

This shark takes its name from the long, conspicuous, serrated teeth that protrude from the lower jaw. It is the largest of the weasel sharks (Hemigaleidae), a family of small to medium groundsharks named for their weasel-like eyes. The snaggletooth shark is usually gray or brown, with undulations on the margins of its spineless dorsal fins. The first dorsal fin begins above the rear margin of the pectoral fins. The second dorsal fin is about two-thirds as high.

**FIELD NOTES**
- Eastern Atlantic, western Indian Ocean, western Pacific
- Up to 8' (2.4 m)
- Harmless
- Day or night, year-round
- Common

The teeth are designed for catching and consuming prey that includes a wide variety of bony fishes, such as anchovies, mackerel, and croakers, as well as other elasmobranchs, namely butterfly rays and small requiem sharks.

The snaggletooth shark is very common in some coastal areas of tropical seas. It frequents waters as shallow as 3⅓' (1 m) and continental and island shelves to depths of 100' (30 m). This is a large but harmless shark, commonly seen by divers close to shore.

Females reach sexual maturity when about 5½' (1.7 m) long. Up to eight embryos are nourished from a yolk sac placenta and born live. This species is fished in many parts of the world for its fins, meat, and liver.

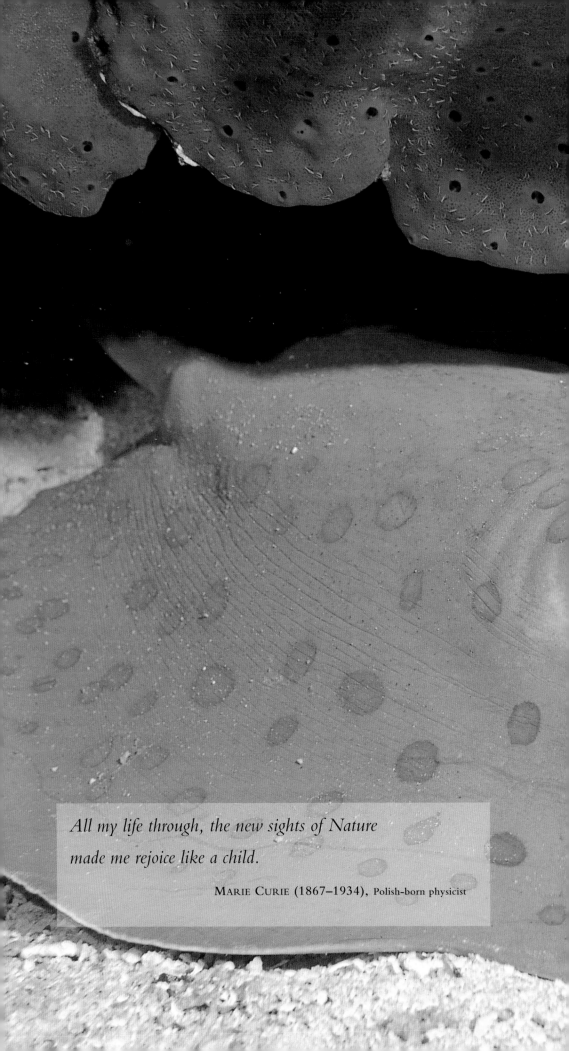

*All my life through, the new sights of Nature
made me rejoice like a child.*

MARIE CURIE (1867–1934), Polish-born physicist

# CHAPTER SEVEN

# RAYS FIELD GUIDE

# USING *the* RAYS GUIDE

*Get to know the rays in all their extraordinary shapes,*

*sizes, shades, and perfectly adapted behaviors.*

This field guide describes and illustrates just a few of the almost 500 species of ray that dwell in the world's oceans, estuaries, and rivers. At least one member of each family is featured here. Some rays are ubiquitous over tropical reefs, drop-offs, and sand flats, and can be curious about, even quite sociable with, snorkelers and divers. Many rays, however, never venture out of the cold, dark depths at the bottom of the ocean. Many more spend most of their days buried up to the eyes and spiracles in mud or sand. Given that they can be hard to find, the biology and behavior of most rays remain something of a mystery. But the next time you're wading in shallow water, watching where you're putting your feet, this guide will give you some insight into the rays you might encounter.

The **main photograph** shows as much of the species as possible, given the constraints of photographing such wild creatures in circumstances and conditions that can be difficult.

The **common** and **scientific names** of each species. The species are grouped according to taxonomy.

The **text** provides information on the appearance of the ray, its common names, habitat, and where and what to look for when you want to find it. It also gives ideas on how to differentiate between similar species, and supplies information, where known, about the ray's migratory habits and methods of reproduction.

Rajidae: Skates

## Rough Skate
Raja nasuta

**FIELD NOTES**

■ Southeastern Pacific off New Zealand

■ Reaches almost 3½' (1 m)

■ Harmless

■ Year-round; rarely seen by divers

■ Common

The rough skate belongs to a group of skates whose common ancestor lived around the shores of the ancient Gondwana supercontinent more than 80 million years ago. This is indicated by the distribution of the modern-day group of skates, which are all found on the continental shelves off New Zealand, Australia, and South America.

The rough skate has a diamond-shaped disc with a very long, pointed snout. Its slender tail has three rows of thorns along its length, while its back is covered with minute prickles. It is usually grayish or brownish, with white spots and darker marbling. It occurs on soft bottoms to about 490' (150 m), although divers will occasionally see one.

Few details are known of the rough skate's biology. It lays horny, rectangular egg cases, which it attaches to the bottom by fine,

*Port Davey skate*

thread-like tendrils. Eggs develop slowly and young after several months. Rece hatched skates can be ide by a belly scar where the sac was attached. Empty egg cases, "mermaid's are found wash beaches after sto A close relative rough skate is the re discovered Port Dave (*Raja* sp.). Of the mo skates in the world, t one that lives in brack is confined to two es the remote southwes off southern Australi stiff snout, more typ ocean skates. This is used for grubbing ar the fine silty bottom on which its restricted distribution, the h this skate left over from the pre likely to be very specific. Its p small, probably no more than individuals. This makes it pa to habitat degradation and o

212

**Color illustrations** supplement the text by showing basic features of the ray, or a related ray species.

This **illustrated banding** at the top of the page is a visual pointer to indicate that the page is about a ray species.

This **panel** refers to the family of rays that the species belongs to.

Platyrhinidae: Thornback Rays

Rhinobatidae: Guitarfishes

Urolophidae: Stingarees

# Thornback
Platyrhinoidis triseriata

**FIELD NOTES**
- Eastern Pacific from California, USA, to Mexico
- Almost 3' (90 cm)
- Harmless; be wary of sharp thorns
- Year-round
- Once plentiful off southern California

...'s take their ...e from the ...horny spines ...metimes ...r to ...arfish ...world. ...ps

...th and nostrils on the underside of the thornback.

around the eyes; the thornback's run along the back and tail.

The thornback lives in temperate and subtropical waters, mainly inshore on sandy and muddy bottoms. Divers occasionally see one around kelp beds, where its brownish upper surface blends well with the dark substrate. It rests in small groups for much of the day, remaining partly buried, with only its thorns protruding. These are sharp, and are probably used defensively against its main predators, small sharks. Although it is ... of ...are of ...the ... re

harmless, this ray should be treated with caution.

Little is known about the thornback's general biology. It is not a powerful swimmer and so it seems unlikely that it undertakes any long migrations. It seems to be more active at night, feeding on sand worms, sea shells, and small crustaceans, such as crabs and shrimps. Mating occurs at the end of summer.

207

# Round Stingray
Urobatis halleri

**FIELD NOTES**
- Eastern Pacific, from northern California to Panama
- Reaches 22" (56 cm)
- Not aggressive; the stinging spine can cause minor injury
- Year-round
- Very common

The round stingray, a member of the stingaree family, is plain brown with ...owish spots and reticulations. It ...a circular disc, the upper ...rface of which is smooth, ...ithout tubercles. The related ...ortez round stingray (*Urobatis maculatus*), from close by in Baja California and the Sea of Cortez, off Mexico, is similar in shape but has large black blotches over the disc. Stingarees can be mistaken for stingrays because of their similar body shape. However, stingarees have a shorter tail, which ends in a long, leaf-shaped caudal fin.

The round stingray lives mainly on muddy and sandy bottoms near the shore, to a depth of about 295' (90 m). In summer, it basks in warm shallow inlets, but remains in coastal waters during winter, only entering inlets to forage. It does not range far, rarely moving beyond an area of about a

*The underside of a juvenile round stingray.*

square mile. It seems sensitive to cold, and lives in water warmer than 50° F (10° C).

This ray feeds during the day on small bottom-dwelling crustaceans, bivalves, and sand worms. An efficient predator, it may use a combination of sight, smell, and vibration to detect prey. It uses its disc and mouth to "dig" for food in the substrate, and has also been seen nipping prey off sea-grass fronds. Divers may see a foraging ray in sheltered bays, or notice the outline of one buried in sediment.

Round stingrays mature early. The sexes segregate before the breeding season, and adult females live offshore until June, when they move in to coastal habitats to mate. Sexually aggressive males patrol the sandy strip between the deep sea-grass beds and the shore to select a suitable mate. He nibbles on her disc, then rolls beneath her and inserts a single clasper. Litters of one to six pups are born inshore in September, where they remain until maturity.

213

**Quick-reference Field Notes panel**
- Distribution range of the ray
- Size
- Possible risks when encountering the ray
- Best time of day or year to observe the species
- Information on population numbers

**Secondary photographs** show details of particular features or amplify some aspect of the ray's habitat or behavior. In some instances, photographs showing other members of the ray's family are included.

# Freshwater Sawfish

Pristis microdon

The sawfish family takes its name from its long, blade-like snout, edged with bony teeth, which resembles a crosscut saw. Sawfishes are easily confused with sawsharks (see p. 140) because they have a similar snout. However, the sawfish's gills are underneath its head rather than on the side, and it is much larger. Indeed, sawfishes are among the biggest fish in the sea.

Unlike most other rays, the sawfishes have a small disc and a shark-like tail. Most of them live inshore, in tropical seas. However, the freshwater sawfish usually inhabits tropical estuaries, rivers, and lakes. This slender, powerful sawfish is yellow to gray in color.

It is rare nowadays, so divers are unlikely to encounter it, and given that it is such a timid creature, it would probably flee at the first sign of a human. Anglers occasionally catch one on lines or in nets. It thrashes around wildly, and its saw teeth can cause serious injury. The saw is

**FIELD NOTES**

■ Tropical Indo-Pacific; possibly Africa and the Americas

■ Up to 21⅓' (6.6 m)

■ Sometimes aggressive in captivity

■ Rarely seen

■ Endangered

thought to be used offensively. The sawfish slashes it from side to side to stun the small fish upon which it feeds. Males also use their saws in battles during the breeding season.

The biology of the freshwater sawfish is not well known. Asian and Australian populations live almost exclusively in fresh water, but in Africa and the Americas, they also live in the sea. They are ovoviviparous. In Central America, they mate during summer in fresh water, where the pregnant females remain until they give birth five months later. Litters number up to 13, with pups being about 2½' (75 cm) at birth.

Sawfish populations have been seriously depleted this century through overfishing and degradation of their habitat. Many species are now rarely seen, and their plight is one of the major conservation issues of the sea.

snout from below

# Bowmouth Guitarfish

Rhina ancylostoma

This unmistakable creature resembles something from prehistory. It has horny ridges with large thorns above and behind the eyes; a broad, flattened head; and gills on the underside of its small disc. All this is typical of a ray, but its powerful body with large, angular fins, and a tail with a pronounced lower lobe, are more shark-like—hence one common name, "shark ray." It is bluish gray to brownish, with large white spots. The shape of its mouth is also distinctive, undulating like a longbow.

The bowmouth guitarfish lives near the coast and around offshore reefs in tropical waters,

**FIELD NOTES**

- Tropical Indo-Pacific, from East Africa to Australia and Japan
- Up to 9½' (2.9 m)
- Not aggressive
- Year-round
- Uncommon

down to about 295' (90 m). Scientists once thought it spent most of its time resting on the bottom, but its behavior in aquariums indicates that this ray swims actively for much of the day and night. Its tail is strong, and well adapted to prolonged swimming. It feeds mainly on crabs and large shellfishes by first restraining the prey against the sea bottom using its large head and pectoral fins. Then, with a series of short, sharp thrusts, it directs the prey into its mouth.

Divers sometimes find individual bowmouths resting near wrecks and coral bommies. They will not attack humans. They produce seven to nine live pups in each litter.

Trawl-net fishers occasionally take bowmouth guitarfish as bycatch. Along with the related whitespotted guitarfish (*Rhynchobatus djiddensis*), it is among the most sought-after elasmobranchs for shark fin soup. Consequently, there are concerns about overfishing.

*The bowmouth guitarfish is likely to avoid humans, and certainly will not attack.*

205

# Atlantic Guitarfish

Rhinobatos lentiginosus

Many of the 40 or so guitarfish species have a shovel-like head and a flattened, tapering tail. With a little imagination, their body shape resembles a guitar, hence their common name. The Atlantic guitarfish looks like some of the sharkfin guitarfishes in its general appearance. However, its dorsal fins are located closer to the tip of the tail (behind the pelvic fin tips), and the lower lobe of its caudal fin is much smaller than the upper lobe. It has a grayish to brownish upper surface with hundreds of small white spots. The adult Atlantic guitarfish differs from the related southern guitarfish (*Rhinobatos percellens*), which occurs from the Caribbean to Argentina, in having enlarged tubercles on the tip of its snout.

This is one of the smaller guitarfishes. It lives in warm temperate and tropical waters, mainly in the shallows from the intertidal zone to about 66' (20 m). Soft, sandy or muddy bottoms, or sea grasses, are its preferred habitats. It eats small, sand-dwelling mollusks and crustaceans, such as amphipods and small crabs. Some guitar-fishes are fussy feeders, selectively ingesting only the

**FIELD NOTES**

■ Northwestern Atlantic, from North Carolina, USA, to southern Mexico

■ Reaches 2½' (75 cm )

■ Harmless

■ Year-round; most common off Florida, USA

■ Reasonably common

nutritious parts of their prey. For example, they will crush clams in their mouth and spit out the shell and gritty bits.

The Atlantic guitarfish is most common off Florida. Swimmers and waders see it at low tide on urban beaches, swimming near the water's edge, its dorsal and caudal fins exposed and its snout probing the sand for food. In the Indo-Pacific region, juvenile plain grayish brown giant guitarfish (*Rhinobatos typus*) are also common inshore, as they search for food over sand flats and in mangrove swamps and estuaries.

Larger guitarfish species may have litters of up to 29, but the Atlantic guitarfish only has about 6 pups, each about 8" (20 cm) long. Males are sexually mature at 19" (48 cm) long. The females bear live young.

The shovel-like head and the tapering tail of an Atlantic guitarfish.

# Thornback

Platyrhinoidis triseriata

Thornback rays take their common name from the rows of large thorny spines along their back and sometimes their tail. They are similar to some round-snouted guitarfish found in other parts of the world. These distantly related groups probably evolved similar body forms to adapt to similar lifestyles in different parts of the world. The thornback's disc is short and broad, and the snout is evenly rounded rather than triangular. The fine segmented cartilages that form the skeleton of the outer disc reach almost as far as the snout tip. Two narrow cartilages link the snout tip to the skull.

The brownish thornback has three rows of pale thorns. Its dorsal fins, near the tail tip, are of similar size, and the tail is much longer than the disc. It is similar to the Japanese thornback ray (*Platyrhina sinensis*), although this ray's thorns are confined to the central part of its disc and

**FIELD NOTES**

- Eastern Pacific from California, USA, to Mexico
- Almost 3' (90 cm)
- Harmless; be wary of sharp thorns
- Year-round
- Once plentiful off southern California

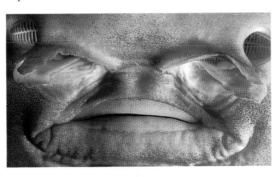

A close-up of mouth and nostrils on the underside of the thornback.

around the eyes; the thornback's run along the back and tail.

The thornback lives in temperate and subtropical waters, mainly inshore on sandy and muddy bottoms. Divers occasionally see one around kelp beds, where its brownish upper surface blends well with the dark substrate. It rests in small groups for much of the day, remaining partly buried, with only its thorns protruding. These are sharp, and are probably used defensively against its main predators, small sharks. Although it is harmless, this ray should be treated with caution.

Little is known about the thornback's general biology. It is not a powerful swimmer and so it seems unlikely that it undertakes any long migrations. It seems to be more active at night, feeding on sand worms, sea shells, and small crustaceans, such as crabs and shrimps. Mating occurs at the end of summer.

207

# Lesser Electric Ray

*Narcine brasiliensis*

Possibly the best known of the numbfishes, the lesser electric ray is small and brownish with dusty blotches. It belongs to a family whose taxonomy and biology are not well understood. It has a flattened, oval-shaped disc, and large pelvic fins. Oversized dorsal and caudal fins cover most of the rear of its tapering tail. It eats mainly sand worms, although it also eats small fishes and crustaceans.

The kidney-shaped electric organs of this ray are located in the middle of the pectoral fins. They account for about a sixth of its body weight. Each organ consists of a honeycomb of 280 to 430 columns, containing several hundred electric plates, which deliver a shock of less than 37 volts. This is so weak that it is unlikely to be a means of defense or even of stunning prey. Nevertheless, some fishers claim to have been knocked off their feet after inadvertently stepping on a ray—probably more from surprise than from the intensity of the shock.

In winter, the lesser electric ray moves farther offshore in warm temperate and tropical waters.

### FIELD NOTES

■ Central-western Atlantic from North Carolina, USA, to northern Argentina, including the Gulf of Mexico

■ To 1½' (45 cm)

■ Capable of delivering a weak electric shock; otherwise, harmless

■ Summer

■ Reasonably common

*The lesser electric ray (below), showing the dusty blotches of its upper surface.*

During summer, it usually inhabits very shallow waters near the shore, where it is often caught in beach and trammel nets. Divers may also see it off sandy beaches if they search carefully. Often, only the eyes and parts of the head are visible because it spends long periods concealed under the sand. Barefoot anglers and waders may accidentally step on a buried ray and receive a minor shock. But this is essentially a harmless creature, and you would have to annoy it before it would discharge its organs in response.

Female lesser electric rays venture into the surf zone in summer to bear 2 to 17 live young. Like many sharks and rays, the color pattern of the pups is more intense than in the adult. Pups average about 4¼" (11 cm) at birth.

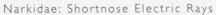

# Spotted Electric Ray

*Narke japonica*

The spotted electric ray, also known as the Japanese numbfish, is one of the shortnose electric rays. This family of at least 12 species of small rays lives in the temperate and tropical Indo-Pacific, mainly on the outer continental shelf and upper slope, although the spotted electric ray does occur inshore. Like all the shortnose electric rays, its disc is almost oval in shape, with a short, thick tail—the general shape is like the numbfish's. It has only one dorsal fin.

The spotted electric ray is reddish brown, with black or white spots on the upper surface. Its snout is short, and like other members of the family, its eyes are small. It lives on sandy bottoms, often near rocky reefs, where it remains hidden for long periods of time. For this reason, although it is quite common, divers are unlikely to come across it. It can become aggressive when annoyed, and is capable of delivering a small electric shock (up to

**FIELD NOTES**

- Northwestern Pacific, from Japan to the South China Sea
- To about 16" (40 cm)
- Capable of delivering a weak electric shock; otherwise, harmless
- Year-round; hard to find
- Not uncommon

80 volts), possibly for defensive reasons or to protect its territory. It feeds on small fish and crustaceans that live in the sand and sediment of its habitat. Its mouth is surrounded by a shallow groove, which allows the mouth to be projected forward to suck up the prey.

The female spotted electric ray gives birth to litters of up to five pups, which are born in early summer.

An unusual New Zealand relative, the blind electric ray (*Typhlonarke aysoni*), lives on the continental slope at depths of 655–2,950' (200–900 m). This little-known ray has minute eyes, concealed beneath a thin covering of skin, making them virtually useless for detecting prey. Instead, it uses electroreceptors. It also has a pelvic fin with a separate anterior lobe, which it can presumably use to prop itself up with when stalking prey.

blind electric ray

# Shorttailed Electric Ray

### Hypnos monopterygium

This ray is unique among the electric rays in having a very large, oval pectoral disc attached to a smaller disc formed from the pelvic fins. The ray takes on a most unusual shape if washed up dead on a beach, swelling in the hot sun to look like a flattened wooden coffin—its other common name is coffin ray. It has a very short tail, with two tiny dorsal fins near the equally small caudal fin. The soft skin lacks spines and denticles, and varies from a rather drab chocolate brown to pinkish or gray.

Shorttailed electric rays live near the coast in warm temperate and subtropical waters. They prefer sheltered habitats, such as muddy bays and estuaries, as well as the continental shelf to 720' (220 m). They are rarely seen because they conceal themselves so well. During the day they remain deeply buried, and they may also change color for camouflage.

This ray's electric organs, located centrally on each pectoral fin, are highly developed. They can deliver a strong shock to stun large prey and may also have a defensive role. Divers who accidentally place a hand on a ray's back will remember the experience for life. Adults feed at night, foraging for fish, worms, and crabs. The mouth of this ray is capable of taking surprisingly large prey, including flounders up to half the size of its body.

Little is known about the biology of this viviparous ray. Females grow larger than males, and bear pups 3–4½" (8–11 cm) long.

> **FIELD NOTES**
> ■ Only in Australian seas
> ■ Probably 16" (40 cm), but reported up to 2' (60 cm)
> ■ Not aggressive, but capable of delivering a powerful shock if touched
> ■ Year-round; mostly seen at night
> ■ Reasonably common

*The underside of a male shorttailed electric ray (above). Only the eyes and spiracles of the ray (left) are visible above the sand.*

# Atlantic Torpedo

Torpedo nobiliana

The Atlantic torpedo is also known as the great or black torpedo ray. It is enormous, and at 200 lb (90 kg), it is certainly the largest of all the electricity-producing rays. It has powerful electric organs in the pectoral disc that can discharge up to 220 volts. The upper surface of its disc is positively charged and the lower surface is negatively charged. During discharge, sea water or an unsuspecting animal creates a path for the current to travel from one side of the "battery" to the other. Without this, the ray could even electrocute itself.

The Atlantic torpedo uses its electric organs in defense and for predation. They may also be used for sensory purposes to detect prey, or as a means of communication. Its back varies in color from dark blue to brown or black, and may be dotted with small white spots and black blotches.

### FIELD NOTES

■ Eastern Atlantic, from United Kingdom to South Africa, including Mediterranean; northwestern Atlantic, from Nova Scotia, Canada, to Florida, USA

■ Recorded up to 6' (1.82 m)

■ If surprised or annoyed, produces a powerful electric shock capable of stunning a diver

■ Year-round; rarely seen

■ Not uncommon; more prevalent in temperate seas

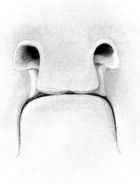

mouth and nostrils

All the torpedo rays have a large, flabby disc, broader than it is long, covered in smooth skin. The short tail has two dorsal fins, the first usually much larger than the second. The caudal fin has tall upper and lower lobes.

The Atlantic torpedo occurs inshore in temperate and tropical waters, to depths of about 1,475' (450 m). While it spends much of its time on the bottom, it is also known to migrate in open water. It is rarely encountered by divers.

Adults are efficient predators of bottom fishes such as small ground sharks, eels, flounders, and soles, whereas young torpedoes feed more on crustaceans. This ray prefers to stalk or ambush its prey under the substrate and eat it live (which makes it difficult to keep in aquariums).

For a ray, the Atlantic torpedo is highly fecund. Females are viviparous, delivering up to 60 pups after almost a year's gestation.

211

# Rough Skate

Raja nasuta

The rough skate belongs to a group of skates whose common ancestor lived around the shores of the ancient Gondwana supercontinent more than 80 million years ago. This is indicated by the distribution of the modern-day group of skates, which are all found on the continental shelves off New Zealand, Australia, and South America.

The rough skate has a diamond-shaped disc with a very long, pointed snout. Its slender tail has three rows of thorns along its length, while its back is covered with minute prickles. It is usually grayish or brownish, with white spots and darker marbling. It occurs on soft bottoms to about 490' (150 m), usually beyond diving depths, although divers will occasionally see one.

Few details are known of the rough skate's biology. It lays horny, rectangular egg cases, which it attaches to the bottom by fine,

**FIELD NOTES**

■ Southeastern Pacific off New Zealand

■ Reaches almost 3⅓' (1 m)

■ Harmless

■ Year-round; rarely seen by divers

■ Common

Port Davey skate

thread-like tendrils. Eggs develop slowly and young hatch after several months. Recently hatched skates can be identified by a belly scar where the yolk sac was attached. Empty egg cases, called "mermaid's purses," are found washed up on beaches after storms.

A close relative of the rough skate is the recently discovered Port Davey skate (*Raja* sp.). Of the more than 280 skates in the world, it is the only one that lives in brackish water. It is confined to two estuarine bays in the remote southwest of Tasmania, off southern Australia. It has a long, stiff snout, more typical of deep-ocean skates. This is presumably used for grubbing around for food in the fine silty bottom on which it lives. Given its restricted distribution, the habitat needs of this skate left over from the prehistoric past are likely to be very specific. Its population is small, probably no more than a few thousand individuals. This makes it particularly vulnerable to habitat degradation and overfishing.

# Round Stingray

Urobatis halleri

The round stingray, a member of the stingaree family, is plain brown with yellowish spots and reticulations. It has a circular disc, the upper surface of which is smooth, without tubercles. The related Cortez round stingray (*Urobatis maculatus*), from close by in Baja California and the Sea of Cortez, off Mexico, is similar in shape but has large black blotches over the disc. Stingarees can be mistaken for stingrays because of their similar body shape. However, stingarees have a shorter tail, which ends in a long, leaf-shaped caudal fin.

The round stingray lives mainly on muddy and sandy bottoms near the shore, to a depth of about 295' (90 m). In summer, it basks in warm shallow inlets, but remains in coastal waters during winter, only entering inlets to forage. It does not range far, rarely moving beyond an area of about a

The underside of a juvenile round stingray.

**FIELD NOTES**

■ Eastern Pacific, from northern California to Panama

■ Reaches 22" (56 cm)

■ Not aggressive; the stinging spine can cause minor injury

■ Year-round

■ Very common

square mile. It seems sensitive to cold, and lives in water warmer than 50° F (10° C).

This ray feeds during the day on small bottom-dwelling crustaceans, bivalves, and sand worms. An efficient predator, it may use a combination of sight, smell, and vibration to detect prey. It uses its disc and mouth to "dig" for food in the substrate, and has also been seen nipping prey off sea-grass fronds. Divers may see a foraging ray in sheltered bays, or notice the outline of one buried in sediment.

Round stingrays mature early. The sexes segregate before the breeding season, and adult females live offshore until June, when they move in to coastal habitats to mate. Sexually aggressive males patrol the sandy strip between the deep sea-grass beds and the shore to select a suitable mate. He nibbles on her disc, then rolls beneath her and inserts a single clasper. Litters of one to six pups are born inshore in September, where they remain until maturity.

213

# Banded Stingaree

Urolophus cruciatus

The banded stingaree is a highly distinctive ray, having smooth grayish to yellowish brown skin with a dark, banded pattern on its back, rather like a crucifix. Its tail is very short, fleshy, and highly flexible, usually with a single, large stinging spine on the upper half. If touched or provoked, the ray thrusts its tail toward its head, driving the spine and its venom into a victim. The pain varies from mild to excruciating, depending on the amount of venom and the location of the wound.

Adults are found concentrated in sheltered muddy bays and estuaries, although they are also common on sand patches near reefs and in caves. Divers and swimmers come across them all the time, frequently finding them with the more widely distributed, sparsely spotted stingaree (*Urolophus paucimaculatus*), a plain gray stingaree with a few white

**FIELD NOTES**

◼ Southwestern Pacific, off southern Australia

◼ Reaches 20" (50 cm)

◼ Not aggressive; however, the stinging spine can cause injury

◼ Year-round

◼ Very common

spots on its upper surface. The banded stingaree is quite inactive, and will often lie hidden under the substrate.

This habit of concealment can cause problems for divers and swimmers, as it's very easy to kneel or place a hand on a ray's back accidentally and become the target of its thrusting tail. Net fishers have been stung when sorting through a catch, so gloves should be used for handling.

Stingarees are viviparous; litters of two to four are born after a gestation of about three months. Male banded stingarees mature at about 10" (25 cm). During spring, small groups of females can be found resting on the bottom with their tails raised over their bodies like scorpions. This behavior may be related to courtship; however, the lives of stingarees are not well understood.

*The venomous barb (right) of the banded stingaree, and the view from below of a spotted stingaree (far right).*

# Ocellate River Ray

Potamotrygon motoro

River rays are members of a small stingray family that lives in the large lakes and river systems of tropical South America. They are confined to freshwater habitats and may be found more than 1,000 miles (1,600 km) from the sea. Many species are similar in appearance but inhabit separate waterways.

**FIELD NOTES**

■ Rivers of Paraguay
■ Up to 1' (30 cm) wide
■ Not aggressive; however, the stinging spine can cause a potentially fatal wound
■ Year-round
■ Probably common

They resemble both stingarees and stingrays in shape. The disc is oval or circular, and the skin is mostly smooth and lacks large thorns. The tail is slender, without dorsal fins but usually with thorns down the middle, and it tapers away beyond a well-developed stinging spine.

The ocellate river ray has a distinctive pattern of dark rings that are biggest on the middle of its back. Smaller, more compact rows of rings are located around the edge. This river ray, from the rivers of Paraguay, lives partly buried in the mud and sand of back eddies and side channels. Once buried, it is very difficult to see, and is therefore easy to step on.

The stinging spine, which is located near the tail tip, can strike well forward, making it a formidable defensive weapon. And despite its small size, the spine can inflict a very nasty wound that produces agonizing pain—it is

dreaded by the local fishermen, who catch this ray with nets. Deaths have been reported from stings on

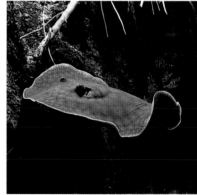

Potamotrygon reticulata, *the reticulated freshwater ray (above), another South American river ray, in its natural habitat.*

the abdomen and from secondary infections that result from unattended wounds.

Ocellate river rays breed between September and October, and the pups are born about five months later. The embryos gain nutrition while inside the mother from the egg yolk and the fluids secreted by her uterine tissues.

Rays that live in the sea need to store high concentrations of urea in the flesh and blood in order to osmoregulate (see p. 122) in their saline environment. However, freshwater river rays use far less urea to osmoregulate.

215

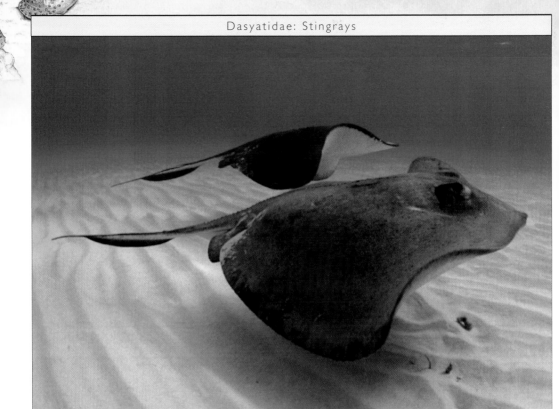

# Southern Stingray

Dasyatis americana

The southern stingray has a large, flattened, somewhat angular disc, with a row of small tubercles running down its gray to brown back. The tail has a long skin fold along its under-surface and a low keel on top.

This stingray lives mainly in sandy habitats off beaches, in lagoons, and around sea-grass beds. It eats large invertebrates such as crabs, shrimps, and worms, and small bottom-dwelling fishes. It feeds mainly at night, remaining almost entirely concealed in the sand during the day. To dig into the substrate, it undulates the disc tips, dispersing the sand evenly.

Often, the first sign a diver notices is a pair of holes on the sandy bottom—the ray's spiracles, easily mistaken for its eyes. If approached with care, the ray usually stays still. The southern stingray is known for its social behavior with humans. At places in the Cayman Islands (see pp. 238–9), divers can hand-feed wild stingrays.

It is the long, dagger-like stinging spines on the tail that have given members of the stingray family their name and brought them unjustified infamy. Stingrays have been responsible for some

**FIELD NOTES**

■ Central-western Atlantic, from New Jersey, USA, to Brazil
■ At least 5' (1.5 m)
■ Not normally aggressive; the stinging spine can cause serious injury
■ Year-round
■ Common in some areas

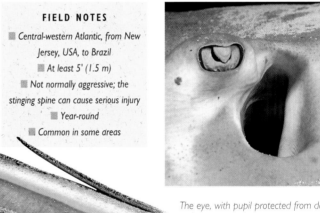

The eye, with pupil protected from day-light by the lappet shield, and spiracle (above), and the venomous spine (left).

human deaths, but in almost all recorded cases, the attacks resulted from the carelessness or stupidity of the victim. Always treat stingrays with respect, and under no circumstances attempt to ride one. As well as delivering venom, the big stinging spines of the largest stingrays are as sharp as a butcher's knife. Cuts from repeated thrusts can cause more damage than the venom, particularly if a vital organ is struck, but such defensive behavior is used only if the animal is threatened or harassed. Stingrays are typically gentle and inquisitive, easily domesticated, and very popular in aquariums.

# Mangrove Whipray

### Himantura granulata

This stingray belongs to a group known as the whiprays, which take their name from their very long, thin, flexible tails. Most of the whiprays, including the attractively patterned leopard whipray (*Himantura undulata*) and reticulate whipray (*Himantura uarnak*), live near tropical coasts throughout the Indo-Pacific. Some species, such as the huge and possibly rare freshwater whipray (*Himantura chaophraya*), have adapted to life in rivers and estuaries, and have been seen flapping around in the shallows of muddy rivers as far as several hundred miles from the open sea.

The mangrove whipray is oval in shape, with a thick disc about as wide as it is long. The rough upper surface is dark brown to grayish brown in the center of the disc, merging to brown to slate gray on the outer edges. This is usually scattered with fine white spots. The ray is white underneath, with dark spots along the edges. It has a distinctive white, whip-like tail without skin folds and with one or more stinging spines. When a ray has

**FIELD NOTES**

■ Indo-West Pacific, from Micronesia, New Guinea, the Java Sea, to northern Australia

■ At least 3' (90 cm) wide, possibly much larger

■ Not aggressive; the stinging spines can cause injury

■ Occasionally seen by divers

■ Uncommon

lost one of these stinging spines, it is usually possible to see a scar on the tail.

As well as occurring close inshore in tropical waters over sand flats and amongst coral, the mangrove whipray sometimes also dwells in mangrove habitats, as its name suggests. Divers occasionally encounter one in shallow waters. However, not a lot is known about the behavior and biology of this unusual stingray. Its diet includes small fishes and small crustaceans, such as crabs and shrimp. Females give birth to young that are about 11" (28 cm) wide and about 30½" (78 cm) in total length.

*The leopard whipray is a large stingray with a distinctive, intricate pattern.*

217

# Bluespotted Ribbontail Ray

Taeniura lymma

The vivid ornamentation of the bluespotted ribbontail ray makes it immediately recognizable. It has bright blue spots on top of its flat, oval-shaped disc, and a distinctive blue stripe along each side of the tail. A broad flap of whitish or bluish skin extends along its undersurface to the tail tip.

The bluespotted ribbontail ray is found alone or in small groups, mostly in shallow water over reef flats. It has also been observed around coral rubble and shipwreck debris at depths of 65' (20 m). It moves over tidal flats, usually at high tide, to feed on sand worms, shrimps, hermit crabs, and small fishes. As the tide recedes, it retires to the protective covering of coral cervices. It rarely buries itself completely in the substrate, and divers and snorkelers will often detect this ray by its distinctive ribbon–like tail poking out from a crack or crevice beneath the coral.

> ### FIELD NOTES
>
> ■ Tropical Indo-Pacific, from southern Africa and the Red Sea to the Solomon Islands
> ■ Up to 2¼' (70 cm) long
> ■ Timid; stinging spines can cause minor injury
> ■ Year-round
> ■ Very common

This is the most abundant of the inshore reef-dwelling rays, and it is often encountered by divers and snorkelers in the Indo-Pacific region. The best viewing sites are over coral reef shallows and on sand patches beneath coral bommies.

Being rather timid, the ribbontail ray will usually swim away frantically if approached or disturbed by divers. The large eyes, which extend above the head on short stalks, give it excellent peripheral vision.

Unlike most other stingrays, its poisonous spines, often two in number, are located closer to the tip than the base of its tail. This enables these rays to strike at potential enemies well forward of their heads.

The bluespotted ribbontail ray produces about seven live young in every litter. Each pup is born with the distinctive blue markings of its parents, in miniature.

*The tail of the bluespotted ribbontail ray is well armed, often with two venomous spines, set back near the tip.*

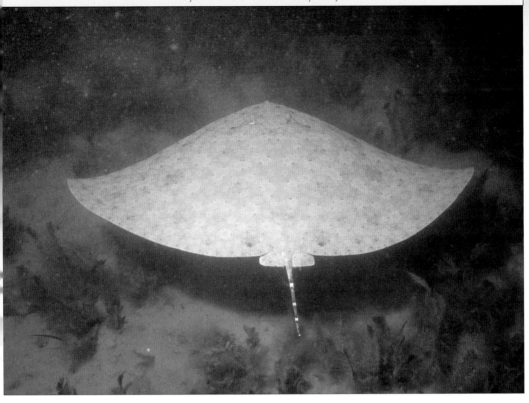

# Australian Butterfly Ray

Gymnura australis

The characteristic features of this unusual fish are best summed up by several of its common names—Australian butterfly ray, and also diamond ray and rattail ray. It has a very large and flat diamond-shaped disc with pectoral "wings" reminiscent of a butterfly. It is ornamented with a delicate greenish gray mosaic overlaid with a peppering of small black spots. The thin, stumpy tail, with its alternating black and white rings, has a small dorsal fin but no caudal fin. It also lacks a stinging spine, although related species may have a short one near the base of the tail.

Little is known about the butterfly rays, but their habits and diet are possibly similar to their relatives, the stingrays. They live mostly on the bottom in tropical waters, to depths of about 165' (50 m). They bury themselves deep into the sediments, their wafer-thin bodies needing only a shallow covering of sand for concealment. Not surprisingly, divers almost never see them. Their main food is a variety of crustaceans and small fishes, such as gobies and dragonets.

### FIELD NOTES

■ *Off northern Australia and New Guinea*

■ *Up to 2⅓' (73 cm) wide*

■ *Harmless; lacks a stinging spine*

■ *Rarely seen by divers*

■ *Reasonably common in some areas*

Males mature at about 14–16" (35–40 cm) and are much smaller than the largest females. Females bear live young, which are nourished while in the uterus partly from their yolk sac but mostly from fluid secreted by the uterine wall. An embryo lies in the uterus with its snout tucked in and its pectoral "wings" folded one over the other below its belly. Pairs wrap around each other head to head. The pups are born in this position and unfold soon after emerging from the mother.

The Australian butterfly ray is regularly caught as bycatch by prawn trawlers. Although they are harmless, they tend to flap around vigorously once on deck. One African species is said to grunt loudly by expelling trapped air from its mouth when brought on deck.

upper tooth

219

# Spotted Eagle Ray

Aetobatus narinari

The spotted eagle ray is the most common and most widely distributed of the eagle rays. Its distinctive pattern of white spots or rings on its greenish to pinkish back makes it easily recognizable. Its flattened snout, like the beak of a duck, gives rise to its alternative common name, duckbill ray. A small stinging spine is located near the tail base.

The spotted eagle ray occurs near continents, islands, and atolls in tropical waters less than 200' (60 m) deep. It is extremely active, swimming for long periods both in the water column and near the bottom. With its graceful action, it appears to fly and glide along, slowly moving its pectoral fins like the wings of a bird. It is powerfully built and can accelerate rapidly, swerving and twisting away from hungry hammerheads or tiger sharks at extraordinary speeds to find

*A spotted eagle ray in full "flight."*

**FIELD NOTES**

- Worldwide in tropical and temperate seas
- Reported to attain 11½' (3.5 m) in width but typically smaller, to 6' (1.8 m)
- Timid; the stinging spine can cause injury
- Year-round
- Common

safety in the shallows. Adults will frolic near the surface, at times leaping well clear of the water in a spectacular display. Their pectoral fins, when thus exposed, resemble a thrashing shark—causing more than one quick evacuation of a swimming beach. For a diver, the sight of a school of 100 or more of these rays cruising through clear blue water is an unforgettable experience. They may be wary if approached.

This ray's teeth, a series of flattened bony plates that form the beak, are designed to crush and mill hard-shelled invertebrates like oysters, clams, and snails. Octopuses, shrimp, and fishes are also eaten. The ray digs up food from the bottom with its flattened snout and pectoral fins.

The spotted eagle ray bears live young after 12 months' gestation. Copulation is brief and takes place belly to belly. Females may mate with up to four males over about an hour, and produce one to four pups per litter. Sharks often follow birthing females to feed on newborn pups.

# Bat Ray

Myliobatis californicus

The bat ray has a broad, angular disc, from which the head protrudes in a rounded, lobe-like snout. It has a long whip-like tail (sometimes damaged by predators), with no caudal fin and up to five short stinging spines just behind the base. The spines, which are preceded by a small dorsal fin, are used to deter predators. Its heavily built body can be either smooth or have small spines along its midline or around the eyes.

This ray occurs alone or in groups, mainly inshore in temperate waters less than 165' (50 m) deep. It spends most time on the bottom, resting on kelp or in large hollows in the sand and mud when it isn't feeding. If disturbed, it will emerge from its hollow and prop itself up on the tips of its pectoral fins with its back arched in a "starting position." It may swim away with explosive acceleration if divers get too close.

The bat ray feeds on a variety of small animals, including shellfishes, crustaceans, and small bony fishes, which it grubs from the bottom. The diet changes with age. Clams are a favorite food of juveniles, while worms are eaten more often by adults. The teeth are fused to form grinding plates. Hard-shelled prey are partly ingested, heavily crushed by the jaws, and spat out. The nutritious flesh is then reingested selectively.

The mating behavior of the bat ray is fairly well known. The male swims in synchrony below the belly of a receptive female. Thorns around his eyes poke into the female's undersurface during mating, helping the couple to maintain position while the male twists a single clasper upward and into the cloaca. Up to 10 pups, each about 1' (30 cm) wide, are born a year later.

**FIELD NOTES**

- Eastern Pacific, from the Sea of Cortez to Oregon, USA
- Up to about 6' (1.8 m)
- Harmless to divers; if handled carelessly, the stinging spine can cause a painful wound
- Year-round
- Common

This school of bat rays, photographed gliding gracefully through Californian waters, is a remarkable sight.

# Javanese Cownose Ray

Rhinoptera javanica

The Javanese cownose ray is dark grayish brown on the back. Its head is separate from the broad, diamond-shaped disc, and has a characteristic pugnose snout. This is concave at the front and overlays the rostral lobe, a lobe with such a marked indentation that it looks like two fleshy lobes rather than one.

**FIELD NOTES**

■ Indo-Pacific, from southern Africa to eastern Indonesia; possibly northern Australia

■ At least 5' (1.5 m) wide

■ One or more small stinging spines on the tail can cause a minor wound

■ Year-round

■ Not uncommon

The Javanese cownose ray flaps its powerful pectoral fins in lazy, lateral undulations to swim almost continuously, rarely ever resting on the bottom. It swims mostly in groups—a related species, the Pacific cownose ray (*Rhinoptera steindachneri*), congregates in schools of more than 1,000. The Javanese cownose is most common along tropical coastlines and in shallow, muddy bays.

This large ray is thought to make daily migrations inshore to feed almost exclusively on bottom-dwelling crustaceans and bivalves. It exposes the buried shellfish by beating its "wings" near the bottom, then grabs it with its rostral lobes. It partly ingests the prey, crushes it between its strong tooth plates, spits it out, then retrieves and swallows the smaller fragments.

Divers sometimes see large schools working their way over shallow sand flats during the day, but this ray's timidity makes encounters rare.

Females copulate belly to belly with several males in succession. The young, one to six per litter, are nourished inside the mother, first by the egg yolk and then by uterine secretions.

*A school of Pacific cownose rays near the Galapagos Islands.*

# Manta Ray

Manta birostris

Mantas are the largest living rays and among the most majestic of fishes. Folklore may have inflated their width to more than 29½' (9 m), but the reality is still very impressive. A 16½' (5 m) manta found in the Bahamas weighed more than 3,000 lb (1,360 kg).

The manta is related to the eagle and cownose rays, and has a similar diamond-shaped disc. But its tail is short and lacks a stinging spine, and its mouth is bordered by two long, lobe-like extensions of the pectoral fins—cephalic lobes. Mantas differ from smaller devilrays in having a relatively larger mouth, located at the snout tip rather than under the head. The color is not uniform, but is usually blackish above and pale below, with light and dark blotches.

Manta rays occur throughout the tropical seas of the world, and populations in each ocean may, in fact, be different species. They live inshore, close to the coast, as well as out in the open sea. They are mostly solitary or swim in small groups. Superbly adapted to pelagic life, they are both graceful and powerful movers, probably swimming almost continuously. They are seen along reef fringes near deep water and are also sighted from boats, as they bask or feed near the surface. Unless harassed, they are harmless.

A manta ray funnels microscopic plankton toward its mouth using the extended cephalic lobes, which remain folded spirally when not in use. Then, with a sophisticated filtering system, it sieves the plankton from the same water that it uses to breathe. Large rays also feed on pelagic crustaceans and small fishes and have been seen in feeding frenzies with sharks and other large predators.

Females produce one or two pups at a time, sometimes ejecting their young into the air when breaching.

A feeding manta displays its huge gill arches.

*Mariana Trench, a deep-sea trench in the western Pacific*

# THE DEEP-WATER RAYS

Almost half of the world's rays occur only in the cool, deep waters of the outer continental shelves and slopes. They are often caught accidentally during deep-sea fishing operations—this is really the only time they are encountered by people. Many of these species are new to science or are known from only a few specimens, so we understand very little about their biology and lifestyle.

## SKATES
Rajidae

Skates are the main group of deep-water rays. While a few true skates (Rajinae), also known as hard-nose skates, live in shallower waters close to shore (see p. 212), most of the 280 or so species live in deeper waters, on soft bottoms down to depths of 9,840' (3,000 m) or more. They are found throughout the world along continental margins, except around coral islands in the Pacific, the only place where they do not occur. Most have rather restricted ranges, and the skates of nearby regions are often quite distinct.

leg skate
*Anacanthobatis* sp.

The family is divided into two primary groups, the softnose skates (Arhynchobatinae) and the true skates (Rajinae). These groups are essentially similar in appearance. Their discs are very flattened and vary according to sex, ranging from round to almost diamond-shaped. They have a rather short, slender tail that usually has two small dorsal fins and a low caudal fin near its tip.

The main difference between the two groups is the flexibility of their snouts, which is based on the shape and strength of the supporting cartilage. As their name suggests, the softnose skates have a floppy snout, while most true skates have a firm and rigid snout supported by cartilage.

One of the most unusual groups of true skates is the leg skates (*Anacanthobatis*). They are small, evolutionally advanced rays with a very flattened, leaf-shaped disc and a thin tail without fins. Each pelvic fin is divided into two distinct lobes. The front lobes resemble thin legs and are presumably used for "walking" over the seabed. Mature males of some species have an extended,

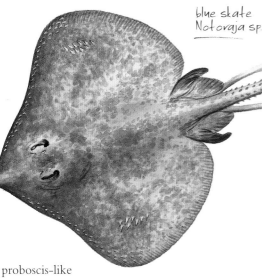

blue skate
Notoraja sp.

embryos may take from several months to more than one and a half years to develop and hatch. Young skates are virtually identical to the mother in shape, although their denticles and thorns develop and harden after birth.

Skates are caught for their meat. The wings, or pectoral flaps, fetch high prices and are eaten in some parts of the world. Given the limited distribution of some skates, they are susceptible to overfishing in certain regions.

## SIXGILL STINGRAYS
Hexatrygonidae

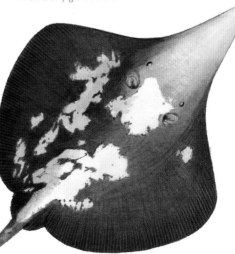

proboscis-like snout, which they use for probing around in the sediments for food. Most of the 18 or so known species of leg skate live on continental slopes. They are rarely caught, even by trawlers.

Skates vary greatly in size. The species of some genera, such as *Pavoraja*, are less than 16" (40 cm) long, with males maturing at about 11" (27 cm). Members of the more ubiquitous genus *Dipturus* may reach 6½' (2 m) long and weigh 200 lb (90 kg) or more.

The skin of skates is either smooth or covered in tiny denticles. Larger denticles, known as thorns, are sometimes present around the eyes and along the back and the upper surface of the tail. Mature males may have additional patches of very sharp thorns beside the eyes (malars) and also in the middle of each pectoral fin (alars), which they use to grasp females during mating. In many species, the alar thorns can be retracted into the disc, making them difficult to notice. However, they are well known to those who handle skates frequently, as is the sight of a careless angler with a skate dangling from a bloody hand.

Skates feed on bottom-dwelling animals, such as soft-shelled mollusks, sand worms, crustaceans, and small fishes. Some species are known to have rudimentary electric organs that may be used to locate prey.

Female skates are fertilized internally by the male's very well developed claspers, which have a series of hooks and spines for grasping the female during mating. The females lay horny egg cases and attach them to the ocean bottom with sticky threads and tendrils. The

The sixgill stingray (*Hexatrygon bickelli*) belongs to the deep-water family of sixgill rays. They live on the midcontinental slopes of the Indo-Pacific, and are more closely related to stingrays than to skates.

The shape of the rear part of the disc and the tail, with one or two stinging spines and a caudal fin, is reminiscent of a stingaree. However, the body is flabby and the features of its head are distinctive and unique.

Unlike all other rays, which have five pairs of gill openings, this ray has six. It has very small eyes and a long, flattened, triangular snout filled with fluid. The snout, which is covered with sensory pores, is highly flexible and is used to detect food. A sixgill ray that had been trawled was observed moving the tip of its snout like a finger.

This ray is likely to bear live young, but like so many of the deep-sea rays, almost nothing is known of its biology.

225

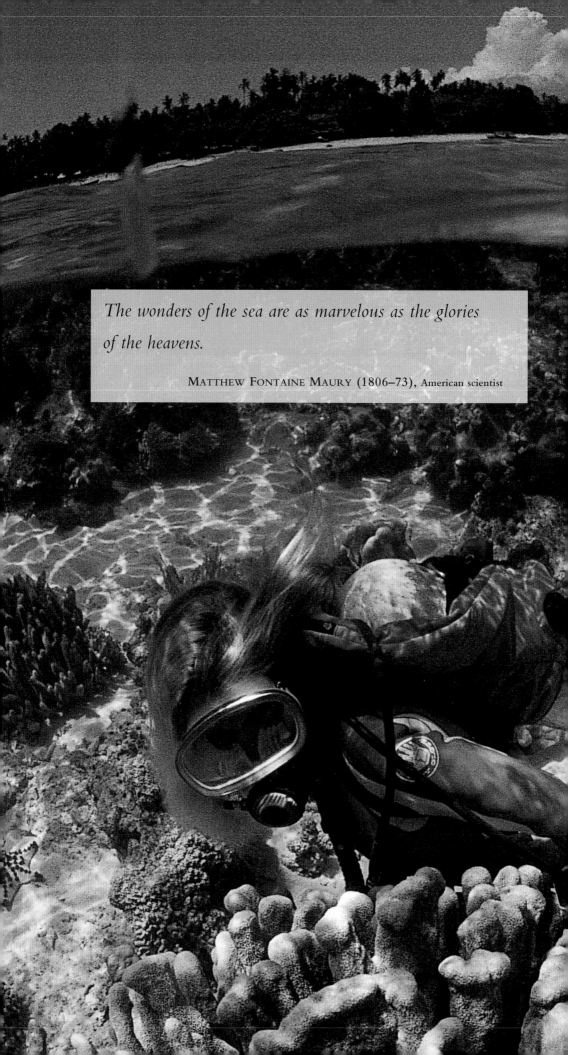

The wonders of the sea are as marvelous as the glories of the heavens.

MATTHEW FONTAINE MAURY (1806–73), American scientist

CHAPTER EIGHT

# ENCOUNTERS *with*
# SHARKS *and* RAYS

# USING ENCOUNTERS
## *with* SHARKS *and* RAYS

*The challenge of observing sharks and rays can take you from*

*the Red Sea to the Galapagos via the Great Barrier Reef.*

The following pages feature 21 marine environments where you have the chance of coming face to face with a shark or ray in its own habitat. Some enthusiasts prefer particular types of encounters, or they become fascinated with certain aspects of the behavior of these mysterious creatures. Whatever your interest, careful planning is essential if you are to have the best chance of seeing sharks and rays in the wild. This guide will help you to choose the destination and diving experience that you seek.

*The **illustrated banding** is a visual pointer to indicate that the page is about a site.*

Encounters with Sharks and Rays

*Vivid color plates give a graphic sense of the principal shark or ray that may be encountered at the site, or of unique features and particular types of flora and fauna that may be of special interest.*

*The **text** describes the habitat at the site, the species that can be seen here, and the behavior you might witness. It warns of possible hazards and advises on equipment that you will need to dive at the site. It also covers the other attractions of the region, the features likely to distract you from looking for sharks and rays.*

## Ras Muhammad
### Egypt

The parched landscape and rugged mountains of the Sinai Peninsula in Egypt seem lifeless. But beneath the sapphire waters of the Red Sea dwells a kaleidoscope of living color. Where the southern tip of the peninsula plunges into the sea at Ras Muhammad, incredible shallow reef flats near the shoreline give way to sheer coral walls disappearing into the depths below. Clouds of Anthias and glassfish shimmer among the undulating soft corals. And shafts of desert sunlight penetrate deep into the blue abyss to reveal patrolling gray reef sharks (see p. 170).

Shark Observatory, one of the best shark sites, is a stretch of the Ras Muhammad coral wall. Divers swimming here will see jacks, tuna, barracuda, and other pelagic marine life traversing the deep ocean. Only the wall is there to orientate you, with the seemingly bottomless sea dropping away beneath you. It is quite common to turn a corner and come face to face with several gray reef sharks searching for food or checking their territory for competitors. It is hard to decide who gets the bigger surprise, as

*Anthias, famous for their vivid color, dart about the coral reef (top); and the Red Sea and Sinai Desert (above).*

the sharks veer out into the limitless blue and the divers kick toward the security of the wall.

Gray reef sharks are curious and territorial, and pay much attention to divers, circling constantly, coming and going, and sometimes even becoming slightly aggressive. But during December and January, you may have the rare privilege of witnessing groups of 5 to 10 gray reef sharks that completely ignore you because they are engrossed in mating behavior. Females circle in the water off the reef, within 30 feet (10 m) of you. A male will dash into the group, single out a female and pursue her, repeatedly biting her flanks. This action is thought to promote ovulation, and the female's thick skin has evolved to deal with it. While you are unlikely to see an actual coupling, these encounters provide opportunities for unique observations and rare photos or video footage.

Shark Reef and Jolanda Reef are two small submerged reefs just below the surface, a short swim from the tip of the peninsula. On their ocean side, these reefs again drop away in coral

248

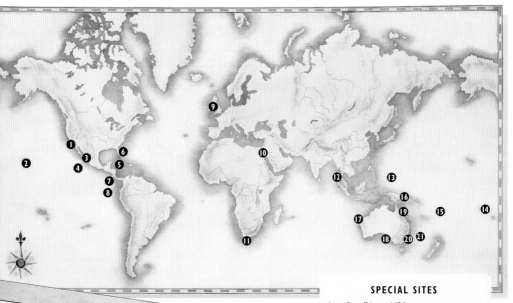

## SPECIAL SITES

1. San Diego, USA
2. Kona Coast, USA
3. Sea of Cortez, Mexico
4. Revillagigedo Islands, Mexico
5. Grand Cayman, Cayman Islands
6. The Bahamas
7. Cocos Island, Costa Rica
8. Galapagos Islands, Ecuador
9. Isle of Man, United Kingdom
10. Ras Muhammad, Egypt
11. Cape Town, South Africa
12. Similan and Surin Islands, Thailand
13. Yap and Palau, Micronesia
14. Rangiroa Atoll, French Polynesia
15. Mamanuca Islands, Fiji
16. Valerie's Reef, Papua New Guinea
17. Ningaloo Reef, Australia
18. Neptune Islands, Australia
19. Great Barrier Reef, Australia
20. New South Wales, Australia
21. Lord Howe Island, Australia

Ras Muhammad

e another
or gray reef
her large
ivers and
ld also look
whitetips
lloped and
eads (see
manta rays
s is one of
any manner of species could
he shallows at Jolanda Reef,
g wreckage from the
sank in 1981, beautiful
tail rays (see p. 218) cruise

Marine Park is considered
est dive sites. With its
allow reefs, coral walls, and
it is a site for both divers
s to the reef is easy. Jeeps,

*A reef shark patrols its territory (left); and a handsome yellowbar angelfish (below).*

live-aboards, and day boats
operate from the nearby resort
town of Sharm El Sheikh.

### EQUIPMENT
Scuba and snorkeling equipment is available for hire or
purchase, but the range is limited and expensive.
If possible, bring your own. The Red Sea can be
cool for a tropical destination, so 5 mm wetsuits
are recommended for the cool season, and 3 mm
wetsuits should be worn at other times.

### SPECIAL FEATURES
Divers and snorkelers can see a spectacular variety
of fish at Ras Muhammad, but two species are
worth special attention. Giant Napoleon wrasse
are particularly striking
and endearing, and are
likely to accompany
divers in the hope of a
handout—a practice
discouraged these
days. They look at you with big
eyes that revolve like ball turrets
as they seek out more generous
divers. Yellowbar angelfish,
unique to Africa and the Red
Sea, have markings on their sides
in the shape of Africa. KD

**TRAVELER'S NOTES**

conditions
Oct; more
ough seas
sharks and
during the

hot days,
ool winds
al and

F

**Dive logistics**
Day boats, live-
aboards, and shore-
based diving from jeeps;
pre-booking recommended
**Accommodation** Excellent range,
from budget hotels to five-star resorts
**Notes** Very cosmopolitan dive travelers;
be prepared for many different diving
techniques and attitudes. Heed any
political advisories for Egypt and
neighboring countries

249

*Traveler's Notes: These provide brief details on when to visit, the weather, water temperature, and possible hazards that might be encountered. They also list the type of diving amenities that are available, live-aboards or day trips, and what level of accommodation to expect.*

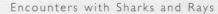

# San Diego
United States of America

The California Bight lies between the southern Californian coast and Channel Islands, which dot the temperate Pacific waters off the American West Coast. The warm temperate marine communities of this region make it one of the world's richest oceanographic areas. Inshore is dominated by golden kelp forests. Offshore are the deeps of the blue-water channel. This is the place for diving with blue sharks (see p. 183).

Dive boats transport groups of divers 12 to 15 miles (19 to 24 km) off the coast from San Diego. The Coronados Islands rise in peaks to the south; the long, rounded mountain of San Clemente Island breaks up the western horizon. All around is the vast Pacific, sometimes green, sometimes blue, some days glassy and sunlit, others choppy and covered in fog. April to September is the best time to dive to avoid the strong winds and big seas of winter.

The dive boat sets a sea anchor, then a roomy shark cage with a door at the rear is lowered over the side. This hangs about 10 to

*A blue shark (above) eyes a diver in a protective chain-mail suit. Forests of giant kelp (left) thrive close to shore.*

15 feet (3 to 4.5 m) below the surface. A divemaster in a protective chain-mail suit (see p. 76) accompanies three divers to the cage. It feels strange to stand in a barred cage suspended in the open ocean, with the clear blue depths falling away, the invisible bottom more than a mile below. You wait, nervously, searching the vast, dimensionless space for a flash of brilliantly blue shark.

As soon as the divemaster, still outside the cage, begins to release bait and chum, they start to arrive—speeding, graceful blues—first 1, then 6, soon as many as 20. The sharks snap at the bait and bump the cage, wanting to test its taste and texture. In the midst of this rush of blue muscle, white teeth, and adrenalin, the practiced (and suit-protected) divemaster allows a small blue shark to bite his chain-mail-clad arm. Photographers, safe inside the cage only inches away, consume film faster

*Harbor seals (right) visit the Channel Islands. Hilton's aeolid (below), a local marine snail.*

than the sharks do bait. You will soon become accustomed to the excitement, and revel in the spectacle. Elegant juveniles barely 2 feet (60 cm) long jet between adults up to 7 feet (2.1 m) and more, all feeding voraciously. A mako might race past in the distance, while strange, seemingly tailless mola molas (ocean sunfish) swim around at a leisurely pace.

The bait and chum are soon gone, and once the ocean current has dispersed any remaining food scraps, the blues begin to slip away, back into the vast ocean. Divers can now return to the boat, being especially careful as they go.

## EQUIPMENT
Only scuba diving is possible in the shark cage. A full 5 mm wetsuit is recommended, but some divers prefer a dry suit as it can get cool waiting in the cage. Dive guides will help you get your weight right for the stationary cage.

## SPECIAL FEATURES
California gray whales migrate through the channel in winter on their way to their calving grounds in Mexico. Blue whales also visit the California Bight, and the second known specimen of the

megamouth shark (see p. 154) was caught in the vicinity.

You should explore the kelp forests close to shore. Beneath the canopy of massed fronds there are colorful fish, lobsters, eels, swellsharks (see p. 163), leopard sharks (see p. 168), California hornsharks (see p. 142), and even the occasional stingray. Watch especially for California's state marine fish, the bright golden (and pugnacious) garibaldi.

The Channel Islands, which can be visited by boat, are a refuge for seals, sea lions, whales, and sea birds. Back on the mainland, Sea World, in San Diego, offers one of the world's best introductions to living sharks. The Steven Birch Aquarium, of the famous Scripps Institution of Oceanography, has exhibits on local sea life and international marine research. **LT**

### TRAVELER'S NOTES

**When to visit** Best diving conditions Apr–Sept
**Weather** Temperate year-round; summer mornings can be foggy, clearing by midday; rain and rough conditions most likely Dec–Feb
**Water temperature** 59–70° F (15–21° C)

**Dive logistics** Cage diving with scuba gear from day boats or live-aboards for trips of three days; pre-booking essential; shore diving and snorkeling around kelp beds and rocky points
**Accommodation** A wide selection is available in San Diego, ranging from budget motels to bed-and-breakfast guesthouses and five-star resorts

# Kona Coast

United States of America

The largest and most diverse of the Hawaiian islands is Hawaii, also called Big Island. Its western coast is known as the Kona Coast, and extends more than 85 miles (135 km). This area is a mecca for divers—calm, clear waters, massive corals, and abundant marine life. Among the many highlights are nightly manta ray "rush hours."

At night, the coastal luxury hotels in the Kona and Kohala districts shine floodlights over nearby rocky points into the shallows below. The powerful beams attract swarms of plankton, the smallest of sea creatures, and the food of choice for giant, filter-feeding manta rays (see p. 223). With the lights and the plankton come the mantas, ready to feed. Undoubtedly, they have been in the area for years, but "Manta Mania," the ad hoc festival of lights, people, and rays, is a recent phenomenon.

While there are no guarantees that the manta rays will show up, they usually do, especially on calm, moonless nights. Those who like to stay dry can watch them from a hotel balcony, or take one of the glass-bottom boats that depart from the harbor at Kailua-Kona. Alternatively, don snorkeling or diving gear and join these huge and graceful creatures in the water. Some snorkelers and divers are dropped off by dive operators' boats, while others simply swim out from shore. Night swims with rays can be enjoyed in many places along the coast. For a more private experience, ask a local diver.

A popular site is the area off Kona Surf Hotel at Keauhou Bay, about 6 miles (9.5 km) south of the town of Kailua-Kona. Here, the water is 15 to 20 feet (4.5 to 6 m) deep, usually with very

*The open mouth of a feeding manta ray (left); and (below) the eastern coastline of Hawaii Volcanoes National Park.*

little surge. Floodlights make the water glow a luminous pale green. To a diver looking up from the bottom, the lights seem to blink occasionally. The blink is really huge mantas passing overhead, their 12 foot (3.6 m) wide bodies eclipsing the light.

The water is often so clear that you can see myriad tiny plankton swarming near the surface, and look into the open mouth of a feeding manta. And you can easily distinguish the gray and black spots on the ray's pure white underside as it passes close overhead in slow, balletic flight. It is a great temptation to touch or hold on to a passing manta, but such behavior is strongly discouraged.

## EQUIPMENT

Snorkeling is the best way to see the manta rays. A Lycra suit or 3 mm wetsuit affords good protection and warmth. Dive operators are based around the Kona district and the town of Kailua-Kona; most offer rentals and sell a range of equipment.

## SPECIAL FEATURES

Hawaii is one of the best served and safest places to dive in the world. Dive boats cover the entire western coast, while

*A convoy of gray reef sharks (above); and a diver checks out a spotted pufferfish (left).*

excellent snorkeling areas also abound. Among bays, coves, lagoons, lava flows, and undersea lava tubes, an alert diver can find almost 600 species of fish—176 of them are found only in Hawaii.

Good encounters with a number of shark and ray species are possible. At particular sites along the western coast, you are likely to see whitetip and blacktip reef sharks, scalloped hammerheads, and eagle rays. You might also see whale sharks, tiger sharks, Galapagos sharks, gray reef sharks, even the occasional oceanic whitetip.

In winter and early spring, huge humpback whales fill these waters with song, vaulting into the air off Hawaii and the nearby island of Maui. Above ground, there is the spectacle of Hawaii Volcanoes National Park to be explored.  LT

### TRAVELER'S NOTES

**When to visit** *Fine year-round; best months for mantas May–Nov; humpback whale season Dec–May*
**Weather** *Warm days and cool nights; 70–85° F (21–29° C); gentle to brisk northeast trade winds; rainy Dec–Feb*
**Water temperature** *74–82° F (23–28° C)*
**Hazards** *Venomous animals include medusae and Portuguese man-of-war*

**Dive logistics** *Snorkeling from shore; day boats and live-aboards for week-long trips (pre-booking essential) offer access to sites along the Kona Coast*
**Accommodation** *A wide range, from beach camping and budget hotels to five-star resorts*
**Notes** *Bernice P. Bishop Museum, the archive of Hawaiian culture in Honolulu, has many artifacts relating to sharks*

# Sea of Cortez

Mexico

The strikingly beautiful Sea of Cortez is formed by the long peninsula of Baja California to the west and the mainland of Mexico to the east. To people who live here or visit, the Gulf is clearly a special place, where stark, rocky desert meets this inland sea's sparkling waters.

*Elephant Rock (above), off Isla Santa Catalina; and scalloped hammerheads approaching (left).*

A complex system of currents divides the Gulf into a cooler northern half and a warmer southern half. Both offer fine diving, but fans of sharks and rays prefer the warmer waters around the major port of the Baja peninsula, La Paz, and adjacent islands. Divers usually fly to La Paz and join a live-aboard boat.

High on the desired site list is a seamount, El Bajo, just east of Isla Espiritu Santo. In this group of rocky pinnacles, 60 feet (18 m) below the surface, moray eels seem to occupy every crevice. Shoals of fish abound and Pacific manta rays (see p. 223), billfish, and an occasional finback whale or whale shark (see p. 151) may also swim by. But schools of hundreds of scalloped hammerhead sharks (see p. 188), with adults up to 12 feet (3.6 m) long, are the main

attraction. The boat uses sonar to locate the underwater pinnacles and divers drop down to look up at the grand fleet of sharks, all headed in the same direction, schooling around the pinnacles.

Despite continued study and many creative explanations, scientists are still not certain why the hammerheads do this.

Isla Las Animas to the north is one of the most exciting and colorful dive spots in the Sea of Cortez. Rock walls are dominated by sea fans and gorgonians and are dense with invertebrate life. Schooling jacks number in the hundreds and there are underwater caves for the adventurous, plus more opportunities for viewing the hammerheads and other pelagic species.

Isla Los Islotes, just north of Isla Espiritu Santo, hosts a sea lion rookery. The island's east end, with a drop-off into deep water with many detached boulders, is good for sighting big fish.

Although spearfishing is not permitted now, years of overfishing and careless practices have

jeopardized the Gulf's ecological health. Baja's dive operators, Mexican and American alike, are dedicated to preserving its fragile beauty. The area is still rich in marine life, although numbers of large groupers and shellfish are declining.

## EQUIPMENT

Dive shops in La Paz are well-equipped but it's best to travel with your own gear. Live-aboards provide weights and tanks. Night-diving is popular and worthwhile. Divers often bring good diving lights, batteries, and "cool light" sticks. On the boat deck, a 5 mm wetsuit can become unbearably warm, but it feels good in the water, especially during winter.

## SPECIAL FEATURES

Isolated small coral heads occur throughout the southern Gulf, but Cabo Pulmo, south of La Paz, can be said to have the only living coral reef on the Pacific coast of North America. Many

reef fish will be recognized as relatives of central and South Pacific species. Farther offshore, fields of garden eels wave sinuously in the current, half their bodies burrowed into the sand while their big eyes search the water for plankton to snatch into mouths the diameter of a soda straw. Where rocks meet the sand at Cabo Pulmo and farther north toward La Paz, a sharp-eyed diver may see the rough-skinned Mexican hornshark, discovered near here in 1972.

In spring, the Sea of Cortez is a good place for sighting whales, including gray whales, finback whales, and the occasional 80 foot (24 m) blue whale. LT

### TRAVELER'S NOTES

**When to visit** Year-round; preferred diving season June–Dec
**Weather** Generally temperate to hot; 100° F (38° C) or more June–Sept; strong winds and tropical storms occur infrequently May–Oct
**Water temperature** 70–80° F (21–27° C) June–Nov; 61–70° F (16–21° C) Dec–May

**Hazards** Variable weather conditions and occasional strong tidal currents
**Dive logistics** Day boats operate from La Paz and Cabo San Lucas; live-aboards offer 3–10 day excursions to Gulf Islands; pre-booking advised
**Accommodation** La Paz has a full range, from pensions, comfortable hotels, to high-rise luxury hotels

Rainbow parrotfish (above left) are a colorful sight; and a rookery of Californian sea lions (above), basking in the Baja sun.

235

# Revillagigedo Islands

Mexico

If a friend asks you to dive at "Revillagigedo," you could end up in the cold waters off Revillagigedo Island in Alaska. Or—and this is our recommendation—you could be diving in warm Mexican waters, far south of the tip of Baja California. Whichever island you visit, most people pronounce it "Ree-vee-yah-hee-hey-do."

The Mexican Revillagigedo archipelago is 300 miles (480 km) south-southwest of the tip of Baja and 370 miles (590 km) west-southwest of Cape Corrientes on the Mexican mainland. The islands, uninhabited except for a Mexican naval installation on Socorro Island, are made up of numerous pinnacles and oceanic rocks. The major islands, spread over a large distance, include San Benedicto, Roca Partida, Clarion, and the largest, Socorro, which rises to 3,707 feet (1,130 m) with 110 square miles (285 sq km) of emergent land. Like most Pacific oceanic islands, the Revillagigedos are volcanic—San Benedicto's last eruption took place in the 1950s.

The great attractions for divers are the large pelagic sharks and schooling tuna that share these remote waters with huge manta rays (see p. 223). As well as the scores of giant mantas, a typical visitor's species list includes large scalloped hammerheads (see p. 188), Galapagos sharks (see p. 173), tiger sharks (see p. 181), and schools of jacks, tuna, and wahoo.

Comfortable live-aboard dive vessels depart from Cabo San Lucas, on the tip of the Baja peninsula, and usually spend 7 to 10 days visiting Socorro and San Benedicto. Boiler Rock, a pinnacle at San Benedicto, is home to "the friendliest manta rays in the world," according to renowned underwater photographer and biologist Norbert Wu. Groups of five or six mantas are common, and they are not shy with divers. Part of the reason for their friendliness may be that they associate this area with fishes that provide a "cleaning

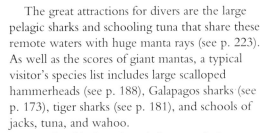

*A school of scalloped hammerheads (top); a Pacific manta ray (left), with remoras and orange Clarion angelfish.*

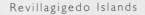

Roca Monument (left), Clarion Island; sightings of humpback whales (below) are often made in spring.

service." Young wrasses, damselfish, and other cleaner fish groom away dead tissue and parasites from the rays' gills, mouths, and body surfaces.

A close pass by a manta with a wingspan of up to 15 feet (4.5 m) may tempt a diver to grab on for a ride, but dive operators discourage this and so does the required permit from the Mexican government. Resist temptation and enjoy the glorious soaring dance of these huge rays as your bubbles caress their pale, muscled undersides.

## EQUIPMENT

This is scuba diving for experienced divers only. A 5 mm wetsuit is recommended. Dive vessels provide weights and tanks and all the comforts of home, but bring reliable, well-tested, gear and a body that's in good physical condition. This is very rigorous diving in remote oceanic waters with strong currents.

## SPECIAL FEATURES

It's a long trip to the Revillagigedo Islands, but worth it, with the adventurous feel of an oceanic expedition. Watch for

sea birds, dolphins, and whales—visitors in May might spot humpback whales.

Keep an eye out for other large pelagics, including schooling yellowfin tuna, and solitary toothy wahoos, 6 feet (1.8 m) blue-water predators that look like a cross between a tuna and a barracuda. Clarion Island gives its name to the rare and beautiful Clarion angelfish, a species unique to these Mexican waters. LT

### TRAVELER'S NOTES

**When to visit** Nov–May only, to avoid stormy Pacific waters and seasonal problems caused by offshore location

**Weather** Tropically warm; often windy

**Water temperature** 70–80° F (21–27° C)

**Hazards** Strong currents, rough water, and the remoteness of the location

**Dive logistics** Large, comfortable live-aboards only; book well in advance; boats depart from San Diego, USA, or Cabo San Lucas, which is closer

**Accommodation** Cabo San Lucas offers a range of accommodation from lodges to luxury hotels

**Notes** This is a very rigorous outing, but it pays off in large numbers of approachable manta rays

# Grand Cayman

Cayman Islands

Three islands make up the Cayman group, islands of dense mangroves and lagoons, powdery beaches set in the Caribbean's aquamarine waters. The steep coral and lime-stone walls of the outer reefs offer grand diving, but the big attraction is inside the barrier reef of Grand Cayman, the opportunity to get close to southern stingrays (see p. 216).

The experience of wading, swimming, snorkeling, or diving with these huge rays is thrilling. They grow to 4 or 5 feet (1.2 or 1.5 m) wide, and have long, whip-like tails, complete with dagger-like stinging spines. They usually spend their days buried in the sand, but Cayman stingrays have overcome their characteristic shyness.

They were originally attracted by scraps from cleaned fish, because fishers and tourists used to clean their catch in the area. People began to feed them regularly, as they came to expect the visits. They are now quite gentle and tame, and seek out interactions with humans, who learn to enjoy the company of these fantastic creatures. Take a deep breath and stretch out on the sandy bottom to watch a ray fly gracefully overhead, its wings and gill slits moving slowly, its extraordinary mouth and

*Southern stingrays (above) of the Caymans show off their tails. Vivid orange cup coral (left).*

nostrils like something from an unknown world. Or simply watch giggling children frolic with rays as wide across as the children are tall.

Cayman stingrays like to be fed, and have developed the manners of a starved dinner guest. If you don't have a squid or ballyhoo ready, the ray will move on after giving you a firm nudge.

There are two popular sites for "dancing" with rays. The most famous is the original Stingray City, on the west side of the Main Channel, close to Barker's Cay. This site is actually a wide, shallow, sandy channel spotted with coral heads. Visibility is usually excellent

over the bright white sand. Tidal currents can cloud the water, but the rays come so close you can't miss them. Water depth varies from 6 to 8 feet (1.8 to 2.4 m). Take a boat to Stingray City, then simply drop off into the water and wade around in sneakers, with mask and snorkel.

Another good site, known as Sandbar, lies at the entrance to Rum Point Channel. The water is shallower here, never reaching more than chest high, and the sea floor is flat and sandy. The conditions are usually ideal.

The main challenge for the photographer is the popularity of the sites. You will have to vie for a prime position with many others. The best way of ensuring that you get clear views and good photos of the stingrays is to stay on the

*A Caribbean collage (above) of fish, corals, and sea fans. Dancing with the rays (left), an experience unique to the Caymans.*

fringe and out of the crowd. The rays will check you out and leave if you offer nothing. By keeping your distance, you will get shots of these friendly rays, with and without people.

## EQUIPMENT

You need only a pair of sneakers and a mask to see these southern stingrays. You can also snorkel or dive with them, and well-equipped dive shops rent and sell all kinds of snorkeling and scuba gear.

## SPECIAL FEATURES

Not to be missed is diving the Cayman Walls, a system of cliffs, slopes, canyons, and valleys encircling the islands. These are encrusted with massive elkhorn coral, bushy black coral, giant sponges, and delicate soft corals, and are home to vast numbers of fish. Look for small creatures, such as a button-sized flamingo tongue cowrie feeding on a purple sea fan. Eagle and manta rays cruise the outer reef walls in this protected marine park. LT

---

### TRAVELER'S NOTES

**When to visit** Year-round; May–Oct offer the best conditions

**Weather** Influenced by trade winds; cooler Nov–Apr, warmest June–Aug; watch weather patterns for tropical storms July–Sept

**Water temperature** Summer, 70–80° F (21–27° C); winter, a bit lower

**Hazards** Clear water and steep walls can tempt divers to dive too deep. Plan your dive and dive your plan.

A recompression chamber is maintained at George Town Hospital, on Grand Cayman Island

**Dive logistics** Day boats to Stingray City; day boats and live-aboards serve the major Cayman dive spots and other islands; booking essential

**Accommodation** A full range, from rented houses and condominiums to luxury resorts; booking essential

**Notes** Holiday periods can be busy

# The Bahamas

The Bahamas

A lone sea star in crystalline Bahaman waters (top). Divers look on as Caribbean reef sharks circle in search of food (above).

The Bahamas consist of about 700 low-lying limestone cays, islands, and islets, only 20 of which are inhabited. Major islands include Grand Bahama, Bimini, Little Abaco, Abaco, Andros, New Providence (Nassau), Eleuthera, the Exumas, Long Island, and Great Inagua. The archipelago extends 600 miles (1,000 km) southeast from Grand Bahama, less than 60 miles (100 km) from the Florida coast of the United States, to Great Inagua Island, within 50 miles (80 km) of Cuba. With such an expanse, the Bahamas offer plenty of variety in dive locations. Every level of diving experience is catered to, and visibility is superb.

Areas that specialize in shark dives are easy to spot from their names: Shark Alley, Shark Arena, Shark Junction, Shark Rodeo. These are open areas to watch free-swimming sharks. Cages are not used. Divers descend 40 to 60 feet (12 to 15 m) to a reef area well known to experienced dive operators. A divemaster joins the group and signals for the boat to lower a bait-filled metal or plastic box. The thawing bait inside soon attracts sharks. Most operators promise from 60 to 100 sharks feeding for an hour.

The old reliables are the graceful but stocky Caribbean reef sharks (see p. 179). These stream in by the dozen, circling the divemaster and bumping each other in their haste and excitement. Sometimes, the bulkier and bossier bull sharks (see p. 174) will move in (these have much larger first dorsal fins set farther forward than the Caribbean reef sharks). Very rarely, a tiger shark (see p. 181) may come by, but big as they are, tiger sharks tend to be shy around bull sharks.

Divemasters are well-trained and careful, but you are in the open with feeding sharks. Follow tips the guides give before the dive; maintain a discreet distance; stay calm and follow instructions.

In the excitement of the feeding, speeding sharks, it's easy to get confused and see only the

240

big picture, but it's a pity to miss the details, so here are some ways to slow down the action in your mind and to help you look more closely at this thrilling spectacle. Count the sharks. Can you tell the species apart? Are they all Caribbean reef sharks or are some bulls? How do the smaller sharks react to the larger sharks? Which are males and which females? (Remember to look at the pelvic fins. Adult males have long, paired claspers extending rearward; in immature males the claspers don't yet reach the margins of the pelvic fins.) Look at the gill slits. Are there any parasitic copepods or juvenile shark suckers there? Such careful and disciplined looking will enrich your shark-watching experience, especially in the Bahamas, where dozens of sharks create such a spectacle.

*Divers are guaranteed close-up views of huge stingrays (above) and Caribbean reef sharks (left).*

## EQUIPMENT

Scuba diving is the only way to see the sharks. Equipment can be purchased or rented in larger centers, such as New Providence. Some gear is available in the more remote areas and on live-aboards, but it's best to bring your own. Weights are always provided. During the winter months, use at least a 3 mm wetsuit as the water cools

considerably. Take your camera. Remember that nothing can be removed from the water.

## SPECIAL FEATURES

Bahaman diving is big and superb, with steep walls, blue holes, large sharks. Take time to really look at the small things, too. Inside sponges lurk tiny golden gobies. Green sea grass shelters slender, delicate pipefish. Purple sea fans tolerate elegant flamingo tongue cowries that feed on the sea fans' soft tissue. Reef squid stare into your eyes, flash a colorful neon signal, then dart off. Don't miss these tiny miracles. LT

### TRAVELER'S NOTES

**When to visit** *Year-round; summer is hot, but the sea refreshes*
**Weather** *Influenced by trade winds; cooler Nov–Apr, warmest June–Sept; watch forecasts for tropical storms*
**Water temperature** *From 70–75° F (21–24° C) in Feb to 82–88° F (28–31° C) in Sept*

**Dive logistics** *Day trips from Grand Bahamas and New Providence; live-aboards also; booking essential*
**Accommodation** *A wide range even on remote cays, from camping and comfortable dive lodges to luxury hotels; Walker Cay on Abaco Island has shore-side accommodation near Shark Rodeo*

# Cocos Island

Costa Rica

Diving Isla del Coco (as the host country of Costa Rica calls it) is a high-seas adventure. A typical dive trip to Cocos begins with a flight to San José, in Costa Rica. An overnight stay in this capital city precedes the morning's three-hour bus trip to the coast, where the dive vessel departs. The 260 mile (420 km) crossing from Puntarenas to Cocos Island, over long, rolling Pacific swells (occasionally shortened to a steep chop), takes 32 to 36 hours. The lush green island, once a favored pirate haunt, is washed by 300 inches (7,620 mm) of rain annually and consequently streams with rivers and waterfalls.

Cocos is famous for what have come to be affectionately called "LLPs" or "Large Legendary Pelagics" ("pelagic" is the oceanographic term for "open sea"). The LLPs of note are silky sharks (see p. 172), scalloped hammerhead sharks (see p. 188), Galapagos sharks (see p. 173), huge manta rays (see p. 223), the occasional whale shark (see p. 151), and schools of tuna and jacks.

Once the vessel arrives, it becomes the mother ship for groups of divers using roving skiffs to reach the diving sites. To justify the long trip to Cocos, most operators stay for a full seven days of diving, with three dives a day. The ship anchors and the skiffs stay mobile to pick up divers surfacing in the strong currents. Deep

diving, fast currents, and plenty of sharks are all thrilling aspects of Cocos diving.

One popular dive spot is a small rock spire on the north side of the island, called Manuelita. This can be a very strenuous and exciting outing. Typically, divers chance the bottom at 140 feet (45 m) to get upward views of schooling scalloped hammerheads shyly aggregating in the murky depths. Currents can be unpredictable, and sometimes flow from different directions at various depths. During your descent to deeper waters, several 12 to 15 foot (3.6 to 4.5 m) manta rays may make lazy barrel rolls close by.

At Punta Ulloa, about 100 whitetip reef sharks are a frequent sight, sharing the area with

*Circling sailfish, just some of the large creatures seen at this site.*

dozens of large marbled ribbontail rays, 4 to 6 feet (1.2 to 1.8 m) across. Whitetips come in all sizes, alone, in pairs, and in groups. Most divers lose count after the first 50. Dirty Rock and Viking Rock usually offer lots of whitetip reef sharks (see p. 186) and numerous scalloped hammerheads too, congregating in water about 120 feet (35 m) deep. The mix often includes a few large Galapagos sharks.

Scalloped hammerheads are abundant on the deep reefs and spires off Cocos. Scuba divers describe them as generally shy, elusive, and difficult to approach within close range. To get good close-up photographs, divers make use of rebreathers (which produce fewer bubbles and make less noise than other types of breathing apparatus). Hammerheads like to stay in deeper, colder, murkier depths, and you can count on seeing them below 120 feet (35 m), although solitary individuals may wander into shallower depths. Most of the LLPs can be seen while diving no deeper than 100 feet (30 m).

*A magnificent manta ray (above) with two remora companions; and countless squirrelfish (left) swimming on a Cocos Island reef.*

## Equipment

This is an active dive trip for experienced divers able to handle strong currents and deep diving. At least a 5 mm wetsuit is essential. Bring reliable gear, a good dive computer, and a body in good physical condition. Nitrox and rebreathers are available on some dive boats that serve Cocos, as are weights and tanks.

## Special Features

An attentive diver can find all kinds of interesting fish and invertebrates, but the big fish are the main attraction. If you tire of open-water sharks, drop to a ledge and get close to a whitetip reef shark. There are hundreds in the area.   LT

### TRAVELER'S NOTES

**When to visit**  Mar–Sept
**Weather**  Cocos Island can be wet; offshore weather can be windy, with rough seas; trust the skipper to make a safe crossing and find the lee
**Water temperature**  Varies with currents; surface can be 80–82° F (27–28° C), with thermoclines dropping to 65–70° F (18–21° C)
**Hazards**  Strong currents and deep diving in a remote area

**Dive logistics**  Live-aboards for 11-day trips, offering 7 full days of diving; advance bookings with dive charter operators are necessary
**Accommodation**  Large, comfortable live-aboard vessels are necessary because of the long ocean passage to Cocos Island; they accommodate between 12 and 22 divers
**Notes**  This is a trip for avid and experienced divers only

# Galapagos Islands
## Ecuador

Politically part of Ecuador, the Galapagos Islands are a remote evolutionary show-case. This archipelago of volcanic islands only five million years old sits astride the Equator and is washed by three major ocean currents. Many of the species of sharks, rays, and reef fishes that live in Hawaii are also here, but only in the Galapagos can you see marine iguanas and penguins basking on a black lava coastline.

Most visitors to this natural treasury fly first to the Ecuadorean capital of Quito, and then west 600 miles (1,000 km) off the coast of South America to the small Galapagos islet of Baltra. Live-aboard charter vessels pick up visitors and, accompanied by a government-licensed naturalist guide, the adventure begins.

Sharks and rays are seen almost anywhere among the many islands, but the favored spots for shark diving are two remote rock islands, Isla Darwin and Isla Wolf, 100 miles (160 km) north of the main group. Here the water is usually warm and clear, and the underwater fauna is large and abundant. Schools of scalloped hammerheads (see p. 188) number in the hundreds; green sea turtles paddle by in their dozens; eagle rays coast above the bottom; and mantas (see p. 223) barrel-roll in

*Crowds of cownose rays (above) gather in sheltered mangrove bays; a marine iguana (below), seen only in the Galapagos Islands.*

midwater, then break the surface. Whitetip reef sharks (see p. 186) rest on the bottom beneath overhangs before venturing forth for a meal of reef fish. A large whale shark (see p. 151) may pass through on its way south. The species list is long and thrilling, and includes sea lions, barracudas, fur seals, and false killer whales. Pacific cownose rays, rare in open waters, gather in large numbers in enclosed mangrove bays. Hot spots include Tortuga Negra on Santa Cruz Island and Elizabeth Bay on Isabella Island. Locals call them *raya dorada*, or golden ray, for their rich color.

244

The first Galapagos shark (see p. 173), collected here in 1904, was named in honor of the islands, but they are now known to occur throughout the world's tropical waters. Graceful and strong, they are seen swimming either alone or in small groups, and should be treated with caution. The Galapagos hornshark, unique to the Galapagos and adjacent South American coastline, lives on the bottom or in rocky crevices. Its large black spots contrast with its cream body.

Divers must pay attention to currents and surging swells. Huge boulders on the bottom look stationary but have only recently been moved by the ocean's power. One diver has described the surging swells as leaving divers "feeling like guppies in a washing machine." The shallower rocky reefs are home to fascinating invertebrates and fishes.

## EQUIPMENT

You are strongly advised to bring your own dive gear. Booking through a dive-travel operator will ensure that your live-aboard vessel is equipped

*Pinnacle Rock (above), Bartolomé Island; a green sea turtle (right).*

for scuba diving (many boats here serve only shore excursions, with limited snorkeling). The mix of currents creates a range of surface water temperatures, and there are marked thermoclines. A 5 mm wetsuit with hood is recommended year-round. Galapagos is not recommended for inexperienced divers because of its remoteness and strong currents.

## SPECIAL FEATURES

Visiting the Galapagos to see only sharks would be worse than visiting Africa to see only lions. There are thousands of reasons to come here; most of them involve animals and plants, both land and marine. Nowhere else can you see coral reef fishes, penguins, sea lions, marine iguanas, and flightless cormorants all on the same day. At the Charles Darwin Research Station at Puerto Ayora, Santa Cruz Island, conservationists are trying to save the endangered giant tortoise.

Prepare for your visit by reading some good books on Galapagos natural history, including young Charles Darwin's accounts of his adventures. LT **245**

---

### TRAVELER'S NOTES

**When to visit** *Year-round, but best in late Feb–May*

**Weather** *Equatorial; warm to hot; cooler season from May–Dec; hotter season Jan–May*

**Water temperature** *Variable with location and depth; from 65–80° F (18–27° C)*

**Hazards** *Blue-water diving with strong currents; this is not for novices*

**Dive logistics** *Live-aboards only; book packages through dive operators*

**Accommodation:** *Live-aboards only, booking essential; hotels and guest-houses at Puerto Ayora, Santa Cruz Island, but little or no diving support*

**Notes** *Be aware of the political climate in Ecuador; check government advisories*

# Isle of Man

United Kingdom

A location with good conditions for the reliable sighting of basking sharks (see p. 157) is found at the Isle of Man. In the heart of the Irish Sea, this is a Celtic island of unspoiled beaches, undulating hills, friendly people, and 10,000 years of history. The area is also popular with shark biologists. A research project was begun here during the 1980s, when a sighting and reporting system for basking sharks was organized.

*The forbidding walls of Peel Castle (above), on the beachfront. Visitors are offered glimpses of the history of the ancient Celtic race on the island.*

The basking shark is one of three species known to feed on plankton. Of the other two, the whale shark (see p. 151) is regularly sighted by divers, while the megamouth (see p. 154) is rarely seen by anyone. The basking shark prefers the colder, plankton-rich waters of the temperate zone. Divers can see them in Monterey Bay along the Californian coast of the United States, off the Scottish west coast, and at sites in the Irish Sea. The place to see large gatherings is the Isle of Man.

The sighting system now extends throughout Britain, and reporters include ferry operators, fishers, divers, charter-boat operators, lighthouse keepers, lifeboat operators, coastguards, and walkers on coastal paths. Information collected over the past 10 years is being used to assess the population and migration patterns of these sharks. They visit British coastal waters from June to early September, but where they go during the winter is as yet unknown.

You can make trips with local dive operators, but a great way to see the "baskers" is to link up with a research group. Biologists welcome volunteers, and organize outings, dedicated to natural history, with Isle of Man travel companies. Headquarters for visitor-volunteers are usually family hotels in the picturesque village of Peel. Venture forth as a volunteer

A small town hugs the coast of the Isle of Man (above). A basking shark (right) feeds in the murky waters of the Irish Sea.

researcher on a scientist's day boat, and listen to the radio crackle with news of shark sightings. Suit up in a warm dry suit as the engine is cut. Slip overboard into the cool blue-green water, sometimes with snorkel gear, sometimes with scuba, and slowly approach the path of a giant plankton feeder.

Perhaps you will be asked to assist in measuring parts of the shark, or to watch for identifying markings or scars. Pause and look into the shark's gaping mouth and see daylight beaming in through the huge gill slits. Visibility is up to 20 feet (6 m), with good opportunities for photographing the sharks.

Basking sharks are still hunted, and researchers estimate that about 5,000 animals are taken each year for their fins. As a result, the species is gradually disappearing from areas in which it was previously common. British biologists are particularly concerned because their observations show that about 95 percent of surface-feeding baskers (the ones killed by hunters) are females. Obviously, the selective removal of this group has severe consequences for a species whose numbers remain unknown.

## EQUIPMENT

The water here is cool and sometimes murky, and you will be most comfortable diving in a dry suit. Dives are made from unanchored boats after basking sharks have been encountered.

## SPECIAL FEATURES

A local dive operator also offers dive outings to see the rich benthic invertebrate fauna on rocky bottoms off the island. Don't miss the chance to experience the history of the island and its people—few dive vacations offer the Celtic warmth of a local pub. The seals, whales, and fish of these waters are at the heart of many a tale you might coax from your companions after a day in and on the Irish Sea. **LT**

### TRAVELER'S NOTES

**When to visit** June to early Sept
**Weather** Cool, maritime climate influenced by the warm Gulf Stream; cool summers, 61–63° F (16–17° C)
**Water temperature** 61° F (16° C)
**Hazards** Avoid becoming chilled
**Dive logistics** Day trips on local dive boats and as volunteers with a well-organized research project, the Isle of Man Basking Shark Project; look up its website at http://www.isle-of-man.com/interests/shark/index.htm
**Accommodation** Hotels and guesthouses; special packages can be pre-booked through travel agents and dive operators

# Ras Muhammad

Egypt

The parched landscape and rugged mountains of the Sinai Peninsula in Egypt seem lifeless. But beneath the sapphire waters of the Red Sea dwells a kaleidoscope of living color. Where the southern tip of the peninsula plunges into the sea at Ras Muhammad, incredible shallow reef flats near the shoreline give way to sheer coral walls disappearing into the depths below. Clouds of Anthias and glassfish shimmer among the undulating soft corals. And shafts of desert sunlight penetrate deep into the blue abyss to reveal patrolling gray reef sharks (see p. 170).

*Anthias, famous for their vivid color, dart about the coral reef (top); and the Red Sea and Sinai Desert (above).*

Shark Observatory, one of the best shark sites, is a stretch of the Ras Muhammad coral wall. Divers swimming here will see jacks, tuna, barracuda, and other pelagic marine life traversing the deep ocean. Only the wall is there to orientate you, with the seemingly bottomless sea dropping away beneath you. It is quite common to turn a corner and come face to face with several gray reef sharks searching for food or checking their territory for competitors. It is hard to decide who gets the bigger surprise, as the sharks veer out into the limitless blue and the divers kick toward the security of the wall.

Gray reef sharks are curious and territorial, and pay much attention to divers, circling constantly, coming and going, and sometimes even becoming slightly aggressive. But during December and January, you may have the rare privilege of witnessing groups of 5 to 10 gray reef sharks that completely ignore you because they are engrossed in mating behavior. Females circle in the water off the reef, within 30 feet (10 m) of you. A male will dash into the group, single out a female and pursue her, repeatedly biting her flanks. This action is thought to promote ovulation, and the female's thick skin has evolved to deal with it. While you are unlikely to see an actual coupling, these encounters provide opportunities for unique observations and rare photos or video footage.

Shark Reef and Jolanda Reef are two small submerged reefs just below the surface, a short swim from the tip of the peninsula. On their ocean side, these reefs again drop away in coral

walls, and are another
favorite area for gray reef
sharks and other large
pelagic fish. Divers and
snorkelers should also look
out for oceanic whitetips
(see p. 176), scalloped and
great hammerheads (see
pp. 188–9), and manta rays
(see p. 223). This is one of
those sites where any manner of species could
turn up. And in the shallows at Jolanda Reef,
amid the remaining wreckage from the
MV *Jolanda*, which sank in 1981, beautiful
bluespotted ribbontail rays (see p. 218) cruise
among the corals.

Ras Muhammad Marine Park is considered
one of the world's best dive sites. With its
crystalline waters, shallow reefs, coral walls, and
wealth of marine life, it is a site for both divers
and snorkelers. Access to the reef is easy. Jeeps,

*A reef shark patrols its territory (left); and
a handsome yellowbar angelfish (below).*

live-aboards, and day boats
operate from the nearby resort
town of Sharm El Sheikh.

## EQUIPMENT
Scuba and snorkeling equipment is available for hire or
purchase, but the range is limited and expensive.
If possible, bring your own. The Red Sea can be
cool for a tropical destination, so 5 mm wetsuits
are recommended for the cool season, and 3 mm
wetsuits should be worn at other times.

## SPECIAL FEATURES
Divers and snorkelers can see a spectacular variety
of fish at Ras Muhammad, but two species are
worth special attention. Giant Napoleon wrasse
are particularly striking
and endearing, and are
likely to accompany
divers in the hope of a
handout—a practice
discouraged these
days. They look at you with big
eyes that revolve like ball turrets
as they seek out more generous
divers. Yellowbar angelfish,
unique to Africa and the Red
Sea, have markings on their
sides in the shape of Africa. **KD** 249

### TRAVELER'S NOTES

**When to visit**  *Best diving conditions
during warm months, June–Oct; more
variable visibility and risk of rough seas
during cool season, Nov–Feb; sharks and
manta rays more in evidence during the
mating season, Dec–Feb*

**Weather**  *Arid desert climate, hot days,
cooler at night; very little rain; cool winds
during Nov–Feb make days cool and
nights quite cold*

**Water temperature**  *70–82° F
(21–28° C)*

**Dive logistics**
*Day boats, live-
aboards, and shore-
based diving from jeeps;
pre-booking recommended*

**Accommodation**  *Excellent range,
from budget hotels to five-star resorts*

**Notes**  *Very cosmopolitan dive travelers;
be prepared for many different diving
techniques and attitudes. Heed any
political advisories for Egypt and
neighboring countries*

# Cape Town
### South Africa

To dive with great white sharks is the ultimate thrill for shark watchers. Dyer Island, a two-hour drive east of Cape Town in South Africa, offers the possibility of viewing and cage diving with great whites. This very special area is actually comprised of two islands. The main island, Dyer, is home to a huge marine bird population; the second, Geyser Island, hosts almost 13,000 Cape fur seals. Separating the two islands is a shallow channel, roughly 160 yards (150 m) wide and 550 yards (600 m) long, nicknamed Shark Alley. Great white sharks patrol this protected channel to hunt fur seals, and this area is without doubt one of the great white shark meccas of the world.

*Jackass penguins (above), Dyer Island; Cape fur seals (left) at Geyser Island.*

Divers are transported the 5 miles (8 km) to the site from nearby Gansbaai by a well-equipped deep-sea cabin cruiser, or in speedboats from Kleinbaai harbor. Once in the channel, most operators deploy a specially designed three-person cage that floats at the surface. Although divers need no fins and don't venture more than 7 feet (2 m) beneath the surface, all are required to have a minimum scuba-diving qualification. Divers can make two to four dives a day, taking turns in the cage. Non-divers can view the activity from the deck or flying bridge of the boat, as the sharks often break the surface in search of bait. One tour operator uses a shark-viewing capsule, which forms part of the boat and offers a 180 degree view of sharks through thick safety glass.

Although sharks are abundant here (on one occasion, researchers working in the area tagged 18 great whites in 7 hours), chumming assures a good turnout. Sometimes the sharks leap boisterously out of the water, but the typical approach is more subdued. First, there is a slight bulge on the glassy surface caused by the shark's bow wave, then two vortices form behind a large dorsal fin as it breaks the surface and a 15 foot (4.5 m) shark heads straight for the bait.

The Twelve Apostles (above), Cape Town. Note the very pointed nose of the great white shark (left), from around Dyer Island.

On deck, watchers are at first mesmerized by the sight, then excited, then eager to jump into the cage and look the creature in the eye. Once in the cool water, the excitement can be elevated by the murky background, out of which the great creatures suddenly emerge. Or, depending on conditions, visibility may permit you to spy a large shark from some distance away.

The high likelihood (claimed to be at least 80 percent) of seeing great white sharks makes Dyer Island and adjacent areas appealing for shark watchers. However, this is also an important research site for the study of the biology and behavior of great whites. Be sure to select a dive operator who cooperates with the ongoing scientific and conservation activities here.

## EQUIPMENT
Some dive operators supply all diving equipment but it is always best to provide your own mask, regulator, and wetsuit—fins are not needed in the cage. A dry suit is best for these waters, but a 6 mm wetsuit will give minimum protection.

## SPECIAL FEATURES
Rocky Dyer Island and the surrounding islands host thousands of Cape fur seals, Cape gannets, jackass penguins, whales, and dolphins. Specially organized dives into the enchanting and balletic world of the Cape fur seal are offered at Seal Island, about 18 miles (30 km) from Cape Town on the Atlantic side of the Cape of Good Hope. Or try whale watching at De Kelders, near Gansbaai, where southern right whales come within 100 feet (30 m) of the rocks. These giant mammals visit this coast to mate and calve from mid June to late December; you can see up to 30 as they come to rub their bodies on the kelp.

The Cape of Good Hope also has more than 50 marked wrecks for divers to explore.  LT

### TRAVELER'S NOTES

**When to visit** High season Feb–Sept, almost 100% likelihood of sightings; low season Oct–Jan, about 80% likelihood

**Weather** Usually pleasant, temperate; sometimes stormy and windy, or still and foggy

**Water temperature** 58–65° F (14–18° C)

**Dive logistics** Day boats; day trips from Cape Town; overnight trips or 10-day excursions based at Gansbaai; book through dive operators

**Accommodation** A range of accommodation in Cape Town; guesthouses at Gansbaai, some self-catering

**Notes** During winter (June–Aug), high shark activity, but weather only permits trips to the island one or two days a week

# Similan and Surin Islands

Thailand

The Similan and Surin Islands are located in the tropical waters of the Andaman Sea, about 70 miles (110 km) northwest of Phuket, Thailand. Huge granite boulders rise out of the aquamarine water like ancient sentinels. On land, there are quiet bays of talcum-powder sand and groves of palm trees. Underwater, the boulders descend 115 feet (35 m) to the sandy sea floor, with every boulder covered in spectacular soft corals, gorgonians, and sponges. These undersea gardens are home to the zebra, or leopard, shark (see p. 150), one of the most endearing and beautiful of sharks.

Divers descend into the warm, calm waters of the Andaman Sea to discover that visibility is excellent, varying from 40 to 100 feet (12 to 30 m). The gentle currents bring nutrient-rich waters to the area, which help create the spectacular diversity of corals and marine life.

Sooner or later, you will come across a zebra shark resting comfortably on the sand floor among the brilliant reefs. They are gentle and harmless, and will let you come quite close,

occasionally even within a few feet. Scuba divers are more likely than snorkelers to see zebra sharks. It is very pleasant to lie on the sand alongside a shark your own size and feel completely safe. This beautiful creature usually stays quite still and you can see remoras moving about on its skin. Eventually, the shark swims off gracefully through the coral canyons, its long tail moving with an undulating, sensuous, almost hypnotic motion.

*A diver takes a very close look (right) at a zebra shark, also known as a leopard shark. Above, a striking clown triggerfish.*

*An underwater seascape of soft corals and lionfish (above), and a bay (below), in the Similan Islands.*

The islands are visited by live-aboard dive boats operating out of Phuket. (Day boats also offer tours to reefs and islands just off Phuket, where zebra sharks and plentiful marine life can be viewed.) Today, the nine islands in the Similan group are mostly uninhabited and are designated the Similan Islands National Park, protecting the flora, fauna, and marine life of the area.

## EQUIPMENT

Scuba and snorkeling equipment can be hired from local dive centers and resorts in Phuket. Lycra suits will suffice, but divers often find a 2–3 mm wetsuit is better, as sometimes cool water thermoclines occur in this region.

## SPECIAL FEATURES

The Similan Islands offer a rare example of differing underwater environments. On the west-facing side, the brilliant colors and unexpected shapes of soft corals and sea fans cover the giant granite boulders. This is in startling contrast to the pastel hues of the hard corals usually populating coral reefs, and which you can find growing prolifically on the eastern side of the islands. Thus, in the

same group of islands, you are able to observe the best of both coral worlds.

As well as the tropical fish you'd expect to see—including butterflyfish, angelfish, and orange Anthias—the reefs of the Andaman Sea contain some unique marine life. The Andaman Sea Crown of Thorns sea star, in iridescent red and purple, can be found eating contentedly and blending in perfectly among the soft corals. These sea stars are a necessary part of the reef's delicate ecosystem. The world's most spectacular triggerfish, the clown triggerfish, is also resident, and can be approached.

Between February and May, the lucky visitor may also encounter a whale shark swimming near Richelieu Rock, in the Surin Islands. KD

### TRAVELER'S NOTES

**When to visit** Best during the dry season, Nov–Apr; sunny, calm seas
**Weather** Tropical climate, 77–89° F (25–31° C)
**Water temperature** 79–82° F (26–28° C)
**Hazards** Very wet during the monsoon season in Sept
**Dive logistics** Snorkeling or scuba diving from live-aboard boats for trips of 2–12 days; pre-booking recommended
**Accommodation** A wide range of resorts, hotels, and guesthouses is available in Phuket

# Yap and Palau

Micronesia

T he island groups of Yap and Palau in the western-central Pacific, along with the outlying Truk (also known as Chuuk) group 1,000 miles (1,600 km) to the east, offer many dive possibilities. Sharks and rays, the abundant tropical marine life, an extraordinary geography, rich local cultural customs, and arguably the best wreck diving in the world, make Micronesia a favored spot for divers.

Sharks patrol the glorious reef (above). The Seventy Islands National Park (left), Palau.

## YAP

Almost unheard of a decade ago, Yap is today renowned for opportunities to get close to manta rays (see p. 223). A combination of tidal barrier-reef channels and favorable weather patterns allows diving with them year-round. Mantas regularly move into two channels for feeding and cleaning. From June through October, locals recommend Goofnuw Channel on the eastern side, where mantas are dispersed over five distinct spots. Milli Channel, on the western side, offers Manta Ridge, where visibility can exceed 100 feet (30 m). Divers cling to the rocks along a ledge about 30 feet (10 m) down while

(see p. 223)

overhead, mantas cruise through the channel.

At both locales, mantas congregate during tidal changes as plankton is funneled out of the lagoon and mangrove areas. Huge volumes of food-rich water are flushed through to the hovering mantas. Some soar directly over your head, close enough to touch, but any such interference with their movements is prohibited.

## PALAU

To many divers, Palau is the top tropical dive spot in the world, while to biologists it is a treasury of both land and sea biodiversity. There are more than 100 different dive sites in the vast coral lagoon and adjacent islands, offering diving unlike anywhere else in the world. Thousands of marine species inhabit the region, including manta rays, barracuda, large and small sharks, and an impressive invertebrate fauna ranging from giant clams to the chambered nautilus.

Palau is unusual in having atolls, high volcanic islands, and its famous uplifted limestone rock

islands all in one area. The edge of the barrier reef is nearby, with magnificent wall diving at such legendary sites as Blue Corner, a pass between lagoon and open sea where sharks abound. Divers share swift-flowing tidal waters with gray reef sharks (see p. 170), blue marlin, manta rays, dogtooth tuna, and Napoleon wrasse. Nearby Big Dropoff and New Dropoff are other favorite spots to drift along in the current, about 30 feet (10 m) down, with the coral-studded bottom passing below and gray reef sharks cruising by in search of a meal.

## EQUIPMENT
Main centers on all island groups have dive shops, but it is best to bring your own gear. This is warm-water diving but Lycra suits and 3 mm

*Longnose hawkfish on a sea fan (left). Some Palau lakes harbor Mastigias jellyfish (below).*

wetsuits protect divers from abrasions and stinging plankton, and on cooler night dives. Scuba diving is the only way to see life in the passes, but the clear waters and glorious reef development also make for superb snorkeling.

## SPECIAL FEATURES
One Micronesian dive experience not to be missed is the wreck diving at Truk. This cluster of 12 tiny volcanic islands and many lesser islets, in a large lagoon girdled by a coral reef, was heavily bombed during the Second World War. The great lagoon is now a graveyard for the wrecks of more than 100 planes and ships, which provide a dramatic background for diving amid the richness of Micronesian marine life.

Inland "lakes" on Palau host large populations of unique jellyfish. Extensive outer reefs offer a phenomenal diversity of invertebrate life, including black corals, giant sea fans, sponges, and stony corals, and some dive operators will even grant your wish to swim with a live chambered nautilus. LT

### TRAVELER'S NOTES

**When to visit** Year-round; manta mating season at Yap, Nov–Mar
**Weather** Good year-round; trade winds May–Nov
**Water temperature** 82–86° F (28–30° C)
**Hazards** Be extra alert when wreck diving; poisonous spiny trees on Palau
**Dive logistics** Day boats and live-aboards from all islands; a live-aboard amphibious airplane based at Palau

visits outer islands, including Yap. Pre-booking before departure essential
**Accommodation** Palau has luxury hotels; Yap and Truk have comfortable hotels and lodge accommodation
**Notes** Yap offers best combination of indigenous culture and dive sites. Nitrox and rebreathers, and training in their use, are available on Yap and Truk

# Rangiroa Atoll

French Polynesia

To the northeast and east of Tahiti is a set of low-lying atolls and islands once known as Tuamotu, the Dangerous Archipelago. The largest of the 80 islands is Rangiroa, some 40 miles (65 km) long and 20 miles (32 km) across. In fact, Rangiroa is the second largest atoll in the Pacific Ocean and its lagoon could accommodate the entire island of Tahiti.

Because of its size, Rangiroa offers far more than the usual excitement of a coral atoll. Steep reef faces drop off to almost 1 mile (1,600 m) deep and swift tidal currents rush through the narrow openings in the reef between lagoon and open sea. At full tidal flood, currents can exceed 5 knots, far too fast to swim against. Although tidal extremes are slight (up to 2 feet [60 cm]), the volume of the lagoon and the narrowness of the passes assure fast-flooding currents when the tide turns. It is these passes that offer Rangiroa's most exciting diving, and that includes sharks.

The order for the day is "go with the flow." Dive boats drop divers off inside the lagoon so

*The lagoon at Rangiroa Atoll (above) stretches away endlessly. Red brick soldierfish (left) shelter in a pass.*

they can swim down 20 to 30 feet (6 to 9 m) and be swept along in the current (to be picked up later out in the open sea by the boat). This is the closest you can get to underwater flying. Imagine soaring from lagoon to open sea while sharing "air space" with a range of sharks, manta rays (see p. 223), and Napoleon fish. Soaring over rich reef growth, you can look down on delicate reef fishes struggling to hold position in the lee of coral heads. You may pass a cave with at least 20 nurse sharks (see p. 149)—perhaps you can return to investigate later.

Outside the reef, where the food-rich and sun-warmed lagoon water meets the water of the open sea, whole food chains are concentrated. Eggs, spawn, larvae, and juveniles born on the reefs of the lagoon meet the predators—sharks, mantas, barracudas, jacks, dogtooth tuna, and mahi-mahi. There is nowhere better to see predation in action than around a flushing pass.

The principal diving spots in Rangiroa include Avatoru Pass, one of the two larger passes at 165 feet (50 m) wide. It is noted for Napoleon fish and manta rays, as well as gray reef sharks (see p. 170), leopard rays, and an impressive fish fauna, especially snappers and jacks.

Tiputa Pass is shorter and not as deep as Avatoru, but it ends with a steep drop-off. Dolphins are often seen in the pass and divers have also reported sailfish and marlin. Drift diving with the current here brings shouts of joy from divers. Photographers are recommended to stay at the end of the group to photograph their buddies in the middle of the action. Gray reef sharks, whitetip reef sharks (see p. 186), and hammerheads guarantee excitement.

Le Failles is a two-hour chartered boat trip across the lagoon. This spectacular dive site on the outer side of the atoll offers rich coral growth and interesting canyons and caves. Shelter in a canyon and see gray reef sharks and perhaps the odd silvertip passing against deep blue space.

### EQUIPMENT
Scuba equipment is available for hire, but if possible, bring your own. Lycra bodysuits or 3 mm

*Gray reef sharks (left) wait outside a reef pass for a meal to be served up to them by the tide. A Titan triggerfish (below).*

wetsuits afford protection from scrapes and keep you warm during long exposures.

### SPECIAL FEATURES
Every fragment of the land on atolls such as Rangiroa was formed by once-living reef plants and animals. Long ago, volcanic Rangiroa was a high island of black lava, like Hawaii or the Galapagos Islands are now. Slowly, the black rock has sunk into the sea and the living reef has continued to grow. Now, the low-lying atoll is just the tip of a thick limestone cap on a basaltic platform far below. LT

## TRAVELER'S NOTES

**When to visit**  Year-round, but best Nov–Apr

**Weather**  Excellent, although trade winds can blow strongly across low-lying atoll; sun protection is always necessary

**Water temperature**  Up to 80° F (27° C)

**Dive logistics**  Day boats essential to dive the passes; pre-book through local Polynesian dive shops; also live-aboards

**Accommodation**  Packages from Tahiti by air include live-aboards or, more frequently, lodge-like shore accommodation; booking essential

**Notes**  Pass diving is a challenge for beginning divers, and local guides expect some experience. Plan your trip carefully to permit ample diving between the infrequently scheduled flights

# Mamanuca Islands

Fiji

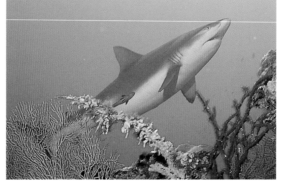

The gray reef shark (above) can be seen in gangs at some sites on the reefs in Fijian waters. A dazzling male blue ribbon eel (far right).

Fiji consists of more than 300 islands scattered over 42,000 square miles (108,800 sq km) of tropical ocean. The only drawback to visiting the region is selecting a single place to stay. Some visitors choose a live-aboard vessel for 7 to 14 days and visit a number of dive sites. Others settle in a shore-based resort and concentrate on the rich variety at hand.

Closest to the visitor's arrival point at Nadi International Airport is the Mamanuca Group (pronounced Mama-nutha). Within this group, Mana Island is a popular choice. The calm, clear waters surrounding the island are protected by a barrier reef, making it an ideal place to learn how to dive or to refine your skills.

One of the best areas for viewing sharks and rays in the Mamanucas is the Supermarket. With coral walls extending about 100 feet (30 m), it is the home of gray reef sharks (see p. 170) and their calmer relatives, nurse sharks (see p. 149) and whitetip reef sharks (see p. 186). Divers drop to the sandy bottom near the reef wall and watch their Fijian dive guide confer with the sharks. Like a generous host at a social gathering, the guide offers chunks of fish on the end of a pole spear. Sharks are cultural resources in Fiji, and some dive guides belong to Fijian shark clans— their job is to protect sharks from entanglement in fishing gear.

Nearby Gotham City is known for its batfish. This rich reef also has abundant triggerfish, barracuda, surgeonfish, and all manner of schooling basslets and damsels. The underwater ecosystem here is typical of the Mamanucas.

The whole Fiji region is full of sharks, and not only the ubiquitous whitetip. Live-aboard vessels have secret spots to share with visiting divers at locations where local Fijian owners have granted permission for diving adventures. These locales offer large gangs of gray reef sharks, both individual and schooling hammerheads and, near reef drop-offs, large silvertip sharks (see p. 169).

Beds of soft coral (above)—the whole area offers wonderful diving; one of Fiji's many islands (left).

## EQUIPMENT

All resorts offer weights and tanks, and many also provide regulators and buoyancy vests. Some resorts rent camera or video gear, but most do not. Lightweight wetsuits, vests, or Lycra dive skins are highly recommended. During warm months, a 3 mm wetsuit is a good idea. For cooler times, a 5 mm wetsuit is better. Scuba diving is necessary to see the sharks, but the reefs can be explored with snorkel gear.

## SPECIAL FEATURES

Located far from major population centers, Fiji's reef system has, for the most part, not been over-exploited, overfished, or damaged. A traditional land-tenure system rigorously protects tribal lands and waters from misuse. This system means, too, that divers and dive operators must have the permission of the owner to dive in a specific area, including sites that may seem remote and unused.

The reefs that this system protects and allows divers to enjoy are glorious. Imagine soaring along the top of a vertical wall, blue water below you, passing under black coral trees and colonies of soft corals taller than you are. Or consider returning to the same spot at night to watch the hundreds of glowing firefly-like lights, which are the headlamps of flashlight fish, emerging from their daytime hiding spots to seek a nocturnal meal of plankton. Shallower reef areas are home to hundreds of species of coral and reef fish, including bright blue ribbon eels. The males have elongate yellow nasal tubes that give them a scary, threatening appearance, but they are lovely creatures, and harmless as well. LT

### TRAVELER'S NOTES

**When to visit** Year-round; best weather in dry season (May–Oct)
**Weather** Daytime temperatures 68–86° F (20–30° C); mild, dry May–Oct; wetter, warmer Nov–Apr (wet season); highest rainfall and humidity in Jan–Feb; east–southwest trade wind
**Water temperature** Temperature 80–83° F (27–28° C) from Nov–Apr; 78–80° F (25–26° C) May–Oct
**Hazards** Stonefish and medusae
**Dive logistics** Snorkeling and scuba diving from the shore, live-aboards or day boats; booking essential
**Accommodation** There is a full range of accommodation, from thatched fales to comfortable lodges and resorts; some resorts cater exclusively to the needs of divers
**Notes** Fiji is friendly and hospitable and has a rich culture

# Valerie's Reef

### Papua New Guinea

The tropical waters and string of islands forming the Bismarck Archipelago lie to the north of the spectacular mountainous mainland of Papua New Guinea. Among the islands of the New Hanover group in the archipelago, hundreds of coral reefs rise to within 30 feet (10 m) of the surface. One of these, Valerie's Reef, is home to a large group of silvertip sharks (see p. 169).

Valerie's Reef had no name until the recent discovery of the silvertips. It was named in honor of Valerie Taylor (see p. 77), renowned shark authority and underwater photographer. Silvertip sharks are the most impressive and largest of the reef shark family, and Valerie's Reef has become the most famous site in the world for guaranteed silvertip shark encounters.

Between 9 and 12 large, female silvertips, ranging in size from 6½–10 feet (2–3 m), live around the reef area. They congregate on the reef as soon as a dive boat appears—they were once fed regularly from visiting dive boats and still associate the sound of the motor with food. It can be a little daunting at first to look into the water and see several sharks waiting for you. But these large, powerful creatures are well behaved. They are waiting to accompany you on what is, initially, a heart-stopping swim to the reef. Once there, you feel less vulnerable, and are able to watch the sharks patrolling their habitat. They cruise slowly and gracefully through the clear, warm water, circling over the beautiful coral gardens and making occasional inquisitive approaches. The silvertips seem to have a social order, and the smaller sharks respect the larger ones.

*Divers (above) admire a gorgonian coral. The lacy scorpionfish (left) can inflict a painful wound with its spines.*

These sharks are calm and confident, and do not harass divers. However, silvertip sharks can be dangerous if overstimulated or provoked. Swim beneath the surface to avoid splashing. Always wear dark gloves and keep your hands

*A female silvertip shark (above) patrols the reef; and (left) a local fishing canoe.*

close to your body to avoid them being mistaken for fish scraps. Dive in buddy teams and give yourself time to get used to the sharks' behavior. Always make your own way back to the live-aboard at the end of a dive rather than signal for a pick-up by the tender. These are small boats with outboards, and the sound of the motor starting excites the sharks, which then dash toward the boat.

The best access to the reef is by live-aboards operating out of Kavieng, on New Ireland, but it is also within range of day boats. The silvertips are accustomed to divers, and photographers will have opportunities for close-ups, wide angles, and even to capture multiple sharks in one shot.

## EQUIPMENT

Scuba diving is recommended rather than snorkeling. The sharks perceive scuba divers as just another predator. But with so many sharks competing for food at one reef, a snorkeler

might attract the wrong kind of attention. You will need normal scuba equipment. The water is very warm so a 2–3 mm wetsuit will be quite adequate for all dives.

## SPECIAL FEATURES

Papua New Guinea is regarded as one of the top 10 dive locations in the world, and it's easy to get distracted from shark and ray encounters. The diversity of corals and fish and the variety of ship and plane wrecks from the Second World War are astounding. The region is also famous for some very rare and bizarre marine species. These include the lacy scorpionfish, an ornately patterned scorpionfish, and the flamboyant cuttlefish, a small, beautiful creature that lays its eggs inside sunken coconuts. *Octopus horridus* is often seen in these waters—no one has yet discovered if it is poisonous or not.

Papua New Guinea also has some of the world's most diverse, unique, and unspoilt indigenous cultures. The people of the Gazelle Peninsula near Kavieng are famous for their fire dancing, so consider a stopover on the way. KD

## TRAVELER'S NOTES

**When to visit** All year round
**Weather** Very warm, tropical; no distinct wet season
**Water temperature** 79–82° F (26–28° C)
**Hazards** Malaria
**Dive logistics** Scuba diving from day boats or live-aboards; the snorkeling is excellent, but is not recommended where there are sharks
**Accommodation** Hotels in Kavieng; excellent live-aboards, booking essential
**Notes** Heed security advisories, particularly in the capital, Port Moresby

# Ningaloo Reef

### Australia

*A whale shark (above) dwarfs a snorkeler. The vast Ningaloo Reef Marine Park (left).*

In the remote far north of Western Australia, 161 miles (260 km) of coral fringing reef are washed by the tropical waters of the Indian Ocean. The reef is protected as Ningaloo Reef Marine Park. Whale sharks (see p. 151), the gentle giants of the oceans, congregate here in large numbers each year from late March to early May.

The higher temperatures of the Indian Ocean in summer and the full moons in March and April trigger a mass explosion of synchronized spawning of the corals of Ningaloo Reef. The coral spawning coincides with the congregation and mass spawning of millions of other marine life forms. This extraordinary phenomenon provides a bountiful food supply, which is what attracts the large numbers of whale sharks to Ningaloo Reef.

The possibility of diving with these huge, slow-moving sharks brings thousands of divers and snorkelers from around the world. Nothing prepares you for the enormous size of one of these creatures, and the feeling of awe as it materializes out of the blue haze, its massive head filling the view, its tiny eye watching. Divers can swim alongside the shark as it moves majestically through the ocean, occasionally opening its cavernous mouth to feed, always accompanied by an entourage of juvenile jacks, pilotfish, cobia, and a mass of remoras. Caution is necessary as the wide sweep of the shark's powerful tail can easily stun or disable a diver.

There are numerous dive tours operating out of Exmouth, the gateway to Ningaloo Reef. A spotter aircraft works with the dive boats to help locate the sharks. Fast and maneuverable, the dive boats repeatedly drop divers off ahead of the shark, picking them up when the shark has moved on, then overtaking the shark to drop them off in front again. Whale sharks may swim slowly, but trying to keep up with them is still tiring. Snorkeling is easier than diving. The sharks spend a great deal of time on the surface, and a snorkeler can swim faster and operate from the dive boat more comfortably than a scuba diver.

Strict rules have been introduced to protect the whale sharks from stress during the season.

There is a total ban on divers touching or riding the sharks, and there are limits on the number of divers in the water with a shark at any one time and on the amount of time they can spend with it. Strobes (flash units) are not allowed. Tour operators must have a permit and boats have a restricted approach zone of 100 feet (30 m).

*Oval butterflyfish (above left) thrive on the reef, and corals caught in the act of spawning (above right), an annual event.*

## EQUIPMENT

Snorkeling is an ideal way to see whale sharks. Consider using a high-tech snorkel and high-performance fins, because you will do a lot of swimming in seas that vary from flat to choppy if the wind picks up. A full-length Lycra suit is also a good idea; it will protect you from marine stingers (nothing deadly) and sunburn.

## SPECIAL FEATURES

Ningaloo Reef does not have world-class coral but it does boast a wealth of marine life. A dive at the Navy Wharf at Exmouth is also very rewarding—the rich artificial reef has an incredible diversity of fish species, including resident tasselled wobbegong sharks (see p. 146).

## CAPE RANGE NATIONAL PARK

Ningaloo Reef Marine Park is parallel to the rugged landscape of North-West Cape and the Cape Range National Park. It was formed when ancient beds of rock were pushed up from the ocean floor between 1.6 and 5 million years ago. The rocks contain fossils of the huge teeth of the prehistoric shark *Carcharodon megalodon*. This awesome predator, estimated to measure more than 40 feet (12 m), is believed to be an extinct relative of the great white shark. It could once be found throughout the oceans of the world. Local rangers and guides conduct tours to these extraordinary fossil sites. **KD**

### TRAVELER'S NOTES

**When to visit** Late Mar to early May
**Weather** Warm, tropical, very sunny; afternoon sea breezes
**Water temperature** 73–79° F (23–26° C)
**Hazards** Occasional cyclones
**Dive logistics** Snorkeling or scuba diving from day boats; some live-aboard boats, but not essential for good access
**Accommodation** Hotels, caravans, and camp sites in Exmouth
**Notes** Avoid operators without spotter planes. Book your dive tours and accommodation before departure. Plan a minimum of five day's diving to guarantee many encounters

# Neptune Islands

Australia

Neptune Islands are situated in the cold, often inhospitable waters of the Great Australian Bight, off the southern coast of Australia. The remote, rocky islands, accessible only by boat from Port Lincoln, South Australia, are home to thousands of Australian sea lions and New Zealand fur seals. It is the abundance of this important food source that draws the great white sharks (see p. 158).

These islands are regarded as the world's best location for encounters with this awesome predator. And although great whites can be found here year-round, January to May is the best time to visit. This is when the seals and sea lions breed, and you avoid the fierce winter weather.

The logistics of organizing a great white shark trip are considerable. A large live-aboard dive boat is required and excursions of at least one to two weeks are recommended. A crew works day and night to spread chum (a mix of products used to attract sharks) across many miles of ocean in the hope that a great white shark will be lured to the boat.

The first sign of this huge fish is its dark shadow beneath the water, with perhaps a dorsal fin

emerging briefly. Large shark cages made of aluminum are lowered into the water and the divers enter the cages via the wide trapdoor in the roof. Jumping from the safety of the dive boat into the cage is frightening, initially. You feel that the walls are too close and the windows too large, and stare into the steel-blue void trying to locate the shark before it sneaks up on you. It materializes slowly, purposefully, swimming straight up to the cage. It will "taste-test" the bars, boat, and anything else it finds to see if it is edible. Then the animal will disappear into the void, only to startle you by suddenly reappearing from another, unexpected direction, to inspect you again and re-test the cage.

Eventually, you will become more used to the unpredictable nature of its presence, and realize that the shark is simply there for the tuna and other chum. It can be very cautious at times, but bold when it wants to feed. Its extraordinary hunting techniques, streamlined beauty, and power command fascination and respect. And it is possible to take excellent photos

*A New Zealand fur seal basks on the rocky shoreline of one of the Neptune Islands.*

*A great white shark (above) approaches the shark cage. Australian sea lions (left) at play.*

or video footage of great whites, both underwater and above water, as it is the only shark that will put its head out of the water and look at you.

If divers are very experienced, some operators will lower the cage to the ocean floor so the great whites can be viewed approaching along the floor or circling overhead. The recent advent of the shark POD (see p. 77) has resulted in successful encounters without a cage, up until now considered out of the question.

Many great white shark trips are undertaken for scientific study and to film educational documentaries. Shark and ray enthusiasts are encouraged to participate to help offset the huge costs and to develop their understanding of and support for the protection of these sharks.

The great white shark is comparatively rare and its numbers are believed to be declining. Sightings cannot be guaranteed. But a trip to the rugged Neptune Islands is a rare opportunity to explore a remote wilderness and to learn more

about this impressive creature. To have good encounters with the sharks is a very lucky bonus.

## EQUIPMENT

Either scuba diving or snorkeling in the shark cage is possible. Some operators provide long hoses that are attached to large onboard air cylinders to allow ease of movement. Extra-heavy weight belts are supplied, and because dive fins are not worn inside the cage, good dive boots are essential. Full-length 5 mm wetsuits with hoods are recommended; however, a dry suit might be preferable as you could be spending long hours in cold water.

## SPECIAL FEATURES

Dives with the fur seals and Australian sea lions are organized away from the chum area or at other islands. Shore excursions to see the seal colonies, busy with newborn pups, are a delight. And it is impossible not to be entranced by the sea lions, particularly when these rare and beautiful blond creatures play. The lucky diver might also see the bizarre leafy sea dragon, unique to southern Australia.  KD

### TRAVELER'S NOTES

**When to visit** Jan–May

**Weather** Temperate; very changeable from calm and hot to windy and cold; calm to quite rough seas

**Water temperature** 61–66° F (16–19° C)

**Hazards** Seals can be aggressive when ashore; seek local advice

**Dive logistics** Cage diving with snorkel or scuba gear from live-aboard dive boats, trips from 3–16 days; pre-booking essential

**Notes** No guarantees; on average, one trip in three is successful

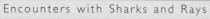

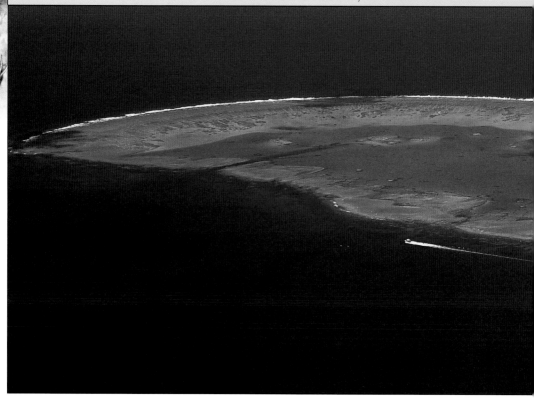

# Great Barrier Reef

Australia

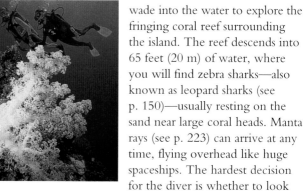

The Great Barrier Reef, off Australia's northeast coast, is the only living thing that can be seen from space. Much of the 1,430 miles (2,300 km) of reef is protected as the Great Barrier Reef Marine Park. It is the pristine home to an extraordinary diversity of coral, invertebrates, and fish—including sharks and rays.

The problem for the enthusiast who wants to see sharks and rays is the enormous choice of sites here. Many dive boats also visit the oceanic reefs of the Coral Sea, 115 miles (185 km) offshore. Some sites virtually guarantee encounters.

Lady Elliot Island is a small coral cay at the southern end of the Great Barrier Reef. It has one of the few resorts actually out on the reef. A dive at Lady Elliot is wonderfully simple. Divers or snorkelers

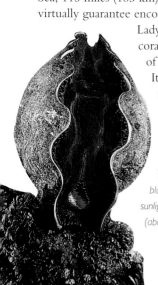

*The giant clam (left), with its blue-green mantle, needs strong sunlight to grow. Yellow soft corals (above) put on a show for divers.*

wade into the water to explore the fringing coral reef surrounding the island. The reef descends into 65 feet (20 m) of water, where you will find zebra sharks—also known as leopard sharks (see p. 150)—usually resting on the sand near large coral heads. Manta rays (see p. 223) can arrive at any time, flying overhead like huge spaceships. The hardest decision for the diver is whether to look up for mantas, down for zebra sharks, or to be distracted by fish, turtles, and coral gardens.

Another extraordinary site—for scuba divers only—is Scuba Zoo at Flinders Reef, out in the Coral Sea. A giant shark cage has been permanently stationed here at a depth of 65 feet (20 m). As soon as the dive boat moors, up to 40 reef sharks appear, cruising the deep reef slope beyond the cage. Divers can feel very vulnerable as they swim down through open water to the cage, but the sharks keep their distance, moving about on the bottom like gray shadows. They are mostly gray reef sharks (see p. 170), with some whitetip reef sharks (see p. 186) and silvertip sharks (see p. 169).

Once everyone is inside the cage, a divemaster hauls down a container of fish. When the

*Looking down over Lady Musgrave Island (above), in the Bunker Group. Gray reef sharks (left).*

A 5 mm suit is recommended for southern Queensland. Bring your own equipment if you are planning a live-aboard excursion, as equipment is generally not available for hire on board.

## SPECIAL FEATURES

The incredible diversity of marine life and the grandeur of the reef are impossible to ignore. Some unique creatures include sea snakes, stone-fish, giant clams, and spider shells. During the Australian spring, turtles come ashore to lay eggs, and the mass, synchronized coral-spawning of the Great Barrier Reef occurs for several nights after the October and November full moons. At the Cod Hole off Lizard Island, up to 20 giant potato cod regularly interact with divers. KD

lid of the container is pulled off and the food is released, dozens of sharks descend on the bait, tearing it apart in a feeding frenzy. They are so close to the cage, you can hear their teeth crunching on bone. Within minutes, the baits are entirely consumed and it is all over. The sharks continue to dash about, excited by the odor of blood and the tiny pieces of fish meat floating in the current. Divers remain in the cage until the current has dispersed all food remnants and the sharks have resumed their normal, relaxed behavior. Only then is it safe to leave the cage and move among the sharks, taking photos in less restricted circumstances.

If your air supply is low because of all the excitement, you can head back to the boat. The sharks will patrol the area and make close passes to inspect divers before dispersing into the deep blue void again.

## EQUIPMENT

A one-piece, 2–3 mm wetsuit will suffice in the warmer waters of northern Queensland.

### TRAVELER'S NOTES

**When to visit** Good conditions almost year-round; occasional strong winds; cyclone season late Dec–Apr
**Weather** Warm to very hot, tropical conditions; consistently dry, except during the cyclone, or wet, season
**Water temperature** 72° F (22° C) in southern Queensland to 82° F (28° C) in northern Queensland; cooler June–Aug
**Hazards** Venomous animals include the lionfish, stonefish, sea snakes, box jellyfish (or sea wasp), cone shell, and blue-ring octopus. None is aggressive and accidents are rare, but learn to identify these species and their behavior
**Dive logistics** Day boats (be prepared for long trips to get out to the reef); live-aboards, trips of 4–8 nights, mostly from Cairns and Townsville, pre-booking recommended
**Accommodation** From camping to five-star resorts ashore or on coastal islands; also on several islands out on the reef; pre-booking recommended
**Notes** Shark feeding not permitted inside the Marine Park

# New South Wales

Australia

The coast of New South Wales, on the eastern seaboard of Australia, is dotted with towns and cities, lined by sandstone cliffs and beaches, and edged by the temperate waters of the Tasman Sea. Here, there are underwater worlds to explore with a diverse range of sharks and rays.

## SEAL ROCKS

Just over 185 miles (300 km) north of Sydney, Seal Rocks is renowned for its large schools of resident sand tiger sharks (see p. 152), also known as gray nurse or spotted raggedtooth sharks. They congregate in packs of 5 to 20, and occasionally even 40, around the spectacular underwater rock formations, in the large reef gutters and sea caves.

Sand tiger sharks have a fearsome appearance, with their long, hooked teeth perpetually protruding from their mouths. However, these are gentle, fish-eating animals that will not attack. They generally have no fear of small groups of divers, and scuba divers can swim safely among them, observing their characteristic circling pattern and photographing them at very

*Jervis Bay (above), on the east coast of Australia. The restless sand tiger shark (left), which feeds only at night.*

close range. Sometimes, they make a sudden, determined approach and the diver has to get out of the way fast. It is quite a thrill to lie on the sea floor and watch that mouth and those teeth pass only a few feet above your head. A careful search in the gutters on the sea floor will often reveal sand tiger shark teeth, shed during mating or feeding.

Day trips from Forster are offered year-round by several dive operators. Although larger congregations occur between November and July, there are always sand tiger sharks to be seen.

## JERVIS BAY

Jervis Bay, a sheltered bay about 115 miles (180 km) south of Sydney, features a rugged sandstone coastline, pure white beaches, and protected coves. Each year during August and September, thousands of Port Jackson sharks (see p. 143) converge on this area to mate and lay their bizarre, spiral-shaped egg cases. Divers

exploring the bay from boats will come across large groups of exhausted females lying about in gutters, caves, and hollows on the reef. Single males patrol the reef, probably looking for receptive females.

During November and December, most of the adult sharks disperse. But a careful search of the bay's sand flats will reveal newly hatched Port Jackson sharks, each a perfect replica of its parents, except for its fins, which seem too large for its tiny body.

These sand flats are covered with many species of algae, sponges, invertebrates, and sea pens—an ideal habitat for angelsharks, eastern fiddler rays, and shorttailed electric rays (see p. 210). Electric rays can give an unwary diver a severe shock if they are touched or harassed.

Jervis Bay also has huge sea caves and giant boulder reefs covered in vividly colored sponge gardens. Spotted and ornate wobbegongs—most unusual sharks with beautifully decorated skin (see p. 147)—lie perfectly camouflaged among the sponges, waiting for passing prey. Divers

*Swimming in the midst of a mating group of Port Jackson sharks (above); and the extraordinary spiral egg case (left) of the Port Jackson shark.*

have occasionally been bitten simply because they disturbed a wobbegong they had not seen.

## EQUIPMENT

Use snorkeling equipment in the shallow coves and foreshores of Jervis Bay to see mating Port Jacksons and also skates, but scuba diving is recommended at all other sites. In summer, wear a one-piece 5 mm wetsuit; in winter, use a two-piece 5 mm wetsuit.

## SPECIAL FEATURES

Around Jervis Bay lives the biggest member of the cuttlefish family, the giant Australian cuttlefish. More than 3⅓ feet (1 m) long, its colors change with its emotions. It will try to bluff by raising its large tentacles if you seem to be a competitor for its territory, but as long as you only observe, encounters are usually spectacular stand-offs. Also look out for the weedy sea dragon, with its delicate coloring. KD

**TRAVELER'S NOTES**

**When to visit** Year-round
**Weather** Warm Oct–Mar, cool Apr–Sept; no distinct rainy season; unpredictable
**Water temperature** 57–70° F (14–21° C)
**Hazards** Rough seas during periods of strong offshore winds
**Dive logistics** Forster: day boats only;

Jervis Bay: live-aboards or day boats, both offering equally good access
**Accommodation** Good-quality hotels, guesthouses, camping, and caravan sites at all locations
**Notes** An excellent region for self-driving, camping, and exploring a diverse range of dive locations and sighting the plentiful marine species

269

# Lord Howe Island

Australia

Tiny Lord Howe Island stands alone in the Tasman Sea, about 745 miles (1,200 km) north-east of Sydney, Australia. It is an extinct volcano, its peaks rising sheer from sapphire-blue subtropical waters that support coral reefs. These corals have formed a beautiful shallow lagoon, home to giant black stingrays and Galapagos sharks (see p. 175), as well as many indigenous species of fish.

At Comet's Hole, groups of giant black sting-rays rest, camouflaged in the sand. When they move, it is an extraordinary sight. They rise languidly off the sea floor, creating a cloud with the sand that was covering them. It streams off their bodies and trails in their wake. Divers and snorkelers can move among the resting rays or follow those that are swimming. Sometimes, you will see a ray pause close to the bottom and use a flapping motion to disturb the sand and uncover prey, which it blankets with its wide body so the prey cannot escape. It then maneuvers itself until its mouth has located the prey.

If you get too close to a ray, it will raise its thick tail high above its back like a lance and make aggressive stabbing movements into the water column. There is no doubt as to the outcome should you venture any closer.

*The flamboyant Spanish dancer (left), a nudibranch, or sea slug. The view of Lord Howe Island (below) from Mount Eliza.*

Young Galapagos sharks enter the lagoon with the rising tide and leave before it falls. The best place to see them is at Erscott's Hole. Because this area is also full of beautiful fish and coral, divers may be concentrating on something else when the sharks first appear. They are fast, frisky, and a little wary, and usually circle on the edge of visibility before dashing in to take a close look at you. A small, sleek shark speeding toward you is bound to get the adrenalin going, but they are simply curious.

A Galapagos shark (above) circles inside the coral lagoon. The rare Lord Howe Island woodhen (left); and a giant black stingray (far left).

Occasionally, divemasters add a little bait to the water to encourage the sharks to come closer, and up to a dozen usually appear. They will continually come up to investigate divers—several sharks approaching at once can be very exciting. If one gets too insistent, a light tap on the nose will result in its rapid departure, leaving you in awe of its speed and streamlined design.

The lagoon is an excellent site for snorkelers and scuba-diving beginners. Even non-divers can view this pristine world from the glass-bottom boats that make daily excursions into the lagoon. Scuba divers can use a fast day boat for single dives in the lagoon or for offshore dives on the reefs surrounding the island.

## EQUIPMENT

Basic snorkeling equipment will suffice and is available for hire, as is scuba equipment. Scuba divers should use a ⅛ inch (3 mm) or ³⁄₁₆ inch (5 mm) wetsuit. Be sure to bring a compact waterproof dive light for night dives.

## SPECIAL FEATURES

Lord Howe Island is a World Heritage Area. Its isolation and its position at the crossroads of the Tasman and Coral Seas have encouraged the development of many unique and endemic species of animal, bird, and marine life. It is an important bird sanctuary, providing a haven for many nesting seabirds, as well as the Lord Howe Island woodhen, one of the world's rarest birds. This flightless creature was almost extinct, but a rescue breeding program has seen its numbers increase gradually.

Divers and snorkelers should also seek out some of the unique fish species, including the doubleheaded wrasse, the wide-band anemonefish, and the Spanish dancer, a red and white nudibranch that resembles the ruffles on a flamenco dancer's dress. KD

### TRAVELER'S NOTES

**When to visit** Nov–May
**Weather** Cool, tropical summer, Oct–May; occasional unpredictable strong winds and regular rainfall; no distinct wet season
**Water temperature** 68–75° F (20–24° C)
**Hazards** The banded scalyfin, a very aggressive small fish, has a bite that can draw blood; swim away from its territory

**Dive logistics** Glass-bottom boats and day boats for snorkeling or scuba diving; pre-book during peak season, Dec–Jan
**Accommodation** Small resorts and guesthouses, fully catered or self-catering; pre-book Dec–Jan
**Notes** Only 400 tourists are allowed on the island at one time. Pack a waterproof coat for rainy spells and a warm jacket for cool evenings

# RESOURCES
# DIRECTORY

*Human life is limited, but knowledge is limitless.*

*The Preservation of Life,*
CHUANG-TZU (4th century BC), Chinese writer

# FURTHER INFORMATION

## Books

*Adventures in Scuba Diving: A Text for the Beginning Diver,* by National Association of Underwater Instructors (NAUI) Staff (Mosby–Year Book, 1994).

*Aqua Expeditions: A Global Travel Guide for the Scuba Diver and Snorkeler,* by Wendy C. Church (Heathcoat Publishing, 1994).

*Cousteau's Great White Shark,* by Jean-Michel Cousteau and Mose Richards (Abradale Books, 1992).

*FAO Species Catalogue. Sharks of the World: An Annotated and Illustrated Catalogue of Shark Species Known to Date,* Fisheries Synopsis No. 125, Vol. 4, Pt 1 & 2, by L. J. V. Compagno (Food & Agriculture Organization of the United Nations, 1984).

*Fossil Sharks of the Chesapeake Bay Region,* by Bretton W. Kent (Egan Rees & Boyer, 1994).

*Great White Shark,* by Richard Ellis and John McCosker (Harper Collins/Stanford University Press, 1991).

*Great White Sharks: The Biology of Carcharodon Carcharias,* by Peter Klimley and David G. Ainley, eds (Academic Press, 1996).

*Guide to the Sharks and Rays of Southern Africa,* by L. J. V. Compagno, D. A. Ebert, and M. J. Smale (New Holland Publishers, London, 1989).

*Half Mile Down,* by William Beebe (Harcourt, Brace and Co., New York, 1934). Documents Beebe's early deep-water explorations of the world's oceans.

*Reef Sharks & Rays of the World: A Guide to Their Identification, Behavior, and Ecology,* by Scott W. Michael (Sea Challengers, Monterey, 1993). Descriptions and identifying photos of sharks and rays that dwell on the world's reefs.

*Scuba Diving,* by Dennis K. Graver (Human Kinetics Books, 1993).

*Scuba Diving Explained: Questions and Answers on Physiology and Medical Aspects of Scuba Diving,* by Lawrence Martin (Lakeside Press, 1995).

*Sea Change: A Message of the Oceans,* by Sylvia A. Earle (G. P. Putnam's Sons, New York, 1995).

*Shadows in the Sea: The Sharks, Skates and Rays,* by Harold W. McCormick, Thomas Allen, and William E. Young (Lyons & Burford, 1996).

*Shark: A Photographer's Story,* by Jeremy Stafford-Deitsch (Headline, London, 1987).

*Shark Attack: How, Why, When and Where Sharks Attack Humans,* by V. Coppleson and P. Goadby (Angus & Robertson, London, 1988). Evaluates the relative dangers and patterns of attacks by various sharks species.

*Shark: Endangered Predator of the Sea,* by Marty Snyderman (Key Porter Book, Toronto, 1995). An exploration of sharks and their threatened world, accompanied by underwater photographer Marty Snyderman's images.

*Shark! Nature's Masterpiece,* by R. D. Lawrence (Chapter's Publishing, 1994). From the Curious Naturalist Series.

*Sharks,* by John Stevens, ed. (Facts on File Publisher, New York, 1987). An introduction to sharks, their biology, habitats, and taxonomy.

*Sharks and Rays of Australia,* by P. R. Last and J. D. Stevens (CSIRO, Australia, 1994). A reference work containing descriptions and illustrations of the shark and ray species that inhabit Australian waters.

*Sharks and Rays of the Pacific Coast,* by Ava Ferguson and Gregor Caillet (Monterey Bay Aquarium, 1990).

*Sharks in Question—The Smithsonian Answer Book,* by V. Springer and J. P. Gold (Smithsonian Institution Press, 1989).

*Sharks: Myth and Reality,* by Gaetano Cafiero and Maddelena Jahoda (Thomasson-Grant, 1994).

*Sharks of Arabia,* by John E. Randall (Immel Publishing, 1990).

*Sharks of Hawaii, their Biology and Cultural Significance,* by Leighton Taylor (University of Hawaii Press, 1993). A well-illustrated account of the sharks found in Hawaiian waters, including material depicting the important role that sharks played in Hawaiian religion and culture.

*Sharks of the World,* by R. Steel (Blanchford, London, 1992).

*Sharks of Tropical and Temperate Seas,* by R. H. Johnson (Gulf Publishing Co., 1995).

*Sharks: Silent Hunters of the Deep,* by Reader's Digest (Reader's Digest, Sydney, 1986). A brief overview of shark biology and ecology.

*Sharks! The Mysterious Killers,* by Discovery Editors (Crown Publishers/Random House, 1996).

*The Book of Sharks,* by Richard Ellis (Grosset & Dunlap, New York, 1989). A revised edition, including Richard Ellis's illustrations.

*The Diver's Handbook,* by Alan Mountain (New Holland, London, UK, 1996).

*The Encyclopedia of Recreational Diving,* by Alex Brylske, Karl Shreeves, and Harry Averill (PADI, USA, 1988). 560-page encyclopedic coverage of diving, with illustrations.

*The Lady and the Sharks,* by Eugenie Clark (Harper & Row, New York, 1969). Details the work of Professor Eugenie Clark, a pioneer shark researcher.

*The Natural History of Sharks,* by Thomas H. Lineaweaver III and Richard H. Backus (Schocken Books/Lyons & Burford, USA, 1986). An illustrated introduction.

*The Scuba Diving Handbook: A Complete Guide to Salt and Fresh Water Diving,* by Paul McCallum (Betterway Books, USA, 1991).

*The Shark: Splendid Savage of the Sea,* by Jacques-Yves Cousteau (Cassell, London, 1989).

*The Sharks of North American Waters,* by José I. Castro (Texas A. & M. University Press, College Station, 1983).

*The Sea Around Us,* by Rachel Carson (Oxford University Press, New York, 1951). A classic conservation book.

## Magazines

*Alert Diver,* North America
*Asian Diver,* Singapore
*Diver,* United Kingdom
*Ocean Realm,* North America
*Rodale's Scuba Diving,* North America
*Scuba Diver,* Australasia
*Scuba Times,* North America
*Shark News: The Newsletter of the IUCN Shark Specialist Group,* United Kingdom
*Skindiving Magazine,* North America
*Sportdiving Magazine,* Australasia
*The Undersea Journal,* North America
*Undercurrents,* North America

## Websites

American Elasmobranch Society, http://www.elasmo.org Research news from shark and ray scholars.

International Shark Attack File, http://www.flmnh.ufl.edu/natsci/ichthyology/shark.htm Information about the attack file, with a summary of worldwide attack data.

Isle of Man Basking Shark Project, http://www.isle-of-man.com/interests/shark/index.htm Details about a basking shark research project in the Irish Sea, with opportunities for volunteers.

Natal Sharks Board, http://goofy.iafrica.com/~carch/ Information about South Africa's major beach-netting service and its research activities and public programs.

Mote Marine Library, http://www.mote.org Information about the research and public programs of a major center for shark research in Florida.

Project Aware (Aquatic World Awareness, Responsibility and Education), http://www.padi.com/ Details of environmental and educational programs of a PADI umbrella organization, to help preserve and protect the underwater environment.

Shark Links Galore, http://www.oceanstar.com/shark/links.htm A comprehensive and frequently updated listing of many websites on sharks, including research, public displays, and diving tours.

Sonny Gruber, http://www.wattcom.com/sharks/ Information and shark research updates.

Tricas Stingray Lab, http://www.fit.edu/~tricas/lab Information about research on stingray behavior and neurobiology, and details of student programs.

US State Department Travel Warnings and Consular Information Sheets, http://www.stolaf.edu/network/travel-advisories.html Information about medical and political security matters.

## Video Cassettes and CD–ROMs

*Great White!,* Discovery Channel, 1992. The great white shark filmed in four oceans around the world.

*Great White Shark,* BBC/National Geographic, 1995.

*Jaws, the True Story,* BBC/Nova, 1984.

*Ocean Planet,* CD–ROM, Discovery Channel, 1995. Explores the world's oceans, aquatic life, and issues related to ecological balance.

*Shark Attack Files,* Discovery Channel, 1994. Scientists, conservationists, and shark hunters look at shark attacks.

*The Ultimate Guide to Sharks,* Discovery Channel, 1996. Examines the most dangerous sharks and their killing cycles.

## Aquariums, Museums, and Universities

The following institutions curate excellent study collections or exhibits of sharks and rays:

Africa Marine World USA, Vallejo, California, USA

Aquarium of the Americas, New Orleans, Louisiana, USA

Australian Museum, Sydney, Australia

Bernice P. Bishop Museum, Honolulu, Hawaii, USA

California Academy of Sciences, San Francisco, California, USA

Living Seas Exhibit, Disney-world, Florida, USA

Monterey Bay Aquarium, California, USA

National Aquarium, Baltimore, Maryland, USA

Okinawa Expo Aquarium, Okinawa, Japan

Osaka Aquarium, Osaka, Japan

Pt Defiance Zoo and Aquarium, Tacoma, Washington, USA

Scripps Institution of Oceanography, University of California, San Diego, California, USA

Sea World, Florida, USA

Sea World, San Diego, California, USA

Smithsonian Museum of Natural History, Washington, DC, USA

South African Museum, Cape Town, South Africa

Waikiki Aquarium, Hawaii, USA

# ORGANIZATIONS

## Shark Research and Environmental Organizations

American Elasmobranch
Society,
Department of Biology,
University of Massachusetts,
Dartmouth,
285 Old Westport Rd,
North Dartmouth, MA
02747-2300, USA

Audubon Ecology Camps and
Workshops,
National Audubon Society,
613 Riversville Rd,
Greenwich, CT 06831, USA,
tel. (203) 869 2017

Center for Marine
Conservation,
1725 DeSales St NW,
Suite 500,
Washington, DC 20036, USA

Chondros,
1003 Hermitage Dr.,
Owensboro, KY 42301-6004,
USA

European Elasmobranch
Association,
Contact: Paddy Walker,
paddy@nioz.nl
Sarah Fowler, SarahFowler@
naturebureau.co.uk

Friends of the Earth,
Global Building, Suite 300,
1025 Vermont Ave NW,
Washington, DC 2005, USA,
tel. (202) 783 7400

Greenpeace,
1436 U St NW,
Washington, DC 20009, USA,
tel. (202) 462 1177,
fax (202) 462 4507, e-mail
info@wdc.greenpeace.org

International Research
Expeditions,
140 University Dr., Menlo
Park, CA 94025, USA,
tel. (415) 323 4288

Oceanic Society
Expeditions,
Fort Mason Center,
Building E, Room 230,
San Francisco, CA
94123-1394, USA,
tel. (800) 326 7491,
(415) 441 1106

Wilderness Society,
900 17th St NW,
Washington, DC 20006,
USA,
tel. (202) 833 2300

World Wildlife Fund,
1250 24th St NW,
Suite 500,
Washington, DC 20037, USA,
tel. (202) 293 4800

## Diving Organizations

American Canadian Underwater
Certification (ACUC),
1264 Osprey Dr.,
Ancaster, Ontario, L9G 3L2,
Canada,
tel. (905) 648 5500,
fax (905) 648 5440,
e-mail acuc@acuc.ca

British Sub Aqua Association
(BSAA),
Northern House,
43–45 Pembroke Place,
Liverpool, Merseyside,
L3 5PH, England,
tel. & fax (44 151) 707 0111,
e-mail mailto:admin@saa.
org.uk

British Sub Aqua Club (BSAC),
Telford's Quay,
Ellesmere Port,
South Wirral,
Cheshire, L65 4FY, UK,
tel. (44 151) 357 1951,
fax (44 151) 357 1250

Confédération Mondiale des
Activités Subaquatiques
(CMAS),
34 Rue de Colisée, 75008
Paris, France,
or Viale Tiziano 74,
00196 Rome, Italy,
tel. (39 6) 368 58480,
fax (39 6) 368 58490,
e-mail cmas@a.cmas.org

Divers Alert Network (DAN)
Europe,
PO Box DAN,
Roseto, Italy,
tel. (39 85) 8930333,
fax (39 85) 8930050,
e-mail mail@daneurope.org

DAN Japan,
c/o Japan Marine Recreation
Association,
3-8 Mejiro, 1-Chome,
Toshima-Ku,
Tokyo 171, Japan,
tel. (81 3) 3590 6501,
fax (81 3) 3590 8325, e-mail
y.mano.ns@med.tmd.ac.jp

DAN North America and
Canada,
PO Box 3823,
Duke University Medical
Center,
Durham, NC 27710, USA,
e-mail dan@dan.ycg.org

DAN Southeast Asia–Pacific,
PO Box 134,
Carnegie, Vic., 3163,
Australia,
tel. (61 3) 9563 1151,
fax (61 3) 9563 1139, e-mail
danseap@c031.aone.net.au

Fédération Française d'Etudes et
de Sports sous Marins
(FFESSM),
24 Quai de Rive-Neuve,
13007 Marseille, France,
tel. (33 91) 33 99 31,
fax (33 91) 58 77 43,
e-mail rebufat@triade.ibp.fra

Fédération Quebeçoise des
Activités Subaquatiques
(FQAS),
PO Box 1000, Succ M,
Montreal, Quebec,
H1V 3R2, Canada,
tel. (514) 252 3009,
fax (514) 254 1363

Handicapped Scuba
Association (HSA),
1104 El Prado,
San Clemente, CA 92672-
4637, USA,
tel. & fax (714) 498 6128,
e-mail 103424.3535@
compuserve.com

International Association for
Handicapped Divers (IAHD)
Box 1076,
S-269 21 Båstad, Sweden,
tel. (46 0431) 69260,
fax (46 0431) 69270,
e-mail iahd@bastad.se

International Association of
Nitrox and Technical Divers
(IANTD),
9628 NE 2nd Ave, Suite D,
Miami Shores, FL 33138,
tel. (305) 751 4873,
fax (305) 751 3958,
e-mail iantdhq@ix.netcom.
com

International Diving Educators
Association (IDEA),
PO Box 8427, Jacksonville,
FL 32239-8427, USA,
tel (904) 744 5554,
fax (904) 743 5425,
e-mail bstier@netrunner.net

International Scuba Educators
Association,
PO Box 17388,
Clearwater, FL
34624, USA,
tel. (813) 539 6491
e-mail j.atsea@ix.
netcom.com

Multinational Diving
Educators Association
(MDEA),
PO Box 3433,
Marathon Shores, FL 33052,
USA,
tel. (305) 743 6188,
fax (305) 743 7499

National Academy of Scuba
Educators (NASE)
1728 Kingsley Ave,
Orange Park, FL 32073,
USA,
tel. (904) 264 4104,
fax (904) 269 2283

National Association of Scuba
Diving Schools (NASDS),
1012 South Yates,
Memphis, TN 38119, USA,
tel. (800) 735 3483,
(901) 767 7265,
fax (901) 767 2798,
e-mail nasds@netten.net

National Association of
Underwater Instructors
(NAUI),
PO Box 14650,
Montclair, CA 91763-1150,
tel. (800) 553 6284,
(909) 621 5801,
fax (909) 621 6405, e-mail
nauimikew@earthlink.net

NAUI Asia-Pacific Services,
71 Ayer Rajah Cres. #03-
01/03, Singapore 0513,
tel. (65) 777 5120,
fax (65) 773 6125

NAUI Australia,
PO Box 183,
Capalaba, Qld, 4157,
Australia,
tel. (61 7) 3390 3233,
fax (61 7) 3390 3159

NAUI Canada,
Divemar Inc.,
37 Bentley Ave,
Ottawa, Ontario,
K2E 6T7, Canada,
tel. (613) 226 8938,
fax (613) 226 1271

NAUI Services (Northern
Europe),
Ohlauer Strasse 5-11,
10999 Berlin, Germany,
tel. (49 30) 612 5392,
fax (49 30) 612 8005

NAUI Services of United
Kingdom,
Cambrian Watersports,
Newbridge-on-Wye,
Llandrindod Wells,
Powys, LD1 6LN, UK,
tel. (44 1597) 860 681,
fax (44 1597) 860 682

National YMCA Scuba
Program (YMCA),
5825-2A Live Oak Pkwy,
Norcross, GA 30093-1728,
USA,
tel. (770) 662 5172,
fax (770) 242 9059,
e-mail scubaymca@aol.com

Professional Association of
Diving Instructors (PADI),
1251 East Dyer Rd,
Suite 100,
Santa Ana, CA 92705-5605,
USA,
tel. (800) 729 7234,
(714) 540 7234,
fax (714) 540 2609,
e-mail bccal@msn.com

PADI Asia,
39 Tampines St,
92 #05-00 Form Building,
Singapore 52883,
tel. (65) 785 9896,
fax (65) 785 8168

PADI Australia,
PO Box 713,
Willoughby, NSW, 2068,
Australia,
tel. (61 2) 9417 2800,
fax (61 2) 9417 1434

PADI Canada,
#3-10114 McDonald Park
Rd, RR#3 Sidney, BC V8L
3X9, Canada,
tel. (604) 656 7234,
fax (604) 656 6221,
e-mail PADICND@direct.ca

PADI International Limited,
Unit 6, Unicorn Park,
Whitby Rd,
Bristol, BS4 4EX, UK,
tel. (44 117) 971 1717,
fax (44 117) 971 0400

PADI Japan,
1-20-1, Ebisu-Minami,
Shibuya-ku,
Tokyo 150, Japan,
tel. (81 3) 57211731,
fax (81 3) 57211735

Professional Diving Instructors
Corporation (PDIC),
PO Box 3633,
Scranton,
PA 18505, USA,
tel. (800) 642 9434,
(717) 342 9434,
fax (717) 342 1276,
e-mail pdicmm@
delphi.com

Scuba Schools International
(SSI),
2619 Canton Ct,
Fort Collins, CO 80525-
4498, USA,
tel. (800) 892 2702,
(970) 482 0883,
fax (970) 482 6157,
e-mail admin@ssiusa.com

Singapore Underwater
Federation (SUF),
100 Guillemard Rd, Room 5,
Singapore Badminton Hall,
Singapore 1439,
tel. & fax (65) 344 4719

South African Underwater
Union,
PO Box 557, Parow, 7500,
Republic of South Africa,
tel. (27 021) 930 6549,
fax (27 021) 930 6541,
e-mail csake@cs.upe.ac.za

Technical Diving International
(TDI),
9 Coastal Plaza, Suite 300,
Bath, ME 04530, USA,
tel. (207) 729 4201,
fax (207) 729 4453,
e-mail doppler@techdiver.com

TDI Canada,
141 Hotchkiss St,
Gravenhurst, Ontario,
Canada,
tel. (705) 687 9226,
fax (705) 687 8251

US State Department
24-hour travel advisory
hotline, tel. (202) 647 5225

# INDEX *and* GLOSSARY

In this combined index and glossary, italic page numbers indicate illustrations and photographs.

## A

**Aborigines** 36
**abyssal** To do with the environment of the ocean depths beyond the continental shelf, with an average depth of about 13,000 feet (4 km) 14, 26, 194
**Adkison, Gary** *61*
**Advanced Open Water Diving course** 83
*Aetobatus narinari* 220, *220*
**alar thorns** Paired patches of thorns on the outer disc of most mature male skates *116*, 124, 225
*Alopias pelagicus* 155, *155*
*A. vulpinus* 156, *156*
**ampullae of Lorenzini** Natural electrical detectors located in the heads of sharks and rays which are sensitive to the electronic signals emitted by potential prey 77, *77*, *100, 102*, 103, 121, 187
*Anacanthobatis* 224, *224*–5
**anal fin** An unpaired fin located on the lower surface of the abdomen. It plays an important part in swimming movements 20, 92, *92*, 93, *93*, 95, 96, 194, 195, 196, 198
**angelsharks**
 body form and function *96*, 97, *97*
 classification 92
 common ancestry with rays 118
 difficulty of holding in aquariums 59
 food and feeding 110
 habitat 104
 injury from nets *89*
 Jervis Bay, New South Wales 269
 Pacific angelsharks *20*, 141, *141*
**angling** 61
**aquaculture** 43, *43*
**aquariums**
 rays in 57, 58, 59, *122*, 123
 sharks in 56–9, *56*–9
 stocking 57
**Arhynchobatinae** 224
**Aristotle** 21, 33, 131
*Atelomycterus macleayi* 162
*A. marmoratus* 162, *162*
**Atlantic guitarfishes** 206, *206*
**Atlantic sharpnose sharks** 185
**Atlantic torpedo rays** 211, *211*
**Australia**
 Great Barrier Reef 266–7, *266*–7
 Lord Howe Island 270–1
 Neptune Islands 264–5
 New South Wales 268–9
 Ningaloo Reef 66, 67, 262–3
**Australian butterfly rays** 219, *219*
**Australian sharpnose sharks** 184

## B

**Bahamas** 66, 240–1
**baiting, of sharks** 29, *29*
**Baja California, Mexico** 234, 236
**baleen whales** 54
**Baltra** 244

**bamboosharks** *106*, 107, 148
**banded stingarees** 214, *214*
**barbel** A slender, fleshy protuberance on the lower jaw; it is equipped with sensory and chemical receptors and is used in the location of food 140, 144, 145, *145*, 146, 147, 149, 150, 164, 165, 199
**barbeled catsharks** 164
**barbeled houndsharks** 199, *199*
**barracuda** 258
**basking sharks**
 as sea monsters *18*, 19
 characteristics 157, *157*
 commercial fishing of 38
 feeding habits 105
 identification by size 93
 in aquariums 59
 Isle of Man 246–7, *247*
 migration 26
**basslets** 258
**bat rays** 27, *129*, 131, 221, *221*
**batfishes** 258
**bathypelagic zone** The bottom of the deep sea, extending from about 3,300 feet (1,000 m), the bottom of the mesopelagic zone, to the ocean floor 17, 27, *104*–5, 105
**batoid** A member of the group of elasmobranch fishes that includes all rays and skates 15, 22, 23, 26, 110

**Beebe, William** 48, *48*
**Belize, Caribbean** *68*
**Benchley, Peter** 46
**bends, the** 69, *69*
**benthic** Living on or near the sea bottom 97, 110, 148, 162, 195, 247
**bigeyed sixgill sharks** 138, *138*
**bioaccumulation** 42
**black torpedo rays** 211
**blackbelly lanternsharks** *192*, 192–3
**blacktip reef sharks** 27, 56, 109, 110, 177, *177*
**blacktip sharks** 107, 112, 175, *175*
**blind electric rays** 209
**blind sharks** 145, *145*
**blue-gray carpetsharks** 145
**blue marlin** 255
**blue sharks**
 body form and function 96, *96*
 characteristics 183, *183*
 distribution 27
 feeding habits 108
 habitat 105
 migration 26, *112*, 113
 reproduction 107
 San Diego, United States 230, *230*
 social organization 109
 teeth *110*
**blue skates** 225
*Blue Water* (film) 77
**bluespotted ribbontail rays** *116*, *123*, 218, *218*
**bluntnose sixgill sharks** 138, *138*
**boats, and sharks** 88–9
**bonito sharks** 159
**bonnethead sharks** 108, 109, 111, 112, 190, *190*
**bony fishes** Fishes with bony skeletons. Other characteristics include scales on the skin, a covering over the gills, and a swim bladder 21, 22, 26, 45, 59, 119, 122, 129, 130, 141, 152, 155, 182, 188, 190, 191, 193, 199, 220
**boroso leather** 36
**bottom-dwelling sharks** 97, *97*
**Bource, Henri** *39*
**bowmouth guitarfishes** 121, 205, *205*
*Brachaelurus colcloughi* 145
*B. waddi* 145, *145*
**bramble sharks** 139, *139*
**broadnose sevengill sharks** 36, 137, *137*
**bronze whaler sharks** 171, *171*
**brownbanded bamboosharks** 148
**bull sharks** 56, 105, *105*, 112, 174, *174*
**bullhead sharks** 47, 142–3, *142*–3
**butterfly rays** 120, 125, 219, *219*

**bycatch** The part of the catch not made up of the targeted species 34, 39, 45, 61, *61,* 62, 88–9, 123, 136, 205, 219

# C

**California hornsharks** 142, *142*
*Callorhynchus* 25
**camcorders** 80–1, *80–1*
**cameras, for underwater photography** 78, *78,* 80, *80*
**Cape fur seals** 250, 251
**Cape Town, South Africa** 250–1, *250–1*
*Carcharhinus albimarginatus* 169, *169*
*C. amblyrhynchos* 170, *170*
*C. brachyurus* 171, *171*
*C. brevipinna* 175
*C. falciformis* 172, *172*
*C. galapagensis* 173, *173*
*C. leucas* 56, 174, *174*
*C. limbatus* 175, *175*
*C. longimanus* 176, *176*
*C. melanopterus* 56, 177, *177*
*C. obscurus* 178, *178*
*C. perezi* 61, 179, *179*
*C. plumbeus* 56, 180, *180*
*Carcharias taurus* 45, 56, 58–9
*Carcharodon carcharias see* great white sharks
*C. megalodon* 94, 95, 263
**Caribbean reef sharks** *29, 61,* 66, 105, 179, *179,* 240–1, *240–1*
**Caribbean sharpnose sharks** 185, *185*
**carpetsharks** 144, *144,* 145
**Carson, Rachel** 49
**cartilaginous fishes** Fishes with skeletons made of cartilage. Sometimes the cartilage is stiffened due to impregnation with calcium salts, but no bone is ever formed. Sharks and rays have a cartilaginous skeleton 20, 23, 33, 38, 94, 96, 115, 118, 121
**catsharks** 27, 28, 104, 107, 108, 109, 162–5, *162–5,* 198, *198*
**caudal fin** An unpaired fin located toward the tail end of the body 15, 20, 21,*92,* 93, 96, *116,* 120, 194, 224
**Cayman Islands** 238–9
**cephalofoil** A head structure in which the front of the skull has a broad, flattened shape, typical of hammerhead sharks 187, 188, 191, *191*
**cephalopods** A class of marine mollusks characterized by a well-developed head surrounded by prehensile tentacles that are used for propulsion through water; includes the octopus, squids, and cuttlefish 17, 25, 105, 111, 139, 156, 164, 179, 187,

188, 198, 199
*Cetorhinus maximus* 19, 38, 59, 93, 157, *157*
**chain-mail suits** 76–7
**Channel Islands, United States** 230, 231
*Chiloscyllium indicum* 148
*C. punctatum* 148
*Chimaera* 24
**chimaeras** 24–5, *24–5,* 45, 94
**Chinese myths** 18
*Chlamydoselachus anguineus* 136, *136*
**Chondrichthyes** 24, 94
**chum** Products used to attract sharks and to feed them once they have arrived 29, 41, 79, 183, 230, 231, 250, 264, 265
**chumming** 41
**"cigar shark"** 196
*Cladoselache* 94–5, *95*
**Clarion Island, Mexico** 236, 237, *237*
**Clark, Eugenie** 49
**claspers** The modified inner edges of the pelvic fins in male sharks, rays, and chimaeras, used for the transferring of sperm to the female 25, *92,* 106, *106,* 109, 116, *116,* 124, *124,* 149, 213, 221, 225, 241
**cleaner fish** *130, 131*
**cloaca** A common opening for the reproductive, digestive, and excretory tracts 25, 106, *106,* 109, *116,* 124, 127, 221
**cobbler wobbegongs** 147
**Cocos Island, Costa Rica** 242–3
**coffin rays** 210
**collared carpetsharks** 104, 144, *144*
**commercial fishing** 38–9
**common honeycomb whiprays** 217
**common sawsharks** 140, *140*
**common thresher sharks** 156, *156*
**conservation** 35, 49, 62–3, *62–3*
**continental shelves** 17

**cookiecutter sharks** 27, *196,* 196–7
**copepods** A major group of small crustaceans, sometimes referred to as sea lice 26, 105, 195, 241
**copper sharks** 171
**coral catsharks** 162, *162*
**Coronados Islands, United States** 230

**Cortez round stingrays** 213
**Costa Rica, Cocos Island** 242–3
**countershading** Protective coloration in which animals are darker on their upper (dorsal) surface than on their lower (ventral) surface so that when lighting is from above they appear evenly colored and inconspicuous 155
**Cousteau, Jacques-Yves** 49, 87, *87*
*Cousteau's Amazon Journey* (Cousteau) 87
**cownose rays** 121, 129, 222, *222,* 244, *244*
**cowsharks** 95
**cowtail stingrays** 36
**crested hornsharks** 143
**crocodile sharks** 27, 197, *197*
**Crown of Thorns sea star** 253
**cryptic coloration** Coloration that makes an animal resemble its background 110
**cusp** A sharp, pointed projection on the tooth 95, 97, 136, 137, 172, 186, *186,* 199
**cuttlefish** 261
*Cyclobatis longicaudatus* 15

# D

**damsels** 258
**DAN insurance** 69
*Dasyatis americana* 46, 216, *216*
**Dean, A**. *39*
**decompression sickness** 69, *69*
**deep-water rays** 224–5, *224–5*
**deep-water sharks** 194–5, *194–5*
**denticle** A scale that resembles a tooth. Dermal denticles give the skin of sharks its sandpaper texture. See also placoid scales 20, 94, 95, 97, 117, 118, 125, *127,* 129, 131, 139, *139,* 163, 192, 195, 210, 225
**devilrays** 15, 23, 59, 118, 119, 123
**diamond rays** 219
*Dipturus* 225
**disc** the distinctive structure of rays and skates, formed by the joining of the enlarged pectoral fins, trunk and sometimes head; typically wider than deep, and may be wedge-shaped, oval, circular, or triangular 23, 116, *116,* 117, *118,* 120, 123, 124, 127, 128, 129, *129,* 224
**dive computers** *84,* 85
**dive magazines** 68
**dive sites**
   Bahamas 240–1
   Cape Town, South Africa 250–1, *250–1*
   Cocos Island, Costa Rica 242–3
   Galapagos Islands, Ecuador 244–5, *244–5*
   Grand Cayman, Cayman Islands 238–9
   Great Barrier Reef, Australia 266–7, *266–7*

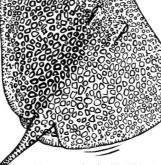

Isle of Man 246–7, *246–7*
Kona Coast, Hawaii 232–3
Lord Howe Island, Australia 270–1
Mamanuca Islands, Fiji 258–9, *258–9*
Neptune Islands, Australia 264–5
New South Wales, Australia 268–9, *268–9*
Ningaloo Reef, Western Australia 262–3
Rangiroa Atoll, French Polynesia 256–7, *256–7*
Ras Muhammad, Egypt 248–9
Revillagigedo Islands, Mexico 236–7
San Diego, United States 230–1
Sea of Cortez, Mexico 234–5, *234–5*
Similan and Surin Islands, Thailand 252–3
Valerie's Reef, Papua New Guinea 260–1
Yap and Palau, Micronesia 254–5
**diving**
approaching sharks and rays 72
dive centers 70–1, 82–3
dive operators 70
dive-travel agents 70
learning how to dive 82–3, *82–3*
protective equipment 76–7, *76–7*
recording observations 72–3
*see also* dive sites; field trips; scuba diving; snorkeling
**dogfishes**
caught as bycatch 45
daily movements 192
dwarf dogfishes 195
evolution 118
identification of 92
in art 32
liver oil from 36
piked dogfishes 37, 38, 193
prickly dogfishes 195, *195*
prickly sharks 139, *139*
spiny dogfishes 98, 104, 107, *192*, 193, *193*
velvet dogfishes 105
**dogtooth tuna** 255
**dolphins** 251
**dorsal fin** The large, unpaired fins located on the back of most fishes 15, 20, 21, 24, 32, *88*, 92, *92*, 93, *93*, 94, 95, 96, 112, *116*, *117*, 120, 126, 194, 195, 196, 197, 198, 224, 240, 250, 264
**Dumas, Frederick** 49
**dusky sharks** 112, 178, *178*
**dusky smoothhound sharks** 167
**dwarf dogfishes** 195
**dwarf dogsharks** 192
**dwarf sharks** *92*
**Dyer Island, South Africa** 250–1

**E**
**eagle rays**
bat rays 221, *221*
distance swimming 129

distribution 27
evolution 118
Galapagos Islands 244
pectoral fins 123
reproduction 124, 125
rudimentary dorsal and caudal fins 15, 120
sociability 130
spotted eagle rays 220, *220*
survival tactics 127, 131
tail spines 23
tooth plates 121, 124
**eastern fiddler rays** 269
**eastern shovelnose stingarees** *124*
*Echinorhinus brucus* 139
*E. cookei* 139, *139*
**ecological niche** The specific role an animal occupies in its ecosystem, generally determined by the way it obtains food 15, 95, 110, 122
**ecosystem** An interdependent community of organisms and the environment in which they live 41, 42, 43, 49, 57, 104, 125, 130, 253, 258
**ecotourism** 41
**Ecuador, Galapagos Islands** 244–5, *244–5*
**Egypt, Ras Muhammad** 248–9
**elasmobranch** A member of a major group of fishes, including sharks and rays 14, 15, 17, 20, 22, 23, 24, 25, 101, 103, 171, 188, 193, 199, 205
**Elasmobranchii** 94
**electric rays**
ability to transmit shocks 23, 33, 59, 126–7
ancestors of skates 118
blind electric rays 209
eyes 116
fins and tail 15, 23
in aquariums 59
lesser electric rays 208, *208*
movement and propulsion 129
Pacific electric rays 17
shortnose electric rays 117, 119, 209, *209*
shorttailed electric rays 59, 119,

120, 210, *210,* 269
spotted electric rays 209, *209*
**elephant seals** *111*
**elephantfishes** 24, 25, *25*
**Endangered Seas Campaign** 49
**endangered species** A species that is considered to be in imminent danger of extinction unless the

factors threatening its survival are removed 45, 62, 88, 183, 245
**endemic species** A species that is restricted to a certain geographical region and is thought to have originated there 119, 140, 270
**environmental changes** 40–1
**environmental degradation** 42–3, *42–3*
**epaulette sharks** 107, 111, 148, *148*
**epipelagic zone** The upper ocean level, starting near the shore and extending out to the open oceans and from the surface down to about 330 feet (100 m). Near-shore areas have rich food resources of plankton and fishes 17, 26, 27, *104–5*
*Etmopterus lucifer* 192, *192–3*
*E. perryi* 192, 195
*Eucrossorhinus dasypogon* 146, *146*
*Eugomphodus taurus* 152, *152*
**euphotic zone** The zone of the sea where light penetration is sufficient for photosynthesis to take place 192
*Euprotomicrus bispinatus* 193, *193*
*Eusphyra blochii* 187, *187*
**exotic species** A species that has been introduced into an area 43

**F**
**false catsharks** 198, *198*
**false killer whales** 244
**fiddler rays** *125*
**field guides** 67
**field trips**
DAN insurance 69
group travel 71
hazards 68–9
live-aboard versus shore-based diving 71
planning for 66–7, 68, 70–1
sources of information 68
travel insurance 69
**Fiji, Mamanuca Islands** 258–9, *258–9*
**film** *see* underwater photography
**filter feeding** Straining of suspended food particles by passing the water across gill rakers, specialized stiff, tooth-like structures located on the inner surface of the gill slits 105, *151*, 157, 232
**finback catsharks** 198, *198*
**finning** 35, *35,* 39
**fish farming** 43, *43*
**fishing**
commercial 38–9
for sharks *see* shark fishing
minimizing damage to sharks and rays 88–9
using bottom-fishing nets *49*
**Fleming, Ian** 46
**Florida Institute of Technology** 60

fossils 94, *94*, 118–19
Fox, Rodney *39*, 50, *50*, 51
French Polynesia, Rangiroa Atoll 256–7, *256–7*
freshwater sawfishes 204, *204*
freshwater whiprays 217
frilled sharks 136, *136*
fur seals *250*, 251, 265

**G**

Galapagos hornsharks 245
Galapagos Islands, Ecuador 66, *66*, 244–5, *244–5*
Galapagos sharks 29, 173, *173*, 236, 242, 243, 245, 270–1, *270–1*
*Galeocerdo cuvier* 181, *181*
*Galeorhinus galeus* 36, 38, 40, 44, 166, *166*
Ganges sharks 45, 174
ghostfishing 40–1
ghostsharks 24, 25
giant black stingrays *75, 124*, 270, *271*
Giddings, Al 47
gill net A curtain-like net suspended vertically in the water to tangle or snare fishes 40, 41, 53, 137
gill rakers *see* filter feeding 157
gill slits The slit-like openings behind the head that connect the gill chamber to the exterior. Oxygen-rich water enters the mouth (and spiracles), passes over the gills, where oxygen is extracted, then out the gill slits 20, 24, 92, *92, 93*, 94, 98, *98*, 116, *116*, 136, 137, 138, 139, 157, 195, 238, 239, 247
*Ginglymostoma cirratum* 149, *149*
*Glyphis gangeticus* 45
goblin sharks 105, 153, *153*
Gondwanaland 119
graceful catsharks 198, *198*
Grand Cayman, Cayman Islands 66, 238–9
gray nurse sharks 67, 152, 268
gray reef sharks
    agonistic display 29, *108*, 109
    approaching 29
    behavior patterns *108*
    characteristics 170, *170*
    daily movements 113
    food and feeding 110
    Great Barrier Reef, Australia 266
    habitat 105
    Kona Coast, United States *232–3*
    Mamanuca Islands, Fiji 258, *258*
    Palau, Micronesia 255
    Rangiroa Atoll, French Polynesia *257*
    Ras Muhammad, Egypt 248–9, *249*
    social organization 109
gray sharpnose sharks 184
Great Barrier Reef, Australia *62*, 266–7, *266–7*
great hammerhead sharks *21*, 93, 105, 189, *189*, 249
great sea turtles 244, *245*

great torpedo rays 211
great white sharks
    attacks by 51, *55*
    "bite and spit" theory 111
    biting action *110–11*
    Cape Town, South Africa 250–1, *251*
    characteristics 158, *158*
    feeding *28*
    habitat 105
    in aquariums 58, 59
    muscles 99
    myths about 46–7
    Neptune Islands, Australia 264–5, *264–5*
    observing 66
    photographing 41
    populations *44*, 44–5
    protection of 35
    relation to *C. megalodon* 95
    size 93
    South Australia 67
    teeth and jaws *110–11*, 111
green sea turtle 50, *50*
Greenland sleeper sharks 26, 36, 93, *194*, 194–5
Greenpeace 63, *63*
group diving vacations 71
Gruber, Dr. Samuel 61
Gruzinski, Rick *51*
guitarfishes
    Atlantic guitarfishes 206, *206*
    bowmouth guitarfishes 121, 205, *205*
    evolution 118, 119
    fins and tail 15, 120
    habitat 27
    movement and propulsion 128
    whitespotted guitarfishes *118*
gulper sharks 105
gummy sharks 40, 44, 167, *167*
gurry sharks 194
*Gymnura australis* 219, *219*

**H**

Haida people 32, *32*
*Halsydrus* 19
hammerhead sharks 187–91, *187–91*
    behavior patterns *108*
    food and feeding 110–11
    great hammerhead sharks *21*, 93, 105, 189, *189*, 249
    habitat 105
    Mamanuca Islands, Fiji 258
    myths about 18–19
    Rangiroa Atoll, French Polynesia 257
    social organization 109
    trapped in nets *39, 53*
hardnose skates 224
*Harriotta* 25
Hass, Hans *48*, 48–9
Hawaii Institute of Marine Biology 61
Hawaii, Kona Coast 232–3
Hawaiian legends, about sharks 19, 33, 47

health, on field trips 69
*Heliobatis* 118, *118*
Hemingway, Ernest 159
*Hemipristis elongatus* 199, *199*
*Hemiscyllium ocellatum* 148, *148*
Herodotus 18
Heterodontidae 47, 57
Heterodontiformes 95
*Heterodontus francisci* 142, *142*
*H. galeatus* 143
*H. portusjacksoni* 143, *143*
*H. zebra* 143
*Hexanchus griseus* 138, *138*
*H. vitulus* 138
*Hexatrygon bickelli* 225, *225*
*Hildebrand Rarity, The* (Fleming) 46
*Himantura* 119, 126
*H. chaophraya* 45, 217
*H. granulata* 123, 217, *217*
*H. uarnak* 217
*H. undulata* 217, *217*
*Historia Animalium* (Aristotle) 21, 33
Holland, Dr. Kim 61
Holocephalii 94
holocephaly 24
Home, Everard 19
hornsharks
    California hornsharks 142, *142*
    crested hornsharks 143
    daily movements 113
    food and feeding 110, 111
    Galapagos hornsharks 245
    habitat 27, *27*, 104
    in aquariums 57
    observing 28
    prehistory 47
    sense of smell *101*
    teeth 95, *110*
    zebra hornsharks 143
houndsharks 27, 28, 104, 166–8, *166–8*, 199, *199*
Hubbs-Sea World Institute 61
hussars 87
hybodont sharks 94, 95
*Hybodus hauffianus* 94
*Hydrolagus* 24
Hypnidae 59, 119, 120
*Hypnos monopterygium* 210, *210*

**I**

Ihuru, Maldives 68
indigenous species A species that occurs naturally within an area 43, 270
*Inner Space* (film) 77
Internet 67, 68
introduced species A species that has been introduced (usually deliberately, by humans) from another area; an exotic species 43
*Isistius brasiliensis* 196, *196–7*
*Isistius plutodus* 196
Isla Darwin, Galapagos Islands 244
Isla Las Animas, Mexico 234
Isla Los Islotes, Mexico 234
Isla Wolf, Galapagos Islands 244

**Isle of Man, United Kingdom**
246–7, *246–7*
**isobath** A line drawn on a chart of
the oceans, connecting points
having the same depth 123
*Isurus oxyrinchus* 36, 159, *159*
*I. paucus* 159

# J, K

**jackass penguins** *250,* 251
**Japanese numbfishes** 209
**Japanese thornback rays** 207
**Javanese cownose rays** 222, *222*
*Jaws* (Benchley) 46, *47*
**Jervis Bay, Australia** 268–9, *268–9*
**Johnson Shark Bag** *54,* 55
**Jonah and the whale** 32, *32*
**Kapa'aheo** 33
**kidney-headed sharks** 188
**Klingit people** 32
**Kona Coast, United States** 232–3

# L

**La Paz, Mexico** 234, 235
**labial furrows** Shallow grooves
around the lips 156, 162, 165,
184, 195, 198, 199
**lacy scorpionfish** 261
*Lady and the Sharks* (Clark) 49
**Lady Elliot Island,**
**Australia** 266
**Lake Nicaragua sharks** 174
**lamella** A thin or plate-like
structure *98, 100,* 101
*Lamna ditropis* 160, *160*
*L. nasus* 38, 161, *161*
**lamnid sharks** 99
**lanternsharks** 105
**largetooth cookiecutter sharks** 196
**leafy sea dragon** 265
**leg skates** *224,* 224–5
**legends** *see* myths
**lemon sharks** *17,* 105, *107,* 108,
109, 113, *113,* 182, *182*
**leopard catsharks** 164
**leopard sharks** 150, 168, *168,*
252, *252*
**leopard whiprays** 217, *217*
*Leptocharias smithii* 199, *199*
**lesser electric rays** 208, *208*
**lighting, in underwater photog-**
**raphy** 78–9, *78–9,* 80
**Linnaeus, Carolus** 92
**lionfishes** 252–3
*The Living Sea* (Cousteau) 87
**longfin mako sharks** 159
**longnose blacktail sharks** 170
**longnose hawkfishes** *255*
**longnose sawsharks** 140
**longtailed carpetsharks** 148, *148*
**Lord Howe Island, Australia** 86,
*86,* 270–1
**Lord Howe Island woodhen** *271*

# M

**mackerel sharks** 158–61, *158–61*
**mako sharks**
body form and function *96,* 97

distribution 27
evolution 47
finding food 105
migration 26, 113
muscles 99
shortfin mako sharks 15, *15, 110,*
159, *159*
teeth and jaws 111
**malaria** 69
**Mamanuca Islands, Fiji** 258–9,
*258–9*
**mangrove stingrays** 128
**mangrove whiprays** 123, 217, *217*
*Manta birostris* 223, *223*
*MANTA* (Hass) 49
**manta rays**
brain of 101, 121
changing attitudes toward 49
characteristics 223, *223*
Cocos Island, Costa Rica
242, *242–3*
contact with

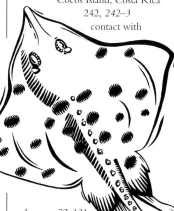

humans 72, 131
distribution 27
Galapagos Islands,
Ecuador 244
Great Barrier Reef, Australia 266
habitat 23, *23*
Kona Coast, United States *232,*
232–3
movement and propulsion 129
Palau, Micronesia 255
pectoral fins 123
photography of *81*
Ras Muhammad, Egypt 249
Revillagigedo Islands, Mexico *236,*
236–7
Sea of Cortez, Mexico *38*
size 117
trapped in nets 49
with cleaner fish *130, 131*
Yap, Micronesia 254
**Manuelita, Cocos Island** 242
**Maoris** 36
**marbled catsharks** 162
**marine iguana** *244*
**marine organisms** 43
**maw** Mouth 163, 195
**McCosker, Dr. John** 47
*Megachasma pelagios* 61, 154, *154*
**megamouth sharks** *16,* 61, 93,
105, 154, *154,* 246
**Melanesians** 74, *74*
**mercury, in sharks and rays** 42
**mesopelagic zone** The mid-level of

the ocean, extending from 330
feet (100 m), the bottom of the
epipelagic (surface) zone, down
about 3,300 feet (1,000 m), the
start of the bathypelagic zone. It is
characterized by low light levels
fading into darkness, a decline in
oxygen and nutrient levels, and
low water temperature *16, 17,*
27, *104–5,* 105, 197,
**Mexico**
Revillagigedo Islands 236–7
Sea of Cortez 234–5, *234–5*
**Micronesia, Yap and Palau** 254–5
**milk sharks** 184, *184*
*Mitsukurina owstoni* 153, *153*
**Mobulidae** 59
**modem sharks** 97
**monkfishes** 141
**Monterey Bay Aquarium** 56, 57
**Mote Marine Laboratory Center**
**for Shark Research** 60, 61
*Mustelus antarcticus* 40, 44, 167, *167*
*M. canis* 167
*Myliobatis californicus* 221, *221*
**myths, about sharks and rays**
18–19, *18–19,* 32–3, 46–7,
*46–7,* 131

# N

*Narcine brasiliensis* 208
**nares** Nasal openings; nostrils 187,
188
*Narke japonica* 209, *209*
**Narkidae** 119
**Natal Sharks Board** 53, 54,
55, 77
**necklace carpetsharks** 144, *144*
*Negaprion acutidens* 182
*N. brevirostris* 182, *182*
*Neoharriotta* 25
**Neptune Islands, Australia** 264–5
**New Hanover Islands, Papua**
**New Guinea** 260
**New South Wales, Australia** 67,
268–9, *268–9*
**nictitating eyelid** A tough, lid-like
membrane that can be closed over
the eye to protect it from damage
93, *93,* 198
**Ningaloo Reef, Western**
**Australia** 66, 67, 262–3
*Notorynchus cepedianus* 36, 137, *137*
**numbfishes** 117, 129, 208, *208,* 209
**nurse sharks**
characteristics 149, *149*
food and feeding 110, 111
habitat 27, 104
Mamanuca Islands, Fiji 258
migration 112
Rangiroa Atoll, French
Polynesia 256

# O

**Ocean Wildlife Campaign** 35
**oceanic whitetip sharks** 27, 105,
176, *176,* 249
**ocellate river rays** 215, *215*

*Octopus horridus* 261
oil spills 42–3, *43, 62*
*Old Man and the Sea, The*
    (Hemingway) 159
Open Water Diving course 82
operculum The bony plate that
    covers the gill 20
*Orectolobus ornatus* 147, *147*
ornate wobbegongs 27, 147, *147*
*Orthacanthus senckenbergianus*
    *14–15*
osmoregulate To maintain control
    over the osmotic pressure of body
    fluids (that is, to prevent the pas-
    sage by osmosis of water or other
    pure solvent through a semi-per-
    meable membrane) by control of
    the amount of salts and/or water
    in the body 215
overfishing 38–9, 44–5, 49, 89
oviparous Egg-laying. Little or no
    development occurs within the
    mother's body, instead the
    embryos develop outside the
    mother's body and each egg
    eventually hatches to a young
    animal. See also ovoviviparous,
    viviparous 107, 124, 144, 150
oviphagous Feeding by older
    embryos on unfertilized eggs and
    smaller embryos within the uterus
    as a means of embryo nutrition
    152
ovoviviparous Giving birth to well-
    developed young which have
    developed from eggs that hatch
    within the mother's body. The
    young are almost exact replicas of
    the adult form. *See also* oviparous,
    viviparous 124, 125, 141, 142,
    149, 166, 167, 181, 192, 193,
    195, 197, 204
*Oxynotus bruniensis* 195, *195*
oyster crusher sharks 143
ozone depletion 41

**P, Q**
Pacific angelsharks *20*, 141, *141*
Pacific cownose rays *26*, 222,
    244, *244*
Pacific electric rays *17*
Pacific manta rays 234
Pacific spotted dolphins *197*
Packard, David 57
Palau, Micronesia 254–5
Papua New Guinea
    silvertip sharks *20, 66, 74,*
    260, *260–1*
    Valerie's Reef 260–1
*Parascyllium variolatum* 144, *144*
parrotfishes 14
*Pastinachus sephen* 36
*Pavoraja* 225
pectoral fins Paired fins, located
    just behind or below the gill
    slits and used for lift and control
    of movement. In rays and
    skates, the greatly enlarged

pectoral fins are attached at the
    back of the skull, and united to
    form a body disc 20, 24, 25, *92,*
    *94, 96, 97,* 109, 110, 116, 121,
    123, 124, 128, 129, 136
pelagic Of the seas, oceans, or open
    water; not associated with the
    bottom 17, 23, 27, 35, 105, 109,
    112, 113, 119, 122, 128, 155,
    156, 172, 223, 234, 236, 237,
    242, 248, 249
pelagic sharks 17, 242
pelagic stingrays 123
pelagic thresher sharks 155, *155*
pelagic zone 17
pelvic fins Paired fins, located on the
    lower part of the body, toward
    the tail 20, *92, 96, 97, 106,* 116,
    *116,* 123, 124, 139, 145, 241
Permian shark fossil *14–15*
photography *see* underwater pho-
    tography
photoperiod The duration of a reg-
    ular exposure to light 16
photophore A light-emitting organ
    found in the skin of fishes of the
    deep 105, 192, 193, 195
photosynthesis A process in which
    green plants use the energy of
    sunlight to combine water and
    carbon dioxide to form sugar and
    starch, at the same time releasing
    oxygen. Photosynthesis is essential
    to life on earth 27, 41, 192
Phuket, Thailand 253
phytoplankton Plant plankton.
    Phytoplankton carries out photo-
    synthesis and is the basis of the
    aquatic food chain 17, 26, 27,
    41, 42
piked dogfishes 37, 38, 193
pit organs 103
placenta An organ formed by the
    fusion of embryonic tissues and
    maternal tissues. It serves for the
    nourishment, respiration, and
    removal of waste products of the
    developing embryo 177
placental viviparity Reproduction
    in which the growth of the
            embryo occurs within
            the mother's
            body which
            nourishes it via
            a placenta
            formed from
            the yolk
            sac.

*See also* yolk sac placenta 107
placoid scales Tooth-like scales that
    make up the sandpaper-like skin
    of sharks. Placoid scales are cov-
    ered by a hard, enamel-like sub-
    stance and the scales project out-
    wards and backwards. Also called
    dermal denticles 94, 97
planktivore An animal that feeds on
    plankton 17, 105
plankton Minute aquatic organisms
    that float or drift in the open sea.
    Plankton comprises plant (phyto-
    plankton) and animal (zooplank-
    ton) organisms 15, 23, 27, 43, 49,
    59, 79, 95, 105, 151, 154, 157,
    *157,* 223, 232, 233, 235, 246,
    247, 254, 255, 259
*Platyrhina sinensis* 207
*Platyrhinoidis triseriata* 207, *207*
*Playing with Sharks* (film) 77
Pliny the Elder 18, 19
POD (Protective Oceanic Device)
    55, 77, *77*
pollution 42–3, *42–3*
Polynesia, French 256–7, *256–7*
Polynesians 18–19, 74, *74*
populations, of sharks and rays
    38–9
porbeagle sharks *26*, 38, 99, 105,
    161, *161*
porcupine rays *127*
*Poroderma africanum* 164, *164*
*P. marleyi* 164
*P. pantherinum* 164
Port Davey skates 212, *212*
Port Jackson sharks *47*, 89, 109,
    143, *143*, 268–9, *269*
Port Phillip Bay, Australia 39
*Potamotrygon motoro* 215, *215*
Potamotrygonidae 119
prickly dogfishes 195, *195*
prickly sharks 139, *139*
*Prionace glauca* 183, *183*
Pristidae 45
Pristiophoriformes *92*
*Pristiophorus cirratus* 140, *140*
*P. nudipinnis* 140
*Pristis microdon* 204, *204*
*Proscyllium habereri* 198, *198*
Protective Oceanic Device 55,
    77, *77*
*Pseudocarcharias kamoharai* 197, *197*
*Pseudotriakis microdon* 198, *198*
*Pteroplatytrygon violacea* 123
Punta Ulloa, Cocos Island 242
pygmy sharks 27, 92, *92,* 105, *193,*
    *193,* 195, *195*
Queensland sharks 105

**R**
*Raja nasuta* 119, 212, *212*
Rajidae 224

            Rangiroa
                Atoll,
                French
            Polynesia
            256–7, *256–7*

**Ras Muhammad, Egypt** 248–9
**ratfishes** *24,* 24–5, 94
**rattail rays** 219
**rays**
  ampullae of Lorenzini 121
  anatomy and biology 22, 120–1,
    *120–1*
  approaching 72, 74–5
  brains of 23, 101
  breathing equipment 22–3
  characteristics 22–3, *22–3*
  classification 116–17, *117*
  close relatives of 24–5, *24–5*
  curiosity of 131
  decline in populations 38–9
  defensive weapons 23
  distribution 26–7, *26–7,* 119
  electrosensory system 103
  evolution 118–19
  fossils of *15*
  gill slits 116
  habitat 15, 16–17, *17,* 122–3,
    *122–3*
  identifying 116–17, *116–17*
  in aquariums 57, 58, 59, *122,* 123
  lateral line 103
  movement and propulsion 128–9,
    *128–9*
  myths about 18–19, *18–19,* 46,
    *46,* 131
  navigation by 127
  parasites on 127
  prehistory 22
  reproduction and life cycle 119,
    124–5, *124–5*
  research into 60
  sense of hearing 103
  sense of sight 101
  sense of touch 101
  social organization 130–1
  sting of 126
  survival and defense 126–7, *126–7*
  symbiotic relationships *130,* 130–1
  teeth of *126*
  uses of 36–7, *36–7,* 131
  *see also specific species of rays*
**red brick soldierfish** *256*
**Red Sea, Egypt** 248, 249
**reef sharks** 75, 86
**requiem sharks** 27, 93, 104–5, 110,
  111, 169–86, *169–86*
  *see also specific species of requiem sharks*
**research, into sharks and rays**
  60–1
**resort courses, in diving** 83
**reticulate whiprays** 217
**Revillagigedo Islands, Mexico**
  236–7
*Rhina ancylostoma* 205, *205*
*Rhincodon typus* 57, 59, 92, 151, *151*
*Rhinobatos lentiginosus* 206, *206*
*R. percellens* 206
*Rhinochimaera* 25
*Rhinoptera javanica* 222, *222*
*R. steindachneri* 222
*Rhizoprionodon acutus* 184, *184*
*R. oligolinx* 184
*R. porosus* 185, *185*

*R. taylori* 184
*R. terraenovae* 185
**ribbontailed rays** *73,* 249
**Ritchie, James** 19
**river rays** 119, 215, *215*
**Roca Monument, Mexico** *237*
**Roca Partida Island, Mexico** 236
**Rogers, B.** *39*
**rough skates** 119, 212, *212*
**roughsharks** 105, 195, *195*
**round stingrays** 27, 28, 131,
  213, *213*

# S

**sailfishes** *242*
**salinity, in rays** 122
**salmon sharks** 105, 160, *160*
**San Benedicto Island, Mexico**
  236
**San Diego, United States** 230–1
**sand tiger sharks**
  characteristics 152, *152*
  in aquariums 56, 58–9
  mating habits 73
  prehistory 47
  protection of *44,* 45
  reproduction 107
  Seal Rocks, Australia 268
  teeth and jaws *47,* 111
**sandbar sharks** 56, 112–13,
  180, *180*
**sawfishes**
  body shape 23
  contrasted with sawsharks 140
  distribution 119
  dorsal and caudal fins 120
  freshwater 204, *204*
  movement and propulsion 128
  nostrils 121
  protective covering on young
    sawfishes 125
  reduction in population 45, *45*
  use of snout 126, *127*
**sawsharks** 15, 23, 92, 97, 98, 118,
  140, *140*
**scalloped hammerhead sharks**
  characteristics 188, *188*
  Cocos Island, Costa Rica 242,
    243
  Galapagos Islands, Ecuador 244
  Ras Muhammad, Egypt 249
  Revillagigedo Islands, Mexico 236,
    *236–7*
  Sea of Cortez, Mexico 234, *234*
**school sharks** 166
**Scripps Institute of**
  **Oceanography** 61, 231
**scuba diving**
  basic rules 84
  equipment 72, 84–5, *84–5*
  invention of regulator 49
  learning how to dive *70,* 82–3,
    *82–3*
  shark attacks on divers 55
**Scuba Zoo, Coral Sea** 266
**scute** A large, bony, external
  plate 126
*Scyliorhinus canicula* 165, *165*

*Sea Around Us, The* (Carson) 49
**sea lions** *111,* 264, 265, *265*
**Sea of Cortez, Mexico** 234–5,
  *234–5*
**sea stars** *87, 240–1,* 253
**sea-water snake** 19
**Seal Rocks, Australia** 268
**senses**
  of rays 103
  of sharks 100–3, *100–3*
**sevengill sharks** 36, 118, 137, *137*
**shagreen** 36
**shark attacks**
  death from 51
  first aid 51
  fishing programs to reduce
    risk of 39
  frequency of 52
  in the period 1990–96 34, 50, 52
  on divers 55
  precautions to take 52–3
  protective equipment 76–7, *76–7*
  reasons for attacks on humans 50–1
  shark bites 51
**shark bags** *54,* 55
**shark fins, in cooking** 36
**shark fishing**
  annual catch 34
  changing attitudes of anglers 61
  commercial fisheries 35, 49
  effects on sharks 15, 40–1
  finning 35, *35,* 39
  overfishing 38–9, 44–5, 49, 89
  sustainability of 44–5
  threatened species 35, 44–5, *44–5*
  to reduce threat of shark attack
    39, 54
  traditional methods 34, *34*
*Shark Hunters* (film) 77
**shark liver oil** 36–7, 38
**shark nets** 53, *53,* 54, 76
**shark products** 36–7, *36–7*
**shark repellents** 55, 76, 77
**sharkfin guitarfishes** 119
**sharks**
  ampullae of Lorenzini 77, *77*
  anatomy 20–1, *92,* 92–3, 97, *97,*
    98–9, *98–9*
  behavior patterns 108–9
  body form and function *95,* 96–7,
    *96–7*
  bottom-dwelling 97, *97*
  brain of 101, *101*
  changing attitudes towards
    48–9, 54
  characteristics 20–1, *20–1*
  classification 21, 92–3, *92–3*
  close relatives 24–5, *24–5*
  courtship 109
  daily movements 113
  decline in populations 35, 38–9
  deep midwater species 192–3,
    *192–3,* 196–7, *196–7*
  deep-water species 194–5, *194–5*
  digestion 98–9
  distribution 26–7, *26–7*
  electrosensory system 103
  evolution 94–5

feeding habits 108, 110–11, *110–11*
gill slits 20, 98, *98*, 99
growth 99, *99*
habitat 14, 16–17, *16–17*, 104–5, *104–5*
habitat changes 40–1, *40–1*
in aquariums 56–9, *56–9*
in history 32–3
interactions with people 15
keeping sharks away from people 54–5, *54–5*
lateral line 103
medical uses 37
migration *112*, 112–13
muscles 99
myths about 18–19, *18–19*, 46–7, *47*
precautions to take when observing 28–9, *28–9*, 72, 74–5
prehistory 14–15, 47, 92, 94–5
reproduction 106–7, *106–7*, 109
research into 60–1
respiration 98, *98*
sense of balance 102, *102*
sense of hearing 102–3
sense of sight 46–7
sense of smell 46, *100*, 101
sense of taste *100*, 101
sense of touch *100*, 101
sense of vision *100*, 100–1
size 93
social organiza-tion 108–9
speed 97
teeth and jaws 21, 36, *36*, *96*, 97, *97*, 110–11, *110–11*, *153*, *154*, *158*, *160*, *167*, *181*, *184*
uses of 36–7, *36–7*
water balance 99
*see also* shark attacks; shark fishing; *specific species of sharks*
**sharpnose sharks** 107, 184–5, *185–6*
**shortfin mako sharks** 15, *15*, *110*, 159, *159*
**shortnose electric rays** 117, 119, 209, *209*
**shortnose sawsharks** 140
**shorttailed electric rays** 59, 119, 120, 210, *210*, 269
**shovelnose rays** 118, *121*, *126*
**shovelnose stingarees** 124
**sicklefin lemon sharks** 182
*Silent World* (Cousteau and Dumas) 49, 87
**silky sharks** 172, *172*
**silvertip sharks**
  characteristics 169, *169*
  Great Barrier Reef, Australia 266
  habitat 105
  Mamanuca Islands, Fiji 258
  Papua New Guinea 20, 66, 74, 260, *260–1*
  pecking order 109
**Similan Islands, Thailand** 252–3
**sixgill sharks** 118, 138, *138*
**sixgill stingrays** 123, 225, *225*

**skates**
  anatomy 120
  blue skates *225*
  characteristics 23, 224–5, *224–5*
  diet 121
  dorsal and caudal fins 15
  evolution 118
  hardnose skates 224
  in aquariums 123
  leg skates *224*, 224–5
  movement and propulsion 128
  Port Davey skates 212, *212*
  reproduction 124–5
  rough skates 119, 212, *212*
  softnose skates 224
  thornback skates *22*, 119
**sleeper sharks** 26, 36, 93, *194*, 194–5
**slender bamboosharks** 148
**smalleye pygmy sharks** 195
**smallspotted catsharks** 165, *165*
**smooth hammerhead sharks** 191, *191*
**smoothhound sharks** 110
**smoothtail mobulas** *128*
**snaggletooth sharks** 199, *199*
**snorkeling** *52*, 86–7, *86–7*
**Socorro Island, Mexico** 236

**softnose skates** 224
*Somniosus microcephalus* 26, 36, *194*, 194–5
*S. pacificus* 26
**soupfin sharks** 36, 38, 39, 40, 44, 166, *166*
**South Africa**
  dive sites near Cape Town 250–1, *250–1*
  shark nets 53
**South Australia** 67
**southern fiddler rays** *23*
**southern guitarfishes** 206
**southern right whales** 251
**southern sawsharks** 140
**southern stingrays** 26–8, *46*, *130–1*, 216, *216*, 238, 238–9
**sparsely spotted stingarees** *119*, *125*, 214, *214*
*Sphyrna lewini* 188, *188*
*S. mokarran* 189, *189*
*S. tiburo* 190, *190*
*S. zygaena* 191, *191*
**spined pygmy sharks** *95*, 195, *195*
**spinner sharks** 175
**spiny dogfishes** 98, 104, 107, *192*, 193, *193*
**spiracle** An auxiliary respiratory opening behind the eye in sharks and rays. It takes in water for breathing when the ray or shark is at rest on the bottom or the

mouth is being used for feeding *92*, 93, 98, *98*, 116, *116*, 125, 130, 139, 141, 144, 145, 149, 162, 193, 195, 198, *210*, 216, *216*
**spookfish** 25, *25*
**spotted eagle rays** *22*, *38*, 220, *220*
**spotted electric rays** 209, *209*
**spotted pufferfish** *233*
**spotted raggedtooth sharks** 152, 268
**spotted stingarees** *119*, *125*
**Squalea** 118
**Squaliformes** 92
*Squaliolus aliae* 195
*S. laticaudus* 92, 195, *195*
*Squalus acanthias* 37, 38, 193, *193*
*S. maximus see Cetorhinus maximus*
*Squatina californica* 141, *141*
**Squatinidae** 59
**Squatiniformes** 92
*Stegostoma fasciatum* 150, *150*
**Steven Birch Aquarium** 231
**stingarees** 23, 119, *119*, 120, 125, 131, 214, *214*
**Stingray City, Cayman Islands** 86
**stingrays**
  anatomy 15, 120–1
  at birth 125
  behavior when approached 131
  bluespotted ribbontail rays 218, *218*
  brain of 101
  distribution 27, 119
  evolution 118
  giant black stingrays *75*, *124*, 270
  Grand Cayman, Cayman Islands 66, 86, 238–9
  habitat 123, *123*
  mangrove stingrays *128*
  movement and propulsion 128, *129*
  myths about 19
  pelagic stingrays 123
  popular perception of 46
  round stingrays 213, *213*
  sixgill stingrays 225, *225*
  southern stingrays *46*, 131, 216, *216*
  venomous spine on tail *121*, 131, *131*
**striped catsharks** 164, *164*
**substrate** The substance forming the bottom of the sea or ocean floor 16, 59, 121, 122, 123, 125, 126, 144, 207, 211, 213, 214, 216, 218
**surgeonfishes** 14, 258
**Surin Islands, Thailand** 252–3
**sustainable fishing** 44–5
*Sutorectus tentaculatus* 147
**swellsharks** *96*, 163, *163*
**swim bladder** A gas-filled, bag-like organ in the roof of the abdominal cavity of bony fish. It enables the fish to achieve neutral buoyancy and so remain at a particular

depth in the water 20, 24, 129
**symbiotic relationship** A situation in which plants or animals of different species live together in a mutually advantageous relationship 130, 193

## T

**tabbigaw sharks** 143
*Taeniura lymma* 218, *218*
**tagging, of sharks** 61, *61,* 112, 113, *113*
**tapetum** (plural tapeta) A reflective layer under the retina which reflects light back to the light receptors, increasing the amount of light that passes across the retina and thereby assisting vision in low-light environments. Species that live in brightly lit shallow waters can darken the tapetum with movable pigments 46, 110
**tasselled wobbegongs** 146, *146*
**Taylor, Ron** 77, 77
**Taylor, Valerie** 77, *77,* 260
**Thailand, Similan and Surin Islands** 252–3
**thermocline** A gradient of temperature change, applied particularly to a zone with rapidly changing temperature between the warm surface waters and cooler deep waters 245, 253
**thickskin sharks** 180
**Thompson, Joe** 51
**thornback rays** 207, *207*
**thornback skates** 22, 119
**threatened species** 44–5, *44–5*
**thresher sharks** 18, 26, 27, 93, 155–6, *155–6*
**tiger sharks**
attacks by 51, *54*
characteristics 181, *181*
daily movements 113
food and feeding 110
habitat 105
migration 112
observing 29
reproduction 107
Revillagigedo Islands, Mexico 236
tagging of *113*
**tope sharks** 166
**Torpedinidae** 59
*Torpedo nobiliana* 211, *211*
**torpedo rays** 27, 59, 121, 124–5, 126
*Torpedo torpedo* 33, *33*
**trammel net** A three-layered net. The middle layer is slack and fine-meshed, the other layers coarse-meshed. Fish passing through a trammel net carry some of the center net into the coarser opposite net and are trapped 208
**travel insurance** 69
**trawl fishing** The dragging of a large conical net behind a boat

along the sea bottom to gather fish and other marine life 38, 40, 45
**tubercles** Projections on the surface of the skin 117, 206, 213, 216
*Triaenodon obesus* 57, 186, *186*
*Triakis semifasciata* 168, *168*
**Tricas, Dr. Timothy** 47, 60
**triggerfishes** 258
**Trùk, Micronesia** 254, 255
*Typhlonarke aysoni* 209

## U

*Undersea World of Jacques Cousteau, The* (TV program) 87
**underwater photography** 48, 48–9, 73, 78–9, *78–9,* 80–1, *80–1*
**United Kingdom, Isle of Man** 246–7, *246–7*
**United States**
Kona Coast 232–3
San Diego 230–1
**United States Navy Shark Chasers** 54
*Urobatis halleri* 131, 213, *213*
*U. maculatus* 213
**Urolophidae** 119
*Urolophus cruciatus* 214, *214*
*U. paucimaculatus* 214

## V

**Valerie's Reef, Papua New Guinea** 260–1
**velvet dogfishes** 105
**ventral** Of the lower part or surface 24, 192
**vitamin A, from shark liver oil** 37
**viviparous** Giving birth to live young; the embryo develops entirely within the uterus. See also oviparous, ovoviviparous 107, 159, 160, 161, 169, 170, 177, 186, 210, 211, 214

## W

**water column** The volume of water between the surface of the sea and the sea bottom. A creature swimming either on the surface or along the sea bottom is not swimming in the water column 16, 23, 27, 29, 96, 138, 166, 175, 187, 189, 220, 270
**weasel sharks** 27
**whale sharks**
characteristics 151, *151*
Cocos Island, Costa Rica 242
commercial fishing of 35
damage from boats 88, *88*
electrosensory system *103*
feeding habits 105
Galapagos Islands, Ecuador 244
habitat *14*
in aquariums 57, 59
Isle of Man, United Kingdom 246

Ningaloo Reef, Australia 67, 262–3, *262–3*
precautions when approaching 72, 79
shape *95*
size *72,* 92, 93, *95*
Surin Islands, Thailand 253
**whales** 251
**whiprays** 45, 119, 123, 126, 127, 129, 131, 217, *217*
**whiptail stingrays** 23, 27, 28
*White Death* (film) 77
**white death sharks** *see* great white sharks
**white pointer sharks** *see* great white sharks
**white sharks** *see* great white sharks
**whitespotted bamboosharks** 106
**whitespotted spurdogs** 193
**whitetip reef sharks**
characteristics 186, *186*
Cocos Island, Costa Rica 242–3
damage from attempted catch *88*
feeding habits 108, 111
Galapagos Islands, Ecuador 244
Great Barrier Reef, Australia 266
habitat *16,* 27, 105, *105*
in aquariums 57
Mamanuca Islands, Fiji 257, 258
social organization 109
**winghead sharks** 187, *187*
**wobbegongs** 27, *27,* 104, 110, 146–7, *146–7*
**World Heritage Area** A natural area considered by UNESCO's World Heritage Convention Committee to be of exceptional interest and universal value 271
**World Wide Fund for Nature** 62
**World Wildlife Fund** 49
**Wu, Norbert** 236

## Y, Z

**Yap, Micronesia** 254–5
**yellowbar angelfishes** *249*
**yolk sac** A membranous sac rich in blood vessels that develops around the yolk; the yolk sac is gradually reduced as nutrients pass from it via the yolk stalk to the developing embryo 107, 177, 219
**yolk sac placenta** In species with placental viviparity, a placenta formed when the spent yolk sac becomes attached to the uterine wall. Nutrients and oxygen are then passed from the mother to the embryo via the yolk stalk; waste products go in the reverse direction 199
**Zambezi sharks** 174
**zebra hornsharks** 143
**zebra sharks** 104, *106,* 107, 150, *150,* 252, *252,* 253, 266
**zooplankton** Animal plankton 17, 26, 105

# CONTRIBUTORS

**Kevin Deacon**, a noted underwater photographer and marine naturalist, is also a PADI underwater instructor. He lives in Australia and is managing director of Dive 2000, which specializes in diving expeditions to some of the world's most fascinating marine environments. His award-winning photographs appear regularly in books and magazines.

**Peter Last**, BSc(Hons), PhD, trained as a marine biologist, but has since developed a major interest in the taxonomy, biogeography, and ecology of Indo-Pacific fishes. He has co-authored three comprehensive identification guides to fishes, including a recent review of the highly diverse shark and ray fauna found in Australian waters.

**John E. McCosker**, PhD, is Senior Scientist and Chair of Aquatic Biology at the California Academy of Sciences, San Francisco. Trained as an evolutionary biologist, his research covers the evolution of marine fishes, and the behavior of sea snakes and sharks. His published works include 170 popular and scientific articles and books.

**Leighton Taylor**, BA (Biology), MS (Zoology), PhD (Marine Biology), is a Fellow of the California Academy of Sciences and a Research Associate of the Bishop Museum of the Waikiki Aquarium in Hawaii. Among his notable achievements during more than 30 years' research, he is credited with discovering the megamouth shark.

**Timothy C. Tricas**, BS, MS (Biology), and PhD (Zoology), is Associate Professor of Biological Sciences at the Florida Institute of Technology, Melbourne, USA. His research focuses on the sensory biology of sharks and rays, and he has also studied the feeding and mating behavior of these animals and coral reef fishes for more than 25 years.

**Terence I. Walker**, BSc, is currently working on a PhD thesis. He is principal marine scientist at the Marine and Freshwater Resources Institute, Queenscliff, Australia, and has more than 25 years' experience in fisheries stock assessment, research, and management. He has published more than 100 scientific and management papers.

# CAPTIONS

*Page 1:* Great white shark from below, Australia.

*Page 2:* Pacific manta ray and diver off the west coast of Mexico.

*Page 3:* Whitetip reef sharks resting on the bottom, Cocos Island, Costa Rica.

*Pages 4–5:* Gray reef sharks at Bikini Atoll.

*Pages 6–7:* Shark silhouetted at a cave entrance, Maui, Hawaii.

*Pages 8–9:* Silhouette of a manta ray, Ningaloo Reef, Western Australia.

*Pages 10–11:* Schooling cownose rays at Galapagos Islands.

*Page 12–13:* Caribbean reef shark swimming over a reef in the Bahamas.

*Pages 30–1:* Manta ray, with remoras attached, encounters a snorkeler on the Great Barrier Reef.

*Pages 64–5:* Caribbean reef shark and diver, New Providence (Nassau), Bahamas.

*Pages 90–1:* Schooling hammerhead sharks at Cocos Island, Costa Rica.

*Pages 114–15:* Pacific manta ray with remora in sunshine, Pacific Ocean, west coast of Mexico.

*Pages 132–3:* Port Jackson shark.

*Pages 200–1:* Bluespotted ribbontail ray.

*Pages 226–7:* Snorkeler on a reef in Indonesia.

*Pages 272–3:* Detail of eye and spiracle of a Port Jackson shark.

# ACKNOWLEDGEMENTS

The publishers wish to thank the following people for their assistance in the production of this book: Garry Cousins, Mark McGrouther (Australian Museum), Margaret McPhee, Craig Sowden, Rod Westblade, and Gordon Yearsley (CSIRO Australia).

# PICTURE AND ILLUSTRATION CREDITS

t = top, b = bottom, l = left, r = right, c = centre, i = inset
A = Auscape International; APL = Australian Picture Library; BCL = Bruce Coleman Limited; CSIRO = Commonwealth Scientific and Industrial Research Organisation (Fisheries), Australia; FLPA = Frank Lane Picture Agency; IV = Innerspace Visions; JR = Jeffrey L Rotman Photography; Minden = Minden Pictures; OEI = Ocean Earth Images; OSF = Oxford Scientific Films; PE = Planet Earth Pictures; TIB = The Image Bank; TPL = The Photo Library, Sydney; TS = Tom Stack and Associates; UGPA = Underwater Geographic Photo Agency

**1** Marty Snyderman/PE **2** Mark Spencer **3** Al Grotell **4–5** James D Watt/PE **6–7** David B Fleetham/TS **8–9** Kelvin Aitken **10–11** David B Fleetham/OSF **12–13** Howard Hall/OSF **13i** Howard Hall/OSF **14–15c** Staatl. Museum für Naturkunde Stuttgart **14b** Ed Robinson/TS **15t** Ken Lucas/PE; b Mike Brock/EarthViews **16t** Bruce Rasner/JR; b David B Fleetham/Silvestris/FLPA **17t** Doug Perrine/PE; c Phillip Colla/IV **18t** Image Library, State Library of NSW; b The Granger Collection, New York **19t** Ben Cropp/A; b Paul Kay/OSF **20t** Mike Turner/TPL; b Mark Conlin/IV **21t** Ron and Valerie Taylor/IV; b Hulton-Deutsch/TPL **22t** Michael Rose/FLPA; b Georgette Douwma/PE **23t** Nigel Marsh/UGPA; c Rudie Kuiter **24** Neil McDaniel/A **25t** Rudie Kuiter; c Rudie Kuiter/IV; b Rudie Kuiter/IV **26–27b** Jeffrey L Rotman/BCL **26c** Tui De Roy/OSF **27tl** Randy Morse/TS; tr Kelvin Aitken/OEI **28l** Jeffrey L Rotman/JR; r Gary Bell/APL **29t** Kevin Deacon/OEI; b Jeffrey L Rotman/JR **30–31** Kevin Deacon/A **31i** Kevin Deacon/A **32t** Frans Lanting/Minden; b AKG Photo, London **33t** D.P. Wilson/FLPA; c Bishop Museum, The State Museum of Natural and Cultural History **34t** Carl Bento/Australian Museum;

br Le Monde à Vos Yeux/Gamma/Picture Media **35**tr Dr Samuel Gruber/IV; bl Ron and Valerie Taylor/Ardea London **36**t Fitzwilliam Museum, University of Cambridge/Bridgeman Art Library; c David B Fleetham/TS; b Toby Adamson/Environmental Images **37**t Stuart Bowey/Ad-Libitum; b P. Morris/Ardea London Ltd **38**t Image Library, State Library of NSW, b Mark Conlin/IV **39**t Doug Perrine/A; c Ron and Valerie Taylor/IV **40**t Brian Alner/PE; c Science Photo Library/TPL; b Randy Morse/TS **41**t Paul Thompson/TPL; b APL **42**t ZEFA/APL; b Dan Guravich/TPL **43**t Alan Levenson/TPL; b Greg Vaughn/TS **44**t Kelvin Aitken/OEI; b David B Fleetham/TS **45**t Jean-Paul Ferrero/A; b Doug Perrine/PE **46** Georgette Douwma/PE **47**t West Stock/APL; c Doug Perrine/IV; b The Kobal Collection **48**tr Topham Picture Library; c Ullstein Bilderdienst **49**t Marty Snyderman/PE; b Le Monde à Vos Yeux/Gamma/Picture Media **50**l Tammy Peluso/TS; r Rodney Fox/JR **51**t Doug Perrine/IV; b Vandystadt/APL **52** David B Fleetham/OSF **53**t Jeffrey L Rotman; b Ron and Valery Taylor/IV **54**t CS Johnson; b CS Johnson **55**t Rebecca Saunders; c Marty Snyderman/IV **56**t Attila A Bicskos; c Attila A Bicskos; b Attila A Bicskos **57** Richard Herrmann/OSF **58**c Kevin Deacon/OEI; b Kevin Deacon/OEI **59**t Kevin Deacon/OEI; b Kevin Deacon/OEI **60**t Doug Perrine/IV; b Giboux/Liaison/Picture Media **61**t Doug Perrine/IV; b Bruce Rasner/JR **62**t Kevin Deacon/OEI; b Paul Steel/Stock Photos P/L **63**t Jean-Paul Ferrero/A; b Joe Sohm/Stock Market Images/Stock Photos P/L **64–65** Mark Spencer/A **65**i Mark Spencer/A **66**t Carl Roessler/IV; b Mike Bacon/IV **67**t Randy Morse/TS; b Randy Morse/TS **68**t Kevin Deacon/OEI; c Kurt Amsler/Vandystadt/ APL; b Kurt Amsler/Vandystadt/APL **69**t Kevin Deacon/A; c Jim Frazier **70**c Kevin Deacon/OEI; b Kevin Deacon/A **71**t Kevin Deacon/OEI; b Kevin Deacon/OEI **72** Tom Campbell/IV **73**t Kurt Amsler/Vandystaat/APL; c Kevin Deacon/OEI; b Doug Perrine/IV **74**c Kevin Deacon/OEI; b Kevin Deacon/OEI **75**t Avi Klapfer/IV; b Kevin Deacon/OEI **76**t Tom Campbell/IV; b Mark Conlin/IV **77**tl F Jack Jackson/PE; tr Kevin Deacon/OEI; b Rory McGuiness/Ron and Valerie Taylor **78**t Kevin Deacon/OEI; c David B Fleetham/TS; b Kevin Deacon/OEI **79**t Kevin Deacon/A; c Leo Collier/PE **80**t Kevin Deacon/OEI; b Ed Robinson/TS **81**t Kevin Deacon/OEI; c Kevin Deacon/OEI; b Mark Spencer/A **82**t Kevin Deacon/OEI; b Pacific Stock/APL **83**t Kevin Deacon/OEI; b Pacific Stock/APL **84**t Kevin Deacon/OEI; b Gary Bell/APL **85**t Kevin Deacon/OEI; b Becca Saunders/A **86**t Kevin Deacon/OEI; c Mike Langford/A; b Gary Bell/APL **87**t Mike Severns/TS; b Flip Schulke/PE **88**t David B Fleetham/TS; b Kevin Deacon/OEI **89**l Kevin Deacon/OEI; r Marty Snyderman/ IV **90–91** Alex Kerstitch/PE **91**i Alex Kerstitch/PE **92** Norbert Wu **94**t Doug Perrine/PE; b Staatl. Museum für Naturkunde Stuttgart **96** Flip Nicklin/Minden **97** James D Watt/EarthViews **98** Kevin Deacon **101** Charles Glatzer/TIB **102** Ken Lucas/PE **103** Ko Fujiwara/TPL **104** TS **105**t Doug Perrine/PE; r Tui De Roy/OSF **106** Mark Conlin/IV **107**t Doug Perrine/PE; b D P Wilson/FLPA **108** Mark I Jones/A **109** Kevin Deacon/OEI **111** Frans Lanting/ Minden **113**t Doug Perrine/IV; bl Doug Perrine/IV; br Doug Perrine/IV **114–115** Kelvin Aitken/OEI **115**t Becca Saunders **116** Becca Saunders/A **118**t John Cancalosi/A; b Kelvin Aitken **119**t George I Bernard/OSF; b Kelvin Aitken **120**t Thor Carter/ CSIRO; cr Thor Carter/CSIRO; b Thor Carter/CSIRO **121**t Thor Carter/CSIRO; b Phillip Colla/IV **122**l George Bingham/ BCL; r Max Gibbs/OSF **123**t David B Fleetham/TS; b Ocean Images Inc./TIB **124**t Kevin Deacon/OEI; b Kelvin Aitken **125**t Rudie Kuiter; c Thor Carter/CSIRO; b Kelvin Aitken **126**t Thor Carter/CSIRO; b Thor Carter/CSIRO **127**t Ron and Valerie Taylor; b Kathie Atkinson/A **128**t Nigel Marsh/UGPA; b Michael S Nolan/IV **129**t Kurt Amsler/PE; c Ed Robinson/EarthViews **130**t Ken Hoppen; b Marty Snyderman/PE **131**t Becca Saunders/ A; b Doug Perrine/A **132–133** Kelvin Aitken/OEI **133**i Kelvin Aitken/OEI **136**t Rudie Kuiter/IV **137**t Kelvin Aitken/OEI; b David B Fleetham/OSF **138**t Saul Gonor/IV; b David B Fleetham/IV **139**t Monterey Bay Aquarium **141**t Daniel Gotshall/ PE **142**t Mark Spencer /A; c Georgette Douwma/PE **143**t Fred Bavendam/OSF; b Kelvin Aitken/OEI **144**t Nigel Marsh/UGPA; b Kelvin Aitken/OEI **145**t Kelvin Aitken/OEI; c Neville Coleman/UGPA; b Neville Coleman/UGPA **146**t Fred Bavendam/OSF; b Cherie Vasas/Nature Travel and Marine Images/OEI **147**t Kelvin Aitken/OEI; b Fred Bavendam/OSF **148**t Kevin Deacon /OEI; b Ron and Valerie Taylor **149**t Doug Perrine/IV; b Doug Perrine/IV **150**t Nigel Marsh/UGPA; b Rod Salm/PE **151**t Kevin Deacon/A; b Kevin Deacon/OEI **152**t Becca Saunders/; b Kelvin Aitken/OEI **154**t Bruce Rasner/JR; b Tom Haight/IV **155**t Ferrari/Watt/IV **156**t Bernie Tershy and Craig Strong/EarthViews **157**t Howard Hall/IV; b Tony Crabtree/OSF **158**t Kelvin Aitken/OEI **159**t David Hall/IV; b Darryl Torckler/ TPL **162**t Rudie Kuiter/IV; b Scott Michael/IV **163**t Ken Lucas/PE; b Mark Conlin/PE **164**t Doug Perrine/IV; b Doug Perrine/IV **165**t Charles and Sandra Hood/BCL; b Charles and Sandra Hood/BCL **166**t Kelvin Aitken/OEI; b Kelvin Aitken/OEI **167**t David B Fleetham/OSF **168**t Mark Conlin/IV; bl Ken Lucas/PE; br Marty Snyderman/PE **169**t Ken Bondy/IV **170**t F. Jack Jackson/PE; b Kurt Amsler/IV **171**t David B Fleetham/OSF; b David B Fleetham/OSF **172**t Doug Perrine/IV; b Doug Perrine/IV **173**t David B Fleetham/OSF; b Kelvin Aitken/OEI

**174**t Doug Perrine/A; b Flip Nicklin/Minden **175**t Doug Perrine/IV; b Gary J Adkison/IV **176** James D Watt/EarthViews **177**t Tom Campbell/IV; b Neville Coleman/UGPA **178**t Neville Coleman/UGPA; b Neville Coleman/UGPA **179**t Kelvin Aitken/OEI; b Doug Perrine/IV **180**t Brian Parker/TS; b David B Fleetham/TS **181**t Doug Perrine/A; b Doug Perrine/A **182**t Doug Perrine/IV; b Jeffrey L Rotman **183**t Richard Herrmann/OSF; b Richard Herrmann/IV **184**t Doug Perrine/IV; b Doug Perrine/IV **186**t Pete Atkinson/PE; b David B Fleetham/OSF **188**t Tui De Roy/A; b Jeffrey L Rotman **189**t Ron and Valerie Taylor; b Gary Adkison/IV **190**t Doug Perrine/IV; b Doug Perrine/IV **191**t Rudie Kuiter/IV; b Warren Williams/PE **192**t Chris Huss/IV **193**t David B Fleetham/OSF; b Gwen Lowe/IV **194**t Verena Tunnicliffe/PE **196**t Norbert Wu/IV **197**b David B Fleetham/IV **200–201** Kevin Deacon/OEI **201**i Kevin Deacon/OEI **204**t Rudie Kuiter/OSF **205**t Mark Strickland/IV; b Ron and Valerie Taylor **206**t Mike Bacon/IV; b Mike Bacon/IV **207**t Randy Morse/TS; b Phillip Colla/IV **208**t Robert Commer/EarthViews; b Ken Lucas/PE **209**t Rudie Kuiter/IV **210**t Kelvin Aitken; bl Neville Coleman/UGPA; br Nigel Marsh/UGPA **211**t Paul Kay/OSF **212**t Scott Michael/IV **213**t Randy Morse/TS; b Norbert Wu/IV **214**t Rudie Kuiter/OSF; bl Neville Coleman/UGPA; br Rudie Kuiter/OSF **215**t Max Gibbs/OSF; b Patrice Ceisel/TS **216**t Georgette Douwma/PE; c Doug Perrine/IV; cr Doug Perrine/A **217**t Ben Cropp/A; b Nigel Marsh/UGPA **218**t Jeffrey L Rotman; b Kevin Deacon/OEI **219**t Nigel Marsh/UGPA **220**t Georgette Douwma/PE; b Nigel Marsh/UGPA **221**t Randy Morse/TS; b Howard Hall/OSF **222**t Rudie Kuiter/IV; b Pacific Stock/APL **223**t Mark Conlin/IV; b Mike Turner/TPL **224**t Robert Hessler/PE **226–227** David B Fleetham/TS **227**i David B Fleetham/TS **230–231** Jeffrey L Rotman/BCL **230**b Richard Herrmann/OSF **231**cr Therisa Stack/BCL; b Randy Morse/BCL **232–233** Ed Robinson/TS **232**c James D Watt/IV; b Stan Osolinski/OSF **233**c Pacific Stock/APL **234–235** Jeff Foott/A **234**c Howard Hall/OSF **235**c Richard Ustinich/TIB; b Pieter Folkens/PE **236–237** Marty Snyderman/PE **236**b Mark Spencer/A **237**cl Richard Herrmann/OSF; cr Kelvin Aitken **238–239** Jeff Hunter/TIB **238**c Kurt Amsler/PE; b Jeff Hunter/TIB **239**b Gary Bell/APL **240–241** Walter Iooss Jr/TIB **240**b Jeffrey L Rotman **241**c Lane Photo/TIB; b Doug Perrine/IV **242–243** Flip Nicklin/Minden **242**b Flip Nicklin/Minden/APL **243**c Flip Nicklin/Minden/APL **244–245** Tui De Roy/A **244**c David B Fleetham/IV; b William S Paton/BCL **245**c Charles and Sandra Hood/BCL **246–247** Andy Williams/Robert Harding Picture Library **246**c Adina Tovy/Robert Harding Picture Library **247**cr Peter Rowlands/PE **248–249** Kevin Deacon/OEI **248**b Kevin Deacon/OEI **249**c Alex Double/PE; b Kevin Deacon/OEI **250–251** Graham Goldin/Stock Photos P/L **250**cr Ron and Valerie Taylor; c Georgette Douwma/PE **251**cl Ron and Valerie Taylor **252–253** Kevin Deacon/OEI **252**c Kevin Deacon/OEI; b Kevin Deacon/OEI **253**cl Max Gibbs/OSF **254–255** Jeff Hunter/TIB **254**c Kelvin Aitken **255**c Steve Rosenberg/Pacific Stock; b Kelvin Aitken **256–257** Lionel Isy-Schwart/TIB **256**b Michael Cufer/TIB **257**c Michael Cufer/IB; b Michael Cufer **258–259** Kelvin Aitken **258**b Dr Heinz Gert de Couet/A **259**c Jean-Paul Ferrero/A; b Max Gibbs/OSF **260–261** Kevin Deacon/OEI **260**bl Kevin Deacon/IV; b Kelvin Aitken/TPL **261**c Kevin Deacon/OEI **262–263** Kevin Deacon/OEI **262**b Cherie Vasas **263**cl Kevin Deacon/OEI; cr Kevin Deacon/OEI **264–265** Jeffrey L Rotman/BCL **264**b Kevin Deacon/OEI **265**c Kevin Deacon/OEI **266–267** Manfred Gottschalk/TS **266**c Kelvin Aitken; b Becca Sauders/A **267**c Doug Perrine/IV **268–269** Attila A Bicskos **268**b Kevin Deacon/OEI **269**cl Kevin Deacon/OEI; cr Kevin Deacon/A **270–271** Neville Coleman/PE **270**c Kevin Deacon/OEI; b Kevin Deacon/OEI **271**cl Kevin Deacon/OEI; cr Kevin Deacon/OEI **272–273** Kelvin Aitken/OEI **273**i Kelvin Aitken/OEI

Illustrations are by: **Martin Camm** 92, 93, 95, 96, 108 (non-aggressive behavior and line), 110, 110–11, 116, 117 (ref. material: 110–11 T. Tricas & J. McCosker, Proceedings of the Californian Academy of Sciences. 43 [14]: 221–38)
**Gino Hasler** 97, 98, 99, 100, 101, 102, 104, 106
**Ngaire Sales** Page trim for Chapters 6, 7, and 8
**Roger Swainston** 136, 139, 140t, 140b, 141, 142, 153t, 153b, 154, 155, 156, 158, 160t, 160b, 161t, 161b, 167, 169, 170, 176, 181, 184t, 184b, 187t, 187b, 192, 194, 195l, 195r, 196, 197, 198t, 198b, 199t, 199b, 204, 209, 211, 212, 219, 224, 225t, 225b (ref. material: 140t, 155 Ken Graham, NSW Fisheries; 153t NSW Fisheries; 204, 212, 224, 225t, 225b CSIRO; 209 Museum of New Zealand Te Papa Tongarewa
**Steve Trevaskis** 112
**Genevieve Wallace** Resources Directory
**Rod Westblade** 108 (aggressive behavior)

Jacket: Front: Paul Humann/JR; Kevin Deacon/A; Becca Saunders; JR; Georgette Douwma/PE; Larry Tackett/TS Back: APL/VOLVOX; Georgette Douwma/PE; Stuart Westmorland/Tony Stone Images/TPL; Neville Coleman/Australasian Marine Photographic Index; Marty Snyderman/PE Front flap: Kevin Deacon/OEI; A; Max Gibbs/OSF Back flap: Phillip Colla/IV; Gary Bell/APL; Neville Coleman/ UGPA.